Lecture Notes in Computer Science 11681

More information about this series at http://www.springer.com/series/7408

Tomas Bures · Laurence Duchien ·
Paola Inverardi (Eds.)

Software Architecture

13th European Conference, ECSA 2019
Paris, France, September 9–13, 2019
Proceedings

 Springer

Editors
Tomas Bures
Charles University
Prague, Czech Republic

Paola Inverardi
University of L'Aquila
L'Aquila, Italy

Laurence Duchien ⓘ
University of Lille
Villeneuve d'Ascq, France

ISSN 0302-9743   ISSN 1611-3349   (electronic)
Lecture Notes in Computer Science
ISBN 978-3-030-29982-8   ISBN 978-3-030-29983-5   (eBook)
https://doi.org/10.1007/978-3-030-29983-5

LNCS Sublibrary: SL2 – Programming and Software Engineering

This Springer imprint is published by the registered company Springer Nature Switzerland AG
The registered company address is: Gewerbestrasse 11, 6330 Cham, Switzerland

Preface

This volume contains the proceedings of the 13th European Conference on Software Engineering (ECSA 2019), held in Paris, France, during September 9–13, 2019. ECSA is the premier European software engineering conference that provides researchers and practitioners with a platform to present and discuss the most recent, innovative, and significant findings and experiences in the field of software architecture research and practice. This edition of ECSA builds upon a series of successful European workshops on software architecture held during 2004–2006, as well a series of European software architecture conferences during 2007–2018. This year was special, as we shared the venue and part of the program with the Systems and Software Product Lines Conference (SPLC) in Paris, France. Some keynotes and tracks were common to both events.

This year's technical program included a main research track, five keynote talks, an industry track, a doctoral symposium track with its own keynote, a Women in Software Engineering (WSE) track focusing on diversity, and a tools and demonstrations track. In addition, we also offered several workshops on diverse topics related to the software architecture discipline. The contributions of all these meetings are included in the companion proceedings, published in the ACM Digital Library.

This volume, assembling just the papers from the main conference, is published by Springer, following a tradition which dates back to its origin in 2004. For this reason, Springer provided 1,000 Euros in funding for the 2019 event. This was used to bestow the ECSA 2019 Best Paper Award, which was announced during the Gala Dinner. Also, for this reason, Springer itself was recognized as a bronze sponsor for the ECSA 2019 edition.

For the main research track, we received 63 submissions in the two main categories: full and short research papers. Based on the recommendations of the Program Committee, we accepted 11 papers as full papers, and 4 additional papers as short papers. Hence the acceptance rate for full research papers was 17,4% for ECSA 2019. For the industrial track, we received 6 submissions and accepted 3 of them. The conference attracted papers (co-)authored by researchers, practitioners, and academia from 28 countries (Algeria, Argentina, Austria, Australia, Belgium, Brazil, Canada, Chile, Columbia, Czech Republic, Equator, Finland, France, Germany, India, Ireland, Italy, the Netherlands, New Zealand, Spain, Poland, Portugal, Romania, Sweden, Switzerland, Turkey, the United Kingdom, and the United States).

It was a great pleasure to have prominent keynote speakers at ECSA 2019. The opening day keynote was delivered by Christian Kästner from Carnegie Mellon University on "Performance Analysis for Highly-Configurable Systems". Professor Carlo Ghezzi from Politecnico di Milano was pleased to accept our invitation to present a keynote for young researchers at the Doctoral Symposium on "Becoming and Being a Researcher: What I Wish Someone Would Have Told Me When I Started Doing Research". The third keynote was presented by Professor Lidia Fuentes from the

University of Malaga on "Variability Variations in Cyber-Physical Systems". These three keynotes were shared with the SPLC program. Rainer Grau from Juropera, Switzerland, delivered the industrial keynote. He spoke about "Good Practices to Identify Bounded Context to Build Agile Organizations in Sync with a Smart System Architecture". The last Keynote was presented by Professor Awais Rashid from University of Bristol. He presented his work on "Secure Software Architectures for a Hyperconnected World: Game Changer or Pipe Dream?".

The role of women in computing has gained more and more attention. To this end, the fourth special track on Women in Software Engineering (WSE) co-located with ECSA 2019 and SPLC 2019 brought together students, junior and senior researchers, as well as practitioners, to present, share, and celebrate their accomplishments and experiences in achieving more diversity in SE/STEM. A large panel was dedicated to this important track. The five panelists, specialized in the field of gender and diversity, were Serge Abiteboul, researcher at Inria and Ecole Normale Supérieure Paris; Isabelle Collet, Professor from University of Geneva; Chiara Condi, activist for women's empowerment and the founder of Led By HER; Elisabeth Kohler, director of the CNRS Mission for Women's Integration; and Florence Sedes, Professor from the University of Toulouse. 33% of ECSA 2019 registered participants were women, which shows the importance of organizing such a track to encourage them to find their place in the community.

We are grateful to the members of the Program Committee for helping us to seek submissions and provide valuable and timely reviews. Their efforts enabled us to put together a high-quality technical program for ECSA 2019. We would like to thank the members of the Organizing Committee of ECSA 2019 for playing an enormously important role in successfully organizing the event with several tracks and collocated events, as well as the workshop organizers, who made significant contributions to this year's successful event.

We also thank our sponsors who provided financial support for the event: Université de Lille, I-Site ULNE, Inria, Missions pour les femmes-CNRS, GDR CNRS Génie de la Programmation et de Logiciel, the Computer Science Lab CRIStAL-UMR CNRS, and the Spirals research group.

The ECSA 2019 submission and review process was extensively supported by the EasyChair conference management system. We acknowledge the prompt and professional support from Springer, that published these proceedings in electronic volumes as part of the *Lecture Notes in Computer Science* series. Finally, we would like to thank the authors of all the ECSA 2019 submissions and the attendees of the conference for their participation, and we look forward to seeing you in L'Aquila, Italy for ECSA 2020.

July 2019

Tomas Bures
Laurence Duchien
Paola Inverardi

Organization

General Chair

Laurence Duchien   University of Lille, France

Steering Committee

Antónia Lopes	University of Lisbon, Portugal
Bedir Tekinerdogan	Wageningen University, The Netherlands
Carlos E. Cuesta	Rey Juan Carlos University, Spain
Danny Weyns	Katholieke Universiteit Leuven, Belgium
David Garlan	Carnegie Mellon University, USA
Flavio Oquendo	University of Brittany, France
Ivica Crnkovic	Mlardalen University, Sweden
Jennifer Pérez	Universidad Politécnica de Madrid, Spain
Muhammad Ali Babar	University of Adelaide, Australia
Paris Avgeriou	University of Groningen, The Netherlands
Patricia Lago	VU University Amsterdam, The Netherlands
Raffaela Mirandola	Politecnico di Milano, Italy
Rogério de Lemos	University of Kent, UK
Uwe Zdun	University of Vienna, Austria

Research Track

Program Committee Chairs

Tomas Bures	Charles University, Czech Republic
Paola Inverardi	University of L'Aquila, Italy

Program Committee

Muhammad Ali Babar	University of Adelaide, Australia
Jesper Andersson	Linnaeus University, Sweden
Anne Koziolek	Karlsruhe Institute of Technology, Germany
Paris Avgeriou	University of Groningen, The Netherlands
Rami Bahsoon	University of Birmingham, UK
Thais Batista	Federal University of Rio Grande do Norte, Brazil
Steffen Becker	University of Stuttgart, Germany
Stefan Biffl	Technical University Wien, Austria
Jan Bosch	Chalmers University of Technology, Sweden
Barbora Buhnova	Masaryk University, Czech Republic
Javier Cámara	University of York, UK
Carlos Canal	University of Malaga, Spain

Ralf Reussner	Karlsruhe Institute of Technology, Germany
Romina Spalazzese	Malmö University, Sweden
Bradley Schmerl	Carnegie Mellon University, USA
Bedir Tekinerdogan	Wageningen University, The Netherlands
Chouki Tibermacine	University of Montpellier, France
Rainer Weinreich	Johannes Kepler University Linz, Austria
Danny Weyns	Katholieke Universiteit Leuven, Belgium
Uwe Zdun	University of Vienna, Austria
Liming Zhu	The University of New South Wales, Australia
Olaf Zimmermann	Hochschule für Technik, Switzerland

Additional Reviewers

Tobias Duerschmid	Peter Mourfield
Andrei Furda	Juergen Musil
Lina Garcés	Roman Pilipchuk
Negar Ghorbani	Martina Rapp
Sara Hassan	Navid Salehnamadi
Chadni Islam	Darius Sas
Reyhaneh Jabbarvand	Stephan Seifermann
Robbert Jongeling	Bruno Sena
Cody Kineer	Dalia Sobhy
Jochen Kuester	Jianhai Su
Jair Leite	Faheem Ullah
Francisca Losavio	Roberto Verdecchia
Carlos Mera Gomez	Tiago Volpato

Industry Track

Program Committee Chairs

Javier Cámara	University of York, UK
Patrick Farail	IRT Saint Exupéry, France

Program Committee

Javier Cámara	University of York, UK
Remco De Boer	ArchiXL, The Netherlands
Patrick Farail	IRT Saint Exupéry, France
María Gómez Lacruz	RavenPack, Spain
K. Eric Harper	ABB, USA
Eric Jenn	Thales, France
Michael Keeling	IBM, USA
Heiko Koziolek	ABB, Germany
Thomas Kropf	Bosch, University of Tuebingen, Germany
Grace Lewis	Carnegie Mellon University SEI, USA

Gonçalo Lopes	D-Orbit, Portugal
Giuseppe Procaccianti	Vandebron B.V., The Netherlands
Magnus Standar	Ericsson, Sweden
Eoin Woods	Artechra, UK

Abstracts of Keynotes

Performance Analysis for Highly-Configurable Systems

Christian Kästner

Carnegie Mellon University

Abstract. Almost every modern software system is highly configurable with dozens or more options to customize behavior for different use cases. Beyond enabling or disabling optional functionality, configuration options often adjust tradeoffs among accuracy, performance, security, and other qualities. However, with possible interactions among options and an exponentially exploding configuration space, reasoning about the impact of configurations is challenging. Which options affect performance or accuracy? Which options interact? What's the optimal configuration for a given workload? In this talk, I will give an overview of different strategies and challenges to learn performance models from highly-configurable systems by observing their behavior in different configurations, looking at sampling and learning strategies, transfer learning strategies, and strategies that analyze the internals or architecture of the system.

Short Bio

Christian Kästner is an associate professor in the School of Computer Science at Carnegie Mellon University. He received his PhD in 2010 from the University of Magdeburg, Germany, for his work on virtual separation of concerns. For his dissertation he received the prestigious GI Dissertation Award. Kästner develops mechanisms, languages, and tools to implement variability in a disciplined way despite imperfect modularity, to understand feature interactions and inter-operability issues, to detect errors, to help with non-modular changes, and to improve program comprehension in software systems, typically systems with a high amount of variability. Among others, Kästner has developed approaches to parse and type check all compile-time configurations of the Linux kernel in the TypeChef project.

Becoming and Being a Researcher: What I Wish Someone Would Have Told Me When I Started Doing Research

Carlo Ghezzi

Politecnico di Milano

Abstract. Why should one wish to become a researcher? What is the role of research and researchers in society? What does one need to do to become a researcher as a PhD student (but also before and after)? What can be the progress of a researcher in his or her career? How to survive and be successful? These are some of the questions I will try to answer in my presentation, based on what I learnt from others and from my own experience.

Very often, young researchers are too busy doing their own research and don't care about the global picture, ignoring these questions. Often, their academic supervisors only focus on the technical side of their supervision, and don't open the eyes of their young research collaborators. But then, sooner or later, these questions emerge and an answer must be given. In particular, I will focus on three issues:

1. *Diffusion of research, through publications and other means.* What does a beginning researcher need to know and what is a good personal strategy?
2. *Evaluation of research and researcher.* Researchers need to understand that they will be subject to continuous evaluation. Why? How? And, most importantly, how should they prepare to live through continuous evaluations?
3. *Ethics.* Researchers need to be aware of the ethical issues involved in doing research. On the one side, integrity is needed in the everyday practice of research. On the other, research is changing the world in which we live. The products of research lead to innovations that can have profound influence on society, and because of the increasingly fast transition from research to practice, they affect the world even before we understand the potential risks. What researchers might see as purely technical problems may have ethical implications, and this requires ethics awareness while doing research.

Short Bio

Carlo Ghezzi is an ACM Fellow (1999), an IEEE Fellow (2005), as well as a member of the European Academy of Sciences and of the Italian Academy of Sciences. He received the ACM SIGSOFT Outstanding Research Award (2015) and the Distinguished Service Award (2006). He has been President of Informatics Europe. He has been a member of the Program Committee of flagship conferences in the software engineering field, such as the ICSE and ESEC/FSE, for which he also served as program and general chair. He has been the editor in chief of the ACM Transactions on Software Engineering and Methodology and an associate editor of IEEE Transactions on Software Engineering, Communications of the ACM and Science of Computer Programming, and Computing. Ghezzi's research has predominately focused on different aspects of software engineering. He co-authored over 200 papers and 8 books. He coordinated several national and international research projects. He has been the recipient of an ERC Advanced Grant.

Variability Variations in Cyber-Physical Systems

Lidia Fuentes

University of Malaga

Abstract. With the increasing size and heterogeneity of systems (e.g., IoT, cyber-physical systems) and enhanced power and versatility of IoT devices (e.g., smart watches, home intelligence sensors), the complexity of managing different kinds of variability for a given vertical domain becomes more difficult to handle. The structural variability of cyber-physical systems becomes more complex, comprising not only the inherent hardware variability of IoT devices and their network access protocols, but also the infrastructure variability derived from modern virtualization technologies, such as microcontainers or unikernels. Variability of software frameworks used to develop domain specific applications and/or services for Cloud/Edge computing environments should not be intermingled with hardware and infrastructure variability modeling. In addition, to exploit the full potential of flexibility in processing, data storage, and networking resource management, experts should define dynamic configuration processes that optimize QoS such as energy efficiency or latency respecting application-specific requirements. In this keynote talk, I will present how QoS assurance in cyber-physical systems implies modeling and configuring different kinds of variability during design, but also at runtime (e.g., user demands, usage context variability), enabling the late binding of dynamic variation points, distributed in IoT/Edge/Cloud devices, and how this can be materialized using current SPL artefacts.

Short Bio

Lidia Fuentes is a professor at the School of Informatics at the University of Malaga, Spain since 2011, with more than 25 years of experience teaching, leading research projects, and supervising thesis. She leads a cross-disciplinary research group CAOSD, focused on applying advanced software engineering technologies to network and distributed systems. Her current research interests include modeling different kinds of variability of Internet of Things (IoT), and cypher-physical systems to support dynamic reconfiguration and green computing. Her scientific production has been very prolific so far, with more than two hundred scientific publications in international forums. Her work has received several best-paper awards at conferences such as ICSR or SPLC-Tools track. She chaired several conferences as general chair (Modularity 2016), program chair (SPLC industry track, VaMoS), served on numerous program committees, and also participated as a panelist at ICSR 2017. She is member of the Steering

Committee of AOSA (Aspect-Oriented Software Association) and VaMoS. She is currently concerned in promoting the STEM careers in girls, participating as a mentor of the Technovation Challenge initiative.

Good Practices to Identify Bounded Context to Build Agile Organizations in Sync with a Smart System Architecture

Rainer Grau

Juropera GmbH

Abstract. The term bounded context describes a (ideal world) technical AND organizational autonomous area of the business model of a company. A bounded context combines three orthogonal aspects: the technology of microservices and DevOps; a functional context with its very specific terminology; an as autonomous as possible organizational unit (a team or a set of teams). The challenge of a company transforming towards the idea of bounded context is the smart design of the orthogonal aspect into a well-balanced overall system. The goal of the well-balanced system to minimize the management overhead required to govern the given complexity of the system.

This talk presents a set of good practices for companies to design a well-balanced overall system addressing the three orthogonal aspects of bounded context. Influencing factors in these good practices are size of the company; complexity and number of different business models; level of organizational complexity such as an international business group with different legal entities; ratio of in-house development versus X-shoring; or existing IT infrastructure dependencies.

Although bounded context are very popular especially in agile environments, this talk will silently communicate that classical methods such as business process modeling or business analysis still are first class citizens in the method toolbox of modern companies.

Short Bio

For over 20 years, Rainer Grau engages with or within companies around the topics of agility, lean leadership, enterprise architecture, and lean organization, or to say it differently, he engages in continuous improvement to integrate modern ideas and new approaches in technology, architecture, and organizational design with the goal to succeed in the market as company and to work with fun as human being.

Steps in his professional life are distinguished consultant and partner at Zühlke Engineering; head of business development at Digitec Galaxus; founder of the Suisse Agile Leader Circle SALC; lecturer at universities in topics around innovation, agility, and digital readiness; founding member and reviewer of the International Requirements Engineering Board (IREB);and speaker at many conferences and venues. Rainer is engaged in the agile community in Switzerland with a long-time passion. Discover more information about Rainer Grau on www.juropera.com.

Secure Software Architectures for a Hyperconnected World: Game Changer or Pipe Dream?

Awais Rashid

University of Bristol

Abstract. The world is experiencing a massive growth in connected cyber-physical systems. Innovations such as smart cities, Internet of Things (IoT), body-area networks, smart grids, and wearable sensors mean that future environments will be hyper-connected, highly open, and regularly collect, process, or disseminate massive amounts of data. It is not difficult to envisage large-scale deployments with hundreds of thousands of nodes that are, in turn, used by a large number of stakeholders to provide a multitude of services. Such shared cyber-physical infrastructures will remain in operation for a long time (potentially decades) and the physical composition, the services provided, and the stakeholders involved will change with time. Software is at the heart of these critical systems that will underpin our society for the foreseeable future. What is the role of software architecture in these emerging hyperconnected environments? In this talk, I will discuss this very question and the challenges of architecting secure software systems when faced with this scale, longevity, and dynamicity.

Short Bio

Awais Rashid is Professor of Cyber Security at the University of Bristol, a Fellow of the Alan Turing Institute, and Director of the EPSRC Centre for Doctoral Training in Trust, Identity, Privacy and Security in Large-scale Infrastructures. His research spans software engineering and cyber security - in particular novel techniques to improve the security and resilience of infrastructures underpinning society. He leads projects as part of the UK Research Institute on Trustworthy, Interconnected, Cyber-Physical Systems (RITICS) and the UK Research Institute on Science of Cyber Security (RISCS). He co-leads the Security and Safety theme within the UK Hub on Cyber Security of Internet of Things (PETRAS) and heads a major international effort on developing a Cyber Security Body of Knowledge (CyBOK) to provide interdisciplinary foundations for education and training programs.

Contents

Quality Attributes

Industry Track

Services and Micro-services

Guiding Architectural Decision Making on Service Mesh Based Microservice Architectures

Amine El Malki[✉] and Uwe Zdun

Faculty of Computer Science, Research Group Software Architecture,
University of Vienna, Vienna, Austria
{amine.elmalki,uwe.zdun}@univie.ac.at

Abstract. Microservices are becoming the de-facto standard way for software development in the cloud and in service-oriented computing. Service meshes have been introduced as a dedicated infrastructure for managing a network of containerized microservices, in order to cope with the complexity, manageability, and interoperability challenges in especially large-scale microservice architectures. Unfortunately so far no dedicated architecture guidance for designing microservices and choosing among technology options in a service mesh exist. As a result, there is a substantial uncertainty in designing and using microservices in a service mesh environment today. To alleviate this problem, we have performed a model-based qualitative in-depth study of existing practices in this field in which we have systematically and in-depth studied 40 reports of established practices from practitioners. In our study we modeled our findings in a rigorously specified reusable architectural decision model, in which we identified 14 architectural design decisions with 47 decision outcomes and 77 decision drivers in total. We estimated the uncertainty in the resulting design space with and without use of our model, and found that a substantial uncertainty reduction can be potentially achieved by applying our model.

Keywords: Microservices · Service meshes · Software design ·
Software architecture · Modeling

1 Introduction

Microservices are a recent approach for designing service architectures that evolved from established practices in service-oriented architectures [13,17,28]. As microservices, especially in large-scale systems, introduce many challenges and high complexity in terms of manageability and interoperability, *service meshes* [15] have been introduced as an infrastructure for managing the communication of containerized microservices and perform many related tasks. For this, they usually use a network of lightweight proxies or sidecars that handle all the communication burden [12,16]. As a result, the coupling between microservices

© Springer Nature Switzerland AG 2019
T. Bures et al. (Eds.): ECSA 2019, LNCS 11681, pp. 3–19, 2019.
https://doi.org/10.1007/978-3-030-29983-5_1

and of microservices to the infrastructure services can get drastically reduced. This also eases establishing interoperability between microservices developed in different programming languages and with different technologies. The proxies or sidecars form a *data plane* that is typically managed by a *control plane* [22].

Unfortunately so far no dedicated architectural guidance exists on how to design and architect microservices in a service mesh environment apart from practitioner blogs, industry white papers, experience reports, system documentations, and similar informal literature (sometimes called gray literature). This includes that so far there is no guidance for users of service mesh technologies or even their implementors to select the right design and technology options based on their respective properties. Very often it is even difficult to understand what all the possible design options, their possible combination, and their impacts on relevant quality properties and other decision drivers are. As a result, there is substantial uncertainty in architecting microservices in a service mesh environment, which can only be addressed by gaining extensive personal experience or gathering the architectural knowledge from the diverse, often incomplete, and often inconsistent existing practitioner-oriented knowledge sources.

To alleviate these problems, we have performed a qualitative, in-depth study of 40 knowledge sources in which practitioners describe established practices. We have based our study on the model-based qualitative research method described in [26], which uses such documented practitioner sources as rather unbiased knowledge sources and systematically codes them using established coding and constant comparison methods [6] combined with precise software modeling, in order to develop a rigorously specified software model of established practices and their relations. This paper aims to study the following research questions:

- **RQ1** What are the established practices that commonly appear in service mesh based designs and architectures?
- **RQ2** What are the dependencies of those established practices? Especially which architectural design decisions (ADDs) need to be made in service mesh based designs and architectures?
- **RQ3** What are the decision drivers in those ADDs to adopt the practices?

In addition to studying and answering these research questions, we have estimated the decision making uncertainty in the resulting ADD design space, calculated the uncertainty left after applying the guidance of our ADD model, and compared the two. Our model shows a potential to substantially reduce the uncertainty not only by documenting established practices, but also by organizing the knowledge in a model.

The remainder of this paper is organized as follows: In Sect. 2 we compare to the related work. Section 3 explains the research method we have applied in our study. Then Sect. 4 explains a precise specification of the service mesh design decisions resulting from our study. The uncertainty estimation is discussed in Sect. 5, followed by a discussion in Sect. 6 and conclusions in Sect. 7.

2 Related Work

Service meshes have been identified in the literature as the latest wave of service technology [12]. Some research studies use service meshes in their solutions. For example, Truong et al. [23] use a service mesh architecture to reduce rerouting effort in cloud-IoT scenarios. Studies on generic architecture knowledge specific to service meshes are rather rare in the scientific literature so far. One example that considers them is TeaStore, which intraffic Control Decision introduces a microservice-based reference architecture for cloud researchers and considers practices used in service meshes [4]. More sources can be found on general microservice best practices. For instance, Richardson [20] provides a collection of microservice design patterns. Another set of patterns on microservices has been published by Gupta [8]. Microservice best practices are discussed in [13], and similar approaches are summarized in a recent mapping study [18]. So far, none of these approaches has put specific focus on the service mesh practices documented in our study.

A field of study related to service mesh architectures are studies on microservice decomposition, as this can lead to decision options and criteria related to the topology of the service mesh. While the microservice decomposition itself is studied in the scientific literature extensively (see e.g. [1,10,25]), its influence on the design of the deployment in a service mesh and its topology are studied only rarely. For instance, Zheng et al. [27] study the SLA-aware deployment of microservices. Selimi et al. [21] study the service placement in a microservice architecture. Both studies are not specific for service meshes, but could be applied to them. In contrast to our study which aims to cover a broad variety of architecting problems, these studies only cover a very specific design issue in a microservice architecture.

The model developed in our study can be classified as a reusable ADD model [29]. Decision documentation models have been used by many authors before, and quite a number of them are focused on services, such as those on service-oriented solutions [29], service-based platform integration [14], REST vs. SOAP [19], microservice API quality [26], big data repositories [7], and service discovery and fault tolerance [9]; however, none of them considers service meshes yet.

3   Research Method

This paper aims to systematically study the established practices in the field of service mesh based architectures. A number of methods have been suggested to informally study established practices, including pattern mining (see e.g. [3]). As in our work, we rather aim to provide a rigorously specified model of the established practices, e.g., to support tool building or the definition of metrics and constraints in our future work, we decided to follow the model based qualitative research method described in [26]. It aims to systematically study the established practices in a particular field and is based on the established qualitative research method Grounded Theory (GT) [6] but in contrast to GT it produces inputs for formal software modeling like model element or relation instances, not just informal textual codes. Like GT, we studied each knowledge source in depth. The method uses descriptions of established practices from the so-called gray literature (i.e., practitioner reports, system documentations, practitioner blogs, etc.). These sources are then used as unbiased descriptions of established practices in the further analysis (in contrast to sources like interviews as used in classic GT). We followed a similar coding process, as well as a constant comparison procedure to derive our model as used in GT. In contrast to classical GT, our research began with initial research questions, as in Charmaz's constructivist GT [2]. Whereas GT typically uses textual analysis, we used textual codes only initially and then transferred them into formal UML models.

A crucial question in GT is when to stop this process; here, theoretical saturation [6] has attained widespread acceptance in qualitative research: We stopped our analysis when 5 to 7 additional knowledge sources did not add anything new to our understanding of the research topic. As a result of this very conservative operationalization of theoretical saturation, we studied a rather large number of knowledge sources in depth (40 in total, summarized in Table 1), whereas most qualitative research often saturates with a much lower number of knowledge sources. Our search for knowledge sources was based on popular search engines (e.g., Google, Bing), social network platforms used by practitioners (e.g., Twitter, Medium), and technology portals like InfoQ and DZone.

Proof-of-Concept Implementation. Our proof-of-concept implementation is based on our existing modeling tool implementation CodeableModels[1], a Python implementation for precisely specifying meta-models, models, and model instances in code with an intuitive and lightweight interface. We implemented all models described in this paper together with automated constraint checkers and PlantUML code generators to generate graphical visualizations of all meta-models and models.

---

[1] https://github.com/uzdun/CodeableModels.

Table 1. Knowledge sources included in the study

Code	Description	Reference
S1	Istio prelim 1.2/traffic management (documentation)	http://bit.ly/2Js3JXj
S2	Using Istio to support service mesh on multiple ... (blog)	http://bit.ly/2FqMce5
S3	Service mesh data plane vs. control plane (blog)	http://bit.ly/2EtC8z6
S4	The importance of control planes with service meshes ... (blog)	http://bit.ly/2He7JYu
S5	Envoy proxy for Istio service mesh (documentation)	https://bit.ly/2HaNdrE
S6	Our move to envoy (blog)	https://bit.ly/2Vyyefd
S7	Envoy proxy 101: what it is, and why it matters? (blog)	https://bit.ly/2HaNhYq
S8	Service mesh with envoy 101 (blog)	https://bit.ly/2UjPuVn
S9	Microservices patterns with envoy sidecar proxy (blog)	https://bit.ly/2tOWo9C
S10	Ambassador API gateway as a control plane for envoy (blog)	http://bit.ly/2TuaZWj
S11	Streams and service mesh - v1.0.x | Kong ... (documentation)	http://bit.ly/2UGX7W1
S12	Istio prelim 1.2/security (documentation)	http://bit.ly/2HyOIkH
S13	Consul architecture (documentation)	https://bit.ly/2ITnhU2
S14	Global rate limiting—envoy ... (documentation)	http://bit.ly/2Js3JXj
S15	Cilium 1.4: multi-cluster service routing, ... (blog)	http://bit.ly/2Cv49pU
S16	Proxy based service mesh (blog)	https://bit.ly/2VzpbL2
S17	Smart networking with consul and service meshes (blog)	http://bit.ly/2Uk14jg
S18	A sidecar for your service mesh (blog)	http://bit.ly/2ThMrvF
S19	Istio prelim 1.2/multicluster deployments (documentation)	http://bit.ly/2udsxI3
S20	Microservices reference architecture from NGINX (blog)	http://bit.ly/2U3tNw1
S21	Comparing service mesh architectures (blog)	http://bit.ly/2tQ2GWd
S22	Istio multicluster on openshift – red hat openshift ... (blog)	https://red.ht/2FcMyn4
S23	Amazon elasticache for Redis FAQs (documentation)	https://amzn.to/2TgGML8
S24	Service mesh for microservices (blog)	http://bit.ly/2TCd6Is
S25	Designing microservices: ... (documentation)	http://bit.ly/2tPQkO4
S26	HashiCorp Consul 1.2: service mesh (blog)	http://bit.ly/2Fnj1It
S27	Connect-Native app integration (documentation)	http://bit.ly/2NEDMlL
S28	Service discovery—envoy ... (documentation)	http://bit.ly/2Tfp59H
S29	Linkerd2 Proxy (open source implementation)	https://bit.ly/2HaiFqa
S30	Multi cluster support for service mesh ... (blog)	http://bit.ly/2Jp6isS
S31	Linkerd architecture (documentation)	http://bit.ly/2Uki3lt
S32	Federated service mesh on VMware PKS ... (blog)	http://bit.ly/2TNRitD
S33	Consul vs. Istio (documentation)	http://bit.ly/2Tdx5gd
S34	Guidance for building a control plane to manage envoy ... (blog)	http://bit.ly/2CCAYRU
S35	Comparing service meshes: Linkerd vs. Istio ... (blog)	http://bit.ly/2TWQAtT
S36	Connect - proxies - Consul by HashiCorp (documentation)	http://bit.ly/2UViLWG
S37	Approaches to securing decentralised microservices ... (blog)	http://bit.ly/2Wp50jn
S38	Istio routing basics – google cloud platform ... (blog)	http://bit.ly/2OoR0Dn
S39	Integrating Istio 1.1 mTLS and Gloo proxy ... (blog)	http://bit.ly/2UTpctm
S40	Kubernetes-based microservice observability ... (blog)	http://bit.ly/2FvE4aT

4   Service Mesh Design Decisions

Following our study results, we identified 14 ADDs for service meshes described
in detail below. *Service Meshes* are usually used together with a *Container
Orchestrator* such as Kubernetes or Docker Swarm. That is, the services in
the mesh, the central services of the service mesh, and service mesh proxies are usually containerized and the containers are orchestrated. Very often

service meshes are used to deal with heterogeneous technology stacks. That is, a major goal is that microservices can be written as HTTP servers with any programming language or technology, and without modification these services get containerized and managed in a mesh, including high-level services like service discovery, load balancing, circuit breaking, and so on. In the first four sections, we describe ADDs that characterize a service mesh as a whole. The remaining section describes ADDs that can be made for specific components of a service mesh.

4.1   Managed Cross-Service Communication Decision

As stated previously, a *Service Mesh* is composed of a set of networked proxies or *Sidecars* that handle the communication between microservices [12,22]. The decision regarding managed communication across the services in a *Service Mesh* is made for the *Service Endpoints* of these microservices, as illustrated in Fig. 1. Not using managed cross-service communication is a decision option for each service endpoint but please note that this essentially means to not follow a service mesh architecture for the endpoint. Alternatively, we can select between the two following design options: *Service Proxy* and *API-Based Service Integration*. *Service Proxy* is the commonly supported option. If the *Service Proxy* is hosted in a container that runs alongside the service container (i.e., in the same pod of the *Container Orchestrator*), the service proxy is called a *Sidecar Proxy*. A few service meshes offer the additional option *API-Based Service Integration*, which means that the service uses a service mesh API to register itself in the mesh and is then integrated without a dedicated proxy. The entire cross-service communication handled by proxies or otherwise integrated services is called the *Data Plane* of the *Service Mesh*. Centralized services of the service mesh are usually called the *Control Plane* (discussed below).

The *Service Proxy* option has the benefit to make it easier to protect the service from malicious or overloaded traffic by achieving *access control, TLS termination, rate limiting and quotas, circuit breaking, load balancing*, and other tasks; this is discussed in more depth in Sect. 4.5. Also, the independence of the service from its proxy increases the *extensibility* and *maintainability* of the service, which is, as a result, not aware of the network at large and only knows about its local proxy. However, this option might produce additional *communication overheads* and *congestions*. The major benefit of choosing an *API-Based Service Integration* over a *Service Proxy* is that it makes the service mesh less *complex* and there is less *communication overhead*. However, doing so limits its *extensibility* and *interoperability*. The option not to manage cross-service communication basically means that all benefits of service mesh are not achievable.

An example realizing the *API-Based Service Integration* is Connect Proxy used in Consul that is implemented using language-specific libraries that are used directly in microservices code. *Service Proxy* and *Sidecar Proxies* are more frequently supported; examples are Envoy Proxy [5] in the Istio Service Mesh [11], Kong Proxy, NGINX Proxy and Linkerd Proxy. Most such service proxy technologies can be deployed as a sidecar or a service proxy running in a different

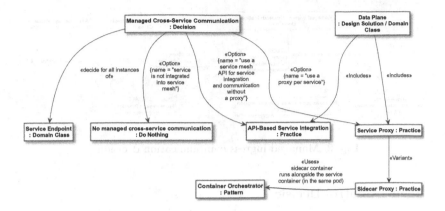

Fig. 1. Managed cross service communication decision

environment (e.g., different server or VM); they usually also offer the option to be used as a *Front Proxy* as discussed in the next section.

4.2 Managed Ingress Communication Decision

In addition to handling cross-service communication, service meshes often intercept incoming traffic, usually called ingress traffic. The decision for managed ingress communication is usually made for the *Service Mesh* as a whole. The ingress traffic then needs to be routed to the containers orchestrated in the mesh. Of course, we might choose not to manage ingress communication but this is a risky and dangerous option since it might expose the service mesh to malicious or overloaded traffic. This option may be adopted in case of a private service mesh, but such meshes seem to be very rare. The typical design option chosen is a *Front Proxy* which is used by the *Control Plane* to intercept ingress traffic as shown in Fig. 2. An *API Gateway* [20], a common microservice pattern with the goal to provide a common API for a number of services, can be realized based on a *Front Proxy* of a service mesh. A *Front Proxy* can protect the service mesh from *malicious traffic*. It can provide *proxy tasks* such as *load balancing* and *multi-protocol support* at the perimeter of the service mesh. Clients are *shielded from details about the inner workings* of the service mesh and are provided with an *API at the client-needed granularity*; this reduces *complexity for clients*. The additional proxy increases *complexity for developers* of the service mesh. The *performance of requests* can be increased, as less roundtrips from clients to services are needed, if the *Front Proxy* can retrieve data from multiple services for one request from a client. However, the additional network hop for accessing the *Front Proxy* decreases the *performance*. An example of this type of proxy is the NGINX Ingress Controller. Most of the proxies from the previous section can also be used as *Front Proxies*.

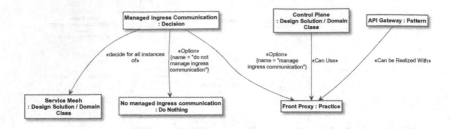

Fig. 2. Managed ingress communication decision

4.3 Traffic Control Decision

Communication in service meshes generates a lot of traffic and data that needs to be controlled and captured e.g. to distribute access control and usage policies, and observe and collect telemetry, traces and metrics. The traffic control decision is usually made for the whole *Service Mesh* as illustrated in Fig. 3. There are four traffic control options:

- *Centralized Control Plane* – A central component, called the *Control Plane*, controls traffic of a service mesh. It is responsible of managing and configuring sidecars in addition to distributing access control and usage policies, observing and collecting telemetry, traces and metrics, in addition to numerous other services like service discovery, as described in Sect. 4.5.
- *Distributed Control Plane* – Each service of a service mesh has its own cache that is efficiently updated from the rest of the services. This helps to enforce policies and collect telemetry at the edge.
- *Front Proxy* – The proxy is responsible for intercepting incoming traffic from outside the service mesh as described in Sect. 4.2. It might also be extended to handle traffic control at the entry point of the service mesh. This option can potentially be combined with the two previous options (for that reasons, the decision is marked with a stereotype that indicates that multiple answers can be selected).
- Finally no dedicated traffic control can be used as well.

The most obvious benefit of using a *Centralized Control Plane* is its *simplicity* and ease of *administration*. However, especially when using one single control plane, it produces a *single point of failure* and is hard to *scale*. Also, it might cause *traffic congestion* which *increases latency*. *Centralized Control Planes* provide policies to the *Service Proxy* on how to perform routing, load balancing and access control. In that case, the next optional decision to take is related to service mesh expansion. Istio service mesh, for example, which is based on *Centralized Control Plane* supports service mesh expansion in a multi-cluster environment. On the other hand, a *Distributed Control Plane* is *highly scalable* and there is *no single point* of failure. However, this option is the most *complex* and thus *risky* option. Using this option, traffic may be forwarded to either a *Service*

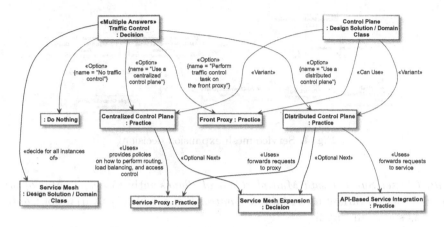

Fig. 3. Traffic control decision

Proxy or directly to a service via *API-Based Service Integration* as described in Sect. 4.1. Consul for example, which implements *Distributed Control Plane*, consists of a set of client agents that are efficiently updated from server agents to control traffic at the edge. An example using *Front Proxy*, described in Source S10 in Table 1, uses Envoy which can be extended to become an *API Gateway*, which then can do traffic control for the service mesh by integrating with Istio. The *Front Proxy* solution does not have the *fine-grained control* offered by the other options, as it is only applied in a central place. It is also a *single point of failure* and is negative for *congestion* and *latency*, but is a *simple* and *non-complex* solution. If used together with one of the other options, it increases the *complexity* of these options even further, but enables more *fine-grained control* for the ingress traffic and thus can reduce the overall traffic in the mesh. These options lead us to the next optional decision regarding distributing traffic control and other tasks among *Control Plane* and *Data Plane* (see Sect. 4.5 for a list of these follow-on decisions, not shown in Fig. 3 for brevity). Figure 3 shows these decision options and their relations.

4.4 Service Mesh Expansion Decision

To *scale* and achieve *redundancy*, service meshes can be expanded and form multi-clustered service meshes, leading to the selection of the option *Multi-Cluster Support* in the decision illustrated in Fig. 4. The service mesh expansion decision is made for the *Service Mesh* itself. Selecting *Multi-Cluster Support* may result in higher *complexity* and increased *network bandwidth* need and *cost*. The decision option *Multi-Cluster Support* is in its simple form just using one *Centralized Control Plane* (see Sect. 4.3) that controls multiple service meshes. The most obvious benefit of this option is its *simplicity* and *ease of administration*. However, it is creating a *single point of failure* and might produce traffic bottlenecks which increase *latency*. *Multi-Cluster Support* has one variant

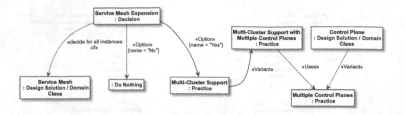

Fig. 4. Service mesh expansion decision

Multi-Cluster Support with Multiple Control Planes with no *single point of failure*. This option variant uses *Multiple Control Planes* which is a variant of *Control Plane* as shown in Fig. 4.

Istio Multicluster on Openshift, described in source S22 of Table 1, is an example that implements *Multi-Cluster Support* using one *Centralized Control Plane*. In this example, one cluster is hosting the *Control Plane* and the others host the *Data Plane* as well as some parts of the *Control Plane* for distributing certificates and *Sidecar Proxy* injection. Another example is NSX service mesh, described in source S32 of Table 1, which is also based on Istio but implements the variant *Multi-Cluster Support with Multiple Control Planes* by enabling a local service mesh per Kubernetes cluster.

4.5   Central Services and Proxy Tasks

As explained above, the *Control Plane* and *Data Plane* provide numerous central services and proxy tasks, and many of those are achieved jointly. The decisions on central services and proxy tasks are usually made for the *Service Mesh* itself but can in many cases be changed for individual services or service clusters from the default configured for the service mesh. Proxy tasks generally can be implemented on the *Service Proxies* or in some cases alternatively on a *Front Proxy*. All solutions relying on a central service or on the *Front Proxy* are introducing a *single point of failure* (not repeated per case below). The decisions, options, and decision drivers for central services and proxy tasks are discussed below. In addition, we have found evidence for decisions that are needed for the basic functioning of the service mesh such as *policy distribution*, which we have not included in our catalog, as the user does not have to make a decision about them. Based on the services and tasks listed below we found evidence for many possible follow-on decisions such as support for *rate limits*, *quotas*, *circuit breaking*, *retries*, *timeouts*, *fault injection*, *dashboards*, *analytics*, and so on. We did not include those in our ADD model either, as the possible list of such higher-level services is excessive and will likely grow over time.

Service Discovery Decision. In order to communicate in a service mesh, services need to locate others based on information like IP address and port number. Of course, this might be simply *hard-coded in each of these services*. If a service changes its address, fails or is unavailable for other reasons like congestion, then it becomes *not reachable* anymore. Then, there is a huge problem since all services code needs to be changed and the mesh needs to be restarted which impacts negatively *availability*. To resolve this issue, the *Control Plane* and *Data Plane* use *service discovery system* usually provided by platforms like Kubernetes for example. An alternative is using a central *Lookup* service [24]. The *distributed service discovery* option requires a consistency protocol and caching of discovery information, i.e. it is more *complex*. However, the lookup is local, thus it offers better *performance*. Without service discovery, the *manageability*, *changeabiltiy*, and *evolvability* of the service mesh would severely suffer.

Load Balancing Decision. Service meshes, especially at scale, have to handle tremendous traffic loads which might overload services, increase their *latency* and decrease their *availability*. In order to avoid such a situation and maintain *scalability*, services are replicated and load is distributed over these instances by both the *Control Plane* and *Data Plane* using a *load balancing* algorithm. *Load balancing* can also be based on geographical location, especially in the case of service mesh expansion described in Sect. 4.4. If load balancing is used, the typical option is *Load balancing on the Service Proxies*. An alternative which offers *balancing loads for the whole ingress traffic* is *Load balancing on the Front Proxy*; this option offers less *fine grained control over the load balancing* than e.g. to balance per service cluster. Both solutions can also be *combined*, offering the benefits of both solutions but also increasing the *complexity*.

Custom Routing Decisions. To manage cross-service and ingress communication, the *Control Plane* and *Data Plane* need to know where each packet should be headed to or routed; routing is usually configured on the *Control Plane* and enacted by the proxies on the *Data Plane*. In addition to such basic routing, the service mesh often offers *Custom Routing* options which can be based on URL path, host header, API version or other application-level rules for *control over the routing* in the mesh. Such routing rules can be dynamically changed, increasing the *flexibility* of the architecture. Custom routing can in follow-on decisions be used for extra tasks, a prominent one is to support continuous experimentation techniques such as *staged rollouts*, *A/B testing* and *canary deployment* (or not). The latter can help for more *controlled deployments* to production, which helps to minimize *deployment risks*.

Health Checking Decision. In highly versatile environment such as service meshes, services go up and down unexpectedly which decreases *availability*. To overcome this issue, periodic *health checks* on services can be applied and e.g. mitigation strategies like service restarts can be applied. Health checks are usually performed by the service proxy and a central service collecting the information. Alternatively, simple health checks like pinging service proxies can also be done solely on the central service, but then *more complex health checking* is not possible. Of course another decision option is to not perform health checks.

Security-Related Decisions. Communication in service meshes usually uses encryption based generated keys and certificates; if not used, the service mesh might be exposed to malicious traffic and manipulations, unless a key and certificate management service outside of the service mesh can or must be used. A simple option is using *API Keys* [26] and local key management. The alternative is to introduce a *central certificate authority*, residing in the *Control Plane*, that takes care of storing and distributing security keys and certificates to the *Data Plane*. This option is more *secure* than the other options and creates in large installations less *maintenance overhead* for managing various *API Keys* in the clients and service proxies, but it is also more *complex* than e.g. *API Keys*. Once authentication is handled, authorization needs to be considered. This can be achieved by setting up access control in the *Control Plane* or in the *Data Plane*. If we choose not to control access after authentication, then services are exposed to unintentional and unwanted modifications. *Security* is the most important driver in this decision; a solution on the data plane supports more *fine-grained control* but is more *complex* than a solution on the control plane. Using encryption in service meshes, usually based on mutual TLS, has to be handled at both ends; not using encryption means *security* is endangered. There are three decision options for *TLS Termination*: either we offer TLS termination directly in the service, at the *Front Proxy*, or – the most common option – in the *Data Plane*. The first option brings *boilerplate code* to the service which might also decrease its *performance*. The second option is only viable if the service mesh is in a private environment in which *internal unencrypted communication* is an option (or another encryption than the one used for communication with clients).

Collect Telemetry, Traces, and Metrics Decision. To observe telemetry, traces and metrics in a service mesh, they first need to be collected. Otherwise, we have to access each of the services and upload this data manually. This is usually done by a *control plane service collecting data from data plane proxies*. With few services, we can choose not to *collect them centrally*. At *large scale*, this might make control and management tasks complex and *central features* such as dashboard or metrics are hard to impossible to build. Some telemetry might also be needed anyway for the functioning of the *service mesh itself*.

Multi-Protocol Support Decision. In heterogeneous environments like service meshes, *multi-protocol support* is required. It helps to have a *unified API interface* that can be used by services using different protocols, which increases *interoperability* and *extensibility* of the service mesh. This can be *offered by data plane proxies* or *on the front proxy*, where the latter option offers less *fine-grained support* and is suitable if *the mesh uses only one protocol inside*. Of course, we might choose not to use this *API interface* and relieve the service mesh from the resulting processing *overhead*. Then, we need to add *boilerplate code* to services to support different protocols or suffer from *interoperability* issues.

5   Estimation of Uncertainty Reduction

There are many different kinds of uncertainties involved in making ADDs in a field in which the architect's experience is limited. The obvious contribution of our ADD model is that it helps to reduce the uncertainty whether all relevant, necessary and sufficient elements for making a correct decision have been found. Another kind of uncertainty reduction is the uncertainty reduction our ADD model provides compared to using the same knowledge, but in a completely unorganized fashion. We want to estimate this kind of uncertainty reduction here, following the approach described in detail in [26]. Here, we estimate the uncertainty reduction only for each individual decision. Please note that in most decisions combinations of options from different decisions need to be taken; but as many decisions in our ADD model have different decision contexts, this can only be calculated precisely for actual decisions made, not for the reusable decisions in the ADD model. But a consequence is that the actually achievable uncertainty reduction is much higher than the numbers below when decisions need to be made in combination. We calculate each number both for using our ADD model (denoted with $\oplus$ below) and not using our model (denoted with $\ominus$ below). Let DEC denote the decisions in our ADD model. For each, $d \in DEC$ there are a number of decision options OPT_d possible to choose for decision d. Finally, there is a set of criteria CRI_d that need to be considered when making a decision d.

Number of Decisions Nodes (ndec): Our ADD model represents each decision separately. So the number of decision nodes for a single decision d is always $ndec_d^\oplus = 1$. Without our ADD model, each decision option in the design space that is not *Do Nothing* is a possible decision node, and it can either be selected or not: $ndec_d^\oplus = |OPT_d \setminus \{Do\ Nothing\}|$. Please note that, if a design solution has variants, OPT_d contains the base variant plus each possible variant.

Number of Required Criteria Assessments in a Decision (ncri): Our ADD model includes explicit decision criteria per decision and for all decisions described above all criteria are pre-decided in the sense that we have assigned a qualitative value $\{++, +, o, -, --\}$ to it, represented in the range: very positive, positive, neutral, negative, and very negative. Thus the required criteria assessments per decision are one assessment per decision, $ncri_d^\oplus = 1$. Without our ADD model, we need to assess each criterion for each decision node (as we have no pre-decided choices): $ncri_d^\ominus = |CRI_d| \times |ndec_d^\ominus|$.

Number of Possible Decision Outcomes (ndo): Our ADD model already models each decision option separately in $|OPT_d|$ including *Do Nothing* options, so $ndo^\oplus$ usually equals $|OPT_d|$ unless the design space allows explicit combinations of solutions as additional outcomes. For instance, in the decision on *managed ingress communication* the *API Gateway* can be combined with the base variant *Front Proxy*. Let the function $solComb()$ return the set of possible solution combinations in the options of a decision; then $ndo_d^\oplus = |OPT_d| + |solComb(OPT_d)|$. The same is true in principle for the decisions made without our ADD model, but as the decision d is here split into multiple separate decision nodes $ndec_d^\ominus$ and without the ADD model no information on which combinations are possible

Table 2. Uncertainty reduction estimation

Decision	$ndec^{\oplus}$	$ndec^{\ominus}$	Imp.	$ncri^{\oplus}$	$ncri^{\ominus}$	Imp.	$ndo^{\oplus}$	$ndo^{\ominus}$	Imp.
Managed cross-service communication	1	3	66.67%	1	24	95.83%	4	8	50.00%
Managed ingress communication	1	2	50.00%	1	16	93.75%	3	4	25.00%
Traffic control	1	5	80.00%	1	45	97.78%	6	32	81.25%
Service mesh expansion	1	2	50.00%	1	16	93.75%	3	4	25.00%
Service discovery	1	2	50.00%	1	16	93.75%	3	4	25.00%
Load balancing	1	3	66.67%	1	21	95.24%	4	8	50.00%
Custom routing	2	4	50.00%	2	8	75.00%	6	10	40.00%
Health checks	1	2	50.00%	1	6	83.33%	3	4	25.00%
Security	3	7	57.24%	3	24	87.50%	10	16	37.50%
Telemetry	1	1	0.00%	1	4	75.00%	2	2	0.00%
Multi protocol support	1	2	50.00%	1	16	93.75%	3	4	25.00%
Total	14	33		14	196		47	96	
Average improvement per decision			49.76%			86.70%			32.59%

is present, we need to consider any possible combination in $ndec_d^{\ominus}$, i.e., the size of the powerset of the decision nodes: $ndo_d^{\ominus} = |\mathcal{P}(ndec_d^{\ominus})| = 2^{|ndec_d^{\ominus}|}$.

Table 2 shows the results of the uncertainty reduction estimation. It can be seen that the number of decisions to be considered $ndec$ can be in total reduced from 33 to 14, with an average improvement of 49.76% when using our ADD model. As all decisions have multiple criteria and when not using our ADD model no decision are pre-decided, the improvement for criteria assessments is higher: on average a 86.70% improvement is possible. Finally, the possible decision outcomes is improved from 96 to 47, with an average 32.59% improvement.

6 Discussion and Threats to Validity

We have studied knowledge on established practices in service mesh architectures, relations among those practices, and decision drivers to answer our research questions **RQ1-3**, respectively, with multiple iterations of open coding, axial coding, and constant comparison to first codify the knowledge in informal codes and then in a reusable ADD model. Precise impacts on decision drivers of design solutions and their combinations were documented as well; for space reasons we only summarized those in the text and did not show them in detailed tables. In addition, we estimated in Sect. 5 the uncertainty reduction achievable through the organization of knowledge in our ADD model. We may conclude that our ADD model (and similar models) has the potential to lead to substantial uncertainty reduction in all evaluation variables due to the additional organization it provides and pre-selections it makes. For individual decisions, mastering and keeping in short term memory the necessary knowledge for design decision making seems very hard for the case without the ADD model (see numbers in Table 2), but quite feasible in case of our ADD model. Our model also helps to maintain an overview of the decisions $ndec^{\oplus}$ and criteria assessments $ncri^{\oplus}$ in the combinations of contexts. Only the number of possible decision outcomes for the combination of multiple decisions seem challenging to handle, both in the $ndo^{\oplus}$ and $ndo^{\ominus}$ case. That is, despite all benefits of our approach, the uncertainty estimations show that a limitation of the approach is that when multiple decisions need to be combined in a context, maintaining an overview of possible outcomes and their impacts remains a challenge – even if a substantial uncertainty reduction and guidance is provided as in our ADD model. Further research and tool support is needed to address this challenge. As our numbers are only rough estimates, further research is needed to harden them and confirm them in empirical studies, maybe based on a theory developed based on such preliminary estimations.

While we believe generalizability of our results beyond the knowledge sources we have studied is possible to a large extent, our results are limited to those sources and to a lesser extent to very similar service mesh architectures. Most of the sources were public Web sources; there might be inhouse practices not reported to the public by practitioners not covered here. Some of the sources were from the technology vendors, which might have introduced bias; but this is mitigated to a certain extent as we considered sources from most major service mesh vendors. Our results are only valid in our set scope; we do not claim any form of completeness. Possible misinterpretations or biases of the author team cannot be fully excluded and might have influenced our results. We aimed to mitigate this threat by our own in-depth experience and by carefully cross-checking among the sources in many iterations.

7   Conclusions

We have performed in this paper a qualitative study in which we have studied service mesh established practices and proposed a formally defined ADD model. In total based on our findings, we modeled 14 architectural design decisions with 47 decision outcomes and 77 decision drivers. In our uncertainty reduction estimations we were able to indicate that the knowledge organization in our ADD model can lead to a significant reduction of uncertainty. We plan in our future work to combine our ADD model with other aspects of microservice design and DevOps practices, and empirically validate a theory based on the preliminary uncertainty reduction estimations. We also plan to validate our ADD model using real life case studies with field practitioners.

18   A. El Malki and U. Zdun

Acknowledgments. This work was supported by: FFG (Austrian Research Promotion Agency) project DECO, no. 846707; FWF (Austrian Science Fund) project ADD-Compliance: I 2885-N33.

References

1. Baresi, L., Garriga, M., De Renzis, A.: Microservices identification through interface analysis. In: De Paoli, F., Schulte, S., Broch Johnsen, E. (eds.) ESOCC 2017. LNCS, vol. 10465, pp. 19–33. Springer, Cham (2017). https://doi.org/10.1007/978-3-319-67262-5_2
2. Charmaz, K.: Constructing Ground Theory. Sage, Thousand Oaks (2014)
3. Coplien, J.: Software Patterns: Management Briefings. SIGS Books & Multimedia, New York (1996)
4. Eismann, S., et al.: A micro-service reference application for cloud researchers. In: 2018 IEEE/ACM International Conference on Utility and Cloud Computing Companion (UCC Companion), pp. 11–12. IEEE (2018)
5. Envoy: Envoy is an open source edge and service proxy, designed for cloud-native applications. https://www.envoyproxy.io/
6. Glaser, B.G., Leonard Strauss, A.: The Discovery of Grounded Theory: Strategies for Qualitative Research, vol. 3. Aldine de Gruyter, Chicago (1967)
7. Gorton, I., Klein, J., Nurgaliev, A.: Architecture knowledge for evaluating scalable databases. In: Proceedings of the 12th Working IEEE/IFIP Conference on Software Architecture (WICSA 2015), pp. 95–104 (2015)
8. Gupta, A.: Microservice design patterns (2017). http://blog.arungupta.me/microservice-design-patterns/
9. Haselböck, S., Weinreich, R., Buchgeher, G.: Decision guidance models for microservices: service discovery and fault tolerance. In: Proceedings of the Fifth European Conference on the Engineering of Computer-Based Systems. ACM, New York (2017)
10. Hasselbring, W., Steinacker, G.: Microservice architectures for scalability, agility and reliability in e-commerce. In: 2017 IEEE International Conference on Software Architecture Workshops (ICSAW), pp. 243–246. IEEE (2017)
11. Istio: What is Istio? https://istio.io/docs/concepts/what-is-istio/
12. Jamshidi, P., Pahl, C., Mendonça, N.C., Lewis, J., Tilkov, S.: Microservices: the journey so far and challenges ahead. IEEE Softw. **35**(3), 24–35 (2018)
13. Lewis, J., Fowler, M.: Microservices: a definition of this new architectural term, March 2004. http://martinfowler.com/articles/microservices.html
14. Lytra, I., Sobernig, S., Zdun, U.: Architectural decision making for service-based platform integration: a qualitative multi-method study. In: Proceedings of WICSA/ECSA, pp. 111–120 (2012)
15. Morgan, W.: The history of the service mesh. https://thenewstack.io/history-service-mesh/
16. Morgan, W.: What's a service mesh? and why do i need one? (4 2017). https://blog.buoyant.io/2017/04/25/whats-a-service-mesh-and-why-do-i-need-one/
17. Newman, S.: Building Microservices: Designing Fine-Grained Systems. O'Reilly, Sebastopol (2015)
18. Pahl, C., Jamshidi, P.: Microservices: a systematic mapping study. In: 6th International Conference on Cloud Computing and Services Science, Rome, Italy, pp. 137–146 (2016)

19. Pautasso, C., Zimmermann, O., Leymann, F.: RESTful web services vs. big web services: making the right architectural decision. In: Proceedings of the 17th World Wide Web Conference (WWW), pp. 805–814, April (2008)
20. Richardson, C.: A pattern language for microservices (2017). http://microservices.io/patterns/index.html
21. Selimi, M., Cerdà-Alabern, L., Sánchez-Artigas, M., Freitag, F., Veiga, L.: Practical service placement approach for microservices architecture. In: IEEE/ACM International Symposium on Cluster, Cloud and Grid Computing. IEEE (2017)
22. Smith, F.: What is a service mesh? April 2018. https://www.nginx.com/blog/what-is-a-service-mesh/
23. Truong, H.L., Gao, L., Hammerer, M.: Service architectures and dynamic solutions for interoperability of IoT, network functions and cloud resources. In: 12th European Conference on Software Architecture: Companion Proceedings, p. 2. ACM (2018)
24. Voelter, M., Kircher, M., Zdun, U.: Remoting Patterns - Foundations of Enterprise, Internet, and Realtime Distributed Object Middleware. Wiley, Hoboken (2004)
25. Zdun, U., Navarro, E., Leymann, F.: Ensuring and assessing architecture conformance to microservice decomposition patterns. In: Maximilien, M., Vallecillo, A., Wang, J., Oriol, M. (eds.) ICSOC 2017. LNCS, vol. 10601, pp. 411–429. Springer, Cham (2017). https://doi.org/10.1007/978-3-319-69035-3_29
26. Zdun, U., Stocker, M., Zimmermann, O., Pautasso, C., Lübke, D.: Guiding architectural decision making on quality aspects in microservice APIs. In: Pahl, C., Vukovic, M., Yin, J., Yu, Q. (eds.) ICSOC 2018. LNCS, vol. 11236, pp. 73–89. Springer, Cham (2018). https://doi.org/10.1007/978-3-030-03596-9_5
27. Zheng, T., et al.: SmartVM: a SLA-aware microservice deployment framework. World Wide Web 22(1), 275–293 (2019). https://doi.org/10.1007/s11280-018-0562-5
28. Zimmermann, O.: Microservices tenets. Comput. Sci. - Res. Dev. 32(3), 301–310 (2017)
29. Zimmermann, O., Koehler, J., Leymann, F., Polley, R., Schuster, N.: Managing architectural decision models with dependency relations, integrity constraints, and production rules. J. Syst. Softw. 82(8), 1249–1267 (2009)

Supporting Architectural Decision Making on Data Management in Microservice Architectures

Evangelos Ntentos[1(✉)], Uwe Zdun[1], Konstantinos Plakidas[1], Daniel Schall[2], Fei Li[2], and Sebastian Meixner[2]

[1] Faculty of Computer Science, Research Group Software Architecture,
University of Vienna, Vienna, Austria
{evangelos.ntentos,uwe.zdun,konstantinos.plakidas}@univie.ac.at
[2] Siemens Corporate Technology, Vienna, Austria
{daniel.schall,fei.li,sebastian.meixner}@siemens.com

Abstract. Today many service-based systems follow the microservice architecture style. As microservices are used to build distributed systems and promote architecture properties such as independent service development, polyglot technology stacks including polyglot persistence, and loosely coupled dependencies, architecting data management is crucial in most microservice architectures. Many patterns and practices for microservice data management architectures have been proposed, but are today mainly informally discussed in the so-called "grey literature": practitioner blogs, experience reports, and system documentations. As a result, the architectural knowledge is scattered across many knowledge sources that are usually based on personal experiences, inconsistent, and, when studied on their own, incomplete. In this paper we report on a qualitative, in-depth study of 35 practitioner descriptions of best practices and patterns on microservice data management architectures. Following a model-based qualitative research method, we derived a formal architecture decision model containing 325 elements and relations. Comparing the completeness of our model with an existing pattern catalog, we conclude that our architectural decision model substantially reduces the effort needed to sufficiently understand microservice data management decisions, as well as the uncertainty in the design process.

1 Introduction

Microservice architectures [14,20] have emerged from established practices in service-oriented computing (cf. [15,18,21]). The microservices approach emphasizes business capability-based and domain-driven design, development in independent teams, cloud-native technologies and architectures, polyglot technology stacks including polyglot persistence, lightweight containers, loosely coupled service dependencies, and continuous delivery (cf. [12,14,20]). Some of these tenets introduce substantial challenges for the data management architecture. Notably,

© Springer Nature Switzerland AG 2019
T. Bures et al. (Eds.): ECSA 2019, LNCS 11681, pp. 20–36, 2019.
https://doi.org/10.1007/978-3-030-29983-5_2

it is usually advised to decentralize all data management concerns. Such an architecture requires, in addition to the already existing non-trivial design challenges intrinsic in distributed systems, sophisticated solutions for data integrity, data querying, transaction management, and consistency management [14,15,18,20].

Many authors have written about microservice data management and various attempts to document microservice patterns and best practices exist [8,12,15,18]. Nevertheless, most of the established practices in industry are only reported in the so-called "grey literature", consisting of practitioner blogs, experience reports, system documentations, etc. In most cases, each of these sources documents a few existing practices well, but usually they do not provide systematic architectural guidance. Instead the reported practices are largely based on personal experience, often inconsistent, and, when studied on their own, incomplete. This creates considerable uncertainty and risk in architecting microservice data management, which can be reduced either through substantial personal experience or by a careful study of a large set of knowledge sources. Our aim is to complement such knowledge sources with an unbiased, consistent, and more complete view of the current industrial practices than readily available today.

To reach this goal, we have performed a qualitative, in-depth study of 35 microservice data practice descriptions by practitioners containing informal descriptions of established practices and patterns in this field. We have based our study on the model-based qualitative research method described in [19]. It uses such practitioner sources as rather unbiased (from our perspective) knowledge sources and systematically codes them through established coding and constant comparison methods [6], combined with precise software modeling, in order to develop a rigorously specified software model of established practices, patterns, and their relations. This paper aims to study the following research questions:

- **RQ1.** What are the patterns and practices currently used by practitioners for supporting data management in a microservice architecture?
- **RQ2.** How are the current microservice data management patterns and practices related? In particular, which architectural design decisions (ADDs) are relevant when architecting microservice data management?
- **RQ3.** What are the influencing factors (i.e., decision drivers) in architecting microservice data management in the eye of the practitioner today?

This paper makes three major contributions. First, we gathered knowledge about established industrial practices and patterns, their relations, and their decision drivers in the form of a *qualitative study on microservice data management architectures*, which included 35 knowledge sources in total. Our second contribution is the codification of this knowledge in form of a *reusable architectural design decision (ADD) model* in which we formally modeled the decisions based on a UML2 meta-model. In total we documented 9 decisions with 30 decision options and 34 decision drivers. Finally, we *evaluated the level of detail and completeness of our model* to support our claim that the chosen research method leads to a more complete treatment of the established practices than methods like informal pattern mining. For this we compared to the by far most complete of our pool of sources, the *microservices.io* patterns catalog [18], and are able to show that our ADD model captures 210% more elements and relations.

The remainder of this paper is organized as follows: In Sect. 2 we compare to the related work. Section 3 explains the research methods we have applied in our study and summarizes the knowledge sources. Section 4 describes our reusable ADD model on microservice data management. Section 5 compares our study with *microservices.io* in terms of completeness. Finally, Sect. 6 discusses the threats to validity of our study and Sect. 7 summarizes our findings.

2   Related Work

A number of approaches that study microservice patterns and best practices exist: The *microservices.io* collection by Richardson [18] addresses microservice design and architecture practices. As the work contains a category on data management, many of them are included in our study. Another set of patterns on microservice architecture structures has been published by Gupta [8], but those are not focused on data management. Microservice best practices are discussed in [12], and similar approaches are summarized in a recent mapping study [15]. So far, none of those approaches has been combined with a formal model; our ADD model complements these works in this sense.

Decision documentation models that promise to improve the situation exist (e.g. for service-oriented solutions [21], service-based platform integration [13], REST vs. SOAP [16], and big data repositories [7]). However, this kind of research does not yet encompass microservice architectures, apart from our own prior study on microservice API quality [19]. The model developed in our study can be classified as a reusable ADD model, which can provide guidance on the application of patterns [21]. Other authors have combined decision models with formal view models [9]. We apply such techniques in our work, but also extend them with a formal modeling approach based on a qualitative research method.

3   Research Method and Modelling Tool

Research Method. This paper aims to systematically study the established practices in the field of architecting data management in microservice architectures. We follow the model-based qualitative research method described in [19]. It is based on the established Grounded Theory (GT) [6] qualitative research method, in combination with methods for studying established practices like pattern mining (see e.g. [4]) and their combination with GT [10]. The method uses descriptions of established practices from the authors' own experiences as a starting point to search for a limited number of well-fitting, technically detailed sources from the so-called "grey literature" (e.g., practitioner reports, system documentations, practitioner blogs, etc.). These sources are then used as unbiased descriptions of established practices in the further analysis. Like GT, the method studies each knowledge source in depth. It also follows a similar coding process, as well as a constant comparison procedure to derive a model. In contrast to classic GT, the research begins with an initial research question, as in Charmaz's constructivist GT [3]. Whereas GT typically uses textual analysis, the method uses textual codes only initially and then transfers them into formal software models (hence it is model-based).

The knowledge-mining procedure is applied in many iterations: we searched for new knowledge sources, applied open and axial coding [6] to identify candidate categories for model elements and decision drivers, and continuously compared the new codes with the model designed so far to incrementally improve it. A crucial question in qualitative methods is when to stop this process. Theoretical saturation [6] has attained widespread acceptance for this purpose. We stopped our analysis when 10 additional knowledge sources did not add anything new to our understanding of the research topic. While this is a rather conservative operationalisation of theoretical saturation (i.e., most qualitative research saturates with far fewer knowledge sources that add nothing new), our study converged already after 25 knowledge sources. The sources included in the study are summarized in Table 1. Our search for sources was based on our own experience, i.e., tools, methods, patterns and practices we have access to, worked with, or studied before. We also used major search engines (e.g., Google, Bing) and topic portals (e.g., InfoQ) to find more sources.

Modelling Tool Implementation. To create our decision model, we used our existing modeling tool CodeableModels[1], a Python implementation for precisely specifying meta-models, models, and model instances in code. Based on CodeableModels, we specified meta-models for components, activities, deployments and microservice-specific extensions of those, as outlined above. In addition, we realized automated constraint checkers and PlantUML code generators to generate graphical visualizations of all meta-models and models.

4 Reusable ADD Model for Data Management in Microservice Architectures

In this section, we describe the reusable ADD model derived from our study[2]. All elements of the model are *emphasized* and all decision drivers derived from our sources in Table 1 are *slanted*. It contains one decision category, *Data Management Category*, relating five top-level decisions, as illustrated in Fig. 1. These decisions need to be taken for the decision contexts *all instances of* an *API*, *Service* instances, or the combination of *Data Objects* and *Service* instances, respectively. Note that all elements of our model are instances of a meta-model (with meta-classes such as *Decision, Category, Pattern, AND Combined Group*, etc.), which appear in the model descriptions. Each of them is described in detail below (some elements may be relevant for more than one decision, but this has been omitted from the figures for ease of presentation).

---

[1] https://github.com/uzdun/CodeableModels.
[2] Replication package can be found at: https://bit.ly/2EKyTnL.

Table 1. Knowledge sources included in the study

Name	Description	Reference
S1[b]	Intro to microservices: dependencies and data sharing	https://bit.ly/2YTnolQ
S2[a]	Pattern: shared database	https://bit.ly/30L1PW2
S3[d]	Enterprise integration patterns	https://bit.ly/2Wr1OHC
S4[b]	Design patterns for microservices	https://bit.ly/2EBmIcQ
S5[b]	6 data management patterns for microservices	https://bit.ly/2K3YMTb
S6[a]	Pattern: database per service	https://bit.ly/2EDDici
S7[b]	Transaction management in microservices	https://bit.ly/2XSKhWL
S8[b]	A guide to transactions across microservices	https://bit.ly/2WpQN9j
S9[b]	Saga pattern – how to implement business transactions using microservices	https://bit.ly/2WpRBuR
S10[b]	Saga pattern and microservices architecture	https://bit.ly/2HF6G3G
S11[b]	Patterns for distributed transactions within a microservices architecture	https://bit.ly/2QqZgUx
S12[b]	Data consistency in microservices architecture	https://bit.ly/2K5G79y
S13[b]	Event-driven data management for microservices	https://bit.ly/2WlSKUs
S14[a]	Pattern: Saga	https://bit.ly/2WpS549
S15[b]	Managing data in microservices	https://bit.ly/2HYIvvY
S16[b]	Event sourcing, event logging – an essential microservice pattern	https://bit.ly/2QusIcb
S17[a]	Pattern: event sourcing	https://bit.ly/2K62TOn
S18[b]	Microservices with CQRS and event sourcing	https://bit.ly/2JK2IZQ
S19[b]	Microservices communication: how to share data between microservices	https://bit.ly/2HCR94u
S20[b]	Building microservices: inter-process communication in a microservices architecture	https://bit.ly/30OVB7U
S21[a]	Pattern: command query responsibility segregation (CQRS)	https://bit.ly/2X80LcM
S22[c]	Data considerations for microservices	https://bit.ly/2WrLeav
S23[b]	Preventing tight data coupling between microservices	https://bit.ly/2WptQmJ
S24[c]	Challenges and solutions for distributed data management	https://bit.ly/2wp5YkO
S25[c]	Communication in a microservice architecture	https://bit.ly/2X7UDkT
S26[b]	Microservices: asynchronous request response pattern	https://bit.ly/2WjAFqb
S27[b]	Patterns for microservices—sync vs. async	https://bit.ly/2Ezhsqg
S28[b]	Building microservices: using an API gateway	https://bit.ly/2EA3AfA
S29[b]	Microservice architecture: API gateway considerations	https://bit.ly/2YUKWqr
S30[a]	Pattern: API composition	https://bit.ly/2WlVqS0
S31[a]	Pattern: backends for frontends	https://bit.ly/2X9I3kQ
S32[c]	Command and query responsibility segregation (CQRS) pattern	https://bit.ly/2wltdMq
S33[b]	Introduction to CQRS	https://bit.ly/2HY0sLm
S34[b]	CQRS	https://bit.ly/2JKI2Rz
S35[b]	Publisher-subscriber pattern	https://bit.ly/2JGtqCx

[a] Denotes a source taken from *microservices.io*
[b] Practitioner blog
[c] Microsoft technical guide
[d] Book chapter

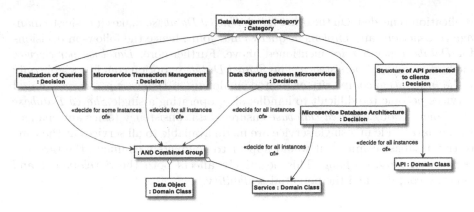

Fig. 1. Reusable ADD model on microservice data management: overview

Microservice Database Architecture (Fig. 2). Since most software relies on efficient data management, database architecture is a central decision in the design of a microservice architecture. Quality attributes such as performance, reliability, coupling, and scalability, need to be carefully considered in the decision making process. The simplest decision option is to choose *service stores no persistent data*, which is applicable only for services whose functions are performed solely on transient data, like pure calculations or simple routing functions. By definition, a microservice should be autonomous, loosely coupled and able to be developed, deployed, and scaled independently [12]. This is ensured by the *Database per Service* pattern [18], which we encountered, either directly or implicitly, in 33 out of 35 sources: each microservice manages its own data, and data exchange and communications with other services are realized only through a set of well-defined APIs. When choosing this option, transaction management between services becomes more difficult, as the data is distributed across the services; for the same reason making queries could become a challenge, too. Thus the optional next decisions on *Microservice Transaction Management* (see sources [S7, S8, S11]) and *Realization of Queries* [18] should be considered (both explained below). The use of this pattern may also require a next decision on the *Need for Data Composition, Transformation, or Management*. Another option, which is recommended only for special cases (e.g., when a group of services always needed to share a data object), is to use a *Shared Database* [18] (see sources [S1, S19]): all involved services persist data in one and the same database.

There are a number of criteria that determine the outcome of this decision. Applying the *Database per Service* pattern in a system results in more *loosely coupled* microservices. This leads to better *scalability* than a *Shared Database* closer to the service with only transient data, since microservices can scale up individually. Especially for low loads this can reduce *performance*, as additional distributed calls are needed to get data from other services and establish *data consistency*. The pattern's impact on *performance* is not always negative: for high loads a *Shared Database* can become a bottleneck, or database replication is needed. On the other hand, *Shared Database* makes it easier to *manage transactions* and *implement queries and joins*; hence the follow-on decisions for *Database per Service* mentioned above. Furthermore, *Database per Service* facilitates *polyglot persistence*. The *Shared Database* option could be viable only if the *integration complexity* or related challenges of *Database per Service*-based services become too difficult to handle; also, operating a single *Shared Database* is simpler. Though *Shared Database* ensures *data consistency* (since any changes to the data made in a single service are made available to all services at the time of the database commit), it would appear to completely eliminate the targeted benefits of *loose coupling*. This negatively affects both the *development and runtime coupling* and the potential *scalability*.

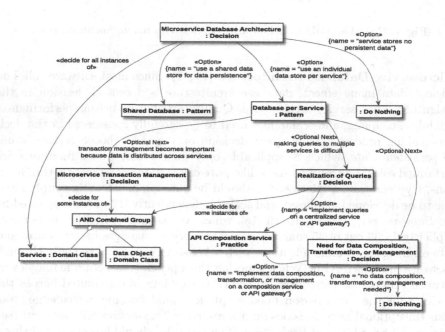

Fig. 2. Microservice database architecture decision

Structure of API Presented to Clients (Fig. 3). When software is decomposed into microservices, many major challenges lie in the structure of the API. This topic has been extensively studied in our prior and ongoing work on API patterns [19]; here we concentrate only on those decision options relevant to data management. Many issues in microservice design are resolved at the API level, such as routing requests to the appropriate microservice, the distribution of multiple services, and the aggregation of results. The simplest option for structuring a system is *Clients Access Microservices Directly*: all microservices are entry points of the system, and clients can directly request the service they need (each service offers its own API endpoint to clients). However, all studied sources recommend or assume the use of the *API Gateway* pattern [18] as a common entry point for the system, through which all requests are routed. An alternative solution, for servicing different types of clients (e.g., mobile vs. desktop clients) is the *Backends for Frontends* pattern variant [18], which offers a fine-grained API for each specific type of client. An *API Gateway* could also be realized as an *API Composition Service* [18], that is a service which invokes other microservices. Furthermore an *API Gateway* can have *Additional centralized data-related functions* (shown in Fig. 3 and discussed below as decision drivers).

The main driver affecting this decision is that *API Gateways* (and thus *API Composition Service* and *Backends for Frontends* in a more limited capacity) can provide a number of centralized services. They can work as a proxy service to *route requests* to the appropriate microservice, *convert or transform requests or data* and deliver the *data at the granularity needed by the client*, and provide the *API abstractions for the data needed by the client*. In addition, they can *handle access management* to data (i.e., authentication/authorization), serve as a *data cache*, and *handle partial failures*, e.g. by returning default or cached data. Although its presence increases the overall *complexity* of the architecture since an additional service needs to be developed and deployed, and increases *response time* due to the additional network passes through it, an *API Gateway* is generally considered as an optimal solution in a microservice-based system. *Clients Access Microservices Directly* makes it difficult to realize such centralized functions. A sidecar architecture [1] might be a possible solution, but if the service should fail, many functions are impeded, e.g. caching or handling partial failures. The same problem of centralized coordination also applies to a lesser extent to *Backends for Frontends* (centralization in each *API Gateway* is still possible). *Use API Gateway to cache data* reduces the *response time*, returning cached data faster, and increases *data availability*: if a service related to specific data is unavailable, it can return its cached data.

Data Sharing Between Microservices (Fig. 4). Data sharing must be considered for each data object that is shared between at least two microservices. Before deciding how to share data, it is essential to identify the information to be shared, its update frequency, and the primary provider of the data. The decision must ensure that sharing data does not result in tightly coupled services. The simplest option is to choose *services share no data*, which is theoretically optimal in ensuring loose coupling, but is only applicable for rather independent services or those that require only transient data. Another option, already discussed above, is a *Shared Database*. In this solution services share a common database; a service publishes its data, and other services can consume it when required. A number of viable alternatives to the *Shared Database* exist. *Synchronous Invocations-Based Data Exchange* is a simple option for sharing data between microservices. *Request-Response Communication* [11] is a data exchange pattern in which a service sends a request to another service which receives and processes it, ultimately returning a response message. Another typical solution that is well suited to achieving *loose coupling* is to use *Asynchronous Invocations-Based Data Exchange*. Unlike *Request-Response Communication*, it removes the

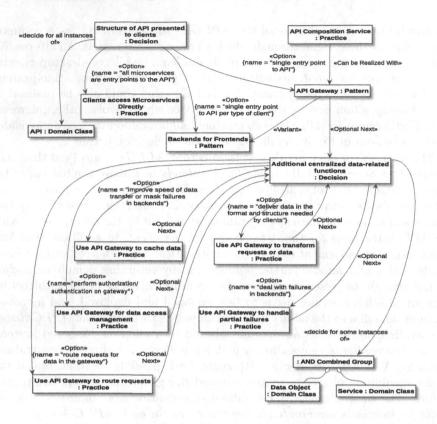

Fig. 3. Structure of API presented to clients decision

need to wait for a response, thereby decoupling the execution of the communicating services. Implementation of asynchronous communication leads to *Eventual Consistency* [17]. There are several possible *Asynchronous Data Exchange Mechanisms*: *Publish/Subscribe* [11], in which services can subscribe to an event; use of a *Messaging* [11] middleware; *Data Polling*, in which services periodically poll for data changes in other services; and the *Event Sourcing* [18] pattern that ensures that all changes to application state are stored as a sequence of events.

The choices in this decision are determined by a number of factors. With a *Shared Database*, the system tends to be more *tightly coupled* and *less scalable*. Conversely, an *Asynchronous Data Exchange Mechanism* ensures that the services are more *loosely coupled*, since they interact mostly via events, use message buffering for queuing requests until processed by the consumer, support *flexible* client–service interactions, or provide an explicit inter-process communication mechanism. It has minimal impact on quality attributes related to network interactions, such as *latency* and *performance*. However, *operational complexity* is negatively impacted, since an additional service must be configured and operated. On the other hand, a *Request-Response Communication* mechanism does not require a broker, resulting in a *less complex* system architecture. Despite this, in a *Request-Response Communication*-based system, the communicating services are more *tightly coupled* and the communication is less *reliable*, as they must both be running until the exchange is completed. Applying the *Event Sourcing* pattern increases *reliability*, since events are published whenever state changes, and the system is more *loosely coupled*. Patterns supporting message persistence such as *Messaging*, *Event Sourcing*, and messaging-based *Publish/Subscribe* increase the *reliability* of message transfers and thus the *availability* of the system.

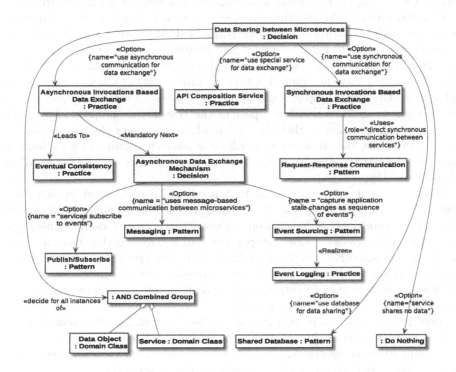

Fig. 4. Data sharing between microservices decision

Microservice Transaction Management (Fig. 5). One common problem in microservice-based systems is how to manage distributed transactions across multiple services. As explained above, the *Database per Service* pattern often introduces this need, as the relevant data objects of a transaction are scattered across different services and their databases. Issues concerning transaction atomicity and isolation of user actions for concurrent requests need to be dealt with. One of the easiest and most efficient options to solve the problem of distributed transactions is to completely avoid them. This can be done through a *Shared Database* (with all its drawbacks in a microservice architecture) or by service redesign so that all data objects of the transaction reside in one microservice. If this is not possible, another option is to apply the *Saga Transaction Management* [18] pattern, where each transaction updates data within a single service, in a sequence of local transactions [S9]; every step is triggered only if the previous one has been completed. The implementation requires an additional decision for the *Saga Coordination Architecture*. There are two possible options for implementing this pattern: *Event/Choreography Coordination* and *Command/Orchestration Coordination* [S9]. *Event/Choreography Coordination* is a distributed coordination approach where a service produces and publishes events, that are listened to by other services which then decide their next action. *Command/Orchestration Coordination* is a centralized approach where a dedicated service informs other involved services, through a command/reply mechanism, what operation should be performed. Moreover, *Saga Transaction Management* supports failure analysis and handling using *Event Log* and *Compensation Action* practices [S12]. Implementing this pattern leads also to *Eventual Consistency*. Another typical option for implementing a transaction across different services is to apply the *Two-Phase Commit Protocol* [2] pattern: in the first phase, services which are part of the transaction prepare for commit and notify the coordinator that they are ready to complete the transaction; in the second phase, the transaction coordinator issues a commit or a rollback to all involved microservices. Here, the *Rollback* [S7] practice is used for handling failed transactions.

There are a number of criteria that need to be considered in this decision. When implementing the *Saga Transaction Management* pattern, the *Event/Choreography Coordination* option results in a more *loosely coupled* system where the services are more *independent* and *scalable*, as they have no direct knowledge of each other. On the other hand, the *Command/Orchestration Coordination* option has its own advantages: it *avoids cyclic dependencies between services*, *centralizes the orchestration of the distributed transaction*, reduces the participants' *complexity*, and makes rollbacks easier to manage. The *Two-Phase Commit Protocol* pattern is not a typical solution for managing distributed transactions in microservices, but it provides a *strong consistency* protocol, guarantees *atomicity* of transactions, and allows read-write *isolation*. However, it can significantly impair system *performance* in high load scenarios.

Realization of Queries (Fig. 6). For every data object and data object combination in a microservice-based system, and its services, it must be considered whether queries are needed. As data objects may reside in different services, e.g., as a consequence of applying *Database per Service*, queries may be more difficult to design and implement than when utilizing a single data source. The simplest option is of course to implement *no queries* in the system, but this is often not realistic. An efficient option for managing queries is to apply the *Command-Query-Responsibility-Segregation* (CQRS) pattern [5]. CQRS is a process of separation between read and write operations into a "command" and a "query" side. The "command" side manages the "create", "update" and "delete" operations; the "query" side segregates the operations that read data from the "update" operation utilizing separated interfaces. This is very efficient if

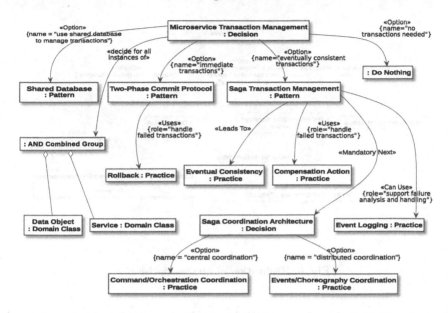

Fig. 5. Microservice transaction management decision

multiple operations are performed in parallel on the same data. The other option is to implement queries in a *API Composition Service* or in the *API Gateway*.

A number of criteria determine the outcome of this decision. The *Command-Query-Responsibility-Segregation* (CQRS) option increases *scalability* since it supports independent horizontal and vertical scaling, improves *security* since the read and write responsibilities are separated. It also increases *availability*: when the "command" side is down the last data update remains available on the "query" side. Despite these benefits, using CQRS has some drawbacks: it adds significant *complexity*, and is not suitable to every system. On the other hand, implementing queries in an *API Composition Service* or *API Gateway* introduces an overhead and decreases *performance*, entails the risk of reduced *availability*, and makes it more difficult to ensure transactional *data consistency*.

5 Evaluation

We used our model-based qualitative research method described in Sect. 3 because informal pattern mining, or just reporting the author's own experience in a field (which is the foundation of most of the practitioner sources we encountered), entail the high risk of missing important knowledge elements or relations between them. To evaluate the effect of our method, we measure the improvement yielded by our study compared to the individual sources; specifically *microservices.io* [18], the by far most complete and detailed of our sources. This is an informally collected pattern catalog based on the author's experience and pattern mining. As such, it is a work with similar aims to this study.

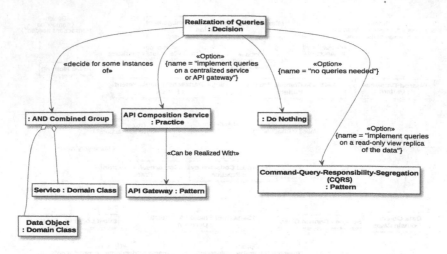

Fig. 6. Realization of queries decision

Of course, our formal model offers the knowledge in a much more systematically structured fashion; whereas in the *microservices.io* texts the knowledge is often scattered throughout the text, requiring careful study of the entire text to find a particular piece of knowledge. For this reason, we believe the formal ADD model to be a useful complement to this type of sources, even if the two contain identical information.

For evaluation of our results, we studied the *microservices.io* texts in detail a second time after completing the initial run of our study, to compare which of the model elements and relations we found are also covered by *microservices.io*. Some parts of this comparison might be unfair in the sense that the *microservices.io* author does not present a decision model and covers the topic in a broad manner, so that some elements or relations may have been excluded on purpose. In addition, there may be some differences in granularity between *microservices.io* and our model, but we tried to maintain consistency with the granularity in the analysis and coding during the GT process. Considering the relatively high similarity of those *microservices.io* parts that overlap with the results of our study, and the general goal of pattern mining of representing the current practice in a field correctly and completely, we nevertheless believe that our assumption that the two studies are comparable is not totally off.

Table 2 shows the comparison for all element and relation types in our model. Only 105 of the 325 elements and relations in our model are contained in *microservices.io*: a 210% improvement in completeness has resulted from systematically studying and formally modeling the knowledge in the larger set of knowledge sources summarized in Table 1. Apart from the trivial *Categories* element type, most elements and relation types display high improvement, most notably, the *Decision driver to patterns/practices relations*. That is mainly because design options (and consequently their relations) are missing entirely. Apart from

Categories, only the *Domain model elements* type shows no improvement, because we only considered those domain elements directly connected to our decisions here. In the larger context of our work, we use a large and detailed microservice domain object model, but as there is nothing comparable in the microservice patterns, we only counted the directly related contexts here (else the improvement of our model would be considerably higher).

Table 2. Comparison of number of found elements and relation types our ADD model and *microservices.io*

Element and relation types	ADD model	*microservices.io*	Improvement
Domain model elements	4	4	0%
Decisions	9	4	125%
Decision context relations	6	3	100%
Patterns/practices	32	15	113%
Decision to option relations	30	13	131%
Relations between patterns/practices	10	4	150%
Patterns/practices to decision relations	12	4	200%
Categories	1	1	0%
Category to decision relations	5	3	67%
Unique decision drivers	34	17	100%
Decision drivers to patterns/practices relations	182	37	392%
Total number of elements	325	105	210%

6   Threats to Validity

To increase internal validity we used practitioner reports produced independently of our study. This avoids bias, for example, compared to interviews in which the practitioners would be aware that their answers would be used in a study. This introduces the internal validity threat that some important information might be missing in the reports, which could have been revealed in an interview. We tried to mitigate this threat by looking at many more sources than needed for theoretical saturation, as it is unlikely that all different sources miss the same important information.

The different members of the author team have cross-checked all models independently to minimize researcher bias. The threat to internal validity that the researcher team is biased in some sense remains, however. The same applies to our coding procedure and the formal modeling: other researchers might have coded or modeled differently, leading to different models. As our goal was only to find one model that is able to specify all observed phenomena, and this was achieved, we consider this threat not to be a major issue for our study.

The experience and search-based procedure for finding knowledge sources may have introduced some kind of bias as well. However, this threat is mitigated to a large extent by the chosen research method, which requires just additional sources corresponding to the inclusion and exclusion criteria, not a specific distribution of sources. Note that our procedure is in this regard rather similar to how interview partners are typically found in qualitative research studies in software engineering. The threat remains that our procedures introduced some kind of unconscious exclusion of certain sources; we mitigated this by assembling an author team with many years of experience in the field, and performing very general and broad searches. Due to the many included sources, it is likely our results can be generalized to many kinds of architecture requiring microservice data management. However, the threat to external validity remains that our results are only applicable to similar kinds of microservice architectures. The generalization to novel or unusual microservice architectures might not be possible without modification of our models.

7   Conclusion

In this paper, we have reported on an in-depth qualitative study of existing practices in industry for data management in microservice architectures. The study uses a model-based approach to provide a systematic and consistent, reusable ADD model which can complement the rich literature of detailed descriptions of individual practices by practitioners. It aims to provide an unbiased and more complete treatment of industry practices. To answer RQ1 we have found in 32 common patterns and established practices. To answer RQ2, we have grouped 5 top-level decisions in the data management category and documented in total 9 *decisions* with 6 *decision context relations*. Further we were able to document 30 *decision to option relations* and 22 (10 + 12) further relations between patterns and practices and decisions. Finally, to answer RQ3, we have found 34 *unique decision drivers* with 182 links to patterns and practices influencing the decisions. The 325 elements in our model represent, according to our rough comparison to *microservices.io*, an 210% improvement in completeness. We can conclude from this that to get a full picture of the possible microservice data management practices, as conveyed in our ADD model, many practical sources need to be studied, in which the knowledge is scattered in substantial amounts of text. Alternatively, substantial personal experiences need to be made to gather the same level of knowledge. Both require a tremendous effort and run the risk that some important decisions, practices, relations, or decision drivers might be missed. Our rough evaluation underlines that the knowledge in microservice data management is complex and scattered, and existing knowledge sources are inconsistent and incomplete, even if they attempt to systematically report best practices (such as *microservices.io*, compared to here). A systematic and unbiased study of many sources, and an integration of those sources via formal modeling, as suggested in this paper, can help to alleviate such problems and provide a rigorous and unbiased account of the current practices in a field (like presently on microservice data management practices).

Acknowledgments. This work was supported by: FFG (Austrian Research Promotion Agency) project DECO, no. 846707; FWF (Austrian Science Fund) project ADD-Compliance: I 2885-N33.

References

1. Sidecar pattern (2017). https://docs.microsoft.com/en-us/azure/architecture/patterns/sidecar
2. Al-Houmaily, Y., Samaras, G.: Two-phase commit. In: Liu, L., Özsu, M.T. (eds.) Encyclopedia of Database Systems, pp. 3204–3209. Springer, Boston (2009). https://doi.org/10.1007/978-0-387-39940-9
3. Charmaz, K.: Constructing Grounded Theory. Sage, Thousand Oaks (2014)
4. Coplien, J.: Software Patterns: Management Briefings. SIGS, New York (1996)
5. Fowler, M.: Command and Query Responsibility Segregation (CQRS) pattern (2011). https://martinfowler.com/bliki/CQRS.html
6. Glaser, B.G., Strauss, A.L.: The Discovery of Grounded Theory: Strategies for Qualitative Research. de Gruyter, Berlin (1967)
7. Gorton, I., Klein, J., Nurgaliev, A.: Architecture knowledge for evaluating scalable databases. In: Proceedings of the 12th Working IEEE/IFIP Conference on Software Architecture, pp. 95–104 (2015)
8. Gupta, A.: Microservice design patterns (2017). http://blog.arungupta.me/microservice-design-patterns/
9. van Heesch, U., Avgeriou, P., Hilliard, R.: A documentation framework for architecture decisions. J. Syst. Softw. **85**(4), 795–820 (2012)
10. Hentrich, C., Zdun, U., Hlupic, V., Dotsika, F.: An approach for pattern mining through grounded theory techniques and its applications to process-driven SOA patterns. In: Proceedings of the 18th European Conference on Pattern Languages of Program, pp. 9:1–9:16 (2015)
11. Hohpe, G., Woolf, B.: Enterprise Integration Patterns: Designing, Building, and Deploying Messaging Solutions. Addison-Wesley, Boston (2003)
12. Lewis, J., Fowler, M.: Microservices: a definition of this new architectural term (2014). http://martinfowler.com/articles/microservices.html
13. Lytra, I., Sobernig, S., Zdun, U.: Architectural decision making for service-based platform integration: a qualitative multi-method study. In: Proceedings of WICSA/ECSA (2012)
14. Newman, S.: Building Microservices: Designing Fine-Grained Systems. O'Reilly, Sebastopol (2015)
15. Pahl, C., Jamshidi, P.: Microservices: a systematic mapping study. In: 6th International Conference on Cloud Computing and Services Science, pp. 137–146 (2016)
16. Pautasso, C., Zimmermann, O., Leymann, F.: RESTful web services vs. big web services: making the right architectural decision. In: Proceedings of the 17th World Wide Web Conference, pp. 805–814 (2008)
17. Perrin, M.: Overview of existing models. In: Perrin, M. (ed.) Distributed Systems, pp. 23–52. Elsevier (2017)

18. Richardson, C.: A pattern language for microservices (2017). http://microservices.io/patterns/index.html
19. Zdun, U., Stocker, M., Zimmermann, O., Pautasso, C., Lübke, D.: supporting architectural decision making on quality aspects of microservice APIs. In: 16th International Conference on Service-Oriented Computing. Springer (2018)
20. Zimmermann, O.: Microservices tenets. Comput. Sci. - Res. Dev. **32**(3), 301–310 (2017)
21. Zimmermann, O., Koehler, J., Leymann, F., Polley, R., Schuster, N.: Managing architectural decision models with dependency relations, integrity constraints, and production rules. J. Syst. Softw. **82**(8), 1249–1267 (2009)

From a Monolith to a Microservices Architecture: An Approach Based on Transactional Contexts

Luís Nunes[iD], Nuno Santos[iD], and António Rito Silva[✉][iD]

INESC-ID/Department of Computer Science and Engineering,
Instituto Superior Técnico, Av. Rovisco Pais 1, 1049-001 Lisbon, Portugal
{luis.a.nunes,nuno.v.santos,rito.silva}@tecnico.ulisboa.pt

Abstract. Microservices have become the software architecture of choice for business applications. Initially originated at Netflix and Amazon, they result from the need to partition, both, software development teams and executing components, to, respectively, foster agile development and horizontal scalability. Currently, there is a large number of monolith applications that are being migrated to a microservices architecture. This article proposes the identification of business applications transactional contexts for the design of microservices. Therefore, the emphasis is to drive the aggregation of domain entities by the transactional contexts where they are executed, instead of by their domain structural inter-relationships. Additionally, we propose a complete workflow for the identification of microservices together with a set of tools that assist the developers on this process. The comparison of our approach with another software architecture tool and with an expert decomposition in two case studies revealed high precision values, which reflects that accurate service candidates are produced, while providing visualization perspectives facilitates the analysis of the impact of the decomposition on the application business logic.

Keywords: Monolith applications · Microservices architecture · Architectural migration · Transactional logic decomposition

1 Introduction

Microservices architecture [22] is increasingly being adopted as the software architecture of business applications. Initially originated at Netflix and Amazon, they result from the need to partition, both, software development teams and executing components. The former promotes the application of software agile approaches, due to smaller loosely dependent teams associated to partitions of the domain model, while the later improves the system horizontal scalability, due to the ability to have different levels of scalability for each execution context. On the other hand, a large number of existing applications are implemented using

© Springer Nature Switzerland AG 2019
T. Bures et al. (Eds.): ECSA 2019, LNCS 11681, pp. 37–52, 2019.
https://doi.org/10.1007/978-3-030-29983-5_3

the monolith architecture, where a single database is shared by all the system functionalities.

A survey done with experts identifies *Wrong Cut*, when microservices are split in the basis of technical layers instead of business capabilities, as one of the two worst bad practices when designing microservices [21]. Therefore, several approaches [12] are being proposed on how to migrate monolith systems to a microservices architecture. Most of these approaches are driven by the identification of structural modules, which have high cohesion and low coupling, in the monolith domain model. However, they do not consider the need to change the application business logic when migrating a monolith to a microservices architecture. This problem is identified in [8] as the *Forgetting about the CAP Theorem* migration smell, which states that there is a trade-off between consistency and availability [6].

We propose the identification of business applications transactional contexts for the design of microservices. Therefore, the emphasis is to drive the aggregation of domain entities by the transactional contexts where they are executed, instead of by their structural domain inter-relationships. This equips software architects to reason about the impacts of the migration on the overall system business logic, due to the relaxing of consistency. Additionally, we define a complete workflow for the identification of microservices together with a set of tools that assist the architects in this process, and apply concepts and techniques such as code analysis and graph clustering.

The comparison of our approach with another software architecture tool and an expert decomposition of the case studies resulted in high precision values, which reflects that accurate service candidates are produced.

The subsequent sections are going to be summarized as follows. Section 2 presents the concepts behind architectural migrations to microservices, Sect. 3 describes the proposed solution, where Sect. 4 evaluates the result of applying the automatic decomposition to a monolith application. Finally, Sect. 5 presents the related work and Sect. 6 the conclusions.

2 Concepts

The migration of a monolith to a microservices architecture comprises three phases: data collection, which collects information about the system that is intended to migrate to microservices architecture; microservices identification, where one, or several, criteria are applied to the collected data to identify microservices candidates; and visualization, which provides a visual representation of the identified microservices, and their relationships, according to different perspectives.

The approaches differ on which technique they use to collect the data, either manual or automatically, the type of data collected, e.g. a call graph or the execution log of the application, and if they are source code based or model-based, which in the latter case the data collection corresponds, actually, to a modeling activity followed by the extraction of information from the model.

The automatic collection of data is based on techniques like, static analysis [20] and dynamic analysis [4], which provide different types of information. Dynamic code analysis can provide richer information, for instance the number of times an entity is accessed, but it is more difficult to obtain, because it is necessary to execute the system according to the adequate execution profiles. For instance, the number of times an entity is accessed depends on the particular usage of the system, which may even be periodic.

On the other hand, the type of collected information is strongly related to how each of the authors characterize a microservice and what they consider as the relevant qualities of a microservices system. For instance, some approaches use the log of the commits in a version control system repository, because they emphasize the team work separation quality of microservices architectures, while other approaches collect the number of invocations between domain entities, because they intend to reduce the communication cost between microservices in order to achieve good performance.

In what concerns the model-based approaches, they define high level representations of the system, for instance use case models and business process models, to represent the information considered necessary for the identification of microservices, arguing that the monolith may have an initial poor design and it is necessary to do some reverse engineering activities. Additionally, these approaches may be applied to the development of a microservices system from scratch. However, the possible mismatch between the source code and its model representation may hinder the microservices extraction to be done by the developer, once the microservices are finally identified by architect. Actually, according to a recent survey [11], industry experts rely on low-level sources of information, like the source code and test suites, which means that even if a model-based approach is followed, the existence of tools that analyze the source code cannot be completely dismissed.

In the microservices identification phase a metric is defined over the collected data. By using this metric a similarity measure between the system elements is calculated, such that a clustering algorithm can be applied to aggregate the monolith entities, maximizing the intra-cluster similarity and minimizing the inter-cluster similarity, where each cluster becomes a microservice candidate. Some of the approaches do not even suggest the application of a clustering algorithm but foster the identification of the microservices by the human observation of a graph, where the similarities between the monolith elements are visually represented.

Obviously, there is a close relationship between the metric and the type of data collected, for instance, if the data is about the invocations between microservices, then the metric gives a high similarity value between two monolith elements, if they have a high number of mutual invocations, such that they can be part of the same cluster.

The visualization phase uses the collected data and, together with the metric of the previous phase, presents a graph that can be analyzed according to different perspectives. For instance, it may be possible to visualize information associated with edges between cluster nodes, for instance, the number of invocations, such that the architect can reason on the impact of these dependencies on the final microservices architecture.

Sixteen microservices coupling criteria are presented in [13]. They extract the coupling information from models and create an indirect, weighted, graph to generate clusters, using two different algorithms that define priorities for each one of the criteria. Finally, the result clusters are visualized. Although they provide the most extensive description of coupling criteria, by being based on models, they require, for some of the criteria, that part of the identification is already done. For instance, for the consistency criticality criteria it is necessary to provide information about the consistency level between the monolith elements, high, eventual, and weak. However, the identification of this information already assumes that the monolith is somehow divided and the impact of the migration in the business logic already identified, because in a monolith the consistency between its elements is always high, due to ACID transactions and their strict consistency.

3   Decomposition by Transactional Contexts

The main objective of this paper is to present a set of tools that support software architects on the process of migrating from a monolithic to a microservices architecture. Our solution relies on the identification of transactional contexts where a business transaction is divided into several transactional contexts.

We assume a software architecture for the monolith that applies the Model-View-Controller (MVC) architectural style, where the business transactions are represented by the controllers. In the monolith, the execution of a controller corresponds to the transactional execution of a request. Therefore, the monolith was designed considering the sequences of these requests, where each one of them is implemented by an ACID transaction and strict consistency. In order to reduce the impact of the migration on the system design we intend to group the domain entities accessed by a controller inside the same microservice, avoiding the introduction of relaxed consistency to the business functionality. Therefore, ideally, a controller would be implemented by a single microservice encapsulating its own database. However, there are domain entities that are accessed by several controllers. Our metric gives lower values to domain entities that are accessed the same controllers, such that they can be located in the same cluster.

Although the tools were developed for an implementation of the monolith in Spring-Boot Java and using the FénixFramework [7] object-relational mapper (ORM), the overall approached can be applied to any monolith that follows the MVC style. The FénixFramework generates a set of classes that represent the domain entities, contain the persistent information, and correspond to the data access layer. Therefore, in the first phase we do a static analysis to the monolith source code to collect, for each controller, which classes generated by the FénixFramework are accessed. This static analysis captures the controllers call graphs using the java-callgraph[1] tool.

The metric is then implement as a similarity measure using the following formula, which returns higher values for pairs of domain entities that are accessed by the same controllers:

$$W_{E1E2} = \frac{N_{Ctrl}(E1E2)}{N_{Ctrl}(E1)} \tag{1}$$

Where, given two domain entities, $E1$ and $E2$, the weight from entity $E1$ to entity $E2$ is the quotient between the number of controllers for which their invocation tree has both, $E1$ and $E2$, as nodes ($N_{Ctrl}(E1E2)$) and the total number of controllers for which their invocation tree has $E1$ as a node ($N_{Ctrl}(E1)$). When applying this measure to a clustering algorithm, in an ideal decomposition, the entities in the same cluster are accessed by the same controllers. The domain entities are clustered using a hierarchical clustering algorithm implemented by the Scipy[2] Python library which generates a dendrogram. Finally, a user interface is used where the software architect can experiment with several cuts in the dendrogram to generate different sets of clusters. After a cut in the dendrogram is done, we support additional experimentation by allowing the architect to rename, merge and split clusters, as well as move an entity between clusters.

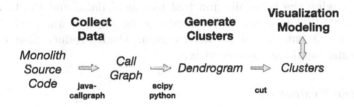

Fig. 1. Data flow schema of the tools to be developed.

The overview of the process behind the examination of the monolithic application can be seen in Fig. 1, and has the following workflow:

1. **Collect Data:** The architect uses a static code analyser implemented using the java-callgraph to generate the text call-graph.
2. **Generate Clusters:** The architect interacts with the web application to generate the dendrogram from the call-graph, using a hierarchical clustering algorithm. Afterwards, cuts the dendrogram, given a value for the maximum distance between domain entities inside each cluster, generating a set of clusters.

---

[1] https://github.com/gousiosg/java-callgraph.
[2] https://www.scipy.org/.

3. **Visualization:** The architect visualizes the generated information according to three views: clusters of entities and how they are accessed by controllers; the accesses pattern of controllers on clusters; the impact of domain entities data on controllers executing in other clusters.
4. **Modeling:** The architect can manipulate each one of the views, which supports informed experimentation because the tool recalculates the weights whenever a change is done.

4   Evaluation and Discussion

The approach was applied to two monolith web applications, LdoD[3] and Blended Workflow[4], but for the sake of space, only the results of the LdoD analysis are presented in the article. The analysis of the Blended Workflow provided similar insights.

4.1   LdoD

The LdoD archive[5] is a collaborative digital archive that contains the Book of Disquiet, originally written by Portuguese poet, Fernando Pessoa. LdoD monolith contains 152 controllers and 55 domain entities, being that 37 of the controllers do not make contact with the domain (24% of the systems controllers).

After applying the java-callgraph tool to collect data, and the hierarchical clustering algorithm to generate the dendrogram, we have analyzed the result according to different cuts of the dendrogram, which produce distinct cluster configurations, candidate microservices.

4.2   Metric Evaluation

As supported by the evaluation of other approaches for software architecture recovery [3,17], an internal and external assessment of the clusters is made.

Internal Evaluation. To perform an intrinsic evaluation of the clustering results for our applications, we have done an ad hoc analysis with metrics proposed by us, except for the silhouette score. These metrics allows us to compare the quality of the clustering resulting from the different cuts.

1. **Number of Singleton Clusters (NSC),** being that having more than 2 singleton clusters is considered negative. Considering a final microservice architecture with clear functional boundaries established, it is likely that there are not two services in which their content is a single domain entity.

---

[3] https://github.com/socialsoftware/edition.
[4] https://github.com/socialsoftware/blended-workflow.
[5] https://ldod.uc.pt.

2. **Maximum Cluster Size (MCS)**, should not be bigger than half of the size of the system. Even with a cluster size inside this range, there is also a dependency regarding the number of entity instances that are part of the aggregate, since invocation of a microservice will bring an aggregate to memory [10]. This aspect is not addressed in this paper.

3. **Silhouette Score (SS)**, given by Eq. 4, where a represents the mean intra-cluster distance (Eq. 2: distance between object o_i and the remaining objects in the cluster) and b the mean nearest-cluster distance (Eq. 3: distance between object o_i and the objects of the neighbor cluster, the one that has the smallest average dissimilarity). This score ranges its values from -1 to 1, representing incorrect clustering (samples on wrong clusters) and highly dense clustering respectively. For every object in a cluster, when this score is high (closer to 1) the mean intra-cluster distance is going to be smaller than the mean nearest-cluster distance, implying that the object is well classified. This metric creates a parallelism with the overall coupling of the clusters of the system, as our objective was to obtain a high intra-cluster similarity and a low inter-cluster similarity, so the partition between clusters is well defined. The silhouette value evaluates exactly this information. In the scope of our problem we calculate the silhouette score for the entire cluster data of the presented cut, meaning that we have to calculate the silhouette of each cluster by averaging the score of all the object inside them and then average the score of all the clusters, reaching a value for the entire dataset.

$$a(o_i) = \frac{1}{|C_A| - 1} \sum_{o_j \in C_A, o_j \neq o_i} d(o_i, o_j) \tag{2}$$

$$b(o_i) = min_{C_b \neq C_A} \frac{1}{|C_B|} \sum_{o_j \in C_B} d(o_i, o_j) \tag{3}$$

$$Silhouette(o_i) = \frac{(b(o_i) - a(o_i))}{max(a(o_i), b(o_i))} \tag{4}$$

In Table 1 we apply the metrics for four cuts of a dendrogram with a max height of 4.0:

Table 1. Internal evaluation results for LdoD.

	Cut(0.01)	Cut(1.5)	Cut(2.5)	Cut(3.5)
Number of Retrieved Clusters (NRC)	40	11	3	2
Number of Singleton Clusters (NSC)	34	3	0	0
Maximum Cluster Size (MCS)	5	18	26	31
Silhouette Score (SS)	0.38	0.48	0.55	0.56

1. The maximization of intra-cluster similarity, given by a cut with the lowest possible value.
2. A cut at an intermediate value, establishing an attempt to make a trade-off between the granularity and the cluster similarity.
3. Two high valued cuts that try to split the system into its main components, usually with a size of 2–4 clusters.

Assessing first our ad-hoc metrics, when increasing the value of the height of the cut on the dendrogram, the NSC and NRC decrease while the MSC increases, which is expected as higher the height less clusters are formed, being that those contain more domain entities. Also, the silhouette score increases with height to a maximum, showing that at that point are formed the ideal clusters according to this metric.

External Evaluation. In this type of evaluation we compare with an expert decomposition both, the results of our approach and the results of applying a software architecture analysis tool, Structure101[6], which uses cyclomatic complexity measures and the identification of cyclic dependencies to define a structural decomposition.

Usually, the computation of evaluation metrics following the use of clustering is done in a pairwise fashion, where, in our case, the pairs of domain entities in the clusters of the decomposition being evaluated are compared with the pairs in the clusters of the domain expert decomposition. The most appropriate metrics for our approach are pairwise precision, recall and f-score, given by Eqs. 5, 6 and 7 respectively.

$$precision = \frac{tp}{tp + fp} \tag{5}$$

$$recall = \frac{tp}{tp + fn} \tag{6}$$

$$F\text{-}score = 2 * \frac{precision * recall}{precision + recall} \tag{7}$$

Where tp (true positives) represents the number of pairs that are in both, the decomposition being evaluated and the expert decomposition, fp (false positives) the number of pairs that are not in the expert decomposition but are in the decomposition being evaluated, and fn (false negatives) the number of pairs that are in the expert decomposition but not in the decomposition being evaluated. Therefore, the precision captures the accuracy whether two domain entities in a cluster actually belong to the same microservice, and the recall the percentage of domain entity pairs correctly assigned to the same microservice.

The pairwise assessment of these metrics for dendrogram cut of 2.5 is presented in Table 2, when comparing the two generated decompositions with the expert decomposition. We can see that the results of our approach for all the presented metrics are higher than Structure101. On the other hand, doing a detailed

---
[6] https://structure101.com/.

analysis, in the three clusters resulting from the 2.5 LdoD cut, we observe that the first is a sub-cluster of a cluster of the expert decomposition, the second is accessed by all controllers, and the third one contains five entities that are responsible for deleting and loading fragments, used by controllers associated with the administration functionalities. Structure101 originates ten clusters from which six are singletons. Of the remaining four, three are sub-clusters of the expert decomposition and the fourth is accessed by all controllers.

Table 2. External evaluation results for 2.5 cut, Structure101 and 1.5 cut.

	Precision	Recall	F-score
Transactional clustering 2.5 cut	73% ($\frac{445}{611}$)	48% ($\frac{445}{926}$)	0.58
Structure101	58% ($\frac{166}{285}$)	18% ($\frac{166}{926}$)	0.27
Transactional clustering 1.5 cut	99% ($\frac{233}{234}$)	25% ($\frac{233}{926}$)	0.40

From this analysis we conclude that, although the use of metrics to identify the best cuts is relevant, it does not exclude the experimentation of other intermediate cuts because smaller clusters may be easily analysed by the expert, which may decided to integrate them with other clusters.

The chosen intermediate cut of the system and its evaluation is also shown in the Table 2. Note that for the 1.5 cut, our precision is much higher, this happens as the smaller clusters formed by a lower cut are almost all subsets of the clusters of the expert decomposition. On the other hand, the recall values are lower, as the singleton clusters are properly penalized by this metric. The only false positive (in 1/11 retrieved clusters) resides in the cluster with the entities LdoD, LdoDUser and VirtualEdition. LdoD is an immutable singleton and the entry point to the domain entities, which can be easily replicated in any cluster. LdoDUser and VirtualEdition were identified by the expert as being used in two different scopes, authentication and virtual edition management, respectively. Our tool classified these entities as being part of the same cluster as they appear together transactionally so, we are going to analyze these cases by using the visualization tool.

4.3   Visualization Analysis

After the metric evaluation of the clusters generated automatically, the software architect uses the visualization tool to do a detailed analysis of the decomposition.

Figure 2(a) shows Cluster0 containing the three entities. It has strong connections with other clusters, the edges thickness represent the number of controllers shared between the two connected clusters. Which means that almost all controllers access Cluster0. The model was already subjected to some changes by

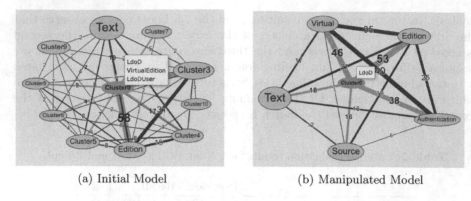

(a) Initial Model   (b) Manipulated Model

Fig. 2. Cluster views presenting clusters and the relations between them

the architect, basically, some of the clusters were renamed to have a domain-specific name, to improve readability. According to the expert these three entities, once created, are not further modified and are frequently accessed because they are the entry point for almost all functionalities. Therefore, since they are immutable, they can be easily replicated. This case constitutes a good example why the visualization tools provide an essential help to the software architect. Part (b) shows the model resulting from several transformation applied to the initial model, cluster rename, merge and split, and entity move between clusters, such that the architect can experiment, and fine tune, the decompositions.

Additionally, our visualization tool allows architects to identify how the business functionality is split between the different clusters. This is particularly relevant because it helps to analyze the impact of the decomposition in the business functionality.

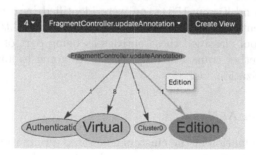

Fig. 3. Controller view of *updateAnnotation* controller and the clusters accessed.

Figure 3 shows the transactional behavior of **Update Annotation** controller occurring in the context of four clusters (candidate microservices). It is possible to identity which entities are accessed in each cluster, whose number is shown in the edge. By analysing the model we can conclude that this decomposition does not have impact on the business logic of this functionality, because all semantically relevant accesses are to cluster Virtual. The accesses to the other clusters are to read immutable information for authentication (Authentication), access the persistent information through the LdoD singleton object (Cluster0), and get the Edition where the annotation is done (Edition). The figure highlights that the only entity accessed in cluster Edition is entity Edition. Note that this cluster contains more entities. It also illustrates that the controllers are selected by the number of clusters they access, 4 in this case (top left corner of the figure), which allows the software architect to easily identify in which controllers the decomposition can have more impact, if they access more clusters it may be necessary to relax their transactional behaviour.

Another visualization that can improve the split of functionalities is to identify which entities are accessed by controllers that also access other clusters, because it may be necessary to relax their consistency, since they are shared between business transactions executing through different microservices. However, when experimenting with this functionality, we realized that the each entity is accessed by all clusters, because there are some controllers, mainly administration controllers that create or delete the domain, and so, they access all domain entities. Therefore, we are considering, in future versions of the visualization tool, to allow the filtering of controllers, and also to use additional information to characterize the relations between clusters, for instance, by also collecting the dataflow between domain entities. Note that currently only the control flow information was collected.

From this discussion, we conclude that it is useful to analyse the relations between clusters through the use of our visualization tool, which shows that it is not enough to rely on the automatic decompositions, but tools should be provided to help to reason about the decomposition and its impacts, in particular, because the decomposition may have impact on the system business logic. Additionally, it is advantageous to enriched the visualization tool with modeling capabilities.

5   Related Work

In [12] it is done an analysis of several approaches for the migration of a monolith to a microservices architecture. Most microservices migration proposals do not consider the need to change the application business logic when migrating a monolith to a microservices architecture, focusing, instead, on the structural aspects related with the high cohesion and low coupling of the microservices. This problem is identified in [8] as the *Forgetting about the CAP Theorem* migration smell, and may have an high impact on the migration of a monolith because it imparts on the users perception of the system operation, which drives our decision to also provide tools for architectural experimentation.

In [23] the authors apply the three migration phases but the clustering phase is not automated, it is based on the observation of a graph. The data is collected from use cases specifications and their decomposition into the domain entities they access. The metric is based on the data shared between operations, the operations that access the same data should belong to the same microservice. It is weighted by the reads and writes from the operations to the data objects, writes have more weight because there is a emphasis on having reads between microservices. They share with our approach the concern in focusing on how business functionalities are decomposed, but their final concern is on the operation level, instead of the controller, because they seek to have high cohesion and low coupling between operations. Their final visualization does not highlight how the business transactions are decomposed into the set of candidate microservices.

To improve performance, in [19], a runtime profiling is used to collect the information about the amount of communication between classes. Additionally, it also supports a semantic clustering that uses a *td-idf* (term frequency/inverse document frequency) to create clusters based on the similarity between names of classes and methods. None of these tactics consider transactional contexts and, so, the decomposition of the business logic. The user starts by deciding which of the two clustering criteria to use, and then visualizes the resulting graph, where a node represents a class and an edge a function call between two classes. Classes belonging to the same cluster have the same color and the edge thickness represents the amount of communication between classes. Representing clusters by colored classes has the advantage of making immediately visible the classes in a cluster, though it may the too confusing if there is a large number of classes. This is one of the few approaches that enhance visualization with modelling capabilities, it allows manipulation of the clusters, e.g. move a class between clusters, which results in the recalculation of the clusters, as we do.

In order to improve the performance of a microservices architecture, in [16], they apply a workload-based feature clustering. The approach is model-based, it uses a feature model, where the microservices identification, each microservice contains one or more features, is driven by a trade-off between performance, which is inversely proportional to the amount of inter-microservices communication, and scalability, which is directly proportional to the number of microservices. They propose the aggregation of features into microservices according to this trade-off in a specific-workload. They focus on feature model aggregation for deploy in a cloud instead of the identification of the microservices in a monolith, and consider that the implementation of the feature model allows features re-combinations, not considering how these impact on the application business logic, because different recombinations may impact differently.

In [9] it is proposed an approach for migrating a monolith implemented using Java Enterprise Edition (JEE). They do static analysis to capture the invocations between the elements. Afterwards, associate a cluster to each session bean and aggregate them according to a threshold, such that the distance between clusters depends on the number of shared entities. Final clusters have one or more session beans and the entities may be shared between different clusters. Finally, it is possible to visualize the clusters, showing the session beans it contains, and the entities shared between two clusters. In our approach we aggregate the data entities that are accessed by the same business transactions, controllers, which is similar to their session beans, but their clusters are formed by session beans instead of domain entities, which hinders the analysis of how the business logic of a business transaction is split between microservices. Therefore, they assume that the microservices interfaces will be preserved, they correspond to the session beans interfaces, while we consider that the migration to the microservices architecture may impact on the application business logic due to the change in the overall consistency of the system, from strict to eventual or weak, which may require the carefully redefinition of the microservices interfaces.

In [1] each functional requirement is a microservice candidate. Afterwards they classify each candidate in terms of scalability and security non-functional requirements and the level of dependency between them. The candidates for which it is expected to have a high volume of requests are considered to require scalability. Then, for those with high and medium scalability requirements it is verified the level of dependency with the other candidates, where a high dependency level corresponds to the frequency of invocations between them. If two microservices are highly dependent and require security, which results in an high overheads, the candidates will be merged into a single microservice. This approach is model-based, which means that the data for the metrics is captured through requirements elicitation and focus on functional composition instead of on a real decomposition of a monolith.

In [15] execution traces analysis are used to generate two types of traces, class-level traces, which capture the classes accessed, and method-level traces, which capture the methods invocations. The microservices are identified by clustering the class-level traces that contain the same classes. Afterwards, the method-level traces are used to identify the interfaces for the candidate microservices. It does not propose any visualization tool. Similarly to our proposal, they aggregate the classes that are shared by the same business capabilities, contrarily to most approaches that focus on structural, coupling and cohesion, and semantic, naming convention, aspects. Their process is automatic, whereas we also propose a visualization tool that allows the experiment with several decompositions, to analyse the impact on the business logic.

In [2] they identify the microservices from a business process point of view. A business processes model is used to identify structural dependency, when there is a direct edge between two activities, and object dependency, when activities have similar data access, assigning a higher weight for writes. These two relations are aggregated in a metric that is use to generate clusters that represent candidate microservices. This model-based approach focus on the structural aspects, aggregate activities that access the same data and are executed next to each other, which result in clusters of activities from which is not possible to assess the impact of the decomposition on the application business logic. Actually, the business process model already describes a business logic between activities, and their aggregation may allow a more strict consistency between the activities that become aggregated in the same microservice, as they will share the same transactional context. Their focus is on composition.

In [5] it is proposed a solution based on semantic similarity that matches the terms used in an OpenAPI specification with a domain vocabulary to suggest decompositions. This is a model-based approach, which requires two models (OpenAPI specification and domain vocabulary), and it is focused on identifying cohesive operations, which access the same data, ignoring the transactional business logic.

In [18] microservice candidates are suggested following an algorithmic approach subsequent to the extraction of data from a version control repository of a monolithic application. They propose three different metrics: single responsibility principle, based on classes that change together in commits; semantic coupling, based on *tfidf* to identify classes that contain code about the same things; and contributor coupling strategy, based on classes accessed by the same team. These metrics focus on the structural aspects, mainly related with the development process and the split of a domain model to control its complexity.

Some approaches propose the analysis of design trade-offs and the dynamic autonomous composition [14], but this is only applicable if the business logic does not vary according to the composition, which does not apply to all types of microservices. Therefore, the transactional contexts approach is particularly suitable for application with a rich domain logic where microservices become logically interdependent, which may require the redesign of the monolith functionality.

6   Conclusions

This paper proposes an approach to the migration of monolith applications to a microservices architecture that focus on the impact of the decomposition on the monolith business logic, an aspect that is not addressed by the existing approaches, and which is described as *forgetting about the CAP Theorem*. Our approach is based on the static analysis of the source code of a monolith, implemented following a Model-View-Controller architectural style, which is enforced by the most popular tools for web development, like Spring-Boot and Django. Therefore, a call graph is obtained for controllers, which are associated to the monolith functionalities. From the call graph are identified the domain entities that are accessed by each controller, and a clustering algorithm is applied to aggregate domain entities that are shared by the same controllers, to reduce the decomposition impact on the monolith business functionality. The resulting decomposition is analysed according to several metrics and an external evaluation, which compares the results with an existing industrial tool and a domain expert. The results are promising, but it is clear that it is necessary to provide more tools to support the experimentation with different candidate decompositions. Therefore, we also propose a visualization tool that allows the rename, merge and split of clusters, and the move of entities between clusters. It also supports different views, cluster, controller and entity, to help on the analysis of the impact of the decomposition on the monolith business logic.

Additionally, and due to the recent research done on the migration from monolith to microservices, the paper presents an extensive description of the related work in order to place our approach in a context that is quickly evolving and which is not yet completely bounded and classified.

The main limitations of this work are: (1) being specific for applications developed using the Fénix Framework; and (2) the java-callgraph tool did not capture calls inside Java 8 streams. Concerning the former limitation, we believe that the results apply to other implementations of web application, as soon as they clearly distinguish controllers from entities. Note that this also includes web applications that do not have views, but which provide a web API, e.g. REST. In what concerns the use of java-callgraph, we have done a manual verification of the collect data to ensure its correctness.

In terms of future work, we are already finishing an Eclipse plugin that captures the controllers call graphs using the Eclipse JDT library. On the other hand, we intend to experiment with decompositions where more information is available, in particular, we intend to distinguish reads from write accesses done by controllers and the dataflows inside controllers, to analyse its impact on cluster generations and in the visualization tools, because, in terms of eventual consistency of an application, the separation of reads from writes and dataflows are crucial for its software architecture design.

The tools source code is publicly available in a github repository[7].

Acknowledgment. This work was supported by national funds through Fundação para a Ciência e Tecnologia (FCT) with reference UID/CEC/50021/2019.

References

1. Ahmadvand, M., Ibrahim, A.: Requirements reconciliation for scalable and secure microservice (de)composition. In: 2016 IEEE 24th International Requirements Engineering Conference Workshops (REW), pp. 68–73, September 2016
2. Amiri, M.J.: Object-aware identification of microservices. In: 2018 IEEE International Conference on Services Computing (SCC), pp. 253–256, July 2018
3. Anquetil, N., Fourrier, C., Lethbridge, T.C.: Experiments with clustering as a software remodularization method. In: Proceedings of the Sixth Working Conference on Reverse Engineering, WCRE 1999, p. 235, IEEE Computer Society, Washington, DC (1999)
4. Ball, T.: The concept of dynamic analysis. SIGSOFT Softw. Eng. Notes **24**(6), 216–234 (1999)
5. Baresi, L., Garriga, M., De Renzis, A.: Microservices identification through interface analysis. In: De Paoli, F., Schulte, S., Broch Johnsen, E. (eds.) ESOCC 2017. LNCS, vol. 10465, pp. 19–33. Springer, Cham (2017). https://doi.org/10.1007/978-3-319-67262-5_2
6. Brewer, E.A.: Towards robust distributed systems (abstract). In: Proceedings of the Nineteenth Annual ACM Symposium on Principles of Distributed Computing, PODC 2000, p. 7. ACM, New York (2000)

---

[7] https://github.com/socialsoftware/mono2micro.

7. Cachopo, J., Rito-Silva, A.: Combining software transactional memory with a domain modeling language to simplify web application development. In: Proceedings of the 6th International Conference on Web Engineering, ICWE 2006, pp. 297–304. ACM, New York (2006)
8. Carrasco, A., van Bladel, B., Demeyer, S.: Migrating towards microservices: migration and architecture smells. In: Proceedings of the 2nd International Workshop on Refactoring, IWoR 2018, pp. 1–6. ACM, New York (2018)
9. Escobar, D., et al.: Towards the understanding and evolution of monolithic applications as microservices. In: 2016 XLII Latin American Computing Conference (CLEI), pp. 1–11, October 2016
10. Evans, E.J.: Domain-Driven Design: Tackling Complexity In the Heart of Software. Addison-Wesley Longman Publishing Co., Inc., Boston (2003)
11. Di Francesco, P., Lago, P., Malavolta, I.: Migrating towards microservice architectures: an industrial survey. In: 2018 IEEE International Conference on Software Architecture (ICSA), p. 29-2909, April 2018
12. Fritzsch, J., Bogner, J., Zimmermann, A., Wagner, S.: From monolith to microservices: a classification of refactoring approaches. In: Bruel, J.-M., Mazzara, M., Meyer, B. (eds.) DEVOPS 2018. LNCS, vol. 11350, pp. 128–141. Springer, Cham (2019). https://doi.org/10.1007/978-3-030-06019-0_10
13. Gysel, M., Kölbener, L., Giersche, W., Zimmermann, O.: Service cutter: a systematic approach to service decomposition. In: Aiello, M., Johnsen, E.B., Dustdar, S., Georgievski, I. (eds.) ESOCC 2016. LNCS, vol. 9846, pp. 185–200. Springer, Cham (2016). https://doi.org/10.1007/978-3-319-44482-6_12
14. Hassan, S., Bahsoon, R.: Microservices and their design trade-offs: a self-adaptive roadmap. In: 2016 IEEE International Conference on Services Computing (SCC), pp. 813–818, June 2016
15. Jin, W., Liu, T., Zheng, Q., Cui, D., Cai, Y.: Functionality-oriented microservice extraction based on execution trace clustering. In: 2018 IEEE International Conference on Web Services (ICWS), pp. 211–218, July 2018
16. Klock, S., Van Der Werf, J.M.E.M., Guelen, J.P., Jansen, S.: Workload-based clustering of coherent feature sets in microservice architectures. In: 2017 IEEE International Conference on Software Architecture (ICSA), pp. 11–20, April 2017
17. Maqbool, O., Babri, H.: Hierarchical clustering for software architecture recovery. IEEE Trans. Softw. Eng. **33**(11), 759–780 (2007)
18. Mazlami, G., Cito, J., Leitner, P.: Extraction of microservices from monolithic software architectures. In: 2017 IEEE International Conference on Web Services (ICWS), pp. 524–531. IEEE (2017)
19. Nakazawa, R., Ueda, T., Enoki, M., Horii, H.: Visualization tool for designing microservices with the monolith-first approach. In: 2018 IEEE Working Conference on Software Visualization (VISSOFT), pp. 32–42, September 2018
20. Nielson, F., Nielson, H.R., Hankin, C.: Principles of Program Analysis. Springer, Heidelberg (1999). https://doi.org/10.1007/978-3-662-03811-6
21. Taibi, D., Lenarduzzi, V.: On the definition of microservice bad smells. IEEE Softw. **35**(3), 56–62 (2018)
22. Thönes, J.: Microservices. IEEE Softw. **32**(1), 116 (2015)
23. Tyszberowicz, S., Heinrich, R., Liu, B., Liu, Z.: Identifying microservices using functional decomposition. In: Feng, X., Müller-Olm, M., Yang, Z. (eds.) SETTA 2018. LNCS, vol. 10998, pp. 50–65. Springer, Cham (2018). https://doi.org/10.1007/978-3-319-99933-3_4

Software Architecture in Development Process

An Exploratory Study of Naturalistic Decision Making in Complex Software Architecture Environments

Ken Power[1]([✉]) [iD] and Rebecca Wirfs-Brock[2]

[1] Independent, Galway, Ireland
ken.power@gmail.com
[2] Wirfs-Brock Associates, Sherwood, OR, USA
rebecca@wirfs-brock.com

Abstract. Architects always make decisions in some context. That context shifts and changes dynamically. Different decision-making strategies are appropriate in different contexts. Architecture decisions are at times made under conditions of time pressure, high stakes, uncertainty, and with too little information. At other times, decision-makers have sufficient time to reflect on the decision and consider alternatives. Understanding context is critical to choosing appropriate approaches to architecture decision making. Naturalistic Decision Making (NDM) explains how people make decisions under real-world conditions. This paper investigates NDM in software architecture and studies architecture decisions in their environment and decision-making context. The research approach includes a case study of large technology organizations consisting of a survey, multiple focus groups, and participant observation. Previous studies that touch on NDM in software architecture have mainly focused on decision-making processes or tools or developing decision models. This paper provides three contributions. First, we build on previous studies by other researchers to produce an in-depth exploration of NDM in the context of software architecture. We focus on Recognition-Primed Decision (RPD) making as an implementation of NDM. Second, we present an examination of the decisions made by experienced architects under conditions that can be considered *naturalistic*. Third, we provide examples and recommendations that help software architects determine when an NDM approach is appropriate for their context.

Keywords: Naturalistic Decision Making ·
Recognition primed decision making · Software architecture · Complexity ·
Decision context · Large-scale

1 Introduction

Architecture decision-making is an inherently complex task because decisions often must satisfy multiple constraints and address multiple stakeholder concerns [1, 2]. Software architects make decisions related to architecture style of the system as well as technological and economical decisions [2]. Several formal, analytic architecture decision-making approaches have been published [3, 4] yet software engineering

© Springer Nature Switzerland AG 2019
T. Bures et al. (Eds.): ECSA 2019, LNCS 11681, pp. 55–70, 2019.
https://doi.org/10.1007/978-3-030-29983-5_4

researchers find few used in practice. One explanation for this may be that complex real-world decisions are not always about making tradeoffs, but instead about finding a decision that satisfices the current situation and allows for action [5]. Naturalistic Decision Making (NDM) originated with the goal of studying how people actually make decisions in a variety of real-world settings, as opposed to in classroom or laboratory settings [6]. These settings include conditions of time pressure, high stakes, experienced decision makers, inadequate information, ill-defined goals, poorly defined procedures, dynamic conditions, and team coordination [7]. There are times where architects need to make decisions under such circumstances. This paper seeks to further contribute to understanding how software architects make decisions under these conditions. In particular we study architecture decision-making in large, complex, software-intensive systems. Such systems are characterized by many components and sub systems developed by geographically-distributed teams, with responsibility for the architecture shared among multiple architects. Interactions among people and systems with emergent properties often result in non-linear, non-deterministic outcomes. This paper presents findings from an exploratory case study of architects making decisions in this context. Section 2 reviews key literature including a comprehensive review of the NDM literature, and studies in software architecture that mention or explore NDM. Section 3 presents the research questions and describes the approach used to answer the questions. Section 4 presents findings from this study. Section 5 is a discussion of the findings, reflecting on the research questions. Section 6 presents conclusions from this study, including a set of recommendations based on the findings, and notes future research that builds on this study.

2 Literature Review

2.1 Naturalistic Decision Making

NDM researchers specifically focus on real-world settings [8]. NDM is a *"pragmatic, realistic approach to understanding decision making"* [9]. NDM researchers have studied many settings, including firefighters, emergency responders, military personnel, police, surgeons, and design engineers [7, 10–12]. Settings under which NDM applies include the following [7]:

- **Time pressure**. NDM is concerned with how decision-makers operate when time is a constraint. Time pressure does not always mean an instantaneous response is required; NDM is cognizant of the context of the decision maker.
- **High stakes**. If a surgeon or firefighter makes a poor decision, lives can be lost. If a software architect makes a poor decision, millions of dollars can be lost. The reputation of the company and the product can be at stake.
- **Experienced decision makers**. NDM assumes experience in the domain as a prerequisite for making high-stakes decisions [7].
- **Inadequate information.** This includes uncertainty about the data, ambiguous data, and missing data. NDM researchers are interested in how decision makers make progress in the face of the uncertainty caused by too little information, or even poor or wrong information [7].

- **Ill-defined goals.** The goal is often poorly defined or poorly structured. There is a lack of clear direction on what to do, and how to do it. The goal might change, or there could be multiple competing goals [13].
- **Poorly defined procedures.** NDM is concerned with poorly defined procedures. In contrast to conventional lab-based studies on decision-making, NDM acknowledges that decision-makers often need to invent novel procedures, or modify existing ones, in order to meet a goal [7].
- **Cue learning.** This refers to the ability of decision-makers to recognize patterns and make distinctions as an aid to decision making [7]. Building on research by Simon [14], Kahneman and Klein [15] equate this ability with intuition, noting that intuition is *"nothing more and nothing less than recognition."*
- **Dynamic and continually changing conditions.** Decision makers need to deal with situations where the conditions around them are changing continually.
- **Group coordination.** The need for coordination among multiple people is a factor in most domains in which NDM has been studied [7].

There are many different models of NDM [16]. All these models have a purpose, and no one model encompasses everything. One of the better-known NDM models is the Recognition Primed Decision (RPD) model [17]. The RPD model focuses on assessing the situation, versus judging one option superior to others. RPD describes how people make decisions using their expertise. Experienced decision makers identify a reasonably good option as the first one they consider (cue learning), rather than generate many options for consideration. Expert decision makers conduct mental simulations of courses of action to determine if it will work, rather than contrasting strengths and weaknesses of multiple options. Where multiple options are considered, they are considered through serial satisficing rather than concurrent deliberation. An advantage of an RPD strategy is the decision maker is always ready to act, rather than waiting for a completed analysis that identifies a winner among multiple options.

The conditions under which NDM applies are, of course, not the only conditions under which architects make decisions. In analytic decision-making models the focus is on identifying situations such strategies are effective or where they fail due to cognitive limitations [18]. In contrast RPD models of decision-making focus on the conditions where people can effectively make decisions without exhaustively considering alternatives [5]. Klein identified three strategies for recognition-primed decision making: when both the details of a situation and an appropriate action are recognized, essentially an if-then-action; when an unknown situation is encountered but there are only a limited set of reasonable actions, gather and fill in enough missing information before taking an appropriate action; and when there is a known situation but the appropriate action to take is unclear, run through a mental simulation of potential actions to find the first acceptable action.

Early decision-making research focused decision-making models based on a rational consideration of alternatives. Given a known, limited set of alternatives, a decision-maker should be able reason about the alternatives. However, Simon [19] proposed that complex situations, limited time and our limited mental computational capacities constrain our decision-making and that consequently our decision-making is "bounded". Instead of collecting and processing all possible information, we necessarily construct a simplified model of the relevant factors contributing to the decision, in order to analyze the consequences of each alternative to select the "best" one. Consequently decision-making is bounded by both the structure of the information in the environment and limits of our mental capabilities [19].

Klein [6] summarizes how core beliefs in decision-making have changed. NDM asserts that experienced decision makers draw on patterns to deal with time pressure, and do not compare options. Expertise primarily depends on tacit knowledge. Projects don't always start with a clear description, particularly if dealing with "wicked problems" [20]. Experienced people in a given situation use their mental models to define what counts as data, rather than systematically building up from data to information to knowledge to understanding. Insights arise by detecting contradictions, anomalies, and connections. Uncertainty is not reduced by gathering more information but can stem from poor framing of data.

NDM research focuses on understanding the conditions under which experts make decisions and how they recognize environmental cues to guide their judgment. Skilled expertise is acquired through practice and developing skilled intuitions in high-validity environments which provide opportunities to learn [15]. Environments have high validity when there are stable relationships between cues and subsequent events, or between cues and the outcomes of actions. High validity does not correlate to certainty; some highly valid environments are also highly uncertain. Kahneman and Klein [12] observe that true experts *"know when they do not know"*, but *"non-experts certainly do not know when they do not know."* The subjective confidence of a decision-maker in a decision is an unreliable indicator of a decision's validity.

Kahneman characterizes two modes of thinking: System 1, which operates automatically and quickly; and System 2, which is slower, effortful, and deliberate [21]. Both systems operate in tandem: System 1 originates impressions and feelings that are the source of beliefs and more deliberate choices made by System 2. Understanding distinctions between these systems helps inform how NDM relates to other decision making approaches [15]. For example, in Recognition-Primed Decision Making (RPDM), System 1 thinking can bring promising solutions quickly to mind, which then are simulated and more deliberately evaluated by System 2. As System 2 monitors environmental cues, System 1 intuitions may be challenged and result in more deliberate reasoning. Schraagen [22] describes the concept of 'inner' and 'outer' environments. The inner environment is about strategies and representations. Klein's Recognition-Primed Decision model is a combination of intuition and analysis [22, 23]. Recognition-based strategies enable decision makers to make decisions continuously [22].

2.2   NDM and Software Architecture

Decision-making in the field of software architecture has been the subject of study for several decades [24]. Researchers have found that most software architectural decisions are made by groups, not individuals, and that while the major factors into a decision are requirements and other constraints, architects report that personal experience and personal preference also contribute to decisions [25]. Tofan, Galster and Avgeriou [26] list 22 factors that contribute to the difficulty of architecture decisions. One of those factors is insufficient information to reduce uncertainty when making the decision.

Decisions made by software architects often require consensus building and gaining trust and decisions are often made under conditions where there is insufficient information, extreme time pressures, and high stakes [27].

There has been some exploration of NDM in software architecture. This paper builds on that earlier work and contributes to a foundation on which future NDM-related research can be based. Zannier, Chiasson and Maurer [5] examine the question of how software designers make decisions. They conclude that the structure of the design problem *"as defined by the decision maker"* determines the aspects of rational and naturalistic decision-making used. Citing that paper [5], Vliet and Tang [28] study the process of making decisions in software architecture and conclude that *"... the structure of the design problem determines which aspects of rational and naturalistic decision making are used. The more structured the design decision, the less a designer considers different options."* Context is key here, and we need to consider not just problem structure, but the context under which the designer is making the decision. Simon [29] defines a set of characteristics that determine what it means for a problem to be well structured. However, Simon [29] also warns that *"definiteness of problem structure is largely an illusion that arises when we systematically confound the idealized problem that is presented to an idealized ... problem solver with the actual problem that is to be attacked by a problem solver with limited (even if large) computational capacities."* Here, Simon [29] (also cited by [5]) warns that definiteness around problem structure is largely an illusion, so care should be taken to not put too much effort into attempting to structure a problem definition in conditions where no such definition is possible.

Falessi et al. mention NDM in the context of comparing software architecture decision-making techniques [24]. They categorize NDM as fitting under one of three types of decision-making, where decision-makers *"keep the first available alternative."* This is not a complete characterization of what occurs. Decision makers do not simply keep the first available option, but rather use pattern matching [30]. Falessi et al. do not mention the expert-informed pattern matching that happens. They do acknowledge the role of intuition, but not explicitly as experience-informed intuition and further characterize NDM as a decision-making technique *"where decisions are studied as the product of intuition, mental simulation, metaphor, and storytelling."* Klein refers to these four elements as the *"sources of power"* needed in naturalistic settings [7].

Manjunath, Bhat, Shumaiev, Biesdorf and Matthes [31] mention NDM in a short paper about decision-making and cognitive biases in software architecture. They state *"evidence has been provided to show that architects either follow rationalistic or naturalistic decision-making process."* Their reference for this statement, and their only reference for NDM, is the work by Vliet and Tang [28] in the section *"Modeling the decision-making process."* In contrast to other NDM studies that focus on expert decision-making in context [8, 22], Manjunath et al. say, *"RPDM is derived from the naturalistic decision-making framework that relies on mental mind maps. It is generally used by inexperienced architects or in scenarios where ADDs are to be made under time pressure and other constraints which affect the decision-making quality."* There are two potential issues with this claim. First, the primary research on NDM refers to *"mental simulation"* but does not refer to *"mental mind maps."* Second, to say that NDM is generally used by inexperienced decision makers is not accurate. NDM emphasizes the requisite expertise of the decision maker [8, 22]. Klein further notes that differences in expertise influence decision strategy [13].

Most of these prior studies of NDM in software architecture reference one of Klein's popular books [7] or [10]. While these two books are useful, this paper cites a wider range of the NDM research literature, contributing to a deeper understanding of how architects decide and the conditions under which they make expert decisions. Other studies of NDM and architecture mentioned above examine the decision process, problem structure, or decision tools. This paper builds on these studies by focusing on the *context* of the architecture problem and the architect as decision maker in a dynamic and complex environment.

3 Research Approach

3.1 Research Setting and Context

This paper studies practicing software architects in their context. This study uses a case study of a large, global technology organization. Initially the researchers conducted an online survey of experienced architects. Of these, 70% had 6 or more years of experience as architects and were located in different sites across a global business group. The goal of the survey was to understand how architects perceived their role and interactions with other architects, engineers, product owners and product management. Following on from the survey, we conducted three focus groups to collect more data about architecture decision-making. Both the survey and focus groups targeted people with expertise in their domain, a defining characteristic of NDM settings, as discussed in Sect. 2. The first part of this study contains details of the study design [27]. Initial observations about architecture decision-making led to a closer look at the survey and focus group data with the goal of gaining a deeper understanding of conditions and contexts under which software architects make decisions.

3.2 Research Questions

This paper is concerned with how Naturalistic Decision Making (NDM), and RPD in particular, applies to decision-making in software architecture, specifically in large and complex environments. In this context, "*large*" relates to large architectures, code bases with tens-to-hundreds of millions of lines of code, large organizations, geographically distributed teams, and products and systems developed by hundreds or thousands of engineers. "*Complex*" in this context refers to the idea that organizations are complex adaptive systems, where behavior of systems is often non-linear and non-deterministic, and the product of the interactions in the system is greater than the sum of the parts [32]. This paper aims to contribute to the body of knowledge on architecture decision-making by answering the following questions:

- **RQ1:** How does NDM apply to Software Architecture decision-making?
- **RQ2:** What are the conditions under which decisions are suited to an NDM approach in software architecture?
- **RQ3:** What are the conditions under which decisions are not suited to an NDM approach in software architecture?

3.3 Research Method

This is a qualitative study. This study uses a case study to *"understand complex social phenomena"* related to how architects make decisions. Case studies are well suited to research in software development because they study contemporary phenomena in their natural setting [33]. This study is concerned with how and why architects make the decisions they do, the context in which they make those decisions. Case studies can *"uncover subtle distinctions and provide a richness of understanding and multiple perspectives"* [34]. This research includes perspectives from multiple stakeholders, not just architects. Yin [35] notes that case studies are suitable when *"the boundaries between phenomenon and context may not be clearly evident."*

3.4 Data Collection and Analysis

Data was collected through an online survey of 62 architects from a business group consisting of approximately 5,000 people worldwide. The survey used an online survey tool to collect responses. The researchers then followed up with three focus groups specifically about architecture decision making with 10, 11, and 12 participants, respectively, from different product lines within the business group. Participants in the focus groups were architects, program managers, engineers, and engineering managers located in Israel, the USA, and India. The focus groups were recorded, and the recordings were transcribed. The authors analyzed the survey data and focus group data independently and reviewed the analyses together through multiple iterations. Additional data was collected through participant observation and follow-up semi-structured interviews. The researchers used NVivo analyze the data.

3.5 Threats to Validity

This section discusses potential threats to the validity of this research study.

- **External Validity**. The researchers do not claim that these findings are universally applicable. They are representative of architects in specific, large global technology organizations. They serve as illustrative examples that others may learn from.
- **Construct Validity**. To mitigate this threat, data were collected from multiple sources. The researchers used triangulation between the survey data, focus groups, and participant observation, thereby converging evidence from multiple distinct data sources. The researchers compared results across multiple groups, where the data was collected at different points in time and in different geographic locations.
- **Reliability**. Relating to the repeatability of the study, the survey instrument and focus group questions were designed over several iterations and involved other subject matter experts and architects to review these and provide feedback. Using respondent validation [36] the researchers reviewed the data with a group of architects to help ensure validity of the data and the findings.
- **Internal validity**. This study does not attempt to establish any causal relationships, so no internal validity threats are described [33].

- **Bias**. People tend to report decision-making experiences where there was a negative sentiment. This could impact the examples that participants chose to share. The researchers encouraged participants to consider both positive and negative experiences and outcomes.

4 Findings

4.1 NDM Conditions Under Which Architects Make Decisions

Architects in the survey report being satisfied with their decisions when they are able to share common goals, collaborate with others, and are involved early and then able follow-through their architecture decision to its implementation [30]. Feedback is important to learning. As one architect notes, "*To me it is very rewarding (for everybody) to work and agree on architecture/design decisions in order to achieve a common goal. The mutual trust and respect is very important as well.*"

When asked about challenges they faced in their role, architects expressed sentiments that exhibit several characteristics commonly found in NDM contexts. Table 1 contains some examples of architects' experiences and how they relate to NDM characteristics. Even with extensive experience, architects don't always feel confident about their expertise. As one architect notes, "*It would be great to focus on one area for certain time to build expertise.*" Here, they are referring to a particular type of expertise, i.e., expertise in the product, system, or subsystem. Dynamic, shifting responsibilities, and changing business demands added to their stress and lack of confidence in their decision-making abilities.

4.2 How Attributes of NDM Decision Making Influence Decision Making

Focus group participants were asked to share their experiences of architecture decisions that they were involved with. A significant number of the examples from the focus groups show evidence of conditions typical of NDM settings as characterized in Sect. 2. Findings are presented here in the same order as the NDM settings in Sect. 2.2.

Time Pressure. The findings show examples of decisions that were made under time pressure. One architect told of a decision made to implement a simple coding change, even though it was known to be inadequate at the time and other alternatives could have been explored. The reason for accepting the solution was, "*because it was urgent. Right now.*" Another architect told of being directed to change their design to "*just make it fit*" time allotted. Although architects acknowledged that decisions need to be made for short-term expediency, e.g. to address an immediate customer need, they aren't always happy about it. One architect described frustrations felt about a decision where, "*The right people were in the room, but there were arguments that were raised for the first time during this meeting. And we came with a proposal, and for some reason, during a very short discussion there were raised new arguments that couldn't be assessed properly. And I think that there was a need to stop the discussion, go and analyze the feedback, but was under a lot of... I'm not sure if it was the real pressure,*"

Table 1. Examples of selected NDM characteristics from the study findings; TC = Team Coordination, II = Inadequate Information, TP = Time Pressures, PDP = Poorly Defined Procedures, DCC = Dynamic Changing Conditions

Architect's experience	NDM characteristic				
	TC	II	TP	PDP	DCC
"Finding time for direct collaboration in calendars"	X		X		
"Getting enough time from the knowledgeable architects is difficult - especially when their agendas are not completely aligned with mine"	X	X	X		
"Time – we're all busy!"			X		
"we spend a lot of time in discussions and speculations of how a feature was designed and implemented, instead of referring to a system spec"		X			
"The transition to feature teams has dissipated in-depth knowledge of our software"		X			X
"Not all the information is shared with architects which could affect some architecture decisions in the initial phase of the project"		X			
"Not being aware of system-wide decisions (guidelines, policies) until long after they are made"		X			
"It would make my job easier if other architects would be concerned with making sure that others know what they are working on, what decisions they have made that affect my work"		X	X		
"Without an agreed process, there is always the tension between the fast and dirty guys and the more structured guys who keep records of requirements and design"				X	
"The developers are encouraged by their managers to provide independent solutions without seeking for an agreed design, and sometimes even against an agreed design"			X	X	
"Feedback on architectural decisions takes years, if ever, to arrive. This makes learning from experience difficult if not impossible"		X			
"Our organization has been in firefighting mode for a long time, and that inhibits the ability to take a step back and look at the bigger picture"					X
"People are so insecure about their jobs … that they are protecting information, not sharing, and are not open to suggestions"	X	X			X

but we wanted to finish up and to get a decision, and I'm not sure that the right decision has been taken, just because of lack of time." Was it actually lack of time, or perceived lack of time? Is there a difference in how action is taken? If the decision-maker feels time pressure, then it is real for them. Options are narrowed when under time pressure. There is also evidence of decisions that were not made under time pressure. Architects shared examples of decisions that were technology focused and strategic or long-term in nature, e.g., API evolution, or creating guidelines for the use of microservice frameworks. These decisions were made more deliberately, involving experimentation and analysis.

High Stakes. The financial stakes are only one perspective of architecture decisions. Architects in this study make decisions that impact products and systems with multi-million- and multi-billion-dollar revenue streams. However, high stakes are not just because of financial concerns. Architects make decisions that impact customer relationships, company reputation, future evolvability of the architecture, and market competitiveness. Trust among peers and colleagues is a further theme that emerged; the stakes are also high if that trust can be damaged. A discussion on how to establish that trust and mutual respect is beyond the scope of this paper.

Experienced Decision Makers. The architects in our study were experienced and generally confident about their decisions. However, occasionally they encountered situations where they felt they lacked expertise. For example, one architect recounted several situations where teams came to him for decisions even though he was not an expert in their particular product area. He expressed feelings of self-doubt *("I don't know all of these things. Winging it most of the time. I don't really understand a lot of this stuff.")*. As the discussion progressed it was clear that the architect was an experienced architect, and familiar with the technology domain. What he felt he lacked was specific experience with the technical components the teams needed help with, which were outside his immediate scope of responsibility. However, his general expertise as an architect and his expertise with the domain resulted in "good enough" decisions that got the team over their immediate hurdle. This also bought them time to fill the gap in organization knowledge. In another situation an architect explicitly sought expertise, in order to make better-informed decisions: *"For example, my team was doing a feature .... They made a lot of changes we're not still really comfortable about, and then ...we went to approach the guy who had left our team. So, he came and he was the one who reviewed."* Developing expertise takes time. An experience was shared of a team that deliberately acquires necessary expertise to competently make decisions in new domains: *"Basically, when they become incompetent, they just close the doors. And they say, 'We will not entertain any request on this component for the next six months. Nothing. Don't come and talk to us if you want us to do a good job...'. ...[And on] the code, they write test cases, they reverse engineer, the whole thing. Then they come back six months later, and it really is like you just changed into a butterfly from a caterpillar. ... At which point, they're really good."*

Inadequate Information. Finding information can be difficult as one architect observed: "so much documentation is missing that ... it becomes very complex to go through the code and do the reverse engineering of what was thought." Yet not every architect expects important details to be recorded: *"Usually, the decision of what was decided will be captured in the document. The decision of why it was decided that way should be captured in somebody's head"*. There are counter examples in the findings where design rationale was documented: *"They do use Confluence for managing everything about the...decision to be taken and conclusions and conversations and thoughts around the decision and everything we've documented, easily to be accessed again... I'm using these sites and these pages. I always find what I'm looking for."*

Ill-defined Goals. Designing the high-level architecture for a feature can be complicated as an architect notes: *"Just the countless numbers of architects that are involved and the lack of clear product ownership because we moved away from component ownership to this feature ownership. Which the lines become blurred because you can own a feature and you're shifting a feature into the solution but then it may impact a number of other things supporting related features and stuff. It's hard to understand where's the start and end of the product that you're supposed to be driving."*

Poorly-defined Procedures. One architect expressed uncertainty about who should be involved in decision-making: *"I think that job description or responsibilities are not well defined. Therefore, I'm talking about myself, you can always ask yourself whether you are the right person to take [a] decision or do you need to consult with someone else, or are you stepping on someone's toes or not."* The shift to agile development has made the process of architecting system infrastructure less obvious; as an architect noted: *"Agile hasn't given an adequate answer to scaffolding or to infrastructure... So as long as we're talking a feature which has some kind of huge impact it's OK. If it's very narrow, end to end, it doesn't impact on the system then it's fine."*

Cue Learning. An architect brought up the issue that sometimes short-term decisions may not be revisited, even when evidence may indicate that this would be judicious: *"The problem is that when what I think is decision making in many, many cases the first decision is accepted as the final one and the project leader [is] not ready to change direction and adjust the decision to problems found."* The discussion continued around what to do with new evidence, as the architecture can't always be in flux. As one architect notes, *"People, in order to develop a solution, in order to develop interfaces, in order to... They need some stability. Even if it's not the ideal solution, we need a consistent solution."*

Dynamic and Continually Changing Conditions. Under pressure to decide, one architect stated they had difficulty finding consensus for the bigger decisions that needed to be made, *"just because things are moving too fast for me, and the organization is too in flux."* Consequently, they made lots of shorter-term decisions to compensate. This person was an experienced architect and recognized the need for considering long-term impacts. Under conditions of uncertainty and time pressure they adopted a strategy that would be good enough in the short term, and keep the team moving towards their longer-term needs. Another architect shared that they adjust their initial decisions based on direct feedback and changing conditions. There are also examples where organization politics can influence decision-making, adding to the volatility and uncertainty of the context. For example, an architect shared that a directive was given and not challenged: *"my feeling was even though that was a* *directive or decision, not enough attention was given to nuance and to actual issues that will arise from the deployment."* Another architect stated that *"there are cases when up to discussion, the people who disagree with mainstream were removed from the discussion."*

Group Coordination. While not all decisions are made by consensus, it often takes time to gain consensus. One architect notes *"because we're focused on consensus over multiple engineering teams and architecture teams all over the place, the process has just gotten more complicated."* Another architect remarks *"To me [it] is very rewarding (for everybody) to work and agree on architecture/design decisions in order to achieve a common goal."*

5 Reflections on the Research Questions

RQ1: How Does NDM Apply to Software Architecture Decision-making?

The study found that experienced software architects make many decisions under dynamically changing business conditions, with time pressure, and having inadequate information. NDM, and RPD in particular, seems suited to decisions that must be made quickly and when fast feedback on the decision allows for course corrections. The conditions under which NDM is appropriate, however, can be short-lived, e.g., the time pressure is temporary. Goals can become clear, or the need for clarity passes. Information becomes available, or the need for that information passes.

RQ2: What are the Conditions Under Which Decisions are Suited to an NDM Approach in Software Architecture?

Decisions that are made collaboratively, where there is mutual respect and trust among decision-makers, and there's enough expertise seem to be well suited to NDM. Kahneman and Klein also observe that true experts know when they don't know and that ability to recognize a situation as novel is one of the characteristics of experts [15]. The case study found examples where architects who didn't know enough to take a decision with confidence either found a way to limit the scope of a decision to what they felt expert in, or found and utilized others' expertise to improve the decision. Given the complexities of the systems they are designing, architects feel more confident in their decision-making when they can learn from engineers and receive feedback on the implementation of their decisions.

RQ3: What are the Conditions Under Which Decisions are Not Suited to an NDM Approach in Software Architecture?

Decisions that require investigation into new technologies or are outside the area of expertise of an architect are not suited to NDM approaches. Other examples where more analytic approaches are appropriate include choosing a new persistence technology or migrating to a microservice architecture. These are conditions where poor information is not tolerable. Environments where there are panels for reviewing architectures generally won't use NDM approaches. In these settings, decisions are made through argumentation, persuasion, and influence – tactics for which there is rarely time in NDM settings. Moreover, even though certain situations may appear conducive to NDM approaches, architects themselves, may question their own expertise, and thus may seek out advice or take a more analytical approach to making an architecture decision.

6 Conclusions

NDM is not a design decision process, but a way of understanding the context in which decisions are made that, in the context of this study, impact architecture. NDM is therefore process-agnostic. This exploratory study concurs with the findings of Klein [17]; namely that recognition primed decisions are more likely when the decision maker is experienced in the domain, time pressure is great, and conditions are less stable. It can be helpful to consider decisions as related to three domains of technology, solution, and product [27]. NDM is more likely to apply to select decisions where new technologies are being introduced. NDM also applies in situations where business and solution contexts are poorly understood, or are being invented, and this has an immediate impact on architecture. Market and competitive pressures can force situations that benefit from NDM. The team needs to decide something quickly and move on. We found evidence that architects learn under conditions of uncertainty when they get feedback. This feedback adds to their expertise and contributes to their learning of important cues. This improves their capability for dealing with future scenarios where recognition-primed decision making is important. These findings are in contrast to other researchers who claim that *"RPDM is generally used by inexperienced architects"* [31]. Working in a complex, distributed environment poses great challenges for naturalistic forms of decision-making. It can be difficult to get meaningful and timely feedback. Decisions that involve a larger group take more time and consensus building. One strategy reported to speed up decision-making was taking decisions that were more limited in scope instead of building consensus. We also found examples where decision-makers, when they felt they lacked expertise, found other experts to help in making decisions or took the time to develop necessary expertise before taking any actions. We also found an example of an architect who was called on to make decisions because he was perceived as being good at making decisions, even though he lacked specific expertise. Our findings concurred with the NDM literature that there often is not enough time to build trust or gain widespread consensus. We observed that authority is granted to architecture decision-makers based on expertise and role. There is often an implicit and immediate and unspoken agreement on granting this trust and authority in a triage situation that requires a rapid architecture decision.

6.1 Recommendations

Based on the findings in this exploratory study into NDM and architecture, the researchers propose the following preliminary recommendations for architects and those responsible for creating the conditions under which architects do their work:

- Experts may not retain their tacit knowledge-informed expert status under dynamically changing conditions. They may quickly and temporarily find themselves operating in an environment where their particular expertise does not apply. Architecture expertise needs to be refreshed in software architecture. Architects are not just doing the same thing over and over again. The context is shifting. Consequently, a lot of learning happens on the job and timely feedback is essential to learning.
- Consider carefully the consequences of using NDM approaches when the necessary expertise is lacking. Expertise is a critical factor to successful decision-making. Growing expertise requires feedback on the consequences of decisions and collaboration with others to share knowledge.
- Most architectural decisions are group decisions. NDM is more challenging in the context of large groups that are distributed. More formality may be required to reach agreement and document decisions in such settings.
- NDM decision-making may not be appropriate for locally optimized architectural decisions. Sometimes seemingly localized decisions have broad system impacts. In these situations, analytic approaches to decision-making may be more appropriate.

6.2 Future Research

This paper describes the first steps in a series of studies that the researchers are working on towards understanding how the software architecture profession can benefit from understanding software architecture through the lens of naturalistic decision making. This has applications for architects, architecting, and architecture. A better understanding of Recognition Primed decisions (RPD) and other NDM models will help architects apply appropriate decision-making strategies in the right context.

While localized decisions may appear expedient, sometimes they can have a broader impact than anticipated. Understanding what conditions under which narrower decision-making contexts are appropriate as well as the potential impacts of a series of micro decisions is a topic of future research.

In addition, the social and political influence on decisions emerged as a point of interest from these findings and is an area worthy of exploring in the context of NDM. The NDM literature says little about the social and political context, e.g., they don't talk about politics of hospitals or fire stations. They focus on expertise. However, in real-world software organizations, political factors are also an influence on decisions.

Klein, Ross, Moon, Klein, Hoffman and Hollnagel [36] report that as people gain experience, they spend more time examining the situation and less on contrasting the options, whereas novices spend more time contrasting options and less on comprehending the situation. We didn't find evidence to support or disprove this finding, as the architects in our study weren't novices; they were experts encountering novel conditions where they needed to make decisions. Further research is needed into how experienced architects approach decision-making under novel conditions.

References

1. Dasanayake, S., Markkula, J., Aaramaa, S., Oivo, M.: Software architecture decision-making practices and challenges. In: 24th Australasian Software Engineering Conference, pp. 88–97 (2015)
2. Rekha V.S., Muccini, H.: Suitability of software architecture decision making methods for group decisions. In: Avgeriou, P., Zdun, U. (eds.) ECSA 2014. LNCS, vol. 8627, pp. 17–32. Springer, Cham (2014). https://doi.org/10.1007/978-3-319-09970-5_2
3. Zalewski, A., Kijas, S.: Beyond ATAM: early architecture evaluation method for large-scale distributed systems. J. Syst. Softw. **86**, 683–697 (2013)
4. Cervantes, H., Kazman, R.: Designing Software Architectures: A practical Approach. Addison-Wesley, Boston (2016)
5. Zannier, C., Chiasson, M., Maurer, F.: A model of design decision making based on empirical results of interviews with software designers. Inf. Softw. Technol. **49**, 637–653 (2007)
6. Klein, G.: Reflections on applications of naturalistic decision making. J. Occup. Organ. Psychol. **88**, 382–386 (2015)
7. Klein, G.A.: Sources of Power. MIT Press, Cambridge (2017)
8. Klein, G.: A naturalistic decision making perspective on studying intuitive decision making. J. Appl. Res. Mem. Cogn. **4**, 164–168 (2015)
9. Gore, J., Banks, A., Millward, L., Kyriakidou, O.: Naturalistic decision making and organizations: reviewing pragmatic science. Organ. Stud. **27**, 925–942 (2006)
10. Klein, G.A.: Streetlights and Shadows: Searching for the keys to Adaptive Decision Making. MIT Press, Cambridge (2009)
11. Klein, G.: Naturalistic decision making. Hum. Factors **50**, 456–460 (2008)
12. Klein, G.A., Calderwood, R.: Decision models: some lessons from the field. IEEE Trans. Syst. Man Cybern. **21**, 1018–1026 (1991)
13. Klein, G.: Naturalistic decision making. In: Human Systems IAC XI, pp. 16–19 (1991)
14. Simon, H.A.: What is an explanation of behavior? Psychol. Sci. **3**, 150–161 (1992)
15. Kahneman, D., Klein, G.: Conditions for intuitive expertise: a failure to disagree. Am. Psychol. **64**, 515 (2009)
16. Flin, R., Salas, E., Straub, M., Martin, L.: Decision Making Under Stress: Emerging Themes and Applications. Routledge, New York (2016)
17. Klein, G.: A Recognition-primed decision (RPD) model of rapid decision making. In: Klein, G.A., Orasanu, J., Calderwood, R., Zsambok, C.E. (eds.) Decision Making in Action: Models and Methods, pp. 138–147. Ablex Publishing, Norwood (1993)
18. Kahneman, D., Tversky, A.: Choices, values, and frames. Am. Psychol. **39**, 341–350 (1984)
19. Simon, H.A.: Invariants of human behavior. Annu. Rev. Psychol. **41**, 1–19 (1990)
20. Sherman, R.O.: Wicked problems. Nurse Leader **14**, 380–381 (2016)
21. Kahneman, D., Egan, P.: Thinking, Fast and Slow (2011)
22. Schraagen, J.M.: Naturalistic decision making. In: Ball, L.J., Thompson, V.A. (eds.) International Handbook of Thinking and Reasoning, pp. 487–501 (2017)
23. Klein, G., Calderwood, R., Clinton-Cirocco, A.: Rapid decision making on the fire ground: the original study plus a postscript. J. Cogn. Eng. Decis. Making **4**, 186–209 (2010)
24. Falessi, D., Cantone, G., Kazman, R., Kruchten, P.: Decision-making techniques for software architecture design. ACM Comput. Surv. **43**, 1–28 (2011)
25. Miesbauer, C., Weinreich, R.: Classification of design decisions – an expert survey in practice. In: Drira, K. (ed.) ECSA 2013. LNCS, vol. 7957, pp. 130–145. Springer, Heidelberg (2013). https://doi.org/10.1007/978-3-642-39031-9_12

70   K. Power and R. Wirfs-Brock

26. Tofan, D., Galster, M., Avgeriou, P.: Difficulty of architectural decisions – a survey with professional architects. In: Drira, K. (ed.) ECSA 2013. LNCS, vol. 7957, pp. 192–199. Springer, Heidelberg (2013). https://doi.org/10.1007/978-3-642-39031-9_17
27. Power, K., Wirfs-Brock, R.: Understanding architecture decisions in context. In: Cuesta, Carlos E., Garlan, D., Pérez, J. (eds.) ECSA 2018. LNCS, vol. 11048, pp. 284–299. Springer, Cham (2018). https://doi.org/10.1007/978-3-030-00761-4_19
28. Vliet, H.V., Tang, A.: Decision making in software architecture. JSS **117**, 638–644 (2016)
29. Simon, H.A.: The structure of ill structured problems. AI **4**, 181–201 (1973)
30. Klein, G.: Naturalistic Decision Making: Implications for Design. Klein Associates Inc., Fairborn (1993)
31. Manjunath, A., Bhat, M., Shumaiev, K., Biesdorf, A., Matthes, F.: Decision making and cognitive biases in designing software architectures. In: 2018 IEEE International Conference on Software Architecture Companion (ICSA-C), Seattle, WA, USA, pp. 52–55 (2018)
32. Bohórquez Arévalo, L.E., Espinosa, A.: Theoretical approaches to managing complexity in organizations: a comparative analysis. Estudios Gerenciales **31**, 20–29 (2015)
33. Runeson, P., Höst, M., Rainer, A., Regnell, B.: Case Study Research in Software Engineering: Guidelines and Examples. Wiley, Hoboken (2012)
34. Kohn, L.T.: Methods in Case Study Analysis. Technical Publication, Center for Studying Health System Change (1997)
35. Yin, R.K.: Case Study Research : Design and Methods, 5th edn. SAGE, London (2014)
36. Klein, G., Ross, K.G., Moon, B.M., Klein, D.E., Hoffman, R.R., Hollnagel, E.: Macrocognition. IEEE Intell. Syst. **18**, 81–85 (2003)

Evaluating the Effectiveness of Multi-level Greedy Modularity Clustering for Software Architecture Recovery

Hasan Sözer[(✉)]

Ozyegin University, Istanbul, Turkey
hasan.sozer@ozyegin.edu.tr

Abstract. Software architecture recovery approaches mainly analyze various types of dependencies among software modules to group them and reason about the high-level structural decomposition of a system. These approaches employ a variety of clustering techniques. In this paper, we present an empirical evaluation of a modularity clustering technique used for software architecture recovery. We use five open source projects as subject systems for which the ground-truth architectures were known. This dataset was previously prepared and used in an empirical study for evaluating four state-of-the-art architecture recovery approaches and their variants as well as two baseline clustering algorithms. We used the same dataset for an evaluation of multi-level greedy modularity clustering. Results showed that MGMC outperforms all the other SAR approaches in terms of accuracy and modularization quality for most of the studied systems. In addition, it scales better to very large systems for which it runs orders-of-magnitude faster than all the other algorithms.

Keywords: Software architecture recovery ·
Software architecture reconstruction · Reverse engineering ·
Modularity clustering · Empirical evaluation

1 Introduction

Software architecture documentation is an important asset for supporting program comprehension, communication and maintenance [16]. This documentation turns out to be usually incorrect or incomplete, especially for old legacy systems [10,24]. It is also very effort-intensive to recover such a documentation manually [14], which can quickly become infeasible as the software size and complexity increases.

Software architecture reconstruction [9] or recovery [21] (SAR) approaches have been introduced to recover software architecture documentation. These approaches essentially analyze dependencies among software modules to group them and reason about the high-level structure of a system. Inter-dependencies

© Springer Nature Switzerland AG 2019
T. Bures et al. (Eds.): ECSA 2019, LNCS 11681, pp. 71–87, 2019.
https://doi.org/10.1007/978-3-030-29983-5_5

among software modules are usually represented with design structure matrices [11] or (un)weighted (un)directed graphs [9,23]. In addition to these different representations, SAR approaches mainly vary with respect to the types of dependencies considered and the types of clustering techniques employed.

In this work, we focus on recovering the high-level structural decomposition of a system based on code dependencies. In that respect, a recent empirical study [21] evaluated the effectiveness of four state-of-the-art SAR approaches and their variants as well as two baseline clustering algorithms. The study was conducted on five open source projects as subject systems, for which the "ground-truth" software architectures were manually recovered. Various types of dependencies extracted from the subject systems were used as input to evaluate their impact on the accuracy of SAR approaches. We used the same dataset for an evaluation of modularity clustering [4,28] as an alternative SAR approach.

Modularity clustering aims at decomposing a graph into cohesive components that are loosely coupled. This aim is aligned with the very basic modularity principle [26] followed in software design. Hence, it makes sense to apply this approach for SAR. In fact, there have been clustering techniques [23] introduced for balancing the tradeoff between coupling and cohesion. However, it was shown that the accuracy of these techniques is low and the utilized modularity metrics are subject to flaws [21]. In this study, we employ the Multi-level Greedy Modularity Clustering (MGMC) approach [25], which borrows metrics and heuristics from the physics literature [7,31]. MGMC combines two heuristics, namely *greedy coarsening* [7] and *fast greedy refinement* [31] to maximize a modularity measure. We evaluate the accuracy of MGMC and compare it with respect to those achieved with other SAR approaches. It was shown that some of these approaches scale to very large systems that contain 10 MLOC, whereas others not [21]. Therefore, runtime performance of MGMC is another important aspect to investiage. We defined the following two research questions based on these concerns:

- *RQ1*: How does the accuracy of MGMC compare to those of other SAR approaches when various types of dependencies are considered?
- *RQ2*: How does the runtime performance of MGMC compare to those of other SAR approaches?

We applied MGMC on dependency graphs regarding five open source projects. These graphs represent different types of dependencies extracted from the source code such as file inclusions and function calls. Then, we measured the quality of the clustering using the corresponding ground-truth architectures and two different metrics proposed before [23,36]. We compared these measurements with respect to the measurements previously reported [21] for the same projects, input files and metrics but for different SAR approaches. Results showed that MGMC outperforms all the other SAR approaches in terms of accuracy and modularization quality [23] for most of the studied systems. In addition, it scales better to very large systems for which it runs orders-of-magnitude faster than all the other algorithms.

This paper is organized as follows. We summarize the related studies on SAR and position our work in the following section. We introduce MGMC in Sect. 3. We explain the experimental setup in Sect. 4. We present and discuss the results in Sect. 5. Finally, in Sect. 6, we conclude the paper.

2 Background and Related Work

There exist many approaches [9] proposed for SAR, some of which are manual or semi-automated. In this study, we focus on approaches introduced for automatically recovering an architecture. The recovered architecture can be in various forms for representing various architectural views [16]. The majority of the existing techniques [21,29,30,33] aim at recovering a *module view* that depicts the structural design-time decomposition of a system [16]. Some of them focus on analyzing the runtime behavior for reconstructing execution scenarios [5] and behavioral views [27]. There are also tools that construct both structural and behavioral views [17,34]. In this work, we focus on SAR approaches that are used for recovering a high-level module view of the system.

SAR approaches also vary with respect to types of inputs they consume [9]. Some of them rely on textual information extracted from source code [8,15]. Many others use dependencies among modules, which are usually represented with design structure matrices [11] or (un)weighted (un)directed graphs [23]. These dependencies can be extracted from a variety of sources as well. For instance, a call graph extracted from the source code can be interpreted as a dependency graph, where each vertex represents a module (e.g., class) and each directed edge represents a dependency (e.g., method call) from the source vertex to the target vertex [23]. As another example, commonly accessed database tables (or other external resources) can be interpreted as (indirect) module interdependencies [2]. The goal of a recent empirical study [21] was to measure the impact of various code dependencies on the accuracy of SAR approaches. These dependencies were represented in the form of unweighted directed graphs, which were extracted based on variable accesses, function calls and file inclusions. We use the same types of dependencies in this work to extend that study with an evaluation of MGMC.

Finally, the employed clustering algorithm/technique is a major variation point among SAR approaches. There are many techniques proposed so far and these techniques have been compared with each other as well. However, an analysis of existing evaluations [21] show that results are not always consistent. In a recent study [13], nine variants of six SAR approaches were compared based on eight subject systems. The overall accuracy of all the evaluated approaches turned out to be low based on their consistency with respect to the ground-truth architectures collected for the subject systems. In that study, ACDC [35] was pointed out as one of the best approaches. In another study, the performance of LIMBO (Scalable Information Bottleneck) [3] was shown to be comparable to that of ACDC. There also exist a study [38] indicating that WCA (Weighted Combined Algorithm) [22] performs better than ACDC. However, in the most recent studies [13,21], ACDC turns out to be superior than others. Results may differ due to the use of different subject systems and assessment measures/criteria.

Bunch [23] employs a hill-climbing algorithm for maximizing modularization quality, while clustering a dependency graph. Its objective function is defined to balance the tradeoff between the cohesion of clusters and coupling among them. However, the best objective function value can be achieved by grouping all the modules in a single cluster [21]. Also, the accuracy of Bunch was shown to be low in recent empirical studies [21]. We adopt a different formulation of modularity in this study and also a different algorithm to maximize it. We previously used another variant of modularity clustering [12] for recovering software architectures of PL/SQL programs. In that approach, dependencies among PL/SQL procedures are extracted based on their common use of database tables. These dependencies are represented in the form of a hypergraph. This representation is converted to a weighted undirected graph, which is then partitioned to maximize modularity. However, that approach was dedicated for PL/SQL programs and its evaluation was based on a single case study. Moreover, it employed a different algorithm [6] to maximize modularity. The effectiveness of MGMC that we introduce in the following section has not been empirically evaluated as a SAR approach.

3   Multi-level Greedy Modularity Clustering

Given a graph $G(V, E)$, modularity clustering aims at grouping the set of vertices $V = \{v_1, v_2, ..., v_n\}$ into a set of k disjoint clusters $C_1, C_2, ..., C_k$ such that the modularity is maximized. The modularity is calculated based on Eq. 1 [28].

$$\mathcal{M} = \frac{1}{2m} \sum_{l=1}^{k} \sum_{i,j | v_i, v_j \in C_l} (w_{ij} - \frac{d_i d_j}{2m}) \qquad (1)$$

In this equation, w_{ij} represents the weight of the edge between v_i and v_j, $d_i = \sum_{j \neq i} w_{ij}$ and $m = \frac{1}{2} \sum_i d_i$. In our dataset, the extracted dependency graphs are not weighted. Hence, w_{ij} can be either 1 or 0, representing the existence of a dependency between v_i and v_j or lack thereof, respectively. However, the objective function and the employed algorithms are generic and they can work on weighted graphs as well. We should also note that graphs are considered as undirected in this formulation. Two vertices, v_i and v_j are adjacent ($w_{ij} = w_{ji} = 1$) if either of these vertices depends on the other.

$\mathcal{M}$ captures the inherent trade-off in maximizing the number of edges among the vertices that take place in the same cluster and minimizing the number of edges among the vertices that take place in different clusters. We can see in Eq. 1 that w_{ij} values are summed up only for pairs of vertices that are in the same cluster. Therefore, decreasing the number of clusters and as such, increasing the size of each cluster is rewarded by taking more pairs into account. On the other hand, the value of w_{ij} will be 0 for pairs of independent vertices that are in the same cluster. Nevertheless, the penalty $\frac{d_i d_j}{2m}$ is paid for each such pair as well. The amount of penalty is proportional to the number of dependencies of these vertices to all the other vertices in the graph.

It was shown that finding a clustering of a given graph with maximum $\mathcal{M}$ is an $\mathcal{NP}$-hard problem [4]. Exact methods can not scale beyond graphs with a few hundred vertices [1,39]. Therefore, many heuristic algorithms have been proposed to address this problem. These are mainly proposed and elaborated in the physics literature [7,31]. MGMC is one of these and it combines two heuristics [25].

The first heuristic is *greedy coarsening* [7], which starts with singleton clusters and iteratively merges cluster pairs as long as the merge operation increases modularity. Hereby, a *merge priority* is assigned to each cluster pair, which determines the order of pairs to be merged at each step. It was empirically shown that the *Significance (Sig)* measure is an effective metric to quantify *merge priority* [25]. *Sig* for a cluster pair *(A,B)* is defined as follows.

$$Sig = \frac{\Delta \mathcal{M}_{A,B}}{\sqrt{deg(A) \times deg(B)}} \tag{2}$$

Hereby, $\Delta \mathcal{M}_{A,B}$ defines the amount of increase in modularity as a result of merging clusters A and B. The *deg* function provides the total weight of edges inside a given cluster.

The second heuristic is called *fast greedy refinement* [31]. This heuristic basically iterates over all the vertices in the graph and finds the *best* target cluster to move for each vertex. The *best* cluster is the one that leads to the largest modularity increase by moving the vertex to this cluster. Iteration stops when the modularity can not be improved further with any vertex movement.

The *coarsening* and *refinement* heuristics do not have to be applied in separate, sequential phases. Moving individual vertices after the completion of coarsening can lead to sub-optimal results. A densely connected group of vertices may not have a chance to move to another cluster because this would involve a series of vertex movements that degrade modularity. However, *refinement* can be applied at any level of the coarsening hierarchy in principle. An entire cluster can be moved rather than an individual vertex. This is the idea behind *multi-level refinement* [18,19], where the application of *coarsening* and *refinement* heuristics are interleaved. Intermediate coarsening results are saved as a *coarsening level* whenever the number of clusters is decreased by a certain percentage called the *reduction factor*. These intermediate results are embodied as a graph where vertices represent clusters obtained at the corresponding coarsening level. The refinement heuristic is applied to every level. It was empirically shown that modularity improves as *reduction factor* decreases; however, the amount of improvement becomes less significant when *reduction factor* incline below 50% [25].

The algorithm [28] we used in this study follows the steps and recommendations described above. The implementation of the overall greedy algorithm is discussed in [25]. Further details of the implementation together with pseudo codes of its various steps are provided in [28].

4   Experimental Setup

In this section, we describe our experimental setup including the properties of our dataset, SAR approaches being compared with MGMC and the evaluation criteria.

4.1   Subject Systems and the Dataset

Table 1 lists information about five open source projects, which were used as subject systems for a previous empirical study [21]. We used the same set of projects because their ground-truth architectures and module dependency information were available.

Table 1. Subject systems.

System	Version	LOC	# of files	Description
Chromium	svn-171054	10 M	18,698	Web Browser
ITK	4.5.2	1 M	7,310	Image Segmentation Toolkit
Bash	4.2	115 K	373	Unix Shell Command Processor
Hadoop	0.19.0	87 K	591	Data Processing Framework
ArchStudio	4	55 K	604	Architecture Development Tool

Table 2 lists the properties of our dataset. Hereby, the second column lists the number of clusters in the ground-truth architecture of each system. The following 3 columns list the numbers of dependencies extracted for 3 basic types of dependencies considered: *(i) Include* dependencies are established between two files if one of them declares that it includes the other. *(ii) Symbol* dependencies are established between two files if one of them makes use of a symbol that is defined in the other. A symbol can be a function or a variable name. *(iii) Function* dependencies constitute a subset of *Symbol* dependencies, just focusing on function calls between modules.

Types of *symbol* dependencies were further varied to observe their impact on the accuracy of SAR approaches. *(i) F-GV* captures function calls and global variables together. *(ii) S-NoDYB* represents *symbol* dependencies extracted by ignoring dynamic bindings. The values listed in Table 2 reflect this type of *symbol* dependencies. *(iii) S-CHA* takes dynamic bindings into account by analyzing the class hierarchies. *(iv) S-Int* is extracted by resolving dynamic bindings based on interfaces only. We used these dependency types in our evaluation. There are two other dependency types that were utilized in the previous empirical study [21], namely *transitive* and *module level* dependencies. We have not used these two since the corresponding dependency information was not available for most of the projects. Information regarding *Include, S-CHA, S-Int, S-NoDyB, Function* and *F-GV* dependencies was available for all the projects. One exception to this was the *Bash* project implemented in C, for which information regarding dynamic bindings could not be extracted. So, dependency information regarding *S-CHA, S-Int* and *S-NoDyB* variants is not available for this project. Dependency information regarding each type of dependency is represented in the form of an unweighted directed graph, so-called a *dependency graph*.

Table 2. Properties of the dataset [21].

System	# of clusters in the ground-truth architecture	# of various types of dependencies		
		Include	Symbol	Function
Chromium	67	1,183,799	297,530	123,422
ITK	11	169,017	75,588	16,844
Bash	14	2,512	2,481	1,025
Hadoop	67	1,772	11,162	2,953
ArchStudio	57	866	5,359	1,411

4.2 Architecture Recovery Approaches

We selected the same variants of SAR approaches, for which we took the results reported [21] regarding their accuracy on the same dataset we use. We only omitted two of these approaches, namely Architecture Recovery Using Concerns (ARC) [15] and Zone Based Recovery (ZBR) [8], which use textual information from source code as input. Results regarding these approaches were missing for dependency graphs that are used as input for MGMC. Most of the results were missing for ARC and ZBR also because they could not scale for large systems [21]. In particular, we included results regarding ACDC [35], two variants of Bunch [23], namely Bunch-NAHC and Bunch-SAHC, two variants of WCA [22], namely WCA-UE and WCA-UENM, and finally, LIMBO [3].

We also included results regarding K-means algorithm used as a baseline for comparison. There was a second baseline derived from the directory structure of the project [21]. However, we omitted that one since most of the corresponding results we missing, just like the case for ARC and ZBR.

4.3 Environment and Parameters

We used a laptop computer with Intel Core i7 1.80 GHz CPU and 16 GB RAM to run the experiments. We used the implementation of MGMC provided by Rossi [28], which is available online[1]. This implementation works on weighted

---

[1] http://apiacoa.org/research/software/graph/index.en.html.

undirected graphs. Hence, in our dataset directions are ignored and all the edge weights are assumed to be 1. We did not provide any of the optional parameters and as such, used the algorithm with its default parameter settings (i.e., *reduction factor* = 25%, *merge priority* = *Sig*).

Input files that store dependency graphs [21] conform to the Rigi Standard Format (RSF) format [32,37]. The clustering results should also be saved in this format to be provided to the implementations of metrics described in the following subsection. However, the input and output formats of the MGMC implementation do not conform to RSF. Hence, we developed programs to preprocess the input and postprocess the output. We did not include the time spent for input/output transformations in our measurements and just report the time elapsed during clustering. We run the algorithm 100 times to observe the variation in running time although the results do not change in these runs.

The reported results for Bunch variants and ACDC are calculated as the average of five runs due to the non-determinism of the employed clustering algorithms [21]. On the other hand, WCA variants, LIMBO and K-means take the number of clusters, k as input. Results reported for these approaches are averages of results obtained from multiple executions, where k is varied in each run. The values of k range from 20 clusters below to 20 clusters above the number of clusters in the ground-truth architecture with step size 5 [21].

4.4   Evaluation Criteria

We used two different metrics to evaluate MGMC and compare it with the other SAR approaches. The first one is the *MoJoFM* metric [36], of which the implementation is available online[2]. This metric is used for measuring the similarity between the recovered architecture and the ground-truth architecture. It has been shown to be more accurate than other representative measures and consistently been used in empirical studies on SAR [13,20,21]. The MoJoFM value for given two clusterings A and B is calculated as follows:

$$MoJoFM = (1 - \frac{mno(A, B)}{max(mno(\forall A, B))}) \times 100\% \tag{3}$$

Hereby, $mno(A, B)$ calculates the minimum number of *move* or *join* operations needed to transform A to B. On the other hand, $max(mno(\forall A, B))$ calculates the maximum $mno(A, B)$ possible for any A. High and low *MoJoFM* values indicate high similarity and high disparity between A and B, respectively.

There might be a lack of consensus on the ground-truth architecture by the domain experts. Hence, there might be multiple such architectures derived [21]. Moreover, the recovery process is by-and-large manual, and as such, error-prone. For these reasons, we used a second metric, namely *normalized TurboMQ* [21], which measures the quality of a clustering independent of any ground-truth architecture. This metric is defined based on the *Cluster Factor (CF)* that is calculated for each cluster, i as follows:

---

[2] http://www.cse.yorku.ca/~bil/downloads/.

Table 3. MoJoFM results for *Bash*.

Method	Include	Symbol	Function	F-GV
MGMC	64	52	57	54
ACDC	52	57	49	50
Bunch-NAHC	53	43	49	46
Bunch-SAHC	57	52	43	49
WCA-UE	34	24	29	30
WCA-UENM	34	24	31	30
LIMBO	34	27	22	22
K-means	59	55	47	46

$$CF_i = \frac{\mu_i}{\mu_i + 0.5 \times \sum_j (\epsilon_{ij} + \epsilon_{ji})} \tag{4}$$

Hereby, μ_i is the number of dependencies among the elements in cluster i. The term $\sum_j (\epsilon_{ij} + \epsilon_{ji})$ defines the sum of dependencies between elements in cluster i and all the elements residing in other clusters. *TurboMQ* measure basically adds up the CF values for all the clusters as shown in Eq. 5.

$$TurboMQ = \sum_{i=1}^{k} CF_i \tag{5}$$

It was observed that *TurboMQ* measure is biased towards architectures with large numbers of clusters [21]. Therefore, it is normalized with respect to the total number of clusters in the recovered architecture. This leads to the *normalized TurboMQ* metric, which we used in our study. The implementation of this metric is available online[3] as well.

We discuss the obtained results in the following section.

5 Results and Discussion

Results for each subject system are listed in Tables 3, 4, 5, 6, 7, 8, 9, 10, 11 and 12. The first and the latter five tables list results regarding the *MoJoFM* metric and the *normalized TurboMQ* metric, respectively. In the following section we first interpret these results to answer *RQ1*. Then, we evaluate the runtime performance as the focus of *RQ2*. We conclude the section with a discussion on threats to validity.

---

[3] https://github.com/hasansozer/Normalized-TurboMQ.

5.1 Accuracy of Modularity Clustering

Tables 3, 4, 5, 6 and 7 list the results for the *MoJoFM* metric. The first column lists the compared SAR approaches, which is followed by results regarding each type of dependency in the respective columns. The best score obtained by any of the SAR approaches for a particular type of dependency is highlighted in light gray. The best score overall is highlighted in dark gray. We can see from these results that the overall best scores are obtained with either ACDC or MGMC. We can also see that best scores per various dependency types are also attributed to these two techniques except a few cases. Overall, MGMC outperforms ACDC in approximately half of the cases.

Table 4. MoJoFM results for *ArchStudio*.

Method	Include	S-CHA	S-Int	S-NoDyB	Function	F-GV
MGMC	61	50	64	66	63	63
ACDC	60	60	77	78	74	74
Bunch-NAHC	48	40	49	47	53	46
Bunch-SAHC	54	39	53	40	53	54
WCA-UE	30	30	32	45	31	31
WCA-UENM	30	30	32	45	31	31
LIMBO	23	23	24	25	24	23
K-means	44	37	39	41	39	38

Table 5. MoJoFM results for *Chromium*.

Method	Include	S-CHA	S-Int	S-NoDyB	Function	F-GV
MGMC	59	56	55	64	67	67
ACDC	64	70	73	71	71	71
Bunch-NAHC	28	31	24	29	29	35
Bunch-SAHC	12	71	43	42	39	29
WCA-UE	23	23	23	27	29	29
WCA-UENM	23	23	23	27	29	29
LIMBO	N/A	23	3	26	27	27
K-means	40	42	43	43	45	45

Tables 8, 9, 10, 11 and 12 list the results for the *normalized TurboMQ* metric. We can see that MGMC is even much better than all the other SAR approaches for this metric. It also consistently outperforms ACDC. In fact, this result is expected because the *normalized TurboMQ* metric evaluates the modularity of the clusters and MGMC aims at maximizing this property although the metrics

Table 6. MoJoFM results for *Hadoop*.

Method	Include	S-CHA	S-Int	S-NoDyB	Function	F-GV
MGMC	27	24	40	42	37	39
ACDC	24	29	41	41	41	41
Bunch-NAHC	23	21	24	24	26	26
Bunch-SAHC	24	26	28	26	29	28
WCA-UE	13	12	15	28	17	17
WCA-UENM	13	12	15	28	17	17
LIMBO	15	13	14	14	13	14
K-means	30	25	29	28	29	29

Table 7. MoJoFM results for *ITK*.

Method	Include	S-CHA	S-Int	S-NoDyB	Function	F-GV
MGMC	50	57	56	54	62	62
ACDC	52	55	52	48	60	60
Bunch-NAHC	37	36	35	35	45	47
Bunch-SAHC	32	46	43	41	54	53
WCA-UE	30	31	44	45	36	36
WCA-UENM	30	31	44	45	36	36
LIMBO	30	31	44	38	36	35
K-means	38	42	39	43	60	61

used for assessing modularity are different. Bunch variants also aim at improving modularity. Hence, it is interesting to see Bunch variants lagging behind for this metric as well. There is one exception to this observation among the results, which is related to the *Archstudio* project (Table 9). Here, Bunch variants outperform all the other SAR approaches in general, although the best overall result is still obtained with MGMC.

We manually analyzed the clustering output provided by MGMC for the *S-CHA* dependency file regarding the *ArchStudio* project in detail. We noticed that there are many clusters in the output that contain a single item only. Then, we checked the occurrence of these items in the input dependency graph. We found out that they are subject to reflexive dependencies. For instance, the following file is specified to be dependent on itself only:

```
edu.uci.isr.archstudio4.comp.archipelago.ObjRefTransfer
```

The output of MGMC is reasonable for such cases. A cluster with no external dependencies may not be merged with other clusters. Also, an item that is dependent on itself only may not be moved to other clusters. These actions would not improve the modularity measure. Indeed, we observed that the TurboMQ value increases from 31 to 70 for MGMC after we remove reflexive dependencies.

5.2   Runtime Performance of Modularity Clustering

Figure 1 depicts a box-plot regarding the execution times of MGMC for the largest set of input files. Hereby, the x-axis lists the four largest dependency graphs in the dataset that are provided as input for clustering. These are all extracted from the *Chromium* project. The total completion time of clustering is indicated by the y-axis in seconds. Recall that we used a laptop computer with Intel Core i7 1.80 GHz CPU and 16 GB RAM to run the experiments. Yet, the execution time do not exceed half a minute even for the largest input file. However, ACDC, which was reported as the most scalable technique, took 70–120 min to run for the same input file on a 3.3 GHz E5-1660 server with 32 GB RAM [21]. Results for the other SAR approaches obtained only after 8 to 24 h of running or a timeout error [21]. Therefore, we conclude that MGMC runs orders-of-magnitude faster than all the other algorithms.

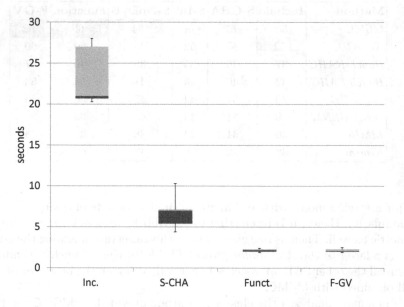

Fig. 1. Runtime performance of MGMC on the largest dependency graphs extracted from the *Chromium* project.

5.3   Threats to Validity

There are several validity threats to our evaluation. First, our evaluation is based on the commonly used *MoJoFM* metric. It was shown that this metric was preferable to other alternatives when the architectures being compared contain the same files [21]. The validity of the ground-truth archtiectures poses another threat for the study. However, actual developers and architects of the projects

Table 8. Normalized TurboMQ results for *Bash*.

Method	Include	Symbol	Function	F-GV
MGMC	74	64	63	63
ACDC	9	22	29	29
Bunch-NAHC	25	31	33	28
Bunch-SAHC	30	30	28	28
WCA-UE	0	7	10	10
WCA-UENM	0	7	5	10
LIMBO	6	13	7	7
K-means	0	17	14	16

Table 9. Normalized TurboMQ results for *ArchStudio*.

Method	Include	S-CHA	S-Int	S-NoDyB	Function	F-GV
MGMC	89	31	50	50	54	37
ACDC	66	41	76	84	72	74
Bunch-NAHC	72	42	74	85	74	75
Bunch-SAHC	71	41	76	85	72	74
WCA-UE	1	11	22	65	10	19
WCA-UENM	1	11	22	65	10	19
LIMBO	2	12	31	38	24	27
K-means	13	21	38	51	35	39

were involved in the extraction of this information [21]. To mitigate these threats, we used a second measure, *normalized TurboMQ*, which measures the quality of a clustering independent of any ground-truth architecture. This measure is based on the modularity metric utilized by the Bunch tool [23] and it is subject to flaws, i.e., it is possible to obtain the maximum score by grouping all the modules in a single cluster. We manually checked results for such cases. Our evaluation is based on five subject systems, which limits the generalizability of conclusions. These systems were selected to be of different size, functionality and design/implementation paradigms to mitigate this threat. It is not easy to extend the dataset due to difficulties in obtaining ground-truth architectures [14].

Table 10. Normalized TurboMQ results for *Chromium*.

Method	Include	S-CHA	S-Int	S-NoDyB	Function	F-GV
MGMC	94	90	80	94	93	93
ACDC	15	19	18	20	24	24
Bunch-NAHC	4	24	9	26	16	19
Bunch-SAHC	2	30	11	23	29	11
WCA-UE	0	2	2	2	2	2
WCA-UENM	0	2	2	2	2	3
LIMBO	N/A	2	2	2	2	2
K-means	0	17	13	19	22	22

Table 11. Normalized TurboMQ results for *Hadoop*.

Method	Include	S-CHA	S-Int	S-NoDyB	Function	F-GV
MGMC	89	45	48	52	54	45
ACDC	48	28	59	65	57	58
Bunch-NAHC	40	26	53	61	52	48
Bunch-SAHC	40	31	53	61	54	56
WCA-UE	1	5	8	34	6	8
WCA-UENM	1	5	8	33	6	8
LIMBO	2	7	19	25	17	17
K-means	11	13	29	34	26	27

Table 12. Normalized TurboMQ results for *ITK*.

Method	Include	S-CHA	S-Int	S-NoDyB	Function	F-GV
MGMC	95	92	80	90	94	94
ACDC	33	24	18	32	40	40
Bunch-NAHC	15	23	23	22	34	37
Bunch-SAHC	10	29	23	21	44	37
WCA-UE	3	9	3	2	10	9
WCA-UENM	3	9	3	2	10	19
LIMBO	7	11	5	1	9	9
K-means	13	24	15	13	31	25

6   Conclusion and Future Work

We introduced an empirical evaluation of MGMC used for SAR. We used five open source projects as subject systems for which the ground-truth architectures were known. Various types of dependencies extracted from these systems were previously used as input to evaluate their impact on the accuracy of state-of-the-art SAR techniques. We used the same dataset to evaluate the accuracy and runtime performance of MGMC and compared the results with respect those achieved with existing techniques. Results showed that the accuracy of MGMC is comparable to that of the best known algorithm so far, namely ACDC [35], outperforming it in approximately half of the cases. In addition, it scales better to very large systems for which it runs orders-of-magnitude faster than all the other algorithms.

As future work, additional metrics can be employed for evaluating the accuracy of clustering results. Other types/variants of greedy, heuristic-based approaches can be employed to maximize modularity. Exact methods can also be applied to obtain the optimal possible outcome as a reference point although they do not scale for large projects. The dataset used for experimentation can also be extended; however, ground-truth architectures are usually not available and it is very effort-consuming to recover them [14].

Acknowledgements. We thank Thibaud Lutellier for providing the extracted dependency data regarding the subject systems.

References

1. Agarwal, G., Kempe, D.: Modularity-maximizing graph communities via mathematical programming. Eur. Phys. J. B **66**(3), 409–418 (2008)
2. Altinisik, M., Sozer, H.: Automated procedure clustering for reverse engineering PL/SQL programs. In: Proceedings of the 31st ACM Symposium on Applied Computing, pp. 1440–1445 (2016)
3. Andritsos, P., Tsaparas, P., Miller, R.J., Sevcik, K.C.: LIMBO: scalable clustering of categorical data. In: Bertino, E., Christodoulakis, S., Plexousakis, D., Christophides, V., Koubarakis, M., Böhm, K., Ferrari, E. (eds.) EDBT 2004. LNCS, vol. 2992, pp. 123–146. Springer, Heidelberg (2004). https://doi.org/10.1007/978-3-540-24741-8_9
4. Brandes, U., et al.: On modularity clustering. IEEE Trans. Knowl. Data Eng. **20**(2), 172–188 (2008)
5. Callo, T., America, P., Avgeriou, P.: A top-down approach to construct execution views of a large software-intensive system. J. Softw.: Evol. Process **25**(3), 233–260 (2013)
6. Çatalyürek, U., Kaya, K., Langguth, J., Uçar, B.: A partitioning-based divisive clustering technique for maximizing the modularity. In: Bader, D.A., Meyerhenke, H., Sanders, P., Wagner, D. (eds.) Graph Partitioning and Graph Clustering. Contemporary Mathematics. AMS, Providence (2012)
7. Clauset, A., Newman, M., Moore, C.: Finding community structure in very large networks. Phys. Rev. E **70**, 066111 (2004)
8. Corazza, A., Martino, S.D., Maggio, V., Scanniello, G.: Investigating the use of lexical information for software system clustering. In: Proceedings of the 15th European Conference on Software Maintenance and Reengineering, pp. 35–44 (2011)
9. Ducasse, S., Pollet, D.: Software architecture reconstruction: a process-oriented taxonomy. IEEE Trans. Softw. Eng. **35**(4), 573–591 (2009)

10. Eick, S., Graves, T., Karr, A., Marron, J., Mockus, A.: Does code decay? Assessing the evidence from change management data. IEEE Trans. Softw. Eng. **27**(1), 1–12 (2001)
11. Eppinger, S., Browning, T.: Design Structure Matrix Methods and Applications. MIT Press, Cambridge (2012)
12. Ersoy, E., Kaya, K., Altınışık, M., Sözer, H.: Using hypergraph clustering for software architecture reconstruction of data-tier software. In: Tekinerdogan, B., Zdun, U., Babar, A. (eds.) ECSA 2016. LNCS, vol. 9839, pp. 326–333. Springer, Cham (2016). https://doi.org/10.1007/978-3-319-48992-6_24
13. Garcia, J., Ivkovic, I., Medvidovic, N.: A comparative analysis of software architecture recovery techniques. In: Proceedings of the 28th International Conference on Automated Software Engineering, pp. 486–496 (2013)
14. Garcia, J., Krka, I., Mattmann, C., Medvidovic, N.: Obtaining ground-truth software architectures. In: Proceedings of the International Conference on Software Engineering, pp. 901–910 (2013)
15. Garcia, J., Popescu, D., Mattmann, C., Medvidovic, N., Cai, Y.: Enhancing architectural recovery using concerns. In: Proceedings of the 26th IEEE/ACM International Conference on Automated Software Engineering, pp. 552–555 (2011)
16. Garlan, D., et al.: Documenting Software Architectures: Views and Beyond, 2nd edn. Addison-Wesley, Boston (2010)
17. Guo, G.Y., Atlee, J.M., Kazman, R.: A software architecture reconstruction method. In: Donohoe, P. (ed.) Software Architecture. ITIFIP, vol. 12, pp. 15–33. Springer, Boston (1999). https://doi.org/10.1007/978-0-387-35563-4_2
18. Hendrickson, B., Leland, R.: A multi-level algorithm for partitioning graphs. In: Proceedings of the ACM/IEEE Conference on Supercomputing, p. 28 (1995)
19. Karypis, G., Kumar, V.: A fast and high quality multilevel scheme for partitioning irregular graphs. SIAM J. Sci. Comput. **20**(1), 359–392 (1998)
20. Kobayashi, K., Kamimura, M., Kato, K., Yano, K., Matsuo, A.: Feature-gathering dependency-based software clustering using dedication and modularity. In: Proceedings of the 28th IEEE International Conference on Software Maintenance, pp. 462–471 (2012)
21. Lutellier, T., et al.: Measuring the impact of code dependencies on software architecture recovery techniques. IEEE Trans. Softw. Eng. **44**(2), 159–181 (2018)
22. Maqbool, O., Babri, H.: The weighted combined algorithm: a linkage algorithm for software clustering. In: Proceedings of the 8th Euromicro Working Conference on Software Maintenance and Reengineering, pp. 15–24 (2004)
23. Mitchell, B., Mancoridis, S.: On the automatic modularization of software systems using the Bunch tool. IEEE Trans. Softw. Eng. **32**(3), 193–208 (2006)
24. Murphy, G., Notkin, D., Sullivan, K.: Software reflexion models: bridging the gap between design and implementation. IEEE Trans. Softw. Eng. **27**(4), 364–380 (2001)
25. Noack, A., Rotta, R.: Multi-level algorithms for modularity clustering. In: Vahrenhold, J. (ed.) SEA 2009. LNCS, vol. 5526, pp. 257–268. Springer, Heidelberg (2009). https://doi.org/10.1007/978-3-642-02011-7_24
26. Parnas, D.L.: On the criteria to be used in decomposing systems into modules. Commun. ACM **15**(12), 1053–1058 (1972)
27. Qingshan, L., Hua, C., Ping, C., Yun, Z.: Architecture recovery and abstraction from the perspective of processes. In: Proceedings of the 12th Working Conference on Reverse Engineering, pp. 57–66 (2005)

28. Rossi, F., Villa-Vialaneix, N.: Représentation d'un grand réseau á partir d'une classification hiérarchique de ses sommets. Journal de la Société Française de Statistique **152**(3), 34–65 (2011)
29. Sangal, N., Jordan, E., Sinha, V., Jackson, D.: Using dependency models to manage complex software architecture. In: Proceedings of the 20th Conference on Object-Oriented Programming, Systems, Languages and Applications, pp. 167–176 (2005)
30. Sangwan, R., Neill, C.: Characterizing essential and incidental complexity in software architectures. In: Proceedings of the 3rd European Conference on Software Architecture, pp. 265–268 (2009)
31. Schuetz, P., Caflisch, A.: Efficient modularity optimization by multistep greedy algorithm and vertex mover refinement. Phys. Rev. E **77**, 046112 (2008)
32. Storey, M.A., Wong, K., Muller, H.: Rigi: A visualization environment for reverse engineering. In: Proceedings of the 19th International Conference on Software Engineering, pp. 606–607 (1997)
33. Sullivan, K., Cai, Y., Hallen, B., Griswold, W.: The structure and value of modularity in software design. In: Proceedings of the 8th European Software Engineering Conference, pp. 99–108 (2001)
34. Sun, C., Zhou, J., Cao, J., Jin, M., Liu, C., Shen, Y.: ReArchJBs: a tool for automated software architecture recovery of JavaBeans-based applications. In: Proceedings of the 16th Australian Software Engineering Conference, pp. 270–280 (2005)
35. Tzerpos, V., Holt, R.: ACDC: an algorithm for comprehension-driven clustering. In: Proceedings of the 7th Working Conference on Reverse Engineering, pp. 258–267 (2000)
36. Wen, Z., Tzerpos, V.: An effectiveness measure for software clustering algorithms. In: Proceedings of the 12th IEEE International Workshop on Program Comprehension, pp. 194–203 (2004)
37. Wong, K.: RIGI User's Manual. University of Victoria (1996)
38. Wu, J., Hassan, A.F., Holt, R.C.: Comparison of clustering algorithms in the context of software evolution. In: Proceedings of the 21st IEEE International Conference on Software Maintenance, pp. 525–535 (2005)
39. Xu, G., Tsoka, S., Papageorgiou, L.: Finding community structures in complex networks using mixed integer optimisation. Eur. Phys. J. B **60**(2), 231–239 (2007)

What Quality Attributes Can We Find in Product Backlogs? A Machine Learning Perspective

Matthias Galster[1(✉)], Fabian Gilson[1], and François Georis[2]

[1] University of Canterbury, Christchurch, New Zealand
{matthias.galster,fabian.gilson}@canterbury.ac.nz
[2] University of Namur, Namur, Belgium
francois.georis@student.unamur.be

Abstract. Automatically identifying quality attributes (e.g., security, performance) in agile user stories could help architects reason about early architecture design decisions *before* analyzing a product backlog in detail (e.g., through a manual review of stories). For example, architects may already get the "bigger picture" of potential architectural key drivers and constraints. Applying a previously developed method to automatically identify quality attributes in user stories, in this paper we investigate (a) what quality attributes are potentially missed in an automatic analysis of a backlog, and (b) how the importance of quality attributes (based on the frequency of their occurrence in a backlog) differs to that of quality attributes identified in a manual review of a backlog. As in previous works, we analyzed the backlogs of 22 publicly available projects including 1,675 stories. For most backlogs, automatically identified quality attributes are a *subset* of quality attributes identified manually. On the other hand, the automatic identification would usually not find more (and therefore potentially irrelevant) quality attributes than a manual review. We also found that the ranking of quality attributes differs between the automatically and manually analyzed user stories, but the overall trend of rankings is consistent. Our findings indicate that automatically identifying quality attributes can reduce the effort of an initial backlog analysis, but still provide useful (even though high-level and therefore potentially incomplete) information about quality attributes.

Keywords: Agile software development · Quality attributes · Product backlog · User stories · Natural language processing

1 Introduction

A key principle of agile software development is to reduce potentially unnecessary upfront work. Nevertheless, it is important to understand the most significant architectural drivers early on to avoid architectural decisions that negatively impact modifiability or performance. If agile teams spend too little time thinking

© Springer Nature Switzerland AG 2019
T. Bures et al. (Eds.): ECSA 2019, LNCS 11681, pp. 88–96, 2019.
https://doi.org/10.1007/978-3-030-29983-5_6

about architecture design upfront, then there is an increased risk of failure [16]. Quality attributes such as performance, security or interoperability impact architecture design decisions, e.g., when selecting architectural patterns, tactics or reference architectures [1]. Therefore, identifying quality attributes early on is part of software architecture analysis [1]. Furthermore, in agile software development we need to balance near-term functional requirements and long-term quality goals [2]. Hence it is crucial to understand which quality attributes are relevant and which quality attributes might be more important than others. Prioritizing quality attributes is difficult in early development iterations and wrong decisions can result in hard-to-modify, unreliable, slow and insecure systems [8].

In agile software development, functional requirements are often specified as textual user stories. For example, for an online store one may define a story like "As a customer, I want to be able to create and edit a customer profile so that I can conveniently use all services of the e-shop." In our previous work [9] we showed that user stories do include information about quality attributes, and explored how to automatically identify user stories that include information about quality attributes. The goal was to better understand potential architectural key drivers and their "bigger picture" *before* analyzing a product backlog in detail (e.g., through a manual and potentially time-consuming review of the initial backlog).[1] As found by others, problems related to architecture are often found late in development projects [13]. Our previous work [9] also showed that we cannot rely on keywords when looking for quality attribute-related information in user stories. We therefore applied machine learning and natural language processing [9].

Machine learning and natural language processing are usually limited regarding precision and recall [7]. Therefore, in this paper we build on our previous work to investigate two exploratory questions: **Q1:** Does an automatic analysis of a backlog miss potentially relevant quality attributes? Answering this question could help understand whether automatic analysis of backlogs potentially misguides the architect's decision making process. **Q2:** How does the importance of quality attributes (based on the frequency of their occurrence in a backlog) differ between an automatic and a manual review of a backlog? Answering this question helps understand whether quality requirements can be reliably prioritized based on an automated analysis. We are interested in a more analytical and exploratory discussion of the implications of identifying quality attributes in user stories, rather than a detailed statistical and experimental evaluation as partially done in our previous work [9]. Thus, in this paper we present a challenge in software architecture research and promising results.

---

[1] We acknowledge that quality attributes are not the only factors with architectural significance; however, other factors are outside the scope of this work.

2   Related Work

In software architecture, there are already examples of using natural language processing, e.g., to extract design decisions from issue management systems [3, 14] or to identify architectural knowledge in developer communities [15].

In 2019, Binkhonain and Zhao conducted a review on machine-learning techniques that classify non-functional requirements [4]. However, most techniques use comprehensive requirement documents (rather than short user stories) written by requirement engineers and rely on keywords. On the other hand, we focus on user stories that are usually written by end users with less training in requirements engineering and writing requirements. Two techniques identified in the review [6,12] deal with mobile app reviews which share some commonalities with user stories (e.g., short and concise sentences), but for a different context. While most of the works discussed in [4] recover design decisions or architecture knowledge *post-hoc* or for reuse, our goal is to inform decisions of architects early on based on architectural drivers that arise from user requirements. Furthermore, our work is also related to prioritizing quality attributes (see e.g., Koziolek [11]). We aim at a lightweight yet useful analysis of architecture-relevant quality attributes in agile development.

3   Research Approach

Below we briefly discuss our approach to explore the two questions outlined in Sect. 1. The **corpus of backlogs and user stories** in our study was a set of 1,775 publicly available stories similar to that used by Dalpiaz *et al.* [5] and in our previous work [9], see Table 1. The number of user stories ranges from 50 to 114 with an average of 76 per backlog. The average length of stories is 24 words.

To **manually identify quality attributes**, two researchers independently labelled user stories to indicate up to two quality attributes per user story (part of our previous work). Then, we merged the labelling and discussed disagreements. We used quality attributes as described in the ISO/IEC 25010 standard [10] (for more details see our previous work [9]). For example, the story "As a repository administrator, I would like to be able to continue to provide access to the repository in the event that the server fails." was labelled as referring to *reliability* since it mentions continuous access to a system even in case of failures. In the following, we use abbreviations for quality attributes (C: compatibility, M: maintainability, PF: performance, PT: portability, R: reliability, S: security).

To **automatically identify quality attributes**, we relied on our previous work [9] which compared different natural language-based machine learning techniques and models using the spaCy library for natural language processing.[2] In this paper we used the best performing model to identify quality attributes (this model had an average precision of *0.65*, average recall of *0.67* and average f_1 score of *0.66* in a k-fold 10 validation) trained on manually labeled stories for all quality attributes.

---

[2] https://spacy.io/.

Table 1. Corpus of product backlogs and user stories.

Backlog	Description	Stories
FederalSpending	Web platform for sharing US government spending data	94
Loudoun	Land management system for Loudoun County, Virginia	57
Recycling	Online platform to support waste recycling	50
OpenSpending	Website to increase transparency of government expenses	53
FrictionLess	Platform for obtaining insights from data	66
ScrumAlliance	First version of the Scrum Alliance website	97
NSF	New version of the NSF website	72
CamperPlus	App for camp administrators and parents	53
PlanningPoker	First version of the PlanningPoker.com website	52
DataHub	Platform to find, share and publish data online	67
MIS	Management information system for Duke University	83
CASK	Toolbox to for fast and easy development with Hadoop	63
NeuroHub	Research data management portal	102
Alfred	Personal interactive assistant for active aging	134
BadCamp	Conference registration and management platform	69
RDA-DMP	Software for machine-actionable data management plans	82
ArchiveSpace	Web-based archiving system	55
UniBath	Institutional data repository for the University of Bath	53
DuraSpace	Repository for different types of digital content	99
RacDam	Software for archivists	100
CulRepo	Content management system for Cornell University	114
Zooniverse	Platform that allows anyone to help with research tasks	60

For each **user story** in each backlog (and following the manual and automatic identification procedures from above) we recorded whether or not it addresses a quality attribute and if so which one(s). For each **backlog**, we collected a ranked list (or sequence) of quality attributes based on (a) the absolute number of occurrences of a quality attribute in all stories of a backlog, (b) the relative occurrence of a quality attribute compared to the number of user stories in a backlog, and (c) the relative occurrence of a quality attribute based on all stories that reference a quality attribute over all backlogs. The rankings were the same using any of these three metrics. We collected this information for manually and automatically identified quality attributes separately. We do not consider other priorities of user stories (e.g., based on value): Priorities are often not known upfront as user stories are usually prioritized by different stakeholders during initial iteration planning and sometimes even re-prioritized later.

To **compare the sequences** of manually and automatically identified quality attributes, we used a simple metric based on the pairwise swaps required to transform one sequence into the other. In case two ranked sequences did not include the same number of quality attributes, the shorter sequence was filled up with empty strings. Then, when transforming one sequence into the other, this empty string in one sequence was moved to the position of the missing quality attribute in the other sequence. For example, the sequence $s_m = \{PF, C, R\}$ from the manual identification and $s_a = \{PF, R\}$ from the automatic identification would lead to a comparison of sequences $s_m = \{PF, C, R\}$ and $s_a = \{PF, R, \epsilon\}$ (where ϵ denotes the empty string). We would require one swap between C and R in s_a to move C to the position of ϵ in s_m. The total number of swaps required in the example would then be 1. The larger the number of swaps, the more different the sequences.

4   Results

In Table 2 we provide the sequences of ranked quality attributes for each backlog (most frequently to least frequently occurring attribute). "Missed" indicates how many quality attributes appear in the sequence from the manual identification, but not in the sequence from the automatic identification. "Additional" indicates the number of quality attributes that appear in the sequence from the automatic identification, but not in the sequence from the manual identification.

Key Findings Regarding Q1 (Missing Quality Attributes): Table 2 (column "Difference") shows that for most backlogs, the automatic classification identified a *subset* of the manually labelled quality attributes. For only two backlogs, the automatic identification found quality attributes that were not identified through manual inspection (security for backlogs of *PlanningPoker* and *NSF*). This means that the amount of false positives on backlog level is rather small (we analyzed false positives at story level in [9]). On the other hand, the most frequently missed quality attributes across all backlogs were security, reliability and portability (eight times each). There are two backlogs for which no quality attribute were automatically identified. *CamperPlus* contained two stories related to security and *BadCamp* contained two stories related to security and one related to compatibility. Still, these attributes were indirectly related to the stories. For example, the story "As a parent, I want to be able to create an account, so that I can sign up my kids for camp online." from *CamperPlus* was annotated with security albeit no obvious reference to security, the manual annotations often being subject to human interpretation.

Key Findings Regarding Q2 (Importance of Quality Attributes): We found that the ranked sequences were quite different mostly because of the missing quality attributes in the automatic classification (column "Difference"). The number of swaps is rather small except for a few backlogs, e.g., *NSF* and *CASK* (see column "Swaps"). On the other hand, the sequences for *NeuroHub* (the only backlog where the quality attributes were the same in both rankings) showed quite a different order. Focusing on the top quality attributes, the differences are rather small (e.g., a quality attribute might be the first ranked in one sequence and the second ranked in another sequence). An exception is the backlog for *CASK*, where compatibility appears least frequently in the manual sequence,

Table 2. Sequences of ranked quality attributes.

Backlog	Sequences	Difference	Swaps
FederalSpending (manual)	$\{M, C, PF, S\}$	Missed: 3	1
FederalSpending (automatic)	$\{C\}$	Additional: 0	
Loudoun (manual)	$\{C, S\}$	Missed: 1	0
Londoun (automatic)	$\{C\}$	Additional: 0	
Recycling (manual)	$\{C, S, M, PT\}$	Missed: 2	1
Recycling (automatic)	$\{S, C\}$	Additional: 0	
OpenSpending (manual)	$\{C, M, S, PT\}$	Missed: 2	1
OpenSpending (automatic)	$\{C, S\}$	Additional: 0	
FrictionLess (manual)	$\{C, PF, R, M\}$	Missed: 1	1
FrictionLess (automatic)	$\{C, PF, S, M\}$	Additional: 1	
ScrumAlliance (manual)	$\{S, C\}$	Missed: 0	0
ScrumAlliance (automatic)	$\{S, C\}$	Additional: 0	
NSF (manual)	$\{C, M, PT\}$	Missed: 1	3
NSF (automatic)	$\{M, S, C\}$	Additional: 1	
CamperPlus (manual)	$\{S\}$	Missed: 1	0
CamperPlus (automatic)	None	Additional: 0	
PlanningPoker (manual)	$\{C, PF, S\}$	Missed: 1	2
PlanningPoker (automatic)	$\{S, C\}$	Additional: 0	
DataHub (manual)	$\{C, R, PT, S, M\}$	Missed: 4	0
DataHub (automatic)	$\{C\}$	Additional: 0	
MIS (manual)	$\{S, C, M, PT, R\}$	Missed: 3	1
MIS (automatic)	$\{C, S\}$	Additional: 0	
CASK (manual)	$\{M, R, PT, C\}$	Missed: 2	3
CASK (automatic)	$\{C, M\}$	Additional: 0	
NeuroHub (manual)	$\{C, S, PT, M, R, PF\}$	Missed: 0	2
NeuroHub (automatic)	$\{C, S, M, PT, PF, R\}$	Additional: 0	
Alfred (manual)	$\{C, S, M, PT, PF\}$	Missed: 1	0
Alfred (automatic)	$\{C, S, M, PT\}$	Additional: 0	
BadCamp (manual)	$\{S, C\}$	Missing: 2	0
BadCamp (automatically)	None	Additional: 0	
RDA-DMP (manual)	$\{S, PF, C, R\}$	Missed: 2	1
RDA-DMP (automatic)	$\{S, C\}$	Additional: 0	
ArchiveSpace (manual)	$\{C, S, R, M\}$	Missed: 2	0
ArchiveSpace (automatic)	$\{C, S\}$	Additional: 0	
UniBath (manual)	$\{C, S, R, M, PF\}$	Missed: 3	0
UniBath (automatic)	$\{C, S\}$	Additional: 0	
DuraSpace (manual)	$\{S\}$	Missed: 0	0
DuraSpace (automatic)	$\{S\}$	Additional: 0	
RacDam (manual)	$\{S, C\}$	Missed: 0	0
RacDam (automatic)	$\{S, C\}$	Additional: 0	
CulRepo (manual)	$\{C, S, R, PF, PT\}$	Missed: 3	0
CulRepo (automatic)	$\{C, S\}$	Additional: 0	
Zooniverse (manual)	$\{C, S\}$	Missed: 1	0
Zooniverse (automatic)	$\{C\}$	Additional: 0	

but most frequently in the automatic sequence. When looking at the number of occurrences of quality attributes in each sequence of *CASK*, we notice that the absolute numbers for compatibility are rather close, but the main difference is related to maintainability.

5 Discussion

Implications: Given our preliminary key findings above, we believe that even though automatically identifying quality attributes may not result in exactly the same quality attributes identified by a human analyst, the automatic approach still provides insights for an initial design space exploration. Considering the time required to manually review a backlog (magnitude of hours) compared to the time of conducting the automatic approach (magnitude of seconds or minutes), we believe that an automated backlog analysis could *complement* rather than *replace* human decision making during architecture design: the automated backlog analysis provides a starting point for problem and solution space exploration (e.g., the automated analysis could identify key architectural drivers).

Limitations: One limitation of our work is that we do not differentiate run-time quality attributes and design time quality attributes. Differentiating types of quality attributes would allow a more detailed analysis of the implications and perhaps the importance of quality attributes. Furthermore, we do not consider the business value of user stories when determining the ranking of quality attributes. Quality attributes that appear in more "valuable" user stories may receive a higher priority (in addition to considering how often these quality attributes appear in a backlog). Also, we do not consider changing and growing backlogs. Our assumption is that quality attributes can be analyzed continuously, but it is important to understand the "bigger picture" early on.

Treats to Validity: In terms of *external validity*, this research relies on a limited number of user stories and backlogs. It is unclear whether these backlogs are representative of industrial practices in general. However, since how user stories are specified in practice varies (e.g., phrasing patterns and writing guidelines) and does not always follow best practices, it may be hard to identify a truly representative set of stories. Also, we only consider stories but no acceptance criteria. Finally, our set of quality attributes is rather limited as it follows the structure of the ISO/IEC 25010 quality model. Future work includes considering more hierarchy levels of that quality model. On the other hand, this will require a much larger set of user stories to train a machine learning classifier, since the number of quality attributes in ISO/IEC 25010 is rather large. Regarding *internal validity*, there could be confounding variables which impact our results and in particular the manual labeling of stories, e.g., the labeling did not involve initial stakeholders. Regarding *conclusion validity*, when comparing quality attributes identified manually and automatically, we treated manually identified attributes as "ground truth". Thus, our findings depend on the quality of the manual classification and consistency across stories.

6 Conclusions

In this paper we presented insights about how automatically identified quality attributes in user stories can provide information for architectural decision making. We found that (a) even though the automatic classification does not identify all quality attributes considered relevant by human experts, at least it identifies a subset rather than a random list of quality attributes, and (b) the rankings of quality attributes identified manually and automatically vary, but trends in sequences are consistent. Future works include analyzing more backlogs and user stories and investigating the impact of distinguishing types of quality attributes on the identified quality attributes and their rankings.

References

1. Bass, L., Clements, P., Kazman, R.: Software Architecture in Practice. Addison-Wesley, Boston (2012)
2. Bellomo, S., Gorton, I., Kazman, R.: Toward agile architecture: Insights from 15 years of ATAM. IEEE Softw. **32**(5), 38–45 (2015)
3. Bhat, M., Shumaiev, K., Biesdorf, A., Hohenstein, U., Matthes, F.: Automatic extraction of design decisions from issue management systems: a machine learning based approach. In: Lopes, A., de Lemos, R. (eds.) ECSA 2017. LNCS, vol. 10475, pp. 138–154. Springer, Cham (2017). https://doi.org/10.1007/978-3-319-65831-5_10
4. Binkhonain, M., Zhao, L.: A review of machine learning algorithms for identification and classification of non-functional requirements. Expert Syst. Appl.: X **1**, 1–13 (2019)
5. Dalpiaz, F., van der Schalk, I., Brinkkemper, S., Aydemir, F.B., Lucassen, G.: Detecting terminological ambiguity in user stories: tool and experimentation. Inf. Softw. Technol. **110**, 3–16 (2019)
6. Deocadez, R., Harrison, R., Rodriguez, D.: Automatically classifying requirements from app stores: a preliminary study. In: Fourth International Workshop on Artificial Intelligence for Requirements Engineering (AIRE). IEEE (2017)
7. Domingos, P.: A few useful things to know about machine learning. Commun. ACM **55**(10), 78–87 (2012)
8. Galster, M., Angelov, S., Martínez-Fernández, S., Tofan, D.: Reference architectures in scrum: friends or foes? In: Joint Meeting of the European Software Engineering Conference and the ACM SIGSOFT Symposium on the Foundations of Software Engineering (ESEC/FSE), pp. 896–901. ACM (2017)
9. Gilson, F., Galster, M., Georis, F.: Extracting quality attributes from user stories for early architecture decision making. In: International Workshop on Decision Making in Software Architecture (MARCH), pp. 1–8. IEEE (2019)
10. ISO/IEC: ISO/IEC 25010 system and software quality models. Technical report, International Organization for Standardization/International Electrotechnical Commission (2010)
11. Koziolek, A.: Architecture-driven quality requirements prioritization. In: IEEE International Workshop on the Twin Peaks of Requirements and Architecture (TwinPeaks), pp. 1–5. IEEE (2012)

12. Lu, M., Liang, P.: Automatic classification of non-functional requirements from augmented app user reviews. In: International Conference on Evaluation and Assessment in Software Engineering (EASE), pp. 344–353. ACM (2017)
13. Martensson, T., Martini, A., Stahl, D., Bosch, J.: Continuous architecture: towards the goldilocks zone and away from vicious circles. In: International Conference on Software Architecture (ICSA), pp. 131–140. IEEE (2019)
14. Shahbazian, A., Lee, Y.K., Le, D., Brun, Y., Medvidovic, N.: Recovering architectural design decisions. In: International Conference on Software Architecture (ICSA), pp. 95–104. IEEE (2018)
15. Soliman, M., Galster, M., Riebisch, M.: Developing an ontology for architecture knowledge from developer communities. In: International Conference on Software Architecture (ICSA), pp. 89–92. IEEE (2017)
16. Waterman, M., Noble, J., Allan, G.: How much up-front? A grounded theory of agile architecture. In: International Conference on Software Engineering (ICSE), pp. 347–357. IEEE (2017)

Architecturing Elastic Edge Storage Services for Data-Driven Decision Making

Ivan Lujic[1]([✉])(iD) and Hong-Linh Truong[2](iD)

[1] Institute of Information Systems Engineering, TU Wien, Vienna, Austria
ivan.lujic@tuwien.ac.at
[2] Department of Computer Science, Aalto University, Espoo, Finland
linh.truong@aalto.fi

Abstract. In the IoT era, a massive number of smart sensors produce a variety of data at unprecedented scale. Edge storage has limited capacities posing a crucial challenge for maintaining only the most relevant IoT data for edge analytics. Currently, this problem is addressed mostly considering traditional cloud-based database perspectives, including storage optimization and resource elasticity, while separately investigating data analytics approaches and system operations. For better support of future edge analytics, in this work, we propose a novel, holistic approach for architecturing elastic edge storage services, featuring three aspects, namely, (i) data/system characterization (e.g., metrics, key properties), (ii) system operations (e.g., filtering, sampling), and (iii) data processing utilities (e.g., recovery, prediction). In this regard, we present seven engineering principles for the architecture design of edge data services.

Keywords: Edge data service · Architectural design · Edge computing · Adaptation · Service computing · IoT · Engineering

1 Introduction

The introduction of edge computing can help dealing with time sensitive requirements for accurate decisions based on Internet of Things (IoT) data [12]. Unlike scalable cloud data repositories, edge systems have limited storage capacity, whereas certain amount of IoT sensor data have to be stored and processed in proximity of the data sources [13]. Consequently, any edge data service must store only the most relevant data for edge analytics (streaming or batch), whereas non-relevant data have to be either discarded or moved to cloud data centers. But the *relevancy* is determined by analytics contexts: these new edge infrastructure conditions and new application analytics requirements, regarding explosive growth of IoT data, force us to explore novel architectural design and further implementations critical for elastic edge data services. By investigating edge data services, we consider strategies, methods, mechanisms and operations for handling and storing constantly generated data at the network edge. We observe that even *within a single edge analytics system:*

© Springer Nature Switzerland AG 2019
T. Bures et al. (Eds.): ECSA 2019, LNCS 11681, pp. 97–105, 2019.
https://doi.org/10.1007/978-3-030-29983-5_7

(**O1**) IoT data are categorized into different model types representing multi-model data, in particular near real-time streaming data and log-based data, thus, requiring different storage types and governance policies. They also include different *significance* levels regarding to storage and edge analytics, especially for critical applications, such as healthcare [6] (e.g., keeping the most important data close to the data source) and smart manufacturing [11] (e.g., keeping significance levels among data streams coming from industrial equipment for maintenance purposes). Hence, *all applications and sensors do not have equal importance*;

(**O2**) Different IoT sensors include *various errors* such as missing data, outliers, noises and anomalies, affecting the designs of edge analysis pipelines and corresponding differently to decision making processes. In this context, incomplete and noisy data can be critical, e.g., for traffic-dependent near real-time route guidance [9], but can be tolerated by intelligent weather forecasts [8];

(**O3**) Data from different IoT sensors appear with *different data generation speed, consequently producing different data volumes for the same time interval*. Simultaneously, different types of monitored sensors require different data volumes to make meaningful analytics. In systems like smart cities, it is crucial, for example, to have big amount of frequent traffic measurements for managing traffic flow in real-time. On the other hand, due to lower volatility, a weather station can require much less data volumes from its sensors for accurate predictions.

Currently, all these highlighted issues are solved outside edge storage services. Solutions for these issues are not included in existing designs of edge data services because, as one might argue, such issues are *analytic context-specific*. However, we argue that they are generic enough that can be customized and must be incorporated into the design of (new) edge data storage systems. These observations indicate crucial changes for enhancing traditional approaches, which have assumptions on consistent low latency, high availability and centralized storage solutions, that cannot be generalized to the edge storage services and unreliable IoT distributed systems. Our first step in solving the above-mentioned issues is to focus on architectural requirements and designs. This paper will contribute: (1) a detailed analysis of edge storage services with application-specific edge analytics support and different utilities and analytics requirements; (2) a specification of necessary principles for engineering highly customized software-defined elastic storage services for dynamic data workload characterizations at the edge.

2   Motivation

In the IoT sensor environment, such as an exemplified university smart building shown in Fig. 1, we can observe data workloads from different IoT applications and decide whether to (1) push data to the cloud data storage, (2) keep relevant data for local edge analytics or (3) discard data if they are not useful for future analytics. In the first case, traditionally, all data are transferred to resource-rich cloud data centers where storage and compute intensive workloads can be handled, resulting in necessary control commands for IoT actuators. However, increasing data streams and latency requirements arising from IoT applications

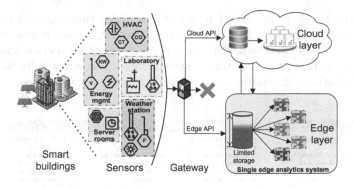

Fig. 1. Traditional single analytics system for university smart buildings use case

makes distant cloud data transfer often impractical. Recent solutions for making crucial fast decisions in IoT systems have increasingly used edge nodes.

In an IoT system, such as a university smart building equipped with many sensors measuring internal subsystems, it is obvious that data from HVAC (Heating, Ventilation, and Air Conditioning) sensors do not have the same importance as data from smart meters and solar panels essential for energy management (O1); incomplete data from weather stations can occur due to external conditions while missing data coming from server room sensors can be caused by some internal failures (O2); an energy management subsystem has higher data generation frequency than a laboratory subsystem (O3). Accordingly, each of these subsystems requires different approach to sensor data analysis, although the same edge storage system is used to integrate data for edge analytics. In addition, limited storage capacities at the network edge prevents us from keeping all generated data. In the third case, due to the limited underlying network infrastructure, some data can be filtered or reduced to save bandwidth usage and storage space, but impacting later degradation of Quality of Service (QoS).

Edge analytics have to meet certain quality of analytics, including amounts of data available, timely decisions and certain levels of data accuracy. Therefore, we must identify which data should be kept at the edge nodes, how long should data be stored, and which processing utilities can assist these problems, providing ability to access the right data at the right time to make data-driven decisions.

3 Engineering Principles for Edge Data Services

Regarding three important aspects of edge storages, namely; edge data/system characterization, application context and edging operations, we present seven principles as guidelines for engineering of elastic edge storage services.

P1: Define and Provide Needed Metrics. To enable efficient customization and adaptation among elements of edge storage systems, it requires a clear definition and flexible monitoring of end-to-end metrics regarding data workloads, application context and system activities.

How: Figure 2 shows end-to-end monitoring metrics that can assist in elastic edge storage management. There are metrics present in four stages of data life cycle, namely data collection, data preprocessing, storage service analysis and data analytics. However, the storage system must also allow definition of new metrics at runtime, depending on application-specific requirements.

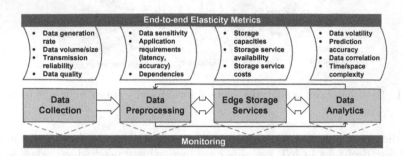

Fig. 2. End-to-end monitoring metrics of elastic edge services through four data stages

Tooling: There are many tools for monitoring cloud systems, e.g., Prometheus[1], and Fluentd[2], but few able to monitor edge data metrics. These tools should be equipped with additional features including pluggable components for edge systems, such as fluentbit[3], providing AI support and tracing instrumentation, as a promising solution for providing end-to-end metrics for elastic storage services.

P2: Support Application-Specific Requirements. Based on sensor-specific metrics and relevancy, we can combine different solutions to deliver appropriate data to local analytics, while meeting application conditions, e.g., clean, complete or normalize sensor data before storage and analysis. Further, customization for secure and verifiable storage is required for applications with sensitive data.

How: Shown in Fig. 3, depending on application information, different sensor data have corresponding data flow routed through the edge architecture to appropriate edge analytics, namely, descriptive, predictive or prescriptive. Interconnected storage nodes, with features including *data recovery* and edge *storage management* mechanisms, ensure access to the relevant data at the right time for different purposes. An algorithm repository contains a set of predefined processing utilities, which usage and order are application-specific and dynamically set at runtime in the elasticity management component. In addition, blockchain integrator component can capture certain types of application-specific data and pass them to the edge blockchain network for verification and auditing.

---

[1] https://prometheus.io/.
[2] https://www.fluentd.org/.
[3] https://fluentbit.io/.

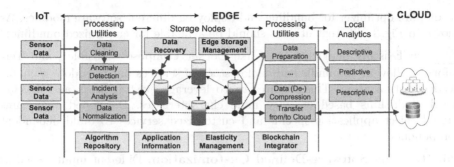

Fig. 3. Application-specific data flows through a holistic edge architecture

Tooling: A repository of available and pluggable microservices can speed up the DevOps of storage services by supplying needed utilities. Different microservices can be used to enable elastic activities, such as data cleaning, normalization and data integration [2]. To keep relevant and complete data in space-limited storage, nodes might incorporate an adaptive algorithm for efficient edge storage management and an automatic mechanism for recovery of incomplete datasets.

P3: Enable Adaptive Data Handling. From a software management standpoint, it is necessary to cope with heterogeneous data workloads including dynamic data streams, batch transfers, QoS critical requirements. Storage service should ensure that stored data are always available, relevant and complete, i.e., keeping data integrity by utilizing different system and data operations.

How: In this context, critical software technology running on the edge can play an important role in storage resources abstraction, supporting communications, configuring suitable data handling features and on-demand data transfers. Techniques for auto-switch data handling algorithms/components should be explored.

Tooling: Fogger[4] could be used to support dynamic allocation and contextual location awareness of storage resources in distributed environment, and featuring blockchain technology. Microservices-based design concepts, such as Edgex[5] open source platform, might enable decentralized and independent data handling as well as reliable data integration supported by on-demand data services.

P4: Highly Customized System Bundling. Edge storage features should be highly customized and application-aware. Considering data workloads and deployment conditions, traditional inflexibility in software modules bundling can produce over- or under-bundled features for supporting edge application analytics. Thus, flexible storage configurations need to meet deployment situations.

How: Based on application-specific information and internal constraints (capacities, resources), the build and deployment process should bundle only components to match these constraints for the right infrastructures. This forces us to

---

[4] https://fogger.io/.
[5] https://www.mainflux.com/.

develop an optimizer for bundling and deploying different software modules. As shown in Fig. 3, different utilities should be available for customized bundling.

Tooling: Existing deploying tools like Docker Compose[6], Ansible[7], and Terraform[8], allow us to bundle and deploy stack of services but they do not enable needed optimization. This requires us to leverage existing work and develop novel algorithms based on edge node characteristics. Developed algorithms should select application-specific and customized services to build dependent components.

P5: Runtime Software-Defined Customization. Different inputs, such as application information and data workload characteristics, have to be combined to support runtime customization of elastic operations and data processing utilities. A way of combining these inputs must enable dynamic, software-defined components for the overall system management. A multi-objective optimization mechanism should enable dynamic prioritization of IoT data and condition evaluation from SLOs at runtime, and thus would impact provided storage service.

How: Figure 4 illustrates potential control flow for elastic storage services. It incorporates a loop for managing internal storage system initially taking valid application information and current storage system metrics. To evaluate a set of defined objectives, dynamic workload characteristics are combined with static knowledge (elastic operations and processing utilities). To decide situational trade-offs for data quality and storage capacities, and utilizing edging system operations, we need to derive an optimization strategy for customized storage with core software-defined APIs for data management and service operations.

Tooling: We need to provide approaches of dynamic configuration, runtime code change (like model@runtime [4]) and services mesh, to combine different inputs from distributed storage nodes. The Kinetic Edge[9] could enable efficient load balancing between distributed storage locations. Multi-objective optimization of customized objectives, e.g., data quality and storage capacities, can be well addressed by using optimized data placement strategies in multi-cloud storage [14].

P6: Support IoT-Edge Continuum. This principle looks at impacting constant data flows between IoT systems and edge storage services, while supporting underlying protocols. According to edge storage performances, it requires triggering different actions with changing data generation frequency on-demand.

How: Both IoT and edge nodes require developing an edge-IoT connector to control data flows that can often be unpredictable. This connector should be able to (1) discard incoming poor quality data; (2) apply various sampling commands for collecting only relevant data; (3) trigger actions for turning off/on sensors in producing data; highly impacting overall performance of edge storage services.

---

[6] https://docs.docker.com.
[7] https://www.ansible.com/.
[8] https://www.terraform.io/.
[9] https://www.vapor.io/kinetic-edge/.

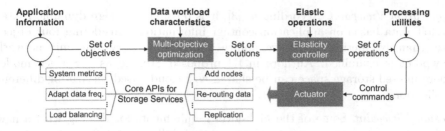

Fig. 4. Elasticity management for customized data flows and edge storage services

Tooling: Novel mechanisms from data viewpoint can be considered allowing IoT sensors to securely receive and perform actuation requests from edge nodes and programmability viewpoint supporting actuation capabilities for remote IoT device programmability. New design patterns for data pipelines should be implemented to control unpredictable data flows and prevent low quality data.

P7: Support Edge-Cloud Continuum. This principle looks at inter-operation and data transmission between edge and cloud storage systems (Fig. 3). Despite the advantages of edge nodes, it is obvious that for many applications, cloud repositories still have to keep large datasets for complex data mining and big data analytics. Thus, we need to support efficient and secure data transfer of large datasets. With an increasing number of data-intensive applications and bandwidth constraints, it will be crucial to reduce data traffic between the edge and the cloud. Further, once large datasets are available in the cloud, analytics models can be trained and then deployed at the edge for better decision making.

How: For efficient edge-cloud cooperation we must build an edge connector to the cloud, supporting: (1) operation viewpoint featuring timely techniques for data approximation, (de)compression and encryption/decryption; (2) network viewpoint featuring mechanism to avoid excessive data traffic through limited network infrastructure; (3) analytics viewpoint featuring coordination mechanism for consistent analytics models employing elasticity and deployment strategies.

Tooling: The approaches to push and pull data on-demand can be investigated for edge-cloud data transfer. Impact of symbolic data representation [10] can be considered as a good starting point to avoid excessive data traffic. There is need for a model to support secure data migration among multi-location data stores.

4   Related Work

System Viewpoint. Various system operations have been used to build efficient edge storage, e.g., authors in [1] discussed a data life cycle while investigating the optimization of storage mechanisms and data management system design for the IoT. The concept of data-centric communication [12] proposed different management strategies to handle stored data from system viewpoint.

Application Viewpoint. According to [3], it is possible to assign dynamic routes for IoT data based on application context information, considering four objectives, namely; lifetime, delay, reliability and data delivery, but only network viewpoint is examined. Authors in [7] proposed Storage as a Service model where unused storage space can be shared as a cloud-based service for different applications.

Design Viewpoint. Some of the high-level requirements for dealing with a new design of the edge storage service in our paper is inline with IoT common design principles [15], but such IoT common principles do not dig into edge storage services and analytics scenarios. High-level self-adaptation for edge computing has been discussed in [5], but it does not focus on edge storage services for application contexts. In our approach, we bridge aforementioned gaps leading to customized software-defined elastic edge storage services.

5   Conclusions and Future Work

IoT data-intensive applications pose big challenges to satisfy their strict requirements for timely and accurate data-driven decision making, while relying on resource constrained edge systems. It is crucial to dynamically define a highly customized optimization strategy to handle incoming data from different perspectives as well as maintaining only the most relevant data for edge analytics. To scale future edge analytics processes, we present engineering principles and demonstrate how they can potentially be implemented. In this context, proposed approaches can help researchers to improve revealed dependencies in edge data services. Although new insights are encouraging, many challenges are still open, considering other application contexts and the implementation of principles.

Acknowledgments. The work in this paper has been partially funded through Rucon project (Runtime Control in Multi Clouds), FWF Y 904 START-Programm 2015 and Ivan Lujic's netidee scholarship by the Internet Foundation Austria.

References

1. Ali, N.A., Abu-Elkheir, M.: Data management for the Internet of Things: green directions. In: 2012 IEEE Globecom Workshops, pp. 386–390. IEEE (2012)
2. Ali, S., Jarwar, M.A., Chong, I.: Design methodology of microservices to support predictive analytics for IoT applications. Sensors **18**(12), 4226 (2018)
3. Silva Araújo, H., Rodrigues, J.J.P.C., Rabelo, R.A.L., Sousa, N.C., Sobral, J.V.V., et al.: A proposal for IoT dynamic routes selection based on contextual information. Sensors **18**(2), 353 (2018)
4. Blair, G., Bencomo, N., France, R.R.: Models@ run.time. Computer **42**(10), 22–27 (2009)
5. D'Angelo, M.: Decentralized self-adaptive computing at the edge. In: International Conference on Software Engineering for Adaptive and Self-Managing Systems, pp. 144–148. ACM (2018)

6. Dimitrov, D.V.: Medical Internet of Things and big data in healthcare. Healthc. Inf. Res. **22**(3), 156–163 (2016)
7. He, W., Yan, G., Da Xu, L.: Developing vehicular data cloud services in the IoT environment. IEEE Trans. Ind. Inform. **10**(2), 1587–1595 (2014)
8. Lai, L.L., et al.: Intelligent weather forecast. In: International Conference on Machine Learning and Cybernetics, vol. 7, pp. 4216–4221 (2004)
9. Lederman, R., Wynter, L.: Real-time traffic estimation using data expansion. Transp. Res. Part B: Methodol. **45**(7), 1062–1079 (2011)
10. Lin, J., Keogh, E., Wei, L., Lonardi, S.: Experiencing sax: a novel symbolic representation of time series. Data Min. Knowl. Disc. **15**(2), 107–144 (2007)
11. O'Donovan, P., Leahy, K., Bruton, K., O'Sullivan, D.T.: An industrial big data pipeline for data-driven analytics maintenance applications in large-scale smart manufacturing facilities. J. Big Data **2**(1), 25 (2015)
12. Psaras, I., Ascigil, O., Rene, S., Pavlou, G., Afanasyev, A., Zhang, L.: Mobile data repositories at the edge. In: Workshop on Hot Topics in Edge Computing (2018)
13. Satyanarayanan, M., et al.: Edge analytics in the Internet of Things. IEEE Pervasive Comput. **14**(2), 24–31 (2015)
14. Su, M., Zhang, L., Wu, Y., Chen, K., Li, K.: Systematic data placement optimization in multi-cloud storage for complex requirements. IEEE Trans. Comput. **65**(6), 1964–1977 (2016)
15. Vogel, B., Gkouskos, D.: An open architecture approach: towards common design principles for an IoT architecture. In: Proceedings of the 11th European Conference on Software Architecture: Companion Proceedings, pp. 85–88. ACM (2017)

Adaptation and Design Space Exploration

Continuous Adaptation Management in Collective Intelligence Systems

Angelika Musil[1,2](✉) [iD], Juergen Musil[1] [iD], Danny Weyns[2,3] [iD], and Stefan Biffl[1]

[1] Christian Doppler Lab SQI, Institute of Information Systems Engineering,
TU Wien, Vienna, Austria
{angelika,jmusil}@computer.org, stefan.biffl@tuwien.ac.at
[2] Department of Computer Science, KU Leuven, Leuven, Belgium
danny.weyns@kuleuven.be
[3] Department of Computer Science, Linnaeus University, Växjö, Sweden

Abstract. Collective Intelligence Systems (CIS), such as wikis and social networks, enable enhanced knowledge creation and sharing at organization and society levels. From our experience in R&D projects with industry partners and in-house CIS development, we learned that these platforms go through a complex evolution process. A particularly challenging aspect in this respect represents uncertainties that can appear at any time in the life-cycle of such systems. A prominent way to deal with uncertainties is adaptation, i.e., the ability to adjust or reconfigure the system in order to mitigate the impact of the uncertainties. However, there is currently a lack of consolidated design knowledge of CIS-specific adaptation and methods for managing it. To support software architects, we contribute an architecture viewpoint for continuous adaptation management in CIS, aligned with ISO/IEC/IEEE 42010. We evaluated the viewpoint in a case study with a group of eight experienced engineers. The results show that the viewpoint is well-structured, useful and applicable, and that its model kinds cover well the scope to handle different CIS-specific adaptation problems.

Keywords: Collective Intelligence Systems · Adaptation · Architecture viewpoint

1 Introduction

In the last decades, *Collective Intelligence Systems* (CIS), such as wikis, social networks, and media-sharing platforms, enable enhanced knowledge creation and sharing at organization and society levels alike. Today, CIS are widely adopted and influence a large number of people in their daily lives. Established CIS platforms have a longevity well over a decade and beyond. Consequently, CIS represent a significant system domain to research from different perspectives.

A CIS is a *complex socio-technical multi-agent system* that realizes environment-mediated coordination based on bio-inspired models in order to

© Springer Nature Switzerland AG 2019
T. Bures et al. (Eds.): ECSA 2019, LNCS 11681, pp. 109–125, 2019.
https://doi.org/10.1007/978-3-030-29983-5_8

create a *perpetual cycle* of knowledge and information *aggregation and dissemination* among its agents (*actors*) [12,18]. The system is heavily driven by its actors who continuously contribute content to a network of information artifacts [15] (*CI artifacts*), which represents the coordinative substrate and is hosted by an adaptive system layer that handles processing [17,23] of aggregated content (*monitoring, analysis, and information filtering*) and information dissemination (using *rules, triggers, and notifications*). This feedback loop between the actor base and the computational system is an essential feature of a CIS and must be carefully designed and maintained and may not be underestimated.

From extensive experience in R&D projects with industry partners and in-house CIS development, we learned that these platforms typically go through a complex evolution process during which they mature, leading to a significant increase of user base size and accumulated content. Thereby, a particular challenge for software architects represents the multiple inherent uncertainties which continuously affect the system. In particular, when designing CIS the available knowledge is not adequate to anticipate all potential changes due to dynamics in the system context, such as changes of conditions, requirements, resources, or the emergence of new requirements and factors to consider. One way to deal with and mitigate the impact of uncertainties is to design systems that adapt or can be adapted when the missing knowledge becomes available [10].

Recent efforts to support software architecture aspects of CIS comprise an architecture pattern as foundation of CIS [13], a reference architecture [17], an architecture framework [14], and an architecture description language [3]. A particular challenging aspect with regard to evolution represents *adaptation of CIS*, which is a multi-dimensional problem that spans the full life-cycle of such platforms. However, the aspect of adaptation has not yet been investigated from a CIS architecture perspective. Traditional adaptation approaches that are applicable to common software system concerns in CIS are not directly applicable to CIS-domain-specific concerns. Examples include adaptation elements in the information dissemination phase of the feedback loop, when in the CIS life-cycle should adaptation activities be performed, or how to address uncertainties effecting the significant CIS perpetual cycle. Based on experiences from stakeholders in industry and our own experiences with studying and developing CIS, we identified a lack of consolidated design knowledge about the adaptation solution space specific to these systems. Current practice in the CIS domain showed that adaptation in CIS is added in an ad-hoc manner as a reaction to certain major incidents, such as rapid decrease of user activities or spam information generated by bots. However, incorporating adaptation mechanisms in an ad-hoc way may lead to unpredictable consequences on the system and unintended system behavior. Furthermore, there is a lack of methods to support software architects to address CIS-specific adaptation with reasonable effort and systematically design, describe and plan it.

To address these challenges, we study the *what*, *when*, and *how* of continuous adaptation management in the CIS domain. Our goal is to provide software architects with CIS-specific adaptation decision-making and management capabilities during the evolution of a CIS software architecture. To achieve this goal, we applied an empirically grounded research approach. We started with a survey of existing CIS to identify if adaptation is a relevant concern and what kind of adaptation is handled in practice. In addition, we reviewed literature regarding research work on adaptation-related concerns and specifics with focus on CIS. Next, we conducted a series of in-depth interviews with companies that have successfully built and operate CIS in order to identify their problems and challenges and to collect best practices on adaptation management in CIS. The collected data provided input for the identification of relevant stakeholders, their concerns during architecture design and requirements for architectural models to address these CIS-specific concerns. Based on the consolidated data and synthesized knowledge, we developed a novel architecture viewpoint, which provides an adaptation-specific view on CIS architectures and is implementation agnostic. The *Continuous Adaptation Management Viewpoint (CIS-ADAPT)* comprises four model kinds and aims at supporting software architects across the CIS life-cycle with a particular focus on the adaptation areas of modeling, scoping, binding time, and evolution of CIS. To evaluate the viewpoint's applicability and usefulness, we conducted a case study with eight experienced engineers.

The remainder of this paper is structured as follows: Sect. 2 summarizes related work. Section 3 describes the research question and methodology we followed. Section 4 presents the proposed architecture viewpoint with its model kinds. Section 5 describes a case study we used to evaluate the viewpoint's applicability and usefulness. Finally, Sect. 7 concludes and suggests future work.

2   Related Work

To the best of our knowledge, CIS-specific adaptation has not been the focus of previous research work. Hence, we discuss a selection of representative work on architecture-based adaptation and related architecture approaches in general.

Architecture-based adaptation [9, 16] is an established approach to engineer adaptive systems that focuses on the central role of software architecture in such systems through abstraction and separation of concerns. Two fundamental concerns of adaptive systems are domain concerns that are handled by the managed subsystem (that realizes the system functionality) and adaptation concerns that are handled by the managing subsystem (i.e., quality concerns about the managed subsystem) [25]. A key approach to realize the managing subsystem is by means of a so called *MAPE* feedback loop (Monitor-Analyze-Plan-Execute) [8]. One well-known architecture-based self-adaptive framework is *Rainbow* [5]. This approach uses an abstract architectural model to monitor software system run time specifications, evaluates the model for constraint violations, and if required, performs global and module-level adaptations. The reference model *FORMS* [26] (FOrmal Reference Model for Self-adaptation) provides a vocabulary for describing and reasoning about the key architectural characteristics of distributed self-adaptive systems and their concerns.

To support reuse of known solutions, [27] consolidated a number of design approaches for decentralized control in self-adaptive systems in form of MAPE

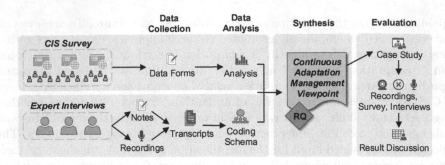

Fig. 1. Applied multi-phase research method

patterns. The authors discussed drivers for the design of self-adaptive systems when choosing one of these MAPE patterns (e.g., optimization, scalability, robustness). [19] presented twelve adaptation-oriented design patterns that are collected from literature and open sources projects. These patterns are clustered around monitoring, decision-making, or reconfiguration. The patterns are at the level of software design in contrast to our architecture-centric perspective that we adopt in this work.

One architecture viewpoint related to our work is the variability viewpoint presented in [4]. However, the focus of that viewpoint was on enterprise software systems and variability in general. Furthermore, [24] presented an approach to augment an architecture viewpoint with a particular variability viewpoint. Although both viewpoints follow ISO/IEC/IEEE42010 [7], they focus on variability concerns but do not consider binding times and system domain specifics.

In conclusion, the proliferation of domain-specific adaptation approaches continues, since the high degree of domain knowledge and complexity widens the gap between general purpose adaptation approaches and the required additional efforts of practitioners to make these approaches work and sustainably manage in specific application domain like CIS.

3   Research Methodology

The main objective of this research is to improve the architectural understanding of CIS and in particular to consolidate design knowledge on adaptation in CIS in order to support software architects to handle it. Based on experiences of stakeholders in the field that built and operate CIS and our own experiences with studying and developing CIS, we identified the following research question: *What are architectural principles to handle CIS-specific adaptation along its life-cycle and how can we codify these principles in a systematic way to make them useful and applicable for software architects?*

To answer this research question, we applied an empirically grounded research method, shown in Fig. 1. We performed a *survey of existing CIS* and a series of *semi-structured interviews* with software architects and senior software engineers of different CIS companies. In the next step the analyzed results and derived knowledge were consolidated in form of an architecture viewpoint for continuous adaptation management in CIS following the ISO/IEC/IEEE 42010 standard [7]. Finally, we evaluated the usefulness and applicability of the proposed viewpoint by conducting a case study with experienced engineers who used the viewpoint to perform adaptation-specific design tasks in CIS key elements. More details, generated material and results of the research activities are available online [11]. In the remainder of this section, we briefly summarize the survey and interviews. The viewpoint and its evaluation are presented in the following sections.

CIS Survey. To investigate different types of CIS-specific adaptation that address key elements and processes in various CIS application contexts, we conducted a system survey based on a defined protocol describing the search strategy, selection and system quality assessment criteria, data extraction process, and data analysis methods. In total, we identified around 100 different CIS based on searches from different sources, such as the web-traffic rankings from Alexa[1], Wikipedia, digital libraries of scientific work, and domain experts from research and industry. We selected 30 CIS based on the quality of the available material to assess the system, including design documentation, user guide, and API specification. We collected data by exploring interaction workflows from an end-user perspective and reviewing available system design and documentation material. Based on subsequent analysis of the collected data and material, we derived initial information about characteristic adaptation points in CIS key elements and processes. Table 1 summarizes the main outcome of the survey in terms of adaptation types in CIS and their refinements.

Expert Interviews. Based on the survey results, we conducted interviews with 10 technical stakeholders covering a variety of roles in CIS engineering, e.g., CTO, software architect, senior engineer, and product manager. The participants come from different Austrian and US companies and organizations that operate a CIS platform in various application domains including medical, societal networking, employer/platform review & rating, and video/music sharing. The participants had 2–10 years experience with CIS engineering and operation. The goal of the interviews was to obtain additional data about stakeholders and adaptation concerns, rationales for adaptation design, and life-cycle aspects. The main selection criteria for participants was their experience in the CIS domain. By applying the guidelines by Hove and Anda [6] and Seaman [22], we designed semi-structured interviews with a combination of specific and open-ended questions (e.g., What are the features of your system that have changed over time? What was your intention of these changes?). We asked them about the different phases they have gone through since the beginning of their software platform and challenges and difficulties they faced during design and engineering activities. The last part dealt with their experiences with respect to platform evolution and CIS-specific adaptation, adaptation management challenges and practices as well as the decision-making process. Each interview took about 50 min and was

---

[1] http://www.alexa.com/topsites/global (last visited at 02/25/2019).

Table 1. Identified adaptation types with examples of elements and their option space

Adaptation type	Adaptation element examples	Element adaptation option examples
Actor	Role & privilege	Editor, administrator, moderator
	Application client	Desktop, web, app, messenger
Aggregation	Artifact attribute	Category, review, votes, tags, comments, actor views
	Interaction rule	Adding, commenting, up-voting, tagging
Processing	Monitoring mechanism	Hot topics monitoring, abnormal behavior monitoring
	Information filtering mechanism	Recommender system, artifact changes, actor activities
Dissemination	Trigger mechanism	Email, app message, on-site notification
	Dissemination rule	Monthly digest, daily report, weekly recommendations

recorded for analysis. For data analysis, we applied coding [21] and grounded theory [2] to transform, structure, and analyze the interview transcripts. The findings of the interviews confirmed and complemented the previous results from the survey and revealed how designing and planning CIS-specific adaptation over the system's life-cycle was managed.

One particular insight is that in later stages changes to adaptation are handled less often than in the beginning and only in a conservative way in order to prevent negative effects on the system's behavior and success. So it is essential to consider the right timing for a CIS's evolution and when to introduce new adaptation elements and options. Changes in CIS-specific elements can have a significant impact on the behavior of the system and consequently on the behavior of the actors.

4   Continuous Adaptation Management Viewpoint

From the data collection and analysis discussed in the previous section, we defined the *architecture viewpoint for continuous adaptation management in collective intelligence systems (CIS-ADAPT)* which unifies CIS-specific aspects with established adaptation approaches. The viewpoint frames the essential concerns of stakeholders with an interest in handling CIS-specific adaptation across the system's life cycle, starting from its inception and during its operation. The viewpoint defines a set of four model kinds for identifying, designing and realizing adaptation in CIS key elements. It is important to note that the focus of this viewpoint is on CIS-specific adaptation and its impact on the system architecture. As such, architects may use additional architectural approaches, such as additional viewpoints or patterns, to deal with adaptation in traditional software system elements and other stakeholder concerns. The architecture viewpoint is structured using the template of the ISO/IEC/IEEE 42010 standard [7].

Table 2 shows an overview of the identified stakeholders and their adaptation concerns addressed by this viewpoint. This viewpoint particularly focuses on the technicalities of adaptation management in CIS, which are no direct concerns of system users, who contribute continuously to it. Thus the users are no stakeholders in terms of this viewpoint, but they are certainly affected by the design decisions made by applying this viewpoint.

The viewpoint comprises four model kinds presented in Tables 3 and 4: *adaptation types, adaptation definition, adaptation in time* and *adaptation workflow*.

Table 2. Continuous Adaptation Management Viewpoint for CIS - Overview

---

Overview: The architecture viewpoint deals with the main stakeholder concerns related to the continuous management of CIS-specific adaptation and defines models for the identification, design and realization of adaptation elements and their space of possible options across the system's life-cycle. The models show the relevant architectural information that is essential to guide a successful preparation for anticipated changes in the system's environment or requirements.

Stakeholders:
Architect(s) who design and describe the CIS architecture and identify the commonalities and the adaptation space in the system.
Owner(s) who define the CIS's purpose and business goals and operate it to provide the service to the users.
Manager(s) who are responsible for overseeing CIS operation.
Analyst(s) who assess the performance of a CIS in terms of quality criteria.

Concerns:
C1 - Adaptation Identification: How can adaptation be exploited to enhance the operation of a CIS? What are possible adaptation elements in a CIS? What are the implications of adaptation elements in the design of a CIS?
C2 - Adaptation Management: What options are available to resolve an adaptation element? What are the effects of different options? What are dependencies between different adaptation elements and options? When are adaptation elements resolved? Who is responsible for handling the adaptation and selecting adaptation options?
C3 - Adaptation Evolution: When are adaptation activities be performed in the CIS life-cycle? How does adaptation influence the CIS evolution?

Adaptation Types Model Kind. This model kind describes the subject of adaptation, comprising four CIS-specific adaptation types along with adaptation elements: (1) *Actor*, (2) *Aggregation*, (3) *Processing*, and (4) *Dissemination*, e.g., an adaptation element of the type *Actor* is *Incentive Mechanism*. Concrete options of this adaptation element can be: awarding badges, up-votes, and likes. Concrete options for adaptation element *Dissemination Rule* of type *Dissemina-*

Table 3. Continuous Adaptation Management Viewpoint for CIS - Model Kinds

---

Model Kinds:

MK1 - Adaptation Types (deals with concern C1): A model that describes *where* adaptation can likely be achieved in a CIS to address uncertainties by identifying potential points of adaptation in CIS-specific system areas along with possible alternatives.

MK2 - Adaptation Definition (deals with concern C2): A model that clarifies *what* adaptation is about in the CIS-of-interest and describes details about the adaptation elements selected for adaptation, the associated element adaptation space of options to address particular uncertainties, and what constraints are applied on their relations.

MK3 - Adaptation in Time (deals with concern C3): A model that describes *when* adaptation activities are applied by responsible entities and how adaptation evolves across the CIS's life-cycle.

MK4 - Adaptation Workflow (deals with concern C2): A model that describes *how* the adaptation elements are realized and resolved, and who is responsible for selecting adaptation options and triggering the changes.

Metamodels:

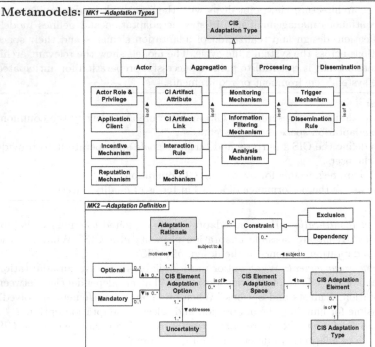

Key: UML

Table 4. Continuous Adaptation Management Viewpoint for CIS - Model Kinds

Metamodels:

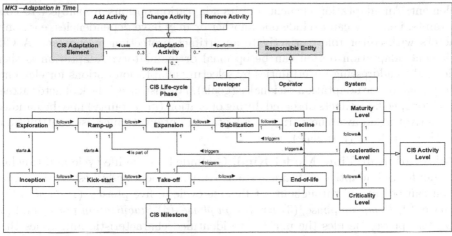

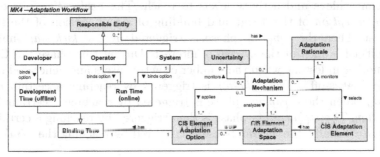

Key: UML

Analyses:

A1 - Adaptation Effect Analysis (using MK1 and MK2): Assesses the effects of different adaptation option selections on the activities of the system and the actor base using a set of scenarios.

A2 - Adaptation Option Conflict Analysis (using MK2, MK3 and MK4): Reviews the relations and dependencies between adaptation elements and their spaces of options that are simultaneously deployed and bound in different life-cycle stages.

tion are artifact change reports, weekly digests, monthly personal recommendations. This model kind supports architects with defining what adaptation types and adaptation elements are relevant to implement in the context of the specific CIS-of-interest based on the concretely identified adaptation types.[2]

---

[2] Gray shaded boxes in model kinds represent links between multiple model kinds.

Adaptation Definition Model Kind. This model kind describes *what* adaptation is. It defines the possible adaptation options of an adaptation element, i.e., the adaptation space, each option representing a particular setting of the element. An adaptation element and its adaptation options are subject to constraints, i.e., they can exclude one another or may have dependencies, e.g., only actors with editor role can activate an artifact protection mechanism. A CIS element adaptation option can be optional or mandatory. Adaptation is then defined as addressing uncertainties by selecting adaptation options for elements according to the adaptation rationales (goals). For instance, a lack of actor attention for specific artifacts observed during operation (uncertainty) may be handled by activating an awareness trigger (adaptation option) to increase contributions to these artifacts (rationale).

Adaptation in Time Model Kind. Grounded on the life-cycle and timeline model for self-adaptive software systems [1], this model describes *when* adaptation can be applied throughout a CIS's life-cycle in five phases: (1) *Exploration* phase, (2) *Ramp-up* phase, (3) *Expansion phase*, (4) *Stabilization* phase, and (5) *Decline* phase. Besides the phases, we identified characteristic milestones that a CIS can achieve and activity levels to reach. The *exploration* phase starts with the *inception* of the design and building of a first version of the system-of-interest. Then the *ramp-up* phase is triggered by the *kick-start* milestone of the official launch of the system-of-interest. During this phase the CIS can reach another milestone when the number of active users and generated content suddenly "takes-off". This *take-off* is triggered by reaching a certain *level of criticality*. Then the *expansion* phase is triggered by reaching a certain *level of acceleration*. The *stabilization* phase is then triggered by reaching a certain *level of maturity*. Finally, the *decline* phase is triggered by reaching the *"end-of-life"* point.

Any responsible entity can perform adaptation activities, i.e., add, change, or remove activities to an adaptation element (by adapting its adaptation options) in different phases of the CIS's life-cycle. For instance, the operator introduces a monitoring mechanism aiming to identify irregular activities in expansion phase. This activity can be affected by reaching a certain CIS milestone (e.g., take-off milestone) or activity level (e.g., criticality level). If an option of an adaptation element is not relevant anymore, a responsible entity can remove it, e.g., the system may turn off a dissemination rule when user activity is increased over a period of time.

Adaptation Workflow Model Kind. This model kind describes *how* CIS-specific adaptations are realized. The adaptation workflow is realized by an adaptation mechanism associated with a responsible entity which can be a developer, an operator, or the system. A developer can apply adaptations offline (and deploy them on the running system), while an operator and the system can apply adaptations online. An adaptation mechanism realizes a feedback loop. The mechanism monitors uncertainties and checks whether the system complies with its goals (rationales). If the system goals may be jeopardized, the adaptation space of the adaptation elements is analyzed, i.e., the options available for adaptation, to mitigate the uncertainties. Based on this analysis, the adaptation mechanism selects adaptation options for adaptation elements. These options are then executed in the system.

Adaptation Effect Analysis. This analysis uses a set of scenarios to assess the effects of selecting different adaptation options on the behavior of the system and the actor base. The analysis results help identifying improvements of the adaptation elements and their adaptation options. The results can also provide insights in the conditions when selected options may improve or degrade the CIS behavior, e.g., in the form of increase/decrease of user activity. In the exploration and ramp-up phases, adaptation effect analysis can be done using simulation or via tool-assisted user testing. In later phases further approaches like A/B testing and/or feature toggles can be added to enable automated, data-driven processes for performance analysis, simulation and selection of adaptation options. Figure 2 shows the effects of adaptation for a CIS pilot that we developed using a NetLogo analysis model. The graphs on the left show results when no dissemination is used. The graphs on the right show results when a slow-cycled global dissemination rule and a short-cycled actor-personalized dissemination rule are activated. The results show that the contribution distribution (top) got a steeper tail at the beginning with the dissemination rules activated, whereby the actor activity (bottom) remained unchanged.

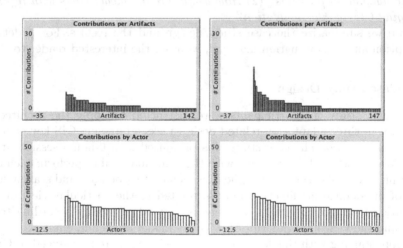

Fig. 2. Analysis results: none (left) or two (right) dissemination rules activated

Adaptation Option Conflict Analysis. This analysis performs a review of the relations and dependencies between adaptation elements, options, and adaptation elements and options that are simultaneously deployed and bound in the different stages of the CIS's life-cycle. The analysis results help to identify possible conflicts and inconsistencies between CIS adaptation elements/options that need to be resolved. In early stage phases, conflict detection and resolution can be performed manually by the architect by using the CIS-specific adaptation definition and workflow models. In later stage phases automated tool-support, such as feature-to-code traceability and consistency checking of the CIS adaptation models, is necessary to make conflict identification and resolution viable.

5   Evaluation of the Viewpoint

To obtain qualitative evidence of the usefulness and applicability of the CIS-ADAPT viewpoint, we performed an in-depth study with eight engineers without any experience in CIS design and development. Participants had between 1 and 7 years of industrial experience in software engineering/software architecture and are active in Austrian companies as project managers, software architects and software developers in various domains. To obtain qualitative data from different perspectives, criteria to select the participants include a mix of male and female engineers as well as a broad range of industry experience to get also insights into how less experienced engineers use the viewpoint.

We applied a *case study* design to plan our qualitative in-depth study and followed the guidelines for case studies in software engineering provided by Runeson et al. [20]. The concrete objective of the case study is answering the following questions: (1) *To what extent does the viewpoint support correct handling of CIS-specific adaptation problems?* (2) *How useful are the model kinds with regard to managing CIS-specific adaptation?*

Here we summarize the case study design and the results. For a detailed description and the evaluation material, we refer the interested reader to [11].

5.1   Case Study Design

In this case study the participants were instructed to apply the architecture viewpoint in three adaptation-related design tasks addressing CIS key elements of a given scenario. The case study was organized as a 6-hours session at TU Wien. We provided all participants with the same material to perform each task, including a general description of the CIS scenario, its domain and stakeholders, a set of pre-defined architecture models related to the particular view on CIS adaptation management which they had to extend or modify according to the tasks, and the viewpoint description with its model kinds and analyses.

Before starting with the design tasks, participants were introduced to CIS in general, software architecture concepts in the context of ISO/IEC/IEEE 42010, and the CIS-ADAPT architecture viewpoint. The participants were also introduced to the CIS scenario and questions were answered to avoid any misunderstanding of the assignment. After the first part, participants were asked to complete a short survey to gather their background information, including their education and experience with (CIS) software architecture design as well as adaptation handling in architecture design.

While the participants performed the design tasks, we video recorded their actions and progression to gather data how they used the viewpoint in the given scenario. At the end of the study session, we collected the modified architecture models and the participants were asked to complete a short survey to assess the applicability, usefulness and understandability of the applied architecture viewpoint and its model kinds. Finally, we conducted individual semi-structured interviews of about 10 min each to collect data about the participant's experiences and challenges during the application of the viewpoint.

We analyzed in total 14 hours of video material as well as the design models that the participants produced while accomplishing the given tasks to identify how they applied the viewpoint and used its model kinds and model elements. The survey results allowed us to better understand and reason about the usefulness and understandability of the viewpoint from an architect's perspective. Finally, the interviews provided us insights into the experiences and challenges the participants had to face as well as feedback for improvement.

5.2 Case Study Results

Eight participants completed 3 tasks, each of which required to use the 4 models of the viewpoint. In total each participant produced 12 models across all tasks, resulting in 96 models in total across all tasks and participants.

Participant	P1	P2	P3	P4	P5	P6	P7	P8	G	Y	R
Task 1 MK1									8	0	0
Task 1 MK2									5	2	1
Task 1 MK3									1	6	1
Task 1 MK4									4	3	1
Task 2 MK1									8	0	0
Task 2 MK2									7	1	0
Task 2 MK3									5	2	1
Task 2 MK4									3	4	1
Task 3 MK1									6	2	0
Task 3 MK2									8	0	0
Task 3 MK3									1	7	0
Task 3 MK4									5	2	1

	P1	P2	P3	P4	P5	P6	P7	P8
Performance	4,33	4,00	4,67	3,33	3,33	2,67	2,67	5,00
Understanding	Easy	Average	Difficult	Difficult	Average	Difficult	Average	Easy
Applicability	Average	Average	Average	Difficult	Difficult	Difficult	Easy	Average
Usefulness	Useful	Average	Average	V. useful	Average	Useful	V. Useful	Useful
Efficiency	Efficient	Efficient	Average	Efficient	Efficient	Efficient	Efficient	Efficient

Fig. 3. Overview of the results of 3 design tasks performed by 8 participants (G = Green: correct solutions; Y = Yellow: partially correct; R = Red: incorrect) (Color figure online)

In task 1, participants extended the space of each of two pre-defined adaptation elements with a new element adaptation option. In task 2, participants modified an existing option from manual to automated application of the option at run time. In task 3, participants defined and introduced a new adaptation element to the system and added two options to its space.

From the created 96 models, 61 (63.5%) were solved correctly, 29 (30.2%) with some deviations, and only 6 (6.3%) models were incorrect. Figure 3 shows an overview of the model defects across all participants and tasks. Hence, in the context of the design tasks, we can answer the first evaluation question (*To what extent does the viewpoint support correct handling of adaptation problems in CIS?*) positively. Nevertheless, some of the participants commented on the complexity of elements of the viewpoint, e.g., *"For me, this [MK3] was the most difficult model, because it has many aspects such as phases and milestones and all interact. Also, this one is more formal. For understanding, you can exactly see how level and phase and milestones are linked."* or *"The workflow model [MK4] was difficult, because it was not clear in the task description specifically when the resolving should actually happen."* In the following, we elaborate on the analysis of the usefulness of each model kind.

MK1. For the *adaptation types model*, 22 of 24 designs were performed without defects, 2 with defects, and none incorrect. The usefulness of MK1 was scored 2.5/5 on average by the participants. Positive feedback includes *"[...] the model provides a good overview about the adaptation types [...]"* and *"[...] it was useful to see the available choices that you have, also when it comes where to add new options and elements [...]"*. Some critical remarks were *"[...] I personally would map the types to my components so that they are not so generic like in the study scenario [...]"* and *"[...] the model was not really necessary for me, because its parts have been repeated already in model 2 [...]"*. In conclusion, the usefulness of MK1 for the tasks at hand is moderate, the opinions among participants differ.

MK2. For the *adaptation definition model*, 20 of 24 designs were performed without defects, 3 with defects, and 1 incorrect. The usefulness of MK2 scored 4.1/5 on average by the participants. Some of the positive feedback of the participants include *"[...] with regards to utility, the definition model was definitely the best."* and *"[...] the most helpful models for me have been models 2 and 3."* One rather negative comment but showing its criticality was *"The definition model was the most challenging for me because it was so central and the following models depend on it. [...] you cannot do much meaningful with the later models if you do not have the definition model straight."* In conclusion, MK2 was regarded as a central model and indicated as highly useful in the tasks at hand.

MK3. For the *adaptation in time model*, 7 of 24 designs were performed without defects, 15 with defects, and 2 incorrect. The usefulness of MK3 was scored 2.4/5 on average by the participants. One of the positive comments was *"Model 3 and 4 have been pretty useful, in particular if you have to consider the run time aspects. That was particularly useful."*. A critical comment was *"The model was tricky for me, because there is no definitive solution when there is the ideal point in time - you know, too early or too late [...]"*. In conclusion, MK3 was the worst performing model kind in terms of correct solutions. Regarding utility the average score was moderate for the given tasks at hand. One recurring comment was that the illustration of the CIS life-cycle that was used during the introduction session would be a beneficial add-on for the viewpoint, e.g., one participant commented *"The life-cycle diagram would make using this model easier. I redraw it* *from memory at the beginning so that I can better envision the life-cycle, instead of just relying on the model kind."*

MK4. For the *adaptation workflow model*, 12 of 24 designs were performed without defects, 9 with defects, and 3 incorrect. The usefulness of MK4 was scored 4/5 on average by the participants. One of the positive comments was *"The workflow model helps to create a more flexible system and you see clearly which risks are covered."* A critical comment was *"It was not always clear when it was run time and when it was development time. Also the dependencies between tasks were rather loose. I think sometimes you cannot sharply discriminate clearly between user tasks and system tasks, as it is suggested in the model kind."* In conclusion, MK4 has shown to be a very useful model for the tasks at hand.

6 Threats to Validity

We briefly discuss potential validity threats of this study and ways how they were mitigated.

Internal Validity. By using well-defined data extraction forms in the CIS survey and an interview guide, we attempted to conduct the study in a consistent and objective way to reduce the risk to affect the validity of the data provided by the study subjects. Especially during the interviews we needed to be very careful when giving specific examples so that we do not influence the given answers. For both data collection methods we performed a pilot study for improvement, e.g., to identify questions/data items that are confusing or do not provide enough informative quality. Also expert feedback was used to counter check the consistency and integrity of the data collection instruments.

To address potential threats of misinterpretation of the collected data, the findings have been derived by two researchers and two additional experienced researchers cross-checked and validated the analysis results and conclusions. Furthermore, during the interviews we regularly summarized the given information and asked the participants to verify the correctness of the interpretation.

External Validity. The presented models are the result of an in-depth analysis of the gathered data but might be limited by the samples we investigated. To increase the generalization of the results to a broader context and strengthen the study results, we plan to conduct a CIS survey with a larger system sample and do more expert interviews. For the evaluation of the viewpoint, we performed a case study with eight participants. To enhance generalization of the results, this qualitative inquiry should be extended with additional cases in other domains.

7 Conclusion

In this paper, we presented an architecture viewpoint for continuous adaptation management in CIS, aligned with ISO/IEC/IEEE 42010. The viewpoint is intended to address CIS-specific adaptation concerns and existing limitations. It was designed to be compatible with other adaptation approaches so that our contribution represents a useful addition to domain-specific adaptation approaches. A qualitative evaluation with eight experienced engineers in a case study shows that the viewpoint is well-structured and particularly useful to handle different CIS-specific adaptation problems. In future work, we plan to refine the viewpoint and extend its evaluation. Furthermore, we plan to further develop the analysis part of the viewpoint and consider to develop tool support for it.

Acknowledgments. The financial support by the Christian Doppler Research Association, the Austrian Federal Ministry for Digital and Economic Affairs and the National Foundation for Research, Technology and Development is gratefully acknowledged.

References

1. Andersson, J., et al.: Software engineering processes for self-adaptive systems. In: de Lemos, R., Giese, H., Müller, H.A., Shaw, M. (eds.) Software Engineering for Self-Adaptive Systems II. LNCS, vol. 7475, pp. 51–75. Springer, Heidelberg (2013). https://doi.org/10.1007/978-3-642-35813-5_3
2. Corbin, J., Strauss, A.: Basics of Qualitative Research: Techniques and Procedures for Developing Grounded Theory, 3rd edn. Sage Publications Inc., Thousand Oaks (2007)
3. Dorn, C., Taylor, R.N.: Coupling software architecture and human architecture for collaboration-aware system adaptation. In: Proceedings of the International Conference on Software Engineering, pp. 53–62. IEEE (2013)
4. Galster, M., Avgeriou, P.: A variability viewpoint for enterprise software systems. In: Proceedings of Joint WICSA/ECSA, pp. 267–271. IEEE Computer Society (2012)
5. Garlan, D., et al.: Rainbow: architecture-based self-adaptation with reusable infrastructure. Computer **37**(10), 46–54 (2004)
6. Hove, S.E., Anda, B.: Experiences from conducting semi-structured interviews in empirical software engineering research. In: Proceedings of the 11th IEEE International Software Metrics Symposium, pp. 23–32. IEEE Computer Society (2005)
7. ISO/IEC/IEEE 42010: Systems and software engineering - architecture description (2011)
8. Kephart, J.O., Chess, D.M.: The vision of autonomic computing. Computer **36**(1), 41–50 (2003)
9. Kramer, J., Magee, J.: Self-managed systems: an architectural challenge. In: Future of Software Engineering, pp. 259–268. IEEE Computer Society (2007)
10. Mahdavi-Hezavehi, S., Avgeriou, P., Weyns, D.: A classification framework of uncertainty in architecture-based self-adaptive systems with multiple quality requirements. In: Managing Trade-Offs in Adaptable Software Architectures, pp. 45–77. Morgan Kaufmann (2017)
11. Musil, A., Musil, J., Weyns, D., Biffl, S.: Supplementary Material: Continuous Adaptation Management in Collective Intelligence Systems (2019). http://qse.ifs.tuwien.ac.at/ci/material/pub/ecsa19/
12. Musil, J., Musil, A., Biffl, S.: Introduction and challenges of environment architectures for collective intelligence systems. In: Weyns, D., Michel, F. (eds.) E4MAS 2014. LNCS (LNAI), vol. 9068, pp. 76–94. Springer, Cham (2015). https://doi.org/10.1007/978-3-319-23850-0_6

13. Musil, J., Musil, A., Biffl, S.: SIS: an architecture pattern for collective intelligence systems. In: Proceedings of the 20th EuroPLoP, pp. 20:1–20:12. ACM (2015)
14. Musil, J., Musil, A., Weyns, D., Biffl, S.: An architecture framework for collective intelligence systems. In: Proceedings of the 12th WICSA, pp. 21–30. IEEE (2015)
15. Omicini, A., Ricci, A., Viroli, M.: Artifacts in the A&A meta-model for multi-agent Systems. Auton. Agent. Multi-Agent Syst. **17**(3), 432–456 (2008)
16. Oreizy, P., et al.: An architecture-based approach to self-adaptive software. IEEE Intell. Syst. **14**(3), 54–62 (1999)
17. Pääkkönen, P., Pakkala, D.: Reference architecture and classification of technologies, products and services for big data systems. Big Data Res. **2**(4), 166–168 (2015)
18. Dyke Parunak, H.: A survey of environments and mechanisms for human-human stigmergy. In: Weyns, D., Van Dyke Parunak, H., Michel, F. (eds.) E4MAS 2005. LNCS (LNAI), vol. 3830, pp. 163–186. Springer, Heidelberg (2006). https://doi.org/10.1007/11678809_10
19. Ramirez, A.J., Cheng, B.H.C.: Design patterns for developing dynamically adaptive systems. In: Proceedings of the ICSE Workshop on Software Engineering for Adaptive and Self-Managing Systems, pp. 49–58. ACM (2010)
20. Runeson, P., Host, M., Rainer, A., Regnell, B.: Case Study Research in Software Engineering: Guidelines and Examples, 1st edn. Wiley Publishing, Hoboken (2012)
21. Saldana, J.: The Coding Manual for Qualitative Researchers, 2nd edn. Sage, Thousand Oaks (2013)
22. Seaman, C.B.: Qualitative methods in empirical studies of software engineering. IEEE Trans. Softw. Eng. **25**(4), 557–572 (1999)
23. Sumbaly, R., Kreps, J., Shah, S.: The "big data" ecosystem at LinkedIn. In: ACM SIGMOD Conference, pp. 1–10. ACM (2013)
24. Tekinerdogan, B., Sözer, H.: Variability viewpoint for introducing variability in software architecture viewpoints. In: Proceedings of the WICSA/ECSA Companion, pp. 163–166. ACM (2012)
25. Weyns, D.: Software engineering of self-adaptive systems. In: Cha, S., Taylor, R., Kang, K. (eds.) Handbook of Software Engineering, pp. 399–443. Springer, Cham (2019). https://doi.org/10.1007/978-3-030-00262-6_11
26. Weyns, D., Malek, S., Andersson, J.: FORMS: unifying reference model for formal specification of distributed self-adaptive systems. ACM Trans. Auton. Adapt. Syst. **7**(1), 8:1–8:61 (2012)
27. Weyns, D., et al.: On patterns for decentralized control in self-adaptive systems. In: de Lemos, R., Giese, H., Müller, H.A., Shaw, M. (eds.) Software Engineering for Self-Adaptive Systems II. LNCS, vol. 7475, pp. 76–107. Springer, Heidelberg (2013). https://doi.org/10.1007/978-3-642-35813-5_4

ADOOPLA - Combining Product-Line- and Product-Level Criteria in Multi-objective Optimization of Product Line Architectures

Tobias Wägemann[1]([✉]), Ramin Tavakoli Kolagari[1], and Klaus Schmid[2]

[1] Technische Hochschule Nürnberg, Keßlerplatz 12, Nuremberg 90489, Germany
{tobias.waegemann,ramin.tavakolikolagari}@th-nuernberg.de
[2] Universität Hildesheim, FB4, Universitätsplatz 1, Hildesheim 31141, Germany
schmid@sse.uni-hildesheim.de

Abstract. Product lines of software-intensive systems have a great diversity of features and products, which leads to vast design spaces that are difficult to explore. In addition, finding optimal product line system architectures usually requires a consideration of several quality trade-offs at once, involving both product-level as well as product-line-wide criteria. This challenge cannot be solved manually for all but the smallest problems, and can therefore benefit from automated support. In this paper we propose ADOOPLA, a tool-supported approach for the optimization of product line system architectures. In contrast to existing approaches where product-level approaches only support product-level criteria and product-line oriented approaches only support product-line-wide criteria, our approach integrates criteria from both levels in the optimization of product line architectures. Further, the approach can handle multiple objectives at once, supporting the architect in exploring the multi-dimensional Pareto-front of a given problem. We describe the theoretical principles of the ADOOPLA approach and demonstrate its application to a simplified case study from the automotive domain.

Keywords: Product line architectures · Design space exploration · Architecture optimization · Multiobjective · Variability modeling · Automotive

1 Introduction

When working with variant-rich product line architectures, it is essential to differentiate between two distinct design spaces that can be present in a given system model. On the one hand, the product line variability (PLV) defines the set of all valid product configurations of an individual product line. On the other hand, design options on the architecture level define a set of architectural degrees of freedom (ADF) for the product line architecture, i.e., they describe the range of potential alternative product line architectures that satisfy the

© Springer Nature Switzerland AG 2019
T. Bures et al. (Eds.): ECSA 2019, LNCS 11681, pp. 126–142, 2019.
https://doi.org/10.1007/978-3-030-29983-5_9

demands of the same product line (as defined by its features). Section 3 gives a detailed description of the differences. For now, it is sufficient to understand that configuring the ADF will result in a specific underlying architecture for the product line (e.g., using an ECU from supplier A instead of the functionally identical ECUs from suppliers B or C, etc.), while configuring the PLV of a product line will result in a specific product.

In order to distinguish our approach from existing work, we first have to consider the purpose of different optimization categories in the field. Optimizing product lines usually aims at finding optimal configurations for the PLV design space, which results in products that are optimal with regard to particular criteria or a specific use case. Another goal of product line optimization can be to shape a PLV design space so that it optimally accommodates (only) a set of given products. Then there is the field of (product) architecture optimization, which aims at making optimal architectural design decisions (i.e., configuring the ADF design space) for single products. Conventional architecture optimization is already a hard combinatorial problem, due to potentially vast design spaces with dependencies among component selections. However, system architects that work with product line architectures face the additional challenge of having to make good design decisions even before the product line variability is resolved. Their decision making process for the architecture must consider not only one specific product, but potentially all products of a product line.

In this paper we present a novel approach named ADOOPLA, short for *Automated Design Option Optimization for Product Line Architectures*, which aims at assisting the system architect in identifying optimal product line system architectures. It is important to understand how ADOOPLA differs from the aforementioned optimization categories. The use case we aim at is different, as it is concerned with finding optimal architectural design decisions for whole product lines at once. In contrast to the aforementioned categories, the result of an ADOOPLA optimization is therefore not a specific optimal product, but rather a product line with optimal architectural design decisions. The purpose of the ADOOPLA approach is—in principle—closer related to architecture optimization than to product line optimization, it must however also take the feature characteristics of the PLV design space into account in order to assess optimality on a product-line-wide scale.

ADOOPLA allows for the optimization of (product) criteria like unit weight and unit cost, which are only really useful when considered at a product level, as well as criteria that can indeed be considered at a product-line-wide level, like the development cost of components. In fact, the ADOOPLA approach allows for mixing both product-level and product-line-wide criteria in a single design space exploration process, as we demonstrate in our case study in Sect. 6. To the best of our knowledge, no other approach has been published that can optimize the architectural design options of product lines with regard to both product-line-wide and product-level criteria, making ADOOPLA a novel contribution in the field of product line architecture optimization. The approach is based on previous publications by the same authors of this paper, which where concerned with representing modeled variability in terms of constraint programming [1], and with generating simple optimization problems from quality criteria annotated in system architectures [2]. In addition, the advancement of the ADOOPLA approach is guided by an evaluation of practitioner needs with regard to automated PLA optimization [3].

The paper is structured as follows. Section 2 gives an overview of related work and shows the difference between ADOOPLA and existing approaches. Section 3 explains the distinction between the PLV and ADF design spaces. Section 4 details the difference product level and product-line-wide criteria. Section 5 illustrates our process of formalizing variant-rich system models into ILP-based optimization problems that can be used to find optimal product line architecture candidates. The formalization process and it's application are demonstrated by means of a simplified automotive case study in Sect. 6. Finally, Sect. 7 concludes the paper and describes our ideas and plans for future work.

2 Related Work

The use case of automated optimization for design space exploration in software engineering can be divided into two distinct fields of research. On the one hand, there is classic system architecture optimization, which is concerned with finding optimal design decisions for a design space defined by architectural design options. On the other hand, there is product line optimization, which deals with the search-based exploration of product line design spaces. The ADOOPLA approach proposed in this paper intersects with both research fields, by aiming at finding optimal architecture design decisions for variant-rich product line system architectures. However, the methods used for classic architecture optimization and product line design space exploration, in particular methods based on generating mathematical formalizations for optimization problems from variability models, are very much related to the ADOOPLA approach.

With regard to classic architecture optimization, Walker et al. [4] present an optimization approach for EAST-ADL[1] models based on multi-objective genetic algorithms which considers system dependability, timing concerns and a simple cost metric. The approach uses HiP-HOPS[2] for fault tree analysis and MAST[3] for response time computation and is therefore coupled to these tools for the evaluation of design objectives. A similar approach for the design objectives cost and dependability is presented by Mian et al. [5] for the AADL[4] language, also using HiP-HOPS for fault tree analysis. Both approaches use similar input models to ADOOPLA, but don't support the optimization of product line architectures and are limited to objectives that can be evaluated by external tooling.

Kugele et al. [6] propose a framework for multi-objective, constraint-based optimization of automotive E/E-architectures based on an intermediate transformation into a domain-specific constraint and optimization language called

---

[1] http://www.east-adl.info.

[2] http://hip-hops.eu.

[3] http://mast.unican.es.

[4] http://www.aadl.info.

AAOL. The framework is concerned in particular with generating optimal solutions for the deployment problem, meaning the automated mapping of software components to available hardware components. Noir et al. [7] propose a tooled manual process for the exploration of architecture design spaces for software-intensive systems, integrating both CVL and the MYRIAD method for assessing the architecture variants. This process does not deal with automated optimization per se, but highlights the relevance of tool support for multi-criteria trade-off analysis of variant-rich system architectures. A manual exhaustive exploration with tool support is very useful for smaller design spaces, but cannot cover the large design spaces that are typical for industrial systems. This is where automated tool support like ADOOPLA, which reduces vast solution spaces to small Pareto-optimal sets, becomes useful instead.

With regard to product line design space exploration, the current research is mostly focused on many-objective feature selection, i.e., the automated configuration of optimal products with regard to multiple criteria. Xiang et al. [8] and Henard et al. [9] propose approaches for finding optimal feature configurations by a combination of multi-objective evolutionary algorithms and SAT solvers, based on a transformation of variability models into conjunctive normal form (CNF), which is similar to the constraint formalization method used in ADOOPLA. Olaechea et al. [10] propose an approach for incorporating design goals into the configuration process for product lines using their own language and tool, and for finding optimal products by means of a multi-objective constraint solver. While this approach is not applicable to industrial models defined in industry standard languages, the usage of annotated quality criteria for the composition of design goals is similar to ADOOPLA.

Thüm et al. [11] propose a classification framework for product line analysis strategies in order to provide systematic guidance to the research in this field. They classify the strategies into four categories: product-based, family-based and feature-based strategies, as well as strategies that use combinations of the three. While the ADOOPLA approach can generate results that are optimal on a product level, it operates only on domain artifacts of the product line architecture itself. ADOOPLA can therefore be classified as a family-based strategy in regard to the classification framework introduced by Thüm et al.

3   Product Line Variability and Architectural Design Options

For the purpose of this paper it is essential to understand the distinction between two kinds of (architectural) variabilities: 1. *Architectural degrees of freedom (ADF)* refers to the set of potential design options for a product (line) architecture. 2. *Product line variability (PLV)* [12,13] describes the variations of proper products that are well-formed with respect to the product line design space. In other words, determining all architectural degrees of freedom will result in a product line architecture (PLA), whereas determining all product line variability (called configuration) will result in a single product. These two kinds of variabilities also have different binding times, i.e., the times at which they must be resolved during the system life cycle. While architectural design options must be resolved at system design time by a system architect, the PLV gets resolved at a later stage in the life cycle [14].

ADF are all design options that architects have available for decision-making. Design options are choices determined exclusively by the architect. This choice is not intended to be made available to the (end) customer. Design options may for example refer to (sub)systems that do not differ in their functionality but are from different suppliers. In the system development process, the architect is required to decide for one alternative and against the other. The architect thereby converts design options into design decisions by successively restricting the originally existent choice. Once all design options have been converted into design decisions, the system created (which can even be a software product line) does no longer have any ADF.

PLV is the system variability required for the software product line, which (usually) is a choice offered to the (end) customer. PLV includes, for example, the choice between two alternative (sub)systems, one of which offers additional equipment (e.g., automatic climate control). The determination of the PLV can usually only be carried out in cooperation with the (end) customer. Once the entire PLV has been determined (configured), the system created no longer contains any variability: it is a single product.

In the ADOOPLA approach, the architectural degrees of freedom are the basis for the optimization process, which intends to produce an optimal product line architecture with respect to (multiple) criteria chosen by an architect. The PLV design space is not resolved as part of the optimization, and is instead used in order to determine a utilization factor for product-level criteria on a product-line-wide scale (cf. Sect. 5.3). Therefore, at the end of our optimization process, no architectural degrees of freedom remain in the system model and the remaining variability is governed only by the product line design space, i.e., the result is a product line with optimal architectural design decisions.

4   Optimality on Product Level and Product-Line-Wide Level

When optimizing design options for product line system architectures, it makes sense to first consider what optimality in this context actually means. First of all, an architect is usually confronted with not only one, but several design goals at once. These design goals are almost always competing with one another; e.g., lowering unit cost will increase unit weight, and vice versa. For automated tool support to be useful in this design task, it must therefore be able to provide a multi-dimensional trade-off analysis for all relevant design goals. In the context of architecture optimization, this effectively means that the optimization process must support multi-objective optimization, resulting in a set of Pareto-optimal architecture candidates. Pareto-optimality is based on the concept of dominance. A candidate is called non-dominated—and is therefore part of the Pareto-optimal set—if and only if there are no other candidates that are better with regard to at least one design goal without degrading one or more of the other design goals [15, p. 414ff].

When considering the quality criteria that can be used as design goals for product line architecture optimization, it becomes obvious that many of the most relevant criteria don't have a lot of useful informative value for product line architectures, as opposed to product architectures. Take for example the criterion unit cost (as the sum of a unit's component piece costs) and consider the use case of finding the (single-objective) optimal architecture candidate for this criterion. The result of such an optimization would be the one product line architecture, that has the lowest piece cost over the sum of all its variable components. The "unit" in unit cost would here refer to the product line itself, not to any particular product. However, a product line can never itself constitute a "unit" per se. The unit-cost-optimization result would therefore be cost-optimal with regard to something that is not—and cannot be—a unit (i.e., the product line), while providing no information whatsoever about the cost-optimality of actual units (i.e., products of the product line). The usefulness of such a result for industrial practice is at least questionable, if not outright useless.

A much more useful outcome would be an optimization result that is (cost-) optimal with regard to the products of the product line, as opposed to the product line itself. This is what we call *product-level optimality*, in contrast to the *product-line-wide-level optimality* shown above. For most design goals, including unit cost, product-level optimality is the key aspect. This is usually the case when the design goal corresponds to a quality of an instantiated unit that can be measured, e.g., the unit cost or unit weight of a specific product.

However, there is good reason for not simply discarding the concept of product-line-wide-level optimality outright. There are certain design goals where a system-wide consideration, instead of a consideration per unit, is actually the more useful approach. An example for such a design goal is the criterion development cost: a development cost for a variable component is due once and only once, no matter how many times that component is present in the product line. In essence, optimizing for the design goal development cost promotes component reuse in the system. Since a consideration of component reuse makes sense on a system-wide basis (as opposed to a per-unit basis), an optimization for a design goal like development cost is indeed most useful on a product-line-wide level.

5   Generating a Useful Optimization Problem

A sound definition of multi-objective optimization is the task of finding the set of *best* solutions for a given problem from the set of all feasible solutions for the problem with regard to certain criteria. *Best* in our case means Pareto-optimal, as introduced in Sect. 4. With regard to our problem domain of product line system architecture optimization, the above definition translates to finding the best architecture candidates within the design space defined by the ADF, i.e., the aggregate of architectural design options.

In this section we present our formalization approach which we realized for formalizing variant-rich product line architectures modeled in EAST-ADL, a domain-specific architecture description language with a focus on variant-rich software-intensive systems [16]. The language was developed in a series of European research projects with strong participation of the automotive industry[5]. Today the EAST-ADL is managed by the EAST-ADL association[6]. The language has been tailored towards compatibility with the well-established AUTOSAR standard[7], which in turn serves as an integral part of the EAST-ADL language by realizing one of its abstraction layers.

In order to constitute a basis for architecture optimization, the optimization problem has to be formalized into a rigorous mathematical form. Our product line architecture optimization problems always have binary decision variables and usually have multiple design objectives. Therefore, our problem domain is that of multi-objective integer linear programming (MOILP) with all decision variables $\in \{0, 1\}$. With all variable system components assigned to decision variables $x_1...x_n$ we can formulate the program as follows:

$$\text{Minimize} \quad Cx$$
$$\text{subject to} \quad Ax \geq a_0 \quad \quad (1)$$
$$x \in \{0, 1\}^n$$

where C is a (m, n)-Matrix of design objective values, A and a_0 are a (p, n)-matrix and a p-vector representing a set of constraints which define the design space of the architecture and x is an n-vector of binary decisions variables; with m being the number of design objectives, n being the number of decision variables and p being the number of ILP-constraints. The matrix Cx is identical to a set of linear objective functions $F(x) = (f_1(x), f_2(x), ..., f_m(x))^T$, one for each design objective. ADOOPLA can generate such MOILPs in the standard formats of OPL[8] and AMPL[9].

In the following sections we describe how we generate an optimization problem in MOILP-form based on a variant-rich PL architecture modeled in EAST-ADL with specific design goals. First, Sect. 5.1 will detail how the variability information of the model is transformed into a set of ILP constraints equivalent to $Ax \geq a_0$ with $x \in \{0, 1\}^n$. Next, Sect. 5.2 will demonstrate the generation of linear objective functions equivalent to Minimize Cx based on the values of modeled quality criteria. At this point we already have a MOILP formalization of an optimization problem, albeit purely on a product-line-wide level (cf. Sect. 4). Therefore, Sect. 5.3 will introduce a method for modifying the MOILP so that objectives with product-level optimality are optimized with regard to the characteristics of products, instead of characteristics of the product line itself.

---

[5] ITEA EAST-EEA (http://www.itea3.org/project/east-eea.html), ATESST, ATESST2 (http://www.atesst.org), MAENAD (http://www.maenad.eu).
[6] http://www.east-adl.info.
[7] http://www.autosar.org.
[8] https://www-01.ibm.com/software/commerce/optimization/modeling.
[9] http://ampl.com.

5.1   Formalizing System Variability

First of all, a formalization must be able to differentiate between product line variability and architecture design options (cf. Sect. 3). As a reminder, what we ultimately want to produce are product line candidates with Pareto-optimal architecture design decisions, as opposed to Pareto-optimal configurations of the product line (i.e., products). We therefore have to omit the product line variability from the optimization process, so that it doesn't get resolved down to a single product automatically.

The ADOOPLA approach can discriminate between product line variability and architecture design options in EAST-ADL models by making use of the language traceability across its abstraction levels [17]. Therefore, if a variation point is part of the system's product line variability, it's origin must always be traceable to the model's Vehicle Level. If however the variation point can not be traced to the Vehicle Level, it must necessarily be part of the architectural degrees of freedom instead. Using this method of distinction, the process assigns decision variables x to all variable components corresponding to architectural degrees of freedom.

The transformation of modeled architecture design options into ILP constraints is done by applying a set of transformation rules proposed by the authors of this paper in a previous publication [2], which use a conversion into propositional logic as an intermediate step. ADOOPLA implements these rules as part of the generation of the MOILP formalization for product line system architecture optimization problems. Table 1 gives an overview of the transformation

Table 1. Transformation rules for EAST-ADL variability into ILP constraints [1].

Variability		Propositional logic	Program constraints
Feature tree	Feature has parent	$f \rightarrow f_{par}$	$f_{par} - f \geq 0$
	Feature is excluded	$!f$	$(1 - f) = 1$
	Feature group	for all m: $f_{par} \rightarrow M_m(f_1, .., f_n)$	for all m: $M_m(f_1, .., f_n) - f_{par} \geq 0$
Feature link	Needs	$f_{start} \rightarrow f_{end}$	$f_{end} - f_{start} \geq 0$
	Optional alternative	$!(f_{start} \wedge f_{end})$	$f_{end} + f_{start} \leq 1$
	Mandatory alternative	$f_{start} \oplus f_{end}$	$f_{start} + f_{end} = 1$
Variation group	Needs	$f_1 \rightarrow (f_2 \wedge \ldots \wedge f_n)$	$\bigwedge_{k=2}^{n} (f_k - f_1 \geq 0)$
	Optional alternative	for all $m : M_m(f_1, .., f_n)$	$f_1 + f_2 + \ldots + f_n \leq 1$
	Mandatory alternative	$f_1 \oplus f_2 \oplus \ldots \oplus f_n$	$f_1 + f_2 + \ldots + f_n = 1$
Configuration decisions		$criterion \rightarrow effect$	$effect - criterion \geq 0$

rules and Sect. 6 demonstrates their application as part of the case study. For a detailed explanation of the rules please refer to the original publication [1].

5.2 Design Objectives for the Product Line

In order to be able to generate objective functions for our optimization problem, the considered design goals must be represented in the system model. For the use case of using EAST-ADL models as input, we evaluate a type of native EAST-ADL annotations[10], which predefine several quantifiable quality criteria that can be annotated to components of the model; e.g., development cost, piece cost, weight, power consumption etc. In case of a design goal that is not natively supported by language annotations, the realization could also be extended in order to process externally held quality criteria information.

To generate objective functions from constraint annotations, we evaluate the matrix of annotated criteria values C and assign them as factors to the decision variables x discovered as part of the process shown in Sect. 5.1. As we already have a mapping of decision variables x to the associated variable components in the model, the assignment of the correct criteria values is a simple table look-up. In case of multi-objective optimization, each decision variable is naturally assigned multiple criteria factors, one per considered design goal. The result is a matrix Cx of criteria factors and decision variables, which is equivalent to a set of linear objective functions $F(x) = (f_1(x), f_2(x), ..., f_m(x))^T$ with $f(x) = c^T x$, where c^T is the transposed vector of the values of annotated criteria for the variable components associated with the decision variables x. For an example how to generate objective functions from annotated criteria values in practice, please refer to the problem formalization of the case study in Sect. 6.1.

At this point, when combining the generated objective functions with the constraints from Sect. 5.1, we already have a fully-fledged optimization problem in MOILP-form that we could use as input for an optimization tool. However, so far our formalization does only take criteria into account, which refer to a product line as a whole (e.g., number of components of the product line architecture). The optimization would thus be able to yield a PLA that is optimized for product-line-wide criteria, which would be similar to some existing approaches. However, this does not yet address the need of optimizing product-level characteristics like the average weight of the actual products should be minimized. In order to correct for this issue, the following section will introduce a method for modifying the program in such a way, that the resulting optimization will instead produce optima over the average quality of valid products (i.e. product-level optimization) for appropriate objectives.

5.3 Design Objectives for Products

Firstly, consider an optimization for the design goal unit cost c_n based on the objective function $\min \sum_{n=1}^{p} c_n^T x$ for p variable components, with the objective

---

[10] EAST-ADL package GenericConstraints [18, p. 170ff].

function generated as shown in the previous section. Optimizing over this function would in essence minimize over the sum of the cost of all variable components in the product line architecture. The resulting optimum would be something akin to the one product line architecture that has the lowest "unit cost". However, it is unclear what this actually means conceptually, since a product line can never itself constitute a "unit". The resulting optimum would in fact *not* carry any information value about potential optimalities of products of the product line. While a result like this is indeed a mathematical optimum, it isn't at all useful for finding a good architecture. For product-level criteria like unit cost or unit weight, we instead need a way of finding optima that are optimal with regard to characteristics of products of the product line, instead of characteristics of the product line itself.

In order to shift optimality to products for product-level design goals, it is necessary to consider the PLV design space in addition to the architecture design options. In essence, objective functions are first determined exactly as with the previous process in Sect. 5.2; i.e. by evaluating annotated quality criteria in the model as criterion values c_n as factors for decision variables x. However, we now introduce an additional set of factors u_n, which results in objective functions in the form of $f_{util}(x) = \sum_{n=1}^{p} u_n^T c_n^T x$ for p variable components. The newly introduced factors u_n account for the degree of utilization of the corresponding variable components in the products of the product line. In other words, components that are used less frequently across the product portfolio are weighted lower for the optimization, whereas components that occur more frequently are weighted higher.

The value for the degree of utilization of variable components results from an evaluation of the product range by means of the product line variability. The values of the utilization factors u_n is determined as follows. Let the number of all valid products of the given product line be G, and the number of all products that make use of a variable component x_k be P_k, then the factor for utilization of this component in the given product line is equal to $u_k = P_k/G$. This of course also means that ADF-variable components that are mandatory with regard to the product line variability have a utilization factor of 1 by default. This makes sense, because components that are not product-line-variable naturally occur in every valid product of the product line, thus P_k is equal to G, ergo $u_k = 1$.

Optimizing over objective functions weighted with these utilization factors will then results in an optimum over the products of the product line, since the design space of the product line variability is the same for all architecture candidates; i.e., the number of valid products G is actually constant for each candidate. This may not be obvious by the way we factorize, however consider the following simple example. A variant-rich product line architecture has $G = 120$ valid products, whereby a variable component x_i is used in $P_i = 80$ of these products, while another variable component x_j is used in $P_j = 30$ products. With our factorization method we get $u_i = P_i/G = 0.67$ and $u_j = P_j/G = 0.25$, so the objective function for criterion c^T would be in the form of $f_{util}(x) = 0.67 * c_i * x_i + 0.25 * c_j * x_j + ... + u_n * c_n * x_n$. In other words, x_i is prioritized over x_j in the optimization by a factor of $u_i/u_j = 2.67$, because it is utilized 2.67-times more frequently in the product portfolio.

By factorizing all variable components of the system architecture accordingly, the components are essentially prioritized relative to each other; with the relative priority governed by how often a component appears in products of the product line. The result of optimizing over an objective function $f_{util}(x)$, factorized by component utilization in the product line, will therefore result in an optimum over the average of valid products of the product line, as opposed to an optimum over the average of all variable components of the product line architecture (cf. Sect. 5.2).

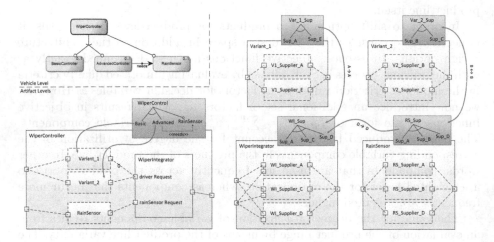

Fig. 1. Case study demonstration model: a wiper control system.

6   ADOOPLA Case Study

In this chapter, we will demonstrate the application and the benefits of the ADOOPLA approach by means of a simplified case study. The small product line architecture is based on an example for a windscreen wiper system proposed by the MAENAD project for demonstrating the variability modeling capabilities of the EAST-ADL language[11]. The existing example has been extended by additional variability both on the vehicle level and on the artifact levels, in order to accommodate a reasonable amount of variation for architecture optimization purposes. The main purpose of this case study is to demonstrate the functionality of the ADOOPLA process for extrapolation to real-world industrial models [3].

Figure 1 shows a variant-rich system architecture for a product line of windscreen wiper control electronics. The wiper system product line can be configured

---

[11] MAENAD Concept Presentation on EAST-ADL Variability: http://www.maenad. eu/public/conceptpresentations/6_Variability_EAST-ADL_Introduction_2013.pdf.

Table 2. Quality criteria values for variable architecture components from different suppliers.

	Development cost/k€	Unit cost/€	Unit weight/g
V1_Supplier_A	28	1.25	70
V1_Supplier_E	30	1.5	65
V2_Supplier_B	41	2.1	120
V2_Supplier_C	39	2.4	105
WI_Supplier_A	25	3.6	50
WI_Supplier_C	27	3.4	35
WI_Supplier_D	29	3.5	45
RS_Supplier_A	22	1.8	125
RS_Supplier_B	24	2.0	110
RS_Supplier_D	22	2.0	105

in either a basic or an advanced configuration, which–on the artifact levels– results in using either variant V1 or V2, respectively. The product line can also support an optional rain sensor component that is mandatory when opting for the advanced configuration. The product line variability is represented by the feature tree on the vehicle level.

The demonstration model also contains design options at the artifact levels, which together define the degrees of freedom for the product line system architecture. Variable components at artifact level are indicated by dashed lines, interdependencies by arrows between variable components. Here, the design options are used in order to represent functionally identical component alternatives from five different suppliers A–E; e.g., the component RainSensor has three different supplier alternatives A, B and D. Some of the component alternatives have interdependencies to other alternatives; i.e., Variant_1 from supplier A requires WiperIntegrator from supplier A, RainSensor from supplier D requires component WiperIntegrator from supplier D, and Variant_2 from supplier B and RainSensor from supplier B require each other.

The alternative components from different suppliers have annotated qualities in regard to the criteria development cost, unit cost and unit weight (cf. Table 2), which are to be considered as design goals for the optimization in our case study. We will demonstrate the usefulness of the ADOOPLA approach by comparing it's results, i.e., mixed product-line-wide and product level Pareto-optimal architecture candidates, with the result of conventional optimization, i.e., purely product-line-wide-level Pareto-optimal candidates.

6.1   Case Study Problem Formalization

In order to formalize the given case study into a sound optimization problem in MOILP form, the ADOOPLA tooling first assigns decision variables to variable architecture components. Remember that we only want to optimize the design space of architectural design options, not the design space of the product line variability. The first challenge is therefore to differentiate between the two different kinds of variation points at the artifact level of our case study model and consider only the ones regarding architectural design options for optimization.

While the variation points for the components Variant_1, Variant_2, WiperIntegrator and RainSensor satisfy this condition, the variation point for the component WiperController does not. This becomes clear when considering that the variation for WiperController can be traced all the way back to the Vehicle Level of the model, which indicates that it is part of the product line variability (cf. Sect. 3).

After selecting for the correct variation points, i.e. only architectural design options, the process assigns decision variables x_i to each of the variable components:

$$x_1 = \backslash WiperController\backslash V1\_Supplier\_A$$
$$x_2 = \backslash WiperController\backslash V1\_Supplier\_E$$
$$x_3 = \backslash WiperController\backslash V2\_Supplier\_B$$
$$x_4 = \backslash WiperController\backslash V2\_Supplier\_C$$
$$x_5 = \backslash WiperController\backslash WI\_Supplier\_A$$
$$x_6 = \backslash WiperController\backslash WI\_Supplier\_C$$
$$x_7 = \backslash WiperController\backslash WI\_Supplier\_D$$
$$x_8 = \backslash WiperController\backslash RS\_Supplier\_A$$
$$x_9 = \backslash WiperController\backslash RS\_Supplier\_B$$
$$x_{10} = \backslash WiperController\backslash RS\_Supplier\_D \qquad (2)$$

Secondly, ADOOPLA formalizes the design space defined by the variation points by transforming them into ILP-constraints. The resulting formalization effectively constitutes our optimization space. Consider the following example for one ILP-constraint. The variants $x_1 = ...\backslash V1\_Supplier\_A$ and $x_2 = ...\backslash V1\_Supplier\_E$ are so-called mandatory alternatives, meaning that one, and only one, must be included in the architecture. This relationship in propositional logic is equal to $x_1 + x_2 = 1$ with $x_1, x_2 \in \{0, 1\}$. ADOOPLA is able to generate ILP-constraints from modeled variability automatically, by applying the transformation rules introduced in Sect. 5.1. Applying these transformation rules to our case study model, the resulting constraints are as follows, with all decision variables $x_i \in \{0, 1\}$:

$$
\begin{aligned}
x_1 + x_2 &= 1 & x_5 - x_1 &\geq 0 \\
x_3 + x_4 &= 1 & x_7 - x_{10} &\geq 0 \\
x_5 + x_6 + x_7 &= 1 & x_3 - x_9 &= 0 \\
x_8 + x_9 + x_{10} &= 1 & & \qquad (3)
\end{aligned}
$$

Next, ADOOPLA generates the objective functions for the design goals development cost, unit cost and unit weight, using the criteria values defined in

Table 2. Note that two of the design goals, namely unit cost and unit weight, are only useful when considered at a product-optimal level, whereas development cost is most useful when considered at a product-line-wide level (cf. Sect. 4). ADOOPLA can account for this difference and can therefore compose the objective functions for unit cost and unit weight as $f_{util}(x) = \sum_{n=1}^{p} u_n^T c_n^T x$ (cf. Sect. 5.3) and the objective function for the design goal development cost as $f(x) = \sum_{n=1}^{p} c_n^T x$ (cf. Sect. 5.2).

The utilization factors are the same for each design goal and therefore have to be calculated by ADOOPLA only once. In our small case study example, there are only three valid products: BasicController without RainSensor, BasicController with RainSensor, and AdvancedController with RainSensor. Calculating the utilization factors for the corresponding variable components follows the method introduced in Sect. 5.3. Therefore, ADOOPLA assigns a utilization factor of $u_{V1} = 2/3 = 0.67$ to BasicController variation point Variant_1, a factor of $u_{V2} = 1/3 = 0.33$ to the AdvancedController variation point Variant_2, and a factor $u_{RS} = 2/3 = 0.67$ to the RainSensor variation point RainSensor. The WiperIntegrator is present in all products of the product line and therefore has a utilization of $u_{WI} = 3/3 = 1$.

With the criteria values from Table 2 and the utilization factors for all variable components, ADOOPLA can now formalize the objective functions for development cost, unit cost and unit weight, in that order, as follows:

$$\min \quad 28 * x_1 + 30 * x_2 + 41 * x_3 + 39 * x_4 + 25 * x_5 + 27 * x_6 + 29 * x_7 + 22 * x_8 + \\ 24 * x_9 + 22 * x_{10}$$

$$\min \quad 0.67 * 1.25 * x_1 + 0.67 * 1.5 * x_2 + 0.33 * 2.1 * x_3 + 0.33 * 2.4 * x_4 + 3.6 * x_5 + \\ 3.4 * x_6 + 3.5 * x_7 + 0.67 * 1.8 * x_8 + 0.67 * 2 * x_9 + 0.67 * 2 * x_{10}$$

$$\min \quad 0.67 * 70 * x_1 + 0.67 * 65 * x_2 + 0.33 * 120 * x_3 + 0.33 * 105 * x_4 + 50 * x_5 + \\ 35 * x_6 + 45 * x_7 + 0.67 * 125 * x_8 + 0.67 * 110 * x_9 + 0.67 * 105 * x_{10} \qquad (4)$$

We now have a complete MOILP formalization of the pursued optimization problem (cf. Sect. 5), which we use as input for an off-the-shelf multi-criteria decision making software. Our tool of choice is the optimization software FINNOPT[12], which allows the user to guide a multi-criteria decision making process towards preferred Pareto-optimal solutions as part of a trade-off analysis. FINNOPT is based on the NIMBUS [19] method that was developed by the Industrial Optimization Group of the University of Jyväskylä, Finland[13]. The tool integrates an external ILP-solver and uses it as part of its decision making process. For this purpose we use the commercial solver CPLEX, which is part of the IBM ILOG CPLEX Optimization Studio[14].

---

[12] http://www.finnopt.com.
[13] http://www.mit.jyu.fi/optgroup.
[14] http://www.ibm.com/software/products/en/ibmilogcpleoptistud.

Table 3. Quality values for valid PLA candidates.

Candidate	Development cost	Unit cost	Unit weight
(A, A, B, B)	118	6.47	210.0
(A, A, C, A)	114	6.43	215.0
(E, A, B, B)	120	6.63	206.7
(E, A, C, A)	116	6.60	211.7
(E, C, B, B)	122	6.43	191.7
(E, C, C, A)	118	6.40	196.7
(E, D, B, B)	124	6.53	201.7
(E, D, C, A)	120	6.50	206.7
(E, D, C, D)	120	6.63	193.3
Product-level		x	x

6.2 Optimization Results and Discussion

The optimization results, i.e., the product line architecture candidates, can be represented using a notation of 4-tuples in the form of $(V1, WI, V2, RS)$; e.g., (A, A, B, B) would be an architecture candidate where the BasicController and the WiperIntegrator use components from supplier A, whereas the Advanced-Controller and the RainSensor use components from supplier B. Table 3 shows the set of all valid architecture candidates for the given architecture design space and their respective qualities with regard to the design goals. Listing (and analyzing) the set of all valid solutions for a design space is not possible for large design spaces, as the number of valid solutions grows exponentially with each variation point.

Even for small design spaces like the one of our case study, finding Pareto-optimal candidates by hand can be a difficult task. It is easy to see that for much larger real-world models, finding optima by hand is practically impossible. However, by using a solver on the MOILP formalization generated by ADOOPLA, it is possible to quickly identify a set of Pareto-optimal architecture candidates. For the case study formalization, the candidates (A, A, C, A), (E, C, C, A) and (E, C, B, B) were identified to be part of the Pareto set.

This result is based on using product-level optimization for the design goals unit cost and unit weight. In comparison, an approach that would not take product-level optima in account would instead have identified the candidates (A, A, C, A), (A, A, B, B) and (E, D, C, D) as Pareto-optimal; a set of candidates much less useful for practical use cases for reasons detailed in Sects. 4 and 5.3.

7 Conclusions

The exploration of design spaces for software product line system architectures is an extremely difficult task due to its inherent complexity. While design space exploration is in most cases non-trivial, the two levels of optimality (product-line-wide criteria vs. product criteria) that are relevant in product line design scenarios make the analysis of such architectures and the corresponding design space exploration particularly difficult for system architects.

In this paper, we presented ADOOPLA, an multi-objective optimization approach for product line architectures that takes both levels of criteria into account and transforms them into an integrated optimization problem. ADOOPLA can therefore help system architects in finding good PLA candidates, that are Pareto-optimal with regard to a set of design objectives. The version of the approach presented in this paper is based on our previous work on identifying optimal product line architectures [2]. However, the inclusion of product-level criteria and their combination with product-line-wide criteria in one combined process is novel in the approach and throughout the literature. We demonstrated the impact of this novel method by applying the ADOOPLA approach to a simplified case study drawn from our work with automotive suppliers. The results of the case study show that by being able to take the difference between the two levels of criteria into account, the approach arrives at different results that represent more adequate candidates for good product line architectures.

The current realization of ADOOPLA supports only linear design objectives derived from the set of quantifiable quality criteria that can be modeled natively in the domain-specific language EAST-ADL. Future work on the approach will be concerned with extending the range of supported design objectives, for example to those defined by the ISO/IEC 25010 standard[15], which comprises multiple quality characteristics as part of a system and software quality model.

References

1. Wägemann, T., Werner, A.: Generating multi-objective programs from variant-rich EAST-ADL product line architectures. In: GI-Jahrestagung, pp. 1673–1685 (2015)
2. Wägemann, T., Tavakoli Kolagari, R., Schmid, K.: Optimal product line architectures for the automotive industry. In: Modellierung 2018 (2018)
3. Wägemann, T., Tavakoli Kolagari, R., Schmid, K.: Exploring automotive stakeholder requirements for architecture optimization support. In: 2019 IEEE International Conference on Software Architecture Companion (ICSA-C), pp. 37–44, March 2019
4. Walker, M., et al.: Automatic optimisation of system architectures using EAST-ADL. J. Syst. Softw. 86(10), 2467–2487 (2013)
5. Mian, Z., Bottaci, L., Papadopoulos, Y., Sharvia, S., Mahmud, N.: Model transformation for multi-objective architecture optimisation of dependable systems. In: Zamojski, W., Sugier, J. (eds.) Dependability Problems of Complex Information Systems. AISC, vol. 307, pp. 91–110. Springer, Cham (2015). https://doi.org/10.1007/978-3-319-08964-5_6
6. Kugele, S., Pucea, G.: Model-based optimization of automotive E/E-architectures. In: Proceedings of the 6th International Workshop on Constraints in Software Testing, Verification, and Analysis, pp. 18–29. ACM (2014)

---

[15] https://iso25000.com/index.php/en/iso-25000-standards/iso-25010.

7. Noir, J.L., et al.: A decision-making process for exploring architectural variants in systems engineering. In: Proceedings of the 20th International Systems and Software Product Line Conference, pp. 277–286. ACM (2016)

8. Xiang, Y., Zhou, Y., Zheng, Z., Li, M.: Configuring software product lines by combining many-objective optimization and SAT solvers. ACM Trans. Softw. Eng. Methodol. **26**(4), 14:1–14:46 (2018)

9. Henard, C., Papadakis, M., Harman, M., Le Traon, Y.: Combining multi-objective search and constraint solving for configuring large software product lines. In: Proceedings of the 37th International Conference on Software Engineering, vol. 1, pp. 517–528. IEEE Press (2015)

10. Olaechea, R., Stewart, S., Czarnecki, K., Rayside, D.: Modelling and multi-objective optimization of quality attributes in variability-rich software. In: Proceedings of the Fourth International Workshop on Nonfunctional System Properties in Domain Specific Modeling Languages, NFPinDSML 2012, pp. 2:1–2:6. ACM, New York (2012)

11. Thüm, T., Apel, S., Kästner, C., Kuhlemann, M., Schaefer, I., Saake, G.: Analysis strategies for software product lines. School of Computer Science, University of Magdeburg, Technical report FIN-004-2012 (2012)

12. Metzger, A., Pohl, K.: Variability management in software product line engineering. In: Companion to the Proceedings of the 29th International Conference on Software Engineering, pp. 186–187. IEEE Computer Society (2007)

13. Clements, P., Northrop, L.: Software Product Lines: Practices and Patterns. Addison-Wesley Professional, Boston (2001)

14. Tischer, C., Boss, B., Müller, A., Thums, A., Acharya, R., Schmid, K.: Developing long-term stable product line architectures. In: Proceedings of the 16th International Software Product Line Conference (SPLC 2012), vol. 1, pp. 86–95. ACM (2012)

15. Burke, E.K., Kendall, G.: Search Methodologies: Introductory Tutorials in Optimization and Decision Support Techniques. Springer, New York (2005). https://doi.org/10.1007/978-1-4614-6940-7

16. Blom, H., et al.: White paper version 2.1.12: EAST-ADL - an architecture description language for automotive software-intensive systems (2013)

17. Reiser, M.O., Tavakoli Kolagari, R., Weber, M.: Compositional variability: concepts and patterns. In: 42nd Hawaii International Conference on System Sciences, pp. 1–10 (2009)

18. EAST-ADL Association: EAST-ADL Domain Model Specification, Version V2.1.12 (2013). http://east-adl.info/Specification/V2.1.12/EAST-ADL-Specification_V2.1.12.pdf

19. Miettinen, K.: IND-NIMBUS for demanding interactive multiobjective optimization. In: Multiple Criteria Decision Making 2005, vol. 1, pp. 137–150 (2006)

Assessing Adaptability of Software Architectures for Cyber Physical Production Systems

Michael Mayrhofer[1]([✉]), Christoph Mayr-Dorn[1,2], Alois Zoitl[2],
Ouijdane Guiza[1], Georg Weichhart[3], and Alexander Egyed[2]

[1] Pro2Future GmbH, Linz, Austria
michael.mayrhofer@pro2future.at
[2] Institute of Software Systems Engineering,
Johannes Kepler University, Linz, Austria
[3] ProFactor GmbH, Steyr, Austria

Abstract. Cyber physical production systems (CPPS) focus on increasing the flexibility and adaptability of industrial production systems, systems that comprise hardware such as sensors and actuators in machines as well as software controlling and integrating these machines. The requirements of customised mass production imply that control software needs to be adaptable after deployment in a shop floor, possibly even without interrupting production. Software architecture plays a central role in achieving run-time adaptability. In this paper we describe five architectures, that define the structure and interaction of software components in CPPS. Three of them already are already well known and used in the field. The other two we contribute as possible solution to overcome limitations of the first three architectures. We analyse the architectures' ability to support adaptability based on Taylor et al.'s BASE framework. We compare the architectures and discuss how the implications of CPPS affect the analysis with BASE. We further highlight what lessons from "traditional" software architecture research can be applied to arrive at adaptable software architectures for cyber physical production systems.

Keywords: Software architectures · Manufacturing ·
Reconfiguration · Cyber-physical production systems · Adaptability

1 Introduction

Cyber Physical Systems (CPS) tightly interweave software and physical components for integrating computation, networking, and physical processes in a feedback loop. In this feedback loop, software influences physical processes and vice versa. CPS in the manufacturing context are referred to as Cyber Physical Production Systems (CPPS). A production cell involving machines, robots, humans, and transport systems such as pick and place units are examples of a CPPS; Not considered are CPS in general: drones, smart buildings, or medical

© Springer Nature Switzerland AG 2019
T. Bures et al. (Eds.): ECSA 2019, LNCS 11681, pp. 143–158, 2019.
https://doi.org/10.1007/978-3-030-29983-5_10

devices. CPPS increase the flexibility and adaptability of industrial production systems which enables reconfiguration of a physical plant layout with little effort and to produce a higher variety of products on the same layout.

Software, and specifically, software architecture plays a central role in achieving this goal. The general capabilities of a production plant depend on its physical layout. Yet, which capabilities are invoked, in which order and under which conditions is controlled mostly by software or human operators. Thus, fast and cheap reconfiguration can only happen through software designed to allow for adaptability and flexibility. Over the last decades, the software architecture community has focused intensely on these concerns in the scope of "traditional" software systems. In these systems physical aspects such as material flow, manipulation of physical objects, and physical layout of machines and humans, play no or only a marginal role. Little of the work in the software architecture community, however, addresses specifically CPPS. We believe that concepts, approaches, and ideas from software architecture are invaluable for guiding the design of CPPS. In return, we would expect that the constraints and characteristics of CPPS raises awareness in the software architecture community about the implications stemming from the physical world. Software systems inevitably will become increasingly fused with physical object as we can already observe with systems described as Smart Devices that are part of the Internet of Things: Software systems that inherently rely on appropriate software architectures for delivering long-term benefit to the user.

In the scope of this paper, we focus only on adaptability of CPPS (and refer for other, equally relevant, properties for example to [1] as well as future work). Adaptability in CPPS comes in two main categories: adaptation of the software (i.e., machine configuration, process configuration, etc.) and adaptation of the physical layout (i.e., relocating machine, mobile robots, autonomous guided vehicles). Both categories imply software adaptability (see Sects. 2 and 3). Whether the goal is assessing the current software architecture of an CPPS or deciding upon a future CPPS software architecture: in both cases we need a mechanism to analyse and compare an architecture's adaptability. Rather than determining criteria from scratch, we apply the BASE framework introduced by Oreizy, Medvidovic, and Taylor [2] (Sect. 4). This framework serves as our basis for evaluating and comparing CPPS architectures. This paper's core contribution is a comparison of five architectures for CPPS with an explicit focus on adaptability: the first three architectures describe the predominant approach to structuring production systems, the latter two architectures are proposed evolutions for increased adaptability (Sect. 5). We complete the paper with an overview of related work (Sect. 6) and an outlook on future work (Sect. 7).

2   Background

Similar to software centric companies, manufacturers aim to remain competitive through a higher innovation rate and an increase in product customization options. The former requires development processes with potential for both agile

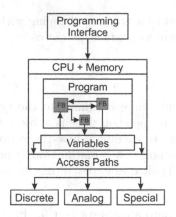

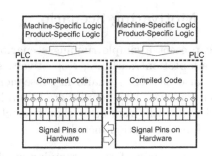

Fig. 1. Simplified PLC architecture layout

Fig. 2. Direct compilation of control code

and parallel development. The ultimate goal is lot-size one: the ability to continuously produce ever-changing product configurations on the same product line at the same low costs as mass production.

From a software architecture point of view, manufacturers face a major challenge: the ability to reconfigure the production environment (the machines, processes, flows, etc) during production time without impairing production pace. At the most extreme end, no two products produced are the same and thus every machine involved in the production needs some (software) adaptation for each product produced.

The foundation of today's manufacturing systems are programmable logic controllers (PLCs). PLCs are microcomputers that read data from sensors in the physical world, process the measurement values, and set output voltages to control drives, valves, etc. (see Fig. 1). They allow the automation of production steps by controlling a variety of machines across the shop floor: conveyor belts, robots, raw material processing machines, measuring devices, packaging, etc. PLC programs consists of function blocks that access and modify variables, and communicate with other function blocks. The variables map via access paths to the input/output ports. PLC-specific programming environments primarily aim to allow efficient and intuitive creation of such control software (mostly control algorithms). Engineers then compile these programs to the target platform and download/deploy them to the PLC for execution. Adaptation with this approach is cumbersome as we will show in Subsect. 5.1.

Software on PLSs fall into two major categories. First, low level control software handles sensor data and actuator signals, that is common for machines of the same type. This software can be compared to a hardware-centric API and its implementation: opening/closing a valve, setting the rotation speed of a drive. We refer to this software as *machine-specific code*. Second, there is software that defines parameters for and calls of low-level control, thereby specifying how a machine must behave on the shop floor: when to open a valve, at which force, how fast to run a drive. This software is tailored to a product, changing with a product revision. We, hence, refer to this software as *product-specific code.*

3   Motivating Scenario

We present a simple running scenario to provide more insights into the type of adaptation machines, respectively, software at the shop floor is subject to. We also use this scenario in subsequent sections to exemplify how the various architectures allow adaptation. In production automation, a machine rarely acts independently from other shop floor elements. Typical examples of machine-to-machine interaction include:

- Parts coming from a stamping machine fall onto a conveyor belt for further transportation.
- A robot feeds raw material to an automated machine tool (e.g., a milling machine) and retrieves the processed product.
- A robot holding a part, while a second robot processes it (e.g., spray painting or welding).

In our scenario, we assume a milling machine controlled with an attached robot arm for removing processed parts and sorting them on trays. Milling machine and robot are controlled by one PLC each for sake of simplicity. Even small scale industrial environments such as the VDMA OPC-UA demonstrator[1] are too complex to be described in adequate detail here, let along discussing its adaptability aspects. Our scenario picks out a part of such a setup that is sufficiently rich for discussing the impact of software architecture on adaptability. Traditionally, with little or no product change, engineers custom tailor the software for the PLCs specifically for a particular product. Here the software controls the movement, speed, and force of the milling machine's cutter as well as the robot arm's gripping position, force, and moving path.

With increasing demand for adaptability, two orthogonal adaptation dimensions emerge. On the one hand, we distinguish between the level of adaptation, and on the other hand we differentiate according to the locality of adaptation. The former describes adaptation of product-specific vs machine-specific code, while the latter separates adaptation within a machine invisible to the outside (local) from adaptations affecting multiple machines (distributed). Adaptation example for resulting four types include:

Machine-specific/Local. Robot manufacturers continuously improve the control algorithms used in robots and offer frequent updates to existing robots on the shop floor. Robot manufacturers may introduce new algorithms that allow for simpler programming of gripping instructions or arm movements.

Product-specific/Local. With lot-size one product customizations, the milling machine might have to cut away at different locations at the raw part, thus requiring different control parameter for each product.

---

[1] https://www.youtube.com/watch?v=pUtSA8g9owY.

Product-specific/Distributed. With lot-size one production, when the raw part size changes between products, then (in addition to the milling machine control software) the robot arm control software needs new parameters for different gripping positions and movement paths to avoid dropping the processed product or bumping it against the milling machine.

Machine-specific/Distributed. The manufacturer decides to switch among the milling machines communications capabilities from WiFi to 5G for communicating with the robot. Assuming that the robot supports both wireless standards, now also the robot control software needs to switch connections.

4 Introduction to BASE

The BASE framework developed by Oreizy, Medvidovic, and Taylor defines four orthogonal criteria to evaluate software systems for their runtime adaptability. In this section we will summarise these criteria and outline how they match CPPS. For a detailed explanation of the framework itself refer to [2].

Behavior: How are changes to the behavior represented and applied? Is behavior limited to a combination of atomic capabilities or is it possible to introduce completely new behavior?

Changes to machine-specific behavior can come in different forms. New functionality (e.g., enabling the milling machine to create curves and arcs) can be introduced, or existing functionality can be improved (e.g., extending the current control algorithm) or replaced. Outdated functionality needs to be removed to create space for new functionality. Changes to the physical architecture (e.g., upgrading to the 5G communication standard) require updates of the drivers.

On the product level, the order of calling the different machine capabilities will change with every product. In addition, the machine configuration (e.g., cutting speeds and control parameters on milling machines, gripping forces and tool tip position on handling robots) needs to be altered, especially when the next product needs different hardware clamps, drills, etc. What looks like a matter of configuration is indeed (physical and software) adaptation (see also Sect. 5.1).

Asynchrony: How does the update process affect the system's execution? Is it necessary to halt the system until the updated has completed, or can it resume after already after a partial update? How would correct execution be guaranteed in case of partial updates?

Given the combination of milling machine and handling robot, it might be desirable to update the robot's motion algorithm or positions for a new product while it is still handling the current product. In general, this aspect focuses on the architecture properties that ideally allow elements of a CPPS to be adapted without negatively affecting others, e.g., enabling the milling machine to start producing while the robot is still under reconfiguration.

State: How does the system react to changes in state? How does it deal with altered types? Does a state change require an interrupt of the system's execution?

In CPPS, we primarily distinguish between managing product-specific state (i.e., which steps/phases are complete, which ones are currently active, what needs to be done next) and machine-specific state (e.g., current drill rotation speed or robot arm position, whether a product is inside the machine).

Execution Context: Constraints on system parts that determine when adaptations are allowed. E.g. the system has to be in a safe state, heap has to be empty, system has to be disconnected from surrounding systems, ... While *Asynchony* focuses on the timing of the ongoing adaptation actions, *Execution context* highlights adaptation pre-conditions. For example, does an architecture allow the algorithm controlling the tools position to be updated during execution or only when the gripper has released the part? Can we update the cutting force estimator on the fly? Do we need to shutdown the robot to alter the path planning? And, if milling machine and robot are working together in one cell, do we have to halt the milling machine while updating the robot? Might such dependencies cascade further across several machines, or even whole cells?

In the next section, we apply the BASE framework to evaluate the adaptability of five architectures: three reference architectures and two proposed evolutions thereof.

5   Architecture Analysis

Our goal is assessing how adaptable various CPPS architectures are. Ideally they are adaptable and response enough to change the behavior in nearly zero time. Recall, that we distinguish software according to product-specific code and machine-specific code. A major difference among the discussed architectures is how intertwined these two code types become at runtime (i.e., on the PLC). We assess each architecture with BASE in general and outline how the adaptation actions from our motivating scenarios may be implemented. Across all architecture Figs. 2, 3, 4, 5 and 6, arrows pointing down indicate transfer of artifacts (code and/or models) while left to right arrows indicate communication among machines.

5.1   Hardcoded and Physically Wired

In the most prevalent solutions, the engineer tightly weaves the product-specific code with the machine-specific code. Machine-specific code is available as include-files at compile time and is transferred upon each software update to the controller together with the product-specific code. Transfer occurs often at runtime when a Manufacturing Execution System (MES) deploys the software before each production process. This process of "direct compilation" is depicted in Fig. 2. Communication among several PLCs occurs primarily via digital pins, thus hard-wired at the hardware level. This approach matches the strict resource limitations of cheap PLCs. Control code is translated directly to machine code, allowing for fast execution and minimizing memory footprint. On the downside, this architectural style comes with significant limitations:

Behavior: An adaptation implies changes to the software regardless whether is product-specific code or machine-specific code. To effect the changes, the complete application needs recompilation and retransfer to the PLC. Unsurprisingly, this approach allows adaptations of existing behavior as well as introduction of completely new behavior.

Asynchrony: The system is unavailable for the duration of shutting down, software replacement, and restarting.

State: Due to wholesale software replacement and system shutdown, any state has to be persisted prior to shutdown or is lost. No separation of machine-specific state from product-specific state exists.

Execution Context: The machine has to reach a safe state for shutdown. During software redeployment, therefore, the machine is unable to continue production or communicate with connected machines. Shutdown needs to be signalled to connected systems to allow them to gracefully react to the unavailable machine undergoing updating. Otherwise connected machines might malfunction due to missing signal values or alternatively have to be shutdown likewise.

Suppose the machines from our motivating scenario are implemented according to this reference architecture, the specific adaptation consequences are the following. The tight coupling of machine-specific and product-specific code implies that regardless whether the changes are new or improved gripping algorithms, or whether these are different milling parameter, the respective machine needs to reach a safe-state and subsequently be shutdown. In addition, the tight coupling among machines on the hardware level requires stopping (or even shutting down) and later restarting of the non-updated machine as well. An engineer, hence, needs to consider how the affected machine-under-adaptation is connected to other machines before effecting an update.

5.2 Central Coordinator Architecture

The *Central Coordinator Architecture* exhibits a clear separation of machine-specific logic and product-specific logic. Each PLC exposes its functionality (e.g., Function Blocks) as higher-level, composable endpoints (i.e., explicit interfaces). The endpoints' granularity depends how the underlying machine is typically used: i.e., how much fine-grained control is needed. See Fig. 3 for an illustration. The defacto protocol for discovery, endpoint provisioning, and invocation in CPPS is OPC-Unified Architecture (OPC-UA) [3] (standardized in IEC 62451). The Centurio Engine [4] is an example for such an architecture.

The machine-specific details behind the exposed endpoints remain opaque to the production process engineer. Typically only engineers at the machine manufacturer—or dedicated integration experts that customize the machine for a particular shop floor—develop and adapt software at the PLC level (including middleware for exposing endpoints).

An engineer discovers the PLCs' endpoints and specifies the control-flow of endpoint invocations and invocation parameter values in a model. The engineer sends the model to the centralized coordinator and triggers its execution. Note that this coordinator is central only with respect to the involved PLCs and not with respect to the overall shop floor. Communication between PLCs occurs indirectly via the centralized coordinator. Production processes with time critical invocation sequences require locating the centralized coordinator close to the involved machines, respectively, PLCs, and/or communication over appropriate network infrastructure such as TSN (time-sensitive networking). Based on BASE, we make the following observations:

Behavior: An engineer specifies product-specific changes as changes to the production process model. The centralized coordinator's capabilities determine whether an updated process model replaces a currently active process wholesale, or whether it applies only the differences. Two options exist to obtain different behavior of machine-specific logic: On the one hand, choosing among different existing behavior occurs via the production process by invoking different endpoints (e.g., for a different algorithm) or using different invocation parameters. On the other hand, radically new functionality needs to be deployed to the PLC via side-channels.

Asynchrony: While switching among pre-existing functionality at the machine-specific level when triggered by the centralized controller is instantaneous, new functionality requires shutting down the machine for the duration of deploying new function blocks and making them available via the middleware. Such a shutdown implies pausing the current product model at the centralized coordinator, and thereby also potentially any other involved machine. However, scheduling an updated production process model for execution at the centralized coordinator upon completion of the currently running process are instantaneous. In-situ changes to running processes may require longer when the process needs to reach a certain stage before updating can safely occur. Changes to the production process become necessary when an interface of the exposed endpoints is affected. However, other machines, respectively PLCs, remain unaffected.

State: Product-specific state is managed in the centralized coordinator while machine-specific state remains within the PLC-level middleware. Updating the product-specific meta-model requires stopping the production, persisting the state, transforming the persisted state to the new meta-model. Such an adaptation typically also requires updating the centralized coordinator but not the machine-specific logic. Machine-specific state is represented by the underlying physical state of the machine and hence readily obtainable via reading from the PLC's hardware signal pins.

Execution Context: Wholesale replacing product-specific logic requires the centralized coordinator to bring the current model to a safe state. A safe state typically describes a situation where the involved machines equally reach a safe state (e.g., idle) or require no input from the coordinator for the duration of the adaptation. In-situ adaptation of the product-specific logic requires product engineering know-how at which state fragments of the model can be updated quickly enough before the coordinator will access them and given the constraints among model fragments. Adaptation of the centralized coordinator itself requires putting all PLCs in a safe state. Switching among pre-existing machine-specific logic is only restricted by the machine-state, i.e., whether the desired invocation of an endpoint is valid at that particular time, but remains independent of the state of other machines. Adding new functionality at the machine-level typically requires PLC shutdown and hence requires the centralized coordinator to reach a safe (product-specific) state first.

Suppose the machines from our motivating scenario are implemented according to this reference architecture, the specific adaptation consequences are the following. Product-specific updates are straight forward implemented via the model and loading this into the centralized coordinator. There is no differences whether the update affects only the milling machine or also the robot arm as neither machines maintain product-specific control software. Machine-specific adaptations are limited to the machine-under-adaptation: updating the gripping algorithm may not even require stopping the milling machine if sufficient time remains to deploy the new algorithm on the robot's PLC and bind it to the endpoint in use by the centralized controller. Alternatively, the centralized controller would bring the milling process to a safe state and wait for continuation once the robot arm becomes operational again. Even machine-specific changes that affected multiple machines in *Baseline Architecture* become strongly decoupled. Switching to 5G on the milling machine, for example, would only affect the communication between the milling machine and the centralized controller (assuming that the controller supports this on the fly), but not the robot.

Overall, this architecture/approach is typically applied in the batch automation domain (e.g., pharma, food, beverages) where the product model is a so-called *recipe* (e.g., recipe for producing aspirin) defined in ISA 88.[2] The *Central Coordinator Architecture*, however, is not limited to this standard.

5.3 *61499 Architecture*

The IEC 61499 standard (and hence this architecture's name, Fig. 4) defines a mechanism for specifying and loading product and machine-specific logic in the form of Function Blocks on the fly. To this end, each PLC hosts a run-time environment (RTE) that executes configurations of function blocks including the communication among function blocks across PLC boundaries. A central model consisting of Function Blocks (algorithmic units for computation, signaling, I/O control etc) and their wiring represent the product and machine-specific logic. Any separation between these to types is implicit and depends on a respective well designed model. While function blocks allow reuse and thus separation of machine-specific functionality, the RTE makes no such distinction and merely requires all logic (of all required function blocks) to be provided in an executable format. The mapping procedure of function blocks across PLCs (and respective RTEs) includes the automatic generation of communication proxies and hence

---

[2] https://www.isa.org/templates/one-column.aspx?pageid=111294&productId=116649.

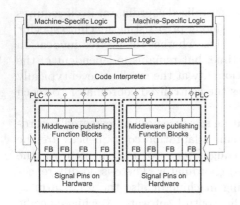

Fig. 3. *Central Coordinator Architecture*

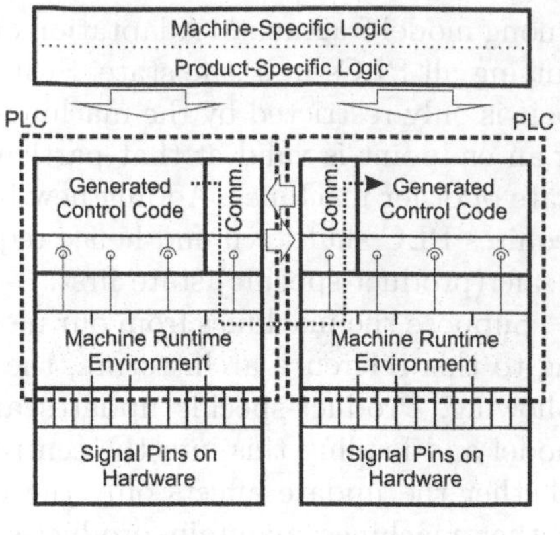

Fig. 4. *61499 Architecture*

allows function blocks to transparently communicate across PLC boundaries. Strasser et al. [5] describe an exemplary implementation of such an architecture. The VMDA demonstrator, referred to in the scenario description, shows the latest state-of-the-art realization of a shop floor by following *61499 Architecture*.

Behavior: The 61499 standard defines the ability how to change, replace, and rewire any function block on the fly.

Asynchrony: Given the finegrained adaptation capabilities, before adaptation, the impact of the adaptation must be evaluated to specify safe condition when to effect a change. Both changes in product and machine logic require compilation to intermediate code and to transfer it to the PLC. The RTE's mechanisms for code transfer support transferring deltas thus, reducing network load.

State: The RTE allows to employ algorithms for complete state transfer. This transfer has to be planned in detail beforehand, together with the code compilation. State required by dependent systems can be kept in memory until the adaptation is complete. This is safely possible as IEC 61499 assumes that physical states (positions, velocities, temperatures, ...) do not jump, thus do only deviate little from one time step to the next.

Execution Context: With the RTE's capabilities of replacing code at runtime while keeping the state in memory (or, if necessary, updating state changes based on estimates) there are no restrictions to adaptation, from the software perspective. The planning of state transfer might become tedious, especially if states are removed or added, but not infeasible. The main limitation is, that the controlled system, the physical system, has to be in a safe state.

Without a clear, dedicated boundary between machine-specific and product-specific logic, any kind of local adaptation are possible on the fly if the timing permits, i.e., the change is completed before the change logic segment is accessed/used by the RTE again. Distributed changes such as switching to 5G or updating product dimension requires to synchronize the changes application on the milling machine and on the robot. Hence, adaptation planning requires in-depth domain knowhow of the milling machine and the robot at product and machine level to identify safe states.

5.4 Coordination Middleware Architecture

Having analysed the properties of these three architectures, we propose *Coordination Middleware Architecture* depicted in Fig. 5 as the next logical evolution step towards more adaptability. Similar to the *Central Coordinator Architecture*, an engineer describes the product-specific logic in a central model and subsequently assigns model fragments to various execution resources (i.e., the PLCs). In contrast to the *61499 Architecture*, there exists a strict separation of product-specific logic and machine-specific logic. A local middleware on each PLC interprets the product model fragments and calls the respective machine-specific code. The model fragments contain information for registering itself at the "shopfloor service bus" (SSB), in essence a coordination middleware. The SSB enables registering endpoints, subscribing to events, and dispatching messages. The SSB is responsible for routing messages and events among the participating PLCs. The local middleware obtains only local view of the overall production process without insights into which other entities are involved as the SSB is the only means for external communication. The SSB thereby constitutes a powerful location for adaptation support due to strong decoupling of machines: information mapping, message/event buffering, machine availability signalling, fail-over handling, etc.

Behavior: Adapting Product-specific logic implies transferring any changes from global model to local fragments. New functionality on machine level requires either recompilation of the middleware, if using a hardcoded interpretation middleware, or transfer of the deltas, if using a RTE as in *61499 Architecture*.

Asynchrony: Distributing updates to local product-specific logic fragments occurs independently from changes to other fragments while the machine continue to produce. Introduction of new machine-specific code without downtime is dependent on the capabilities of the middleware/RTE.

State: Product state needs to be persisted when adaption implies replacing a complete product fragment during production. Alternatively, applying deltas to the product model fragment preserves such state. For impact on machine-state, see *Central Coordinator Architecture*.

Execution Context: Updating (or replacing) a process fragment requires it to be in an safe state, i.e., where it is not expected to react before the end of the adaptation procedure. The SSB enables PLCs to deregister during non-instantaneous adaptations or maintenance (both at product fragment level and machine logic level). The SSB may then signal other participants to suspend, involve a failover machine (e.g., use another robot), or it temporarily stores events and messages until the adapting PLC becomes available again. This limits the impact on other machines when a PLC needs to be shutdown for machine-level adaptations.

The specific adaptation consequences for our motivating scenario are very similar to *Central Coordinator Architecture* for machine-specific and product-specific adaptations. With respect to product-logic adaptation: adaptations can be effected on the fly. However, while distributed product-specific adaptations such as different product dimensions requiring different gripping locations may be distributed to machine and robot at different times, these adaptations have to be made effective simultaneously which incurs coordination overhead. Machine-specific distributed adaptation such as switching to 5G requires also the SSB seamlessly use that communication means, making the change transparent to the robot.

5.5   *Distributed Middleware Architecture*

A further evolution of *Coordination Middleware Architecture* results in *Distributed Middleware Architecture*. It merges the strong separation of product-specific and machine specific logic of the *Central Coordinator Architecture* with the peer-to-peer communication and on-the-fly updating capabilities of the *61499 Architecture*, without having a central communication bottleneck as in the *Coordination Middleware Architecture* (see Fig. 6. An SSB is often not feasible due to performance reasons (latency, throughput) or infrastructure availability. It effectively becomes distributed across the participating systems and integrated in the local middleware there. This implies that participating systems need to discover other participants, become aware of their role in the product-specific model, subscribe for events, and track their availability. Consequently adaptation support such as message caching, fail-over, etc becomes more complex. Given the similarities to the other architectures, the analysis with BASE yields few differences.

Behavior: Similar to *Coordination Middleware Architecture*.

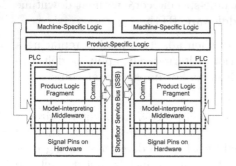

Fig. 5.   *Coordination   Middleware Architecture*

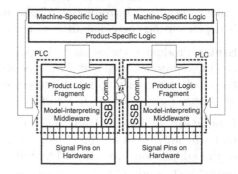

Fig. 6. *Distributed Middleware Architecture*

Asynchrony: Similar to *Coordination Middleware Architecture*, despite the fact, that there is no central, consistent view on the machine availability (formerly available at the SBB) but is maintained distributed and hence typically only eventually consistent.

State: Similar to *Coordination Middleware Architecture*.

Execution Context: Similar to *Coordination Middleware Architecture*, Adaptation that requires multiple model fragments to be simultaneously updated for correct production requires a dedicated coordinator mechanism for the adaptations in sync. The middleware/coordinators now need to reach an agreement when to adapt, rather than merely exposing an simple adaptation endpoint for synchronization.

The adaptation implications for our motivating scenario are almost the same as for the *Coordination Middleware Architecture* architecture. Here, machine-specific distributed adaptation such as switching to 5G now requires all communicating parties to complete the switch at the same time.

5.6 Discussion

In the authoritative papers on the BASE framework [6,7], highlight that Behavior, Asynchrony, State, and Execution identify the central techniques for achieving adaptability: In CPPS separating product and machine specific logic enables defining more precisely what should change, and how that can be changed while keeping the (side) effects local, and managing machine state separate from product(ion) state (see also [2]).

The two general strategies underlying these techniques are making bindings adaptable and using explicit events or messages for communication. These observations also hold true in CPPS. Malleable bindings imply that machines and robots are allocated to the individual production steps as late as possible, e.g., which robot instance maneuvers the product into and out of a particular milling machine instance. In CPPS the physical world limits the bindings to physically available machines, but having the flexibility at the software (architecture) level enables for increased flexibility at the physical level, e.g., replacing a robot, adding one to increase production pace, integrating autonomous transport vehicles. Architectures 2 to 5 make such late binding possible. Architecture 2 allows late binding of the machines to the production process steps, Architecture 3 explicitly focuses on the ability to change the bindings at runtime, Architecture 4 introduces an SSB with capabilities for dynamically routing messages to the right endpoints, with Architecture 5 doing the same but in a distributed manner.

Similarly, events/message achieve strong decoupling among components. There is no shared memory or tight binding. Events allow monitoring and thus provide feedback on the system state, informing adaptation mechanisms when and where to engage. Events further allow replaying, transforming, and enhancing to turn systems interoperable, see architectures 4 and 5.

Maintaining a model of the system (product-specific and/or machine-specific) is a key towards adaptability. Several approaches demonstrate the runtime adaptation based on linking a model, i.e., the system's architecture with its implementation, e.g., [6,8,9].

Ultimately, what architecture to select depends on the desired level of adaptability subject to the constraint of the physical properties of the production process and involved machines. An injection molding machine typically will produce many similar parts before the molding form is exchanged (a slow procedure) to produce a different product and thus has different requirements for run-time adaptation compared to a laser cutter that potentially cuts out a different form every time. A second selection criterion is whether the architecture meets the real-time requirements of two communicating machines. When two robots need to interact to jointly lift a physical object, exchanging messages via an SSB in Architecture D might not be able to deliver messages quickly enough.

6   Related Work

Software architecture research is an active topic in the cyber physical (production) systems community. Ahmad and Babar [1] show that the last decades has seen adoption of software development paradigms in robotics. As robots are a specialisation of CPS, we expect a similar development for the CPS and CPPS community. Pisching et al. [10] propose to use service-oriented architectures for CPPS and define a layout for CPS to behave as services. Thramboulidis et al. [11] investigate the usage of CPS as microservices. Others develop architectures, usually based on patterns studied well already in software architectures [12,13]. Their goal is to improve the compatibility between components, there is only little focus on runtime adaptation. None of the above works analysed considers frequent software reconfiguration or in-situ adaptation. This is a topic heavily investigated in the software architecture community. Several papers propose a plethora of approaches with many of them being relevant to CPS.

Oreizy, Medvidovic and Taylor [2] gathered an extensive survey on existing solutions and styles for flexible software. Michalik et al. [14] determine which code needs to be updated on a system, based on software product lines. The technology would be a key enabler for lot size one, yet it is left open how the actual software update is executed. Holvoet, Weyns and Valckenaers [15] identify patterns for delegate multi-agent systems that allow great reconfigurability at the level of replacing and rewiring components. They are great visions for future shopfloors, but might need several steps to be introduced in existing manufacturing environments. Fallah, Wolny and Wimmer [16] propose a framework that uses SysML to model and execute a production process. Their approach has a strong distinction between machines and machine operators, which we consider hampering when it comes to mixed scenarios, where machines should be replaced by humans or vice versa. Moreover, the tools of SysML are less suited to model dynamic processes compared to e.g. BPMN or SBPM. Other approaches introduce platform-specific "connectors" [17] or "bindings" [18] and platform-independent coordination middleware. Prehofer and Zoitl [19] extend this concept of platform-specific access layer (a.k.a. "thin controller") with the capability to receive control code at runtime. Though various architectures exist for robotic systems [1, 20], CPPS go in scope beyond a single machine or robot and hence have to satisfy stricter requirements [21, 22].

7   Conclusions

We motivated the need for architectural adaptability in cyber physical production systems. Using the BASE framework, we showed how Behavior, Asynchrony, State, and Execution aspects affect an architecture's adaptability. We presented three existing and two novel architectures and discussed what makes them adaptable. While not the only architecture selection criterion, being aware of the limits of adaptability of a particular architecture is of uttermost importance when designing for future CPPS.

While this paper focused on the small scale interactions and adaptability of a few machines (and/or robots) for production, the adaptability on higher levels such as covering the complete shop floor are not very well understood yet. Our next steps focus on investigating how architectural styles and patterns apply for adapting at such higher-levels, especially in the presence of the various architectures presented in this paper.

Acknowledgement. Supported in part by ENGEL Austria GmbH and Pro2Future, a COMET K1-Centre of the Austrian Research Promotion Agency (FFG), grant no. 854184.

References

1. Ahmad, A., Babar, M.A.: Software architectures for robotic systems: a systematic mapping study. J. Syst. Softw. **122**, 16–39 (2016)
2. Oreizy, P., Medvidovic, N., Taylor, R.N.: Runtime software adaptation: framework, approaches, and styles. In: Companion of the 30th International Conference on Software engineering, pp. 899–910. ACM (2008)
3. Mahnke, W., Leitner, S.-H., Damm, M.: OPC Unified Architecture. Springer, Heidelberg (2009)
4. Pauker, F., Mangler, J., Rinderle-Ma, S., Pollak, C.: Centurio.work - modular secure manufacturing orchestration. In: 16th International Conference on Business Process Management 2018, pp. 164–171 (2018)
5. Strasser, T., et al.: Framework for distributed industrial automation and control (4diac). In: 2008 6th IEEE International Conference on Industrial Informatics, pp. 283–288 (2008)
6. Oreizy, P., Medvidovic, N., Taylor, R.N.: Architecture-based runtime software evolution. In: Proceedings of the 20th International Conference on Software Engineering, pp. 177–186. IEEE Computer Society, Washington, DC (1998)
7. Taylor, R., Medvidovic, N., Oreizy, P.: Architectural styles for runtime software adaptation. In: 2009 Joint IEEE/IFIP Conference on Software Architecture European Conference on Software Architecture, pp. 171–180 (2009)

8. Garlan, D., Cheng, S., Huang, A., Schmerl, B., Steenkiste, P.: Rainbow: architecture-based self-adaptation with reusable infrastructure. Computer **37**(10), 46–54 (2004)
9. Dorn, C., Taylor, R.N.: Coupling software architecture and human architecture for collaboration-aware system adaptation. In: Proceedings of the 2013 International Conference on Software Engineering, pp. 53–62. IEEE Press (2013)
10. Pisching, M.A., Junqueira, F., Filho, D.J., Miyagi, P.E.: An architecture based on IoT and CPS to organize and locate services. In: 2016 IEEE 21st International Conference on Emerging Technologies and Factory Automation (ETFA), pp. 1–4 (2016)
11. Thramboulidis, K., Vachtsevanou, D.C., Solanos, A.: Cyber-physical microservices: an IoT-based framework for manufacturing systems. In: 2018 IEEE Industrial Cyber-Physical Systems (ICPS), pp. 232–239 (2018)
12. Hussnain, A., Ferrer, B.R., Lastra, J.L.M.: Towards the deployment of cloud robotics at factory shop floors: a prototype for smart material handling. In: 2018 IEEE Industrial Cyber-Physical Systems (ICPS), pp. 44–50 (2018)
13. Spinelli, S., Cataldo, A., Pallucca, G., Brusaferri, A.: A distributed control architecture for a reconfigurable manufacturing plant. In: 2018 IEEE Industrial Cyber-Physical Systems (ICPS), pp. 673–678 (2018)
14. Michalik, B., Weyns, D., Boucke, N., Helleboogh, A.: Supporting online updates of software product lines: a controlled experiment. In: 2011 International Symposium on Empirical Software Engineering and Measurement, pp. 187–196 (2011)
15. Holvoet, T., Weyns, D., Valckenaers, P.: Patterns of delegate MAS. In: 2009 Third IEEE International Conference on Self-Adaptive and Self-Organizing Systems, pp. 1–9 (2009)
16. Fallah, S.M., Wolny, S., Wimmer, M.: Towards model-integrated service-oriented manufacturing execution system. In: 2016 1st International Workshop on Cyber-Physical Production Systems (CPPS), pp. 1–5 (2016)
17. Malek, S., Mikic-Rakic, M., Medvidovic, N.: A style-aware architectural middleware for resource-constrained, distributed systems. IEEE Trans. Softw. Eng. **31**, 256–272 (2005)
18. Hallsteinsen, S., et al.: A development framework and methodology for self-adapting applications in ubiquitous computing environments. J. Syst. Softw. **85**(12), 2840–2859 (2012)
19. Prehofer, C., Zoitl, A.: Towards flexible and adaptive productions systems based on virtual cloud-based control. In: Proceedings of the 2014 IEEE Emerging Technology and Factory Automation (ETFA), pp. 1–4 (2014)
20. Georgas, J.C., Taylor, R.N.: An architectural style perspective on dynamic robotic architectures. In: Proceedings of the IEEE Second International Workshop on Software Development and Integration in Robotics (SDIR 2007), Rome, Italy, p. 6 (2007)
21. Hu, L., Xie, N., Kuang, Z., Zhao, K.: Review of cyber-physical system architecture. In: 2012 IEEE 15th International Symposium on Object/Component/Service-Oriented Real-Time Distributed Computing Workshops, pp. 25–30 (2012)
22. Sadiku, M., Wang, Y., Cui, S., Musa, S.: Cyber-physical systems: a literature review. Eur. Sci. J. **13**(36), 52–58 (2017). ISSN 1857-7881

Quality Attributes

Optimising Architectures
for Performance, Cost, and Security

Rajitha Yasaweerasinghelage[1,2]($\boxtimes$), Mark Staples[1,2], Hye-Young Paik[1,2],
and Ingo Weber[1,2]

[1] Data61, CSIRO, Level 5, 13 Garden Street, Eveleigh, NSW 2015, Australia
{rajitha.yasaweerasinghelage,mark.staples,
hye-young.paik,ingo.weber}@data61.csiro.au
[2] School of Computer Science and Engineering, University of New South Wales,
Sydney, NSW 2052, Australia

Abstract. Deciding on the optimal architecture of a software system is difficult, as the number of design alternatives and component interactions can be overwhelmingly large. Adding security considerations can make architecture evaluation even more challenging. Existing model-based approaches for architecture optimisation usually focus on performance and cost constraints. This paper proposes a model-based architecture optimisation approach that advances the state-of-the-art by adding security constraints. The proposed approach is implemented in a prototype tool, by extending Palladio Component Model (PCM) and PerOpteryx. Through a laboratory-based evaluation study of a multi-party confidential data analytics system, we show how our tool discovers secure architectural design options on the Pareto frontier of cost and performance.

Keywords: Software architecture · Software performance ·
Data security · Architecture optimisation

1 Introduction

Many software systems today are complex, with thousands of deployed components and many stakeholders [19]. With increasing complexity, there is increasing development cost. Non-functional requirements for systems often include response time, cost of development and operation, and security. When developing systems, software architecture should support these requirements effectively.

There are inter-dependencies and trade-offs between quality attributes like performance, cost, and security. For example, secure components are generally more costly than non-secure components. Prior work reports costs of $10,000 per line of code to develop highly-secure components, compared to $30–$40 per line of code for less-secure components [7,11]. When designing systems with critical requirements for performance, cost, and security, architects try to achieve optimal trade-offs between them. In a large design space, with many components

T. Bures et al. (Eds.): ECSA 2019, LNCS 11681, pp. 161–177, 2019.
https://doi.org/10.1007/978-3-030-29983-5_11

and design options, finding designs with good trade-offs is challenging, even for experienced architects. Manually assessing and comparing quality attributes for even a small number of design alternatives is difficult and error-prone.

Model-based design is now a common practice, and helps architects explore options during design. Many architecture modelling and optimisation methods have been studied [2–4]. There are well-established methods for optimising deployment architecture based on the performance of the system [13,16], costs of development, deployment, and maintenance [16], and other constraints such as energy consumption [21]. However, security constraints and policies are not yet well-treated in existing literature on architectural optimisation [1].

In this paper, we propose a new approach for optimising for performance, cost, and security in architectural design. We demonstrate the feasibility of the approach by implementing a prototype which extends the Palladio Component Model [4] and PerOpteryx optimisation tool [13] to support static *taint* analysis. One challenge in designing secure systems is defining and evaluating system security. Optimisation techniques require automated assessments. Static taint analysis is a simple automatic security analysis approach. Taint analysis is not a perfect model of security, but is a popular technique for identification of architecture-level vulnerabilities related to data propagation in the design phase [22]. Although our prototype uses taint analysis, our approach is more general and we discuss the use of other techniques for security analysis.

The main contributions of this paper are: an approach for architectural optimisation for cost, performance, and security; a model and method for taint analysis for security analysis for Palladio and PerOpteryx; and an evaluation of the approach on an industrial use case demonstrating feasibility and the ability to generate useful insights: in the case study, best performance and cost were achieved by non-secure architectures, but secure architectures were not far behind. Also, the approach discovered distinctive design options on the Pareto frontier of cost and performance for secure designs.

The paper structured is as follows. In Sect. 2, we introduce existing technologies relevant to the proposed approach. Then we provide an overview of the proposed method in Sect. 3. Section 4 provides details about modelling and optimisation through a running example. We discuss and compare literature closely related to this work in Sect. 5, propose suggestions for future work in Sect. 6 and conclude the paper with Sect. 7.

2   Background

This section reviews: architecture performance modelling; architecture design space exploration and deployment optimisation; and static taint analysis.

2.1   Architecture Performance Modelling

Architectural models capture the system structure by representing the links between components. Performance characteristics are associated with these components and their composition. Popular frameworks for architectural modelling are the Palladio Component Model (PCM) [18], and Descartes Modelling Language [12]. Architectural models can incorporate additional non-functional attributes associated with the system structure, such as latency, resource usage, cost and throughput. The resulting models can be used by simulation engines or analytical solvers to analyse non-functional properties [5]. Simulation-based prediction can be time-consuming, but provides more flexibility for modelling.

Palladio Component Model (PCM). [18] is the platform used in this paper to model architecture performance characteristics. Palladio was selected as it is freely available, supports simulation, provides a familiar 'UML-like' interface for model creation, and has the flexibility to incorporate extensions such as architectural optimisation tools [8,13], new qualities [21], and new kinds of systems [23]. The modelling concepts in Palladio align with component-based development paradigm and support component reuse across models.

2.2 Architecture Design Space Exploration and Deployment Architecture Optimisation

Automated software architecture exploration based on architecture models is increasingly popular in industry. Aleti et al. [1] surveys existing methods.

PerOpteryx. [13] is an automated design space exploration tool for PCM, capable of exploring many degrees of freedom. PerOpteryx starts with a PCM instance and a set of design decision models that describe how the architecture can be changed. Automated search over this design space is performed using a genetic algorithm. For each generation in the search, a Palladio instance is generated and analysed to evaluate quality attributes such as performance and cost.

PerOpteryx is capable of optimising multiple quality attributes by searching for Pareto-optimal candidates. A candidate is Pareto optimal if there exists no other candidate that is better across all quality metrics. A set of Pareto-optimal candidates approximate the set of globally Pareto-optimal candidates [8].

2.3 Static Taint Analysis

Defining meaningful quantitative metrics for security is challenging. There have been a number of approaches proposed, but in our opinion, there is no single generic method suitable for all applications (see Sect. 5). In this paper, to simplify our demonstration of security analytics for optimisation, we use taint analysis. Taint analysis results in a binary secure/not-secure evaluation for a system, which is arguably the most challenging kind of metric for use in optimisation. Taint analysis is simple but useful in identifying fundamental issues in the data flow of the system, as a form of information flow analysis [17,22].

Taint is used to represent the reach of an attack within a system. As shown in Fig. 1, taint starts at a taint source (node 1), which could be a component exposed to the external environment, then flows to connected components. Taint

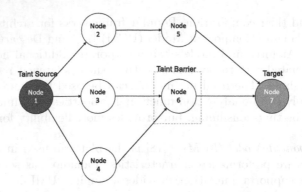

Fig. 1. Graph taint analysis, illustrating an insecure system. Bad 'taint' from the source Node 1 to the critical target Node 7, via a path through Node 2, despite being blocked from flowing through the taint barrier at Node 6.

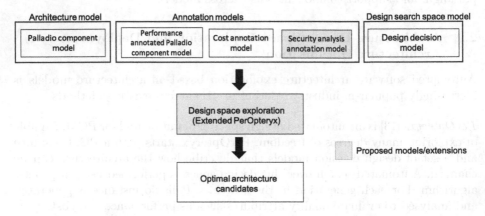

Fig. 2. Method overview, highlighting extensions proposed in this paper.

blockers (e.g. node 6) are secure components which prevent further propagation of taint. A system security property defines the set of critical components (e.g. node 7) which must remain free of taint after maximal propagation of taint through the system. The system in Fig. 1 is not secure, because taint can flow through non-secure components (e.g. nodes 2, 5) to the critical component.

3   Method Overview

Our approach, shown in Fig. 2, combines architecture-level performance modelling, simulation and optimisation. We use three types of models to represent the system: the initial architecture model, annotation models, and the design search space model. We use the Palladio Component Model (PCM) tool for the underlying architecture model. To define annotation models, we annotate PCM with information about three quality attributes; performance, cost, and security.

The performance annotation model is supported directly in PCM, and the Palladio cost extension is used for cost annotations. The security model is defined separately. In Sect. 3.1, we describe how each quality attribute is modelled.

For the design search space model, we used Palladio Design Decision Diagrams. These are used to generate candidate architectures in the optimisation phase. Some design options are specific to security architecture. For example, a component might be modelled as being a secure component that works as a taint barrier. So, the default Palladio Design Decision Diagrams need to be extended to accommodate these model elements.

For design space exploration, we use PerOpteryx optimisation tool with modifications to use these extended security annotation models. The output is a set of generated Pareto-optimal candidate architectures, which can be used by experts to select the final design.

3.1   Quality Attribute Modelling for the Optimisation

The first step of the proposed approach is to model each quality attribute.

Performance Modelling. We used PCM performance analysis, as discussed in the literature [9], which has been shown to be sufficiently accurate for various types of applications, including the example system discussed in this paper. This demonstrates that our approach allows the reuse of previously-developed Palladio performance models.

The security level of a component may affect the resource utilisation of the component, impacting the overall performance of the system. (For example, encrypting communications may incur a performance overhead.) In such cases, a component with one kind of functionality is modelled with different performance (and security) properties as design alternatives, and are used for design exploration during optimisation.

Cost Modelling. We use the existing and well-studied Palladio cost modelling extension for modelling cost attributes. This can capture different types of costs such as component costs, variable and fixed resource costs, and networking costs.

The security level of a component can impact its cost. For example, secure components are more expensive to develop than less-secure components. We model a component with one kind of functionality as multiple alternative components that represent different levels of security each with a corresponding cost in the cost model. Then we use those component alternatives when exploring options during optimisation.

Security Modelling. A key contribution of this paper is integrating security analysis into automatic design space exploration. Unlike other quality attributes such as performance and cost, security is not easily quantifiable. Security analyses often only make Boolean judgements about system security (i.e., secure, or not), but some analyses give continuous metrics of security (e.g., expected time to next attack). In this paper, we demonstrate our approach using taint analysis as the basis for security analysis. However, our general approach could be adapted to use other security analysis metrics, as discussed in Sect. 5.

4   Modelling and Optimising

The prototype for our approach uses taint analysis (see Sect. 2.3) as the security analysis technique. As our goal is to optimise performance and cost while satisfying a security requirement, we developed an extension for integrating taint analysis with existing Palladio Models and incorporating taint properties into the PerOpteryx optimisation. To describe the modelling and optimisation process, we use a running example based on a privacy-preserving computing system called N1Analytics[1] [9]. This section provides details about the extension and how it works for the running example. Finally, we discuss how the architecture of the N1 Analytics system can be optimised for performance, cost, and taint properties.

4.1   Running Example

N1Analytics is a platform that allows statistical analyses using data distributed among multiple providers, while maintaining data confidentiality between the providers. Following the main principles of N1Analytics systems, we designed an initial abstract architecture, to illustrate some of the critical features of our proposed approach. It should be noted that this abstract architecture differs from actual N1Analytics implementations.

Base Deployment Architecture. Figure 3 presents the federated deployment architecture of the N1Analytics platform. Data providers and coordinators are the two main building blocks. In an analytics operation, the coordinators have the private key to decrypt the computed results but do not have access to plain or encrypted input data. They only have a partial output that is not itself capable of revealing plaintext results.

The private key is not accessible to the data providers, so they cannot violate the privacy of the encrypted input data shared with them. Data providers and coordinators may have a set of worker nodes to perform their operations. It is possible to move data between nodes, as long as they preserve the protocol: the coordinator should not have access to the encrypted data, and data providers should not have access to the private keys.

---

[1] https://www.n1analytics.com.

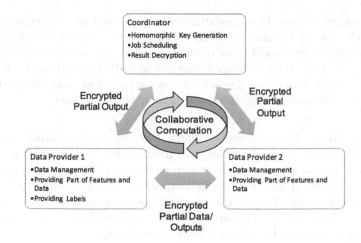

Fig. 3. N1Analytics platform distributed architecture

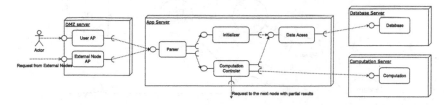

Fig. 4. N1Analytics component architecture in UML notation

Component Architecture. To simplify the demonstration, we modify the architecture of the N1Analytics system used in our earlier work [24] by assuming that the basic component architecture of the coordinator and each data provider is similar. Even so, the resource utilisation and the functionality of each node are different. Notably, the computation overhead and workflow of each node are significantly different. We model each node separately to reflect those differences. Figure 4 presents the architecture model we considered.

4.2 Modelling System for Optimisation

Performance Modelling. We modelled performance characteristics following the general Palladio approach. Our model of the N1Analytics system is similar to that presented in our earlier work [24], but introduces changes to demonstrate cost-based optimization and security-critical components.

In [24], the N1Analytics system was deployed in a test environment, and the resource utilisation of each development component was measured. Then, each development component was mapped to a functional component to be used in the model architecture. The architecture is modelled in PCM using functional components, and the resource utilisation of each component is derived from microbenchmark results. Resource utilisation is defined as a function of work-load and the size of the data set. The resource environment definition, usage model, and allocation model were defined based on the design specification of the system. We reuse their published abstract model[2], but with minor modifications to introduce a user access point component, a parser, and database access component for demonstrating data propagation design options.

Cost Modelling. We used the standard Palladio Cost modelling approach. Note that if a single component can have multiple levels of security, it needs to be modelled as multiple alternative components with different cost properties. Similarly, when introducing additional components such as secure load balancers and secure bridging interfaces, base costs and operating costs need to be specified accordingly. There will also be an overhead for operation cost, because some secure components may have higher resource utilisation.

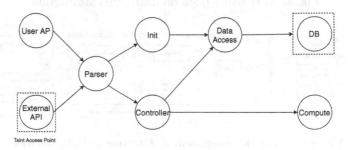

Fig. 5. Taint graph

Security Modelling - Modelling Taint Properties. We extended PCM to define taint properties of the system. These properties are then used in the optimisation algorithm. First, the extension retrieves the candidate system architecture and converts to a taint graph as shown in Fig. 5.

In the proposed method, each software component can be *taint safe* or *taint unsafe*. Assigning this state to a component, based on whether it is secure or not, is a decision for the model designer, as discussed further in Sect. 6. Taint safe components act as a taint barrier preventing taint propagation from that point onwards. In this study, our cost models assume that taint safe components cost more than their taint unsafe counterparts.

From an initial taint setting, we analyse the graph by graph search, spreading taint except through taint safe components. The search includes cyclic dependencies which might spread taint over multiple passes. The results about whether security critical components become tainted are provided to the optimisation engine (see Sect. 4.4).

---

[2] https://doi.org/10.6084/m9.figshare.5960014.v1.

When modelling the N1Analytics architecture, we represent each component twice, with secure and non-secure alternatives, each with a different cost. Our not-unrealistic assumption is that a secure component is ten times more expensive than its non-secure version. Additionally, to explore the impact of security-specific design patterns, we define two optional secure bridge components in front of the parser and the data access component. Our experiments are executed with and without these secure bridging components.

4.3 Additional Design Options

We modelled additional architectural design alternatives related to data propagation of the system and basic security policies in Design Decision Diagrams. These define the exploration space for architecture optimisation.

In this paper, we include design options directly related to the security properties. The design options model their impact on the overall performance, cost, and security of the analysed architecture. These design options are used alongside other general architecture design options.

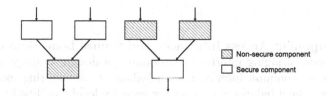

Fig. 6. Design option - taint blockers/secure components

Taint Blockers/ Secure Components. Developing a secure component is significantly more expensive than developing a component using a standard development process. To be cost-optimal, only a limited number of components can be secure.

As illustrated in Fig. 6, a component can be made taint safe to act as a taint barrier protecting critical components and thus ensuring system security. A secure component may have higher resource utilisation compared to less-secure components due to validity checks, or encryption, and this is also reflected in the performance models.

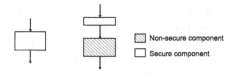

Fig. 7. Design option - secure bridging interfaces

Secure Bridging Interfaces. There is a significant cost of securing components if those components are large. One design strategy to prevent taint propagation is to implement secure bridging interfaces in-between components, as shown in Fig. 7. A typical bridging interface component is small compared to major functional components because it focuses on enforcing key security properties. Being smaller, their development cost can be significantly lower. On the other hand, introducing a bridging interface component adds new fundamental cost for developing the component, increases resource utilisation, and may act as a performance bottleneck.

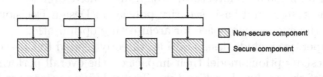

Fig. 8. Design option - secure component access interfaces and secure load balancers

Secure Component Access Interfaces and Secure Load Balancers. Similar to the secure bridging interface components, a design strategy might be to introduce secure common interfaces/load balancers, or to bring existing common interfaces/ load balancers to a higher security level (see Fig. 8). Generally, these components are smaller than major functional components, and so have significantly lower development cost. However, these components also can be bottlenecks to the system and incur additional base development cost. In addition, as load balancer interfaces can be concurrently accessed by multiple components with different resource utilisation, we have to consider such interactions when optimising the system under different workloads.

4.4   Model Optimisation

We started the optimisation with the architecture shown in Fig. 4. Even though the proposed approach can handle multiple components defined as taint starting points or security critical systems, for the simplicity of illustration we define the *external access* component as the taint starting point and the *database* component as the only security-critical component. In the initial architecture, all components are non-secure.

In the Design Decision Model, we allow every component except access points and databases to be made taint safe or taint unsafe. Additionally, we defined optional trusted bridge components before the parser and computation controller. Access points, databases, and computation components should only be allocated to the DMZ server, database server, and computation server respectively. Other components can be allocated to any server.

We modelled the example system using Palladio Workbench version 4.0 using SimuCom Bench for performance analysis with Sensor Framework as the persistence framework. For design space exploration we used PerOpteryx version 4.0 with slight modifications for accommodating taint analysis when optimising. We executed the optimisation on a machine with a 2.7 GHz Intel Core i5 CPU and 8 GB main memory. It took approximately 4 h to run 500 iterations of the simulation.

4.5 Results

The selection of optimal components for a system depends on its requirements. Here we assume the reasonable goal is the *lowest-cost secure architecture that achieves a response time above a given threshold.*

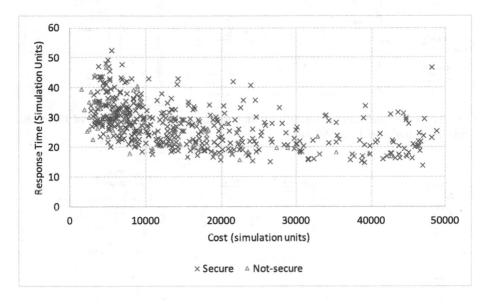

Fig. 9. Response time and cost of candidate architectures generated by PerOpteryx. (Color figure online)

Figure 9 plots the identified candidate architectures as a distribution of response time and cost. The red dot indicates the initial architecture configuration (i.e. Fig. 4) fed into the system. Secure candidates are shown as blue diagonal crosses, and non-secure candidates are shown with an orange plus. As can be seen, the genetic algorithm generated fewer non-secure candidates than secure candidates. Importantly, the results show that when the architecture is secure the system tends to be more expensive and have inferior performance. In other words, *if security is ignored when picking a candidate architecture, one would likely pick a non-secure architecture.* However, there are secure alternatives with just slightly inferior cost and performance.

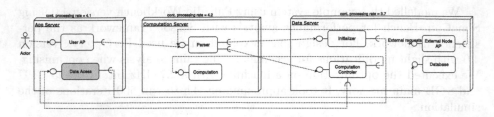

Fig. 10. Secure candidate architecture with low cost where the simulated cost is 2,778 units. Simulated response time of this architecture is 33.9 units.

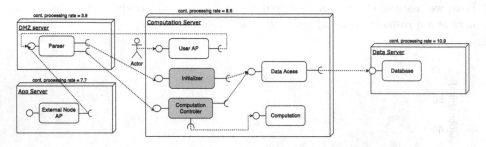

Fig. 11. Secure candidate architecture with low simulated response time of 13.4 units where simulated cost is 46,692 units.

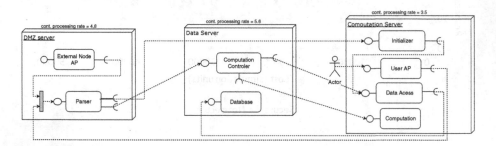

Fig. 12. Secure intermediate point where a bridge component has been introduced. Cost is 2,832 units and response time is 32.1 units.

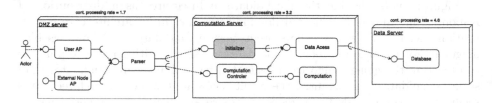

Fig. 13. Generated non-secure architecture. Simulated cost is low as 1,580 and response time is 37.8 units. The system is non-secure despite one component being secure.

For some concrete examples, Fig. 10 shows the cheapest secure architecture that costs 2,778 units but has 33.9 units response time. Figure 11 illustrates the best performing secure architecture identified, which has a response time of 13.4 units but costs of 46,692 units. Figure 13 shows a non-secure architecture which has cost low as 1,580 while response time is 37.8. From these examples, it is evident that this method is capable of generating wide range of feasible candidate architectures based on given design options. This is true for all the candidates.

Identifying vastly different architectures with similar performance, cost and security can be beneficial in some cases. The difference between those architectures can be measured by calculating the edit distance between two Palladio instances by aggregating the weighted difference of each design option. We assigned a lower weight for differences in the resource environment and higher weight for structural changes to identify architectures with vastly different structural changes. Figures 10 and 12 show a pair of such alternative architectures we identified by comparing distance between alternatives, i.e., structurally quite different but with similar performance and cost, and both secure.

5 Related Work

Here we compare our work to related security modelling and analysis approaches.

Design Space Exploration for Security. Eunsuk Kang [10] identifies the importance of design space exploration for security and outlines key elements of a framework intended to support it. The main focus of his work is on low-level system design and configuration, which is not directly applicable to architecture level design exploration.

Security Modelling Using Palladio Component Model. Busch et al. [6] provide a Palladio extension to predict the mean time to the next security incident. Their methodology is to model what to protect (e.g., data of a database), different ways to access the protected data (e.g., hacking the fronted and then hacking the non-public database), attacker's experience, available knowledge about the system, and the quality of the components in the system. The model can then predict the mean time to the next security incident.

Busch et al.'s approach facilitates security comparison of different architectures and can be used to identify secure architectures. The main limitation is the difficulty of identifying specific model parameters such as the experience of an attacker or quality of a component. It is also complicated to model insider attacks. Nonetheless, the approach defines a metric for system security that might be able to be incorporated into the general approach proposed in this paper.

Quantifying Security. Sharma et al. [20] propose to use Discrete-Time Markov Chains (DTMCs) to model software architecture. This is a hierarchical model that captures quality attributes of components, including security. They quantify security through a model that represents the probability of exposing the vulnerability of a component in a single execution and its effect on system security. This model considers how often a certain component is accessed, which is ignored in our approach based on the assumption that an attacker accesses a component as often as needed. Sharma et al. [20] designed the model to consider the system as broken if at least one component is successfully attacked. Yet, as the systems we consider are typically deployed on several machines, a broken component does not mean that the whole system is compromised. Hence, we designed our approach to consider the control flow of a system as could be followed by an attacker.

Madan et al. [15] propose a Semi-Markov process-based model to quantify security for intrusion-tolerant systems. This model is based on two state-transition models describing how the system behaves under attack. Their scope is Denial-of-Service (DoS) and attacks to compromise the system. The objective of the models is to calculate the Mean Time To Security Failure, to quantify the security of the system. In contrast to this model, our approach can assess the security of component-based architectures and is not restricted to monolithic systems.

SECOMO. SECOMO (Security Cost Model) [14] is a cost modelling technique associated with a framework for risk management in telecommunications. It estimates the effort required to conduct a risk management project in a networked environment. This estimation forms a basis for other task estimations such as the cost, human resources and duration of the project. The estimations are calculated using network size and parameters called scale factors and effort multipliers, which combined together can provide a measure for the security task complexity.

6   Discussion and Future Work

Unlike performance and cost, security is not easily quantifiable. Although security must be considered when making architecture design decisions, the complicated nature of security makes it difficult to follow traditional automated design optimisation practices. In this paper, we demonstrated that, instead of directly modelling the security of architecture, it is possible to perform architecture optimisation using security analysis techniques in conjunction with other quantifiable system properties (cost, performance). We used taint analysis as an example architecture security analysis technique to demonstrate the proposed approach.

Based on system security requirements and a domain of operation, we expect it would be possible to use alternative security analysis techniques such as those discussed in Sect. 5 in place of taint analysis. By using alternative security analysis techniques, users may better identify security vulnerabilities relevant to their domain. We plan to extend this work by developing a wider range of security analysis techniques to be used along with Palladio component model, covering different aspects of security analysis.

In an architectural model, secure components may have higher cost, because of the time and resources required to secure and provide assurance for that component. This may include formal security evaluation techniques such as Evaluation Assurance Level (EAL). These assumptions of increased cost are reasonable, but could be refined or tailored in specific industries or organisations if empirical cost data is available. The security of a component can also depend on the domain. For example, a component might be sufficiently secure for a small-scale software system with no significant security threats, but be non-secure for a highly security-critical system in a hostile environment.

PerOpteryx performs a heuristic search on the design space. So it is not guaranteed to find the optimal or simplest viable architecture. Different initial architectures may converge to different sub-optimal Pareto candidates. The system also does not find a single optimal architecture, but instead defines a range of optimal alternatives on the Pareto frontier. It is the architect's responsibility to choose the final architecture. The architectures discussed here are for illustration purposes only. In real-world scenarios, all the relevant components need to be modelled with higher detail in order to get more accurate results.

Taint analysis technique we chose for the evaluation of the proposed approach outputs a binary value for the security. In the real world, architects may want to use continuous values such as mean time for an attack (see Sect. 5). In such cases, they can apply the same principles we propose and optimise the system for multi-objectives considering security as another dimension because PerOpteryx inherently supports multi-objective optimisations.

7   Conclusion

This paper proposes a new method that incorporates security analysis techniques, in addition to cost and performance (latency), when automatically exploring and optimising system architecture designs. We demonstrate our approach using taint analysis, a basic architecture security analysis technique where secure components stopped propagation of taint from attackers to security-critical components, as the basis for security analysis. We prototyped the approach by extending the Palladio Component model and PerOpteryx systems. The extensions include support for our security modelling and analysis. We reported on the experiment and demonstrate the feasibility of using the approach, illustrating contrasting examples of generated secure system architectures on the cost/performance Pareto frontier.

The evaluation was performed on an industrial example of a secure system architecture for a privacy-preserving computing system. The case study highlighted the usefulness of the approach, by finding that best performance and cost were achieved by non-secure architectures – secure architectures were not far behind, and a variety of distinct design options were identified. Our approach is aimed at supporting architects in identifying and selecting good architecture during the design phase, considering security, cost and performance. In future work, we plan to augment the prototype with support for other security models and analysis techniques.

References

1. Aleti, A., Buhnova, B., Grunske, L., Koziolek, A., Meedeniya, I.: Software architecture optimization methods: a systematic literature review. IEEE Trans. Softw. Eng. **39**(5), 658–683 (2013)
2. Ardagna, D., Casale, G., Ciavotta, M., Pérez, J.F., Wang, W.: Quality-of-service in cloud computing: modeling techniques and their applications. J. Internet Serv. Appl. **5**, 5–11 (2014)
3. Balsamo, S., Di Marco, A., Inverardi, P., Simeoni, M.: Model-based performance prediction in software development: a survey. IEEE Trans. Softw. Eng. **30**(5), 295–310 (2004)
4. Becker, S., Koziolek, H., Reussner, R.: The Palladio component model for model-driven performance prediction. J. Syst. Softw. **82**(1), 3–22 (2009)
5. Brunnert, A., et al.: Performance-oriented DevOps: a research agenda. arXiv preprint arXiv:1508.04752 (2015)
6. Busch, A., Strittmatter, M., Koziolek, A.: Assessing security to compare architecture alternatives of component-based systems. In: International Conference on Software Quality, Reliability and Security. IEEE (2015)
7. Colbert, E., Boehm, B.: Cost estimation for secure software & systems. In: ISPA/SCEA 2008 Joint International Conference (2008)
8. De Gooijer, T., Jansen, A., Koziolek, H., Koziolek, A.: An industrial case study of performance and cost design space exploration. In: International Conference on Performance Engineering. ACM (2012)
9. Djatmiko, M., et al.: Privacy-preserving entity resolution and logistic regression on encrypted data. In: Private and Secure Machine Learning (PSML) (2017)
10. Kang, E.: Design space exploration for security. In: 2016 IEEE Cybersecurity Development (SecDev), pp. 30–36. IEEE (2016)
11. Klein, G., et al.: seL4: formal verification of an OS kernel. In: Symposium on Operating Systems Principles. ACM (2009)
12. Kounev, S., Brosig, F., Huber, N.: The Descartes modeling language. Department of Computer Science, University of Wuerzburg, Technical report (2014)
13. Koziolek, A., Koziolek, H., Reussner, R.: PerOpteryx: automated application of tactics in multi-objective software architecture optimization. In: Proceedings of the QoSA & ISARCS. ACM (2011)
14. Krichene, J., Boudriga, N., Fatmi, S.: SECOMO: an estimation cost model for risk management projects. In: International Conference on Telecommunications, ConTEL 2003, vol. 2. IEEE (2003)
15. Madan, B.B., Goševa-Popstojanova, K., Vaidyanathan, K., Trivedi, K.S.: A method for modeling and quantifying the security attributes of intrusion tolerant systems. Perform. Eval. **56**(1–4), 167–186 (2004)

16. Martens, A., Koziolek, H., Becker, S., Reussner, R.: Automatically improve software architecture models for performance, reliability, and cost using evolutionary algorithms. In: International Conference on Performance Engineering (ICPE) (2010)
17. Newsome, J., Song, D.X.: Dynamic taint analysis for automatic detection, analysis, and signature generation of exploits on commodity software. In: NDSS, vol. 5. Internet Society (2005)
18. Reussner, R.H., et al.: Modeling and Simulating Software Architectures: The Palladio Approach. MIT Press, Cambridge (2016)
19. Safwat, A., Senousy, M.: Addressing challenges of ultra large scale system on requirements engineering. Procedia Comput. Sci. **65**, 442–449 (2015)
20. Sharma, V.S., Trivedi, K.S.: Architecture based analysis of performance, reliability and security of software systems. In: International Workshop on Software and Performance. ACM (2005)
21. Willnecker, F., Brunnert, A., Krcmar, H.: Predicting energy consumption by extending the Palladio component model. In: Symposium on Software Performance (2014)
22. Yang, Z., Yang, M.: LeakMiner: detect information leakage on android with static taint analysis. In: 2012 Third World Congress on Software Engineering (WCSE). IEEE (2012)
23. Yasaweerasinghelage, R., Staples, M., Weber, I.: Predicting latency of blockchain-based systems using architectural modelling and simulation. In: International Conference on Software Architecture (ICSA) (2017)
24. Yasaweerasinghelage, R., Staples, M., Weber, I., Paik, H.Y.: Predicting the performance of privacy-preserving data analytics using architecture modelling and simulation. In: International Conference on Software Architecture (ICSA) (2018)

QoS-Based Formation of Software Architectures in the Internet of Things

Martina De Sanctis[1], Romina Spalazzese[2], and Catia Trubiani[1][✉]

[1] Gran Sasso Science Institute, L'Aquila, Italy
{martina.desanctis,catia.trubiani}@gssi.it
[2] Department of Computer Science and Media Technology,
Internet of Things and People Research Center,
Malmö University, Malmö, Sweden
romina.spalazzese@mau.se

Abstract. Architecting Internet of Things (IoT) systems is very challenging due to the heterogeneity of connected objects and devices, and their dynamic variabilities such as mobility and availability. The complexity of this scenario is exacerbated when considering Quality-of-Service (QoS) constraints. Indeed, reasoning about multiple quality attributes, e.g., power consumption and response time, makes the management of IoT systems even more difficult since it is necessary to jointly evaluate multiple system characteristics. The focus of this paper is on modelling and analysing QoS-related characteristics in IoT architectures. To this end, we leverage on the concept of Emergent Architectures (EAs), i.e., a set of things temporarily cooperating to achieve a given goal, by intertwining EAs with QoS-related constraints. Our approach provides the automated formation of the *most suitable EAs* by means of a QoS-based optimisation problem. We developed an IoT case study and experimental results demonstrate the effectiveness of the proposed approach.

1 Introduction

The Internet of Things (IoT) refers to a complex network of interactive *things*, i.e., heterogeneous tags, sensors, actuators, objects, and devices that dynamically cooperate [1–3]. The IoT is exploited for the development of many applications spanning multiple domains, such as natural disasters, industrial automation, smart homes [4]. The IoT attracted the attention of companies, governments, and citizens, and has given rise to research in both industry and academia [5]. A recent estimation of the IoT market in the upcoming years has been quantified of being $1.7 trillion including nearly 50 billion things [6].

Nonetheless, building software architectures that support the execution of IoT systems brings new challenges, in fact non trivial choices are required when heterogeneous objects and devices must dynamically cooperate. The IoT environment changes dynamically, e.g., due to devices' availability or the user's mobility. Given the uncertainty in the operational environment (e.g., faulty things, capabilities appearing/disappearing at any moment), and the high diversity of things

© Springer Nature Switzerland AG 2019
T. Bures et al. (Eds.): ECSA 2019, LNCS 11681, pp. 178–194, 2019.
https://doi.org/10.1007/978-3-030-29983-5_12

dynamically available in different and often unknown places, it is not feasible to define a priori a unique software architecture. Moreover, communicating things may be also potentially resource-constrained. The peculiarity of the IoT domain is that services may show QoS-based characteristics that are platform-specific (e.g., the sensing of light level may be offered by multiple sensor devices, each of them showing a different QoS) and time-varying (e.g., actuators may be constrained by the battery level that changes at runtime), and this heterogeneity makes more complex the QoS-based evaluation of IoT software architectures. This paves the way for considering Quality-of-Service (QoS) concerns in IoT as first class citizens.

In the literature, several QoS-based methodologies have been proposed at various layers of the IoT architecture and different QoS factors, such as performance and reliability, have been considered [7]. However, there is still need for models, metrics, and tools that facilitate the interaction with the dynamically available things, thus to satisfy QoS-related goals, besides the functional ones. This paper focuses on the challenge of specifying IoT architectural models including QoS aspects and providing support for the *automatic* formation of the Emergent Architectures (EAs). EAs stem from Emergent Configurations (ECs), i.e., a set of things that connect and cooperate temporarily through their functionalities, applications, and services, to achieve a user goal [8,9]. Things are possibly smart connected objects (e.g., curtains) and devices (e.g., temperature sensors). More specifically, we are interested to derive the *most suitable* EAs, i.e., an *optimal set* of connected things cooperating to jointly address functional and extra-functional requirements.

In our previous work [10], we make use of Domain Objects (DOs), i.e., a service-based formalism [11], for forming and enacting ECs in the IoT domain. However, despite its proved effectiveness in the dynamic and automatic formation of ECs, we experienced improper usage of resources, even reflecting to end-users unsatisfaction. To tackle these issues, in this paper we extend both the DOs formalism and the approach in [10] where purely functional requirements can be specified, and QoS-related concerns were not considered at all. The specific contributions of this paper are: (i) a model-based approach that embeds the specification of QoS-related properties at the level of things; (ii) the automated formation of the most suitable EAs in the IoT relying on the selection of QoS-based optimal devices; (iii) a case study demonstrating the feasibility and effectiveness of the proposed approach.

The remainder of this paper is organised as follows. Section 2 describes an IoT scenario that we use throughout the paper, and some background information. Section 3 illustrates our approach. Section 4 presents the case study, explains experimental results, and discusses threats to validity. Section 5 reports related work, and Sect. 6 concludes the paper pointing out future research directions.

2 Motivating Example and Foundations

In this section we give a motivating scenario that will guide us through the paper and we describe some relevant background notions.

2.1   Smart Light Scenario

In this section we describe the IoT Smart Light (SL) scenario, where things cooperate to achieve a predefined light level in a lecture room. This scenario extends the one described in [10] by further including and managing extra-functional requirements. Consider, for instance, a university campus made by different buildings hosting diverse types of rooms, e.g., libraries, dormitories, classrooms, offices. Each room is equipped with several IoT things, i.e., light sensors, curtains, and lamps. The things, along with their functionalities, are configured to be controllable via a mobile application allowing authorized users to increase/decrease the light level while moving in different rooms, based on their needs. For instance, in a lecture room, the lecturer can decide to decrease the light level when giving a presentation through a projector or, to the contrary, to increase it when using the blackboard. As opposite, in a dormitory room, a student can decide to have a higher light level when studying and a lower one when resting. A possible way to achieve such goals is to dynamically identify an EA made, for instance, by the user's smartphone, a light sensor, and available curtain(s) and lamp(s). The selected light sensor measures the current light level in the room, and subsequently the lamps are turned on/off, and the curtains can be opened or closed.

Besides fulfilling the functional goals of this scenario (e.g., adjusting the light level), the mobile application committer and the final users are also interested in fulfilling extra-functional requirements. For instance, the committer may want to minimise the power consumption of all the devices installed in the campus, i.e., to positively impact on the campus energy bill, while guaranteeing users satisfaction. This means that users can set their own preferences modifying the default settings. Specifically: (i) light sensors display different sensing accuracy and users may require a certain accuracy level to get trustable estimations; (ii) curtains expose a time required for opening/closing them, and users may be interested in minimising it; (iii) lamps contribute with different light intensities, and users may select the ones that better match with the required light level.

2.2   Background

This work builds upon an existing approach called IoT-FED (Forming and enacting Emergent configurations through Domain objects in the IoT) [10] that exploits the Domain Object (DO) model, i.e., the building block of a design for adaptation [11].

Domain Objects. DOs allow the definition of independent and heterogeneous things/services in a uniform way. This means that developers can work at an abstract level without dealing with the heterogeneity of things and their communication protocols. Since the actual system can vary in different execution contexts, as it can be constituted by disparate things (e.g., sensors, actuators, smartphones) dynamically available, the DO model supports the systems realization at runtime, when the execution context is known.

To model things, developers wrap them as DOs. This task is done only *una tantum*, i.e., when a new device type/brand is available. Each DO implements its own behavior (i.e., the *core process*), which is meant to model its capability (e.g., the sensing capability of a sensor). At the same time, for its nominal execution, a DO can optionally require capabilities provided by other DOs (e.g., the lamp and curtain actuating capabilities are externally required by the SL application). In addition, it exposes one or more *fragments* (e.g., the sense light level fragment) describing offered services that can be *dynamically* discovered and used by other DOs. Both core process and fragments are modelled as processes, by means of the Adaptive Pervasive Flows Language (APFL) [12].

The dynamic cooperation among DOs is performed by exploiting a *refinement* mechanism. At design time, APFL allows the partial specification of the expected behaviour of a DO through *abstract activities*, i.e., activities that the DO does not implement itself; they are defined only in terms of a goal labelling them (e.g., sense the light) and they represent open points in DOs' processes and fragments. At runtime, the refinement mechanism makes abstract activities *refined* according to the (composition of) fragments offered by other DOs, whose execution leads to achieve the abstract activity's goal. This enables a *chain of refinements*, as will be later discussed (see Fig. 5). We adopt a refinement mechanism that makes use of advanced techniques for the dynamic and incremental service composition, and it is based on Artificial Intelligence (AI) planning [13]. For further details on DOs, we refer to [14] describing the prototype of a travel assistant application developed by using DOs technologies.

IoT-FED. The IoT-FED approach supports the formation and enactment of ECs by means of the DOs technologies. Given the *user goal type* (e.g., adjust light level) and the *goal spatial boundaries*, such as the location where the EC must be formed and enacted (e.g., the lecture room), the execution starts (e.g., from the SL application's DO). If existing, the EC is made up by the set of things whose corresponding DOs have been involved in the refinement process of all the encountered abstract activities, through the selection of their fragments.

Figure 1 shows an abstract framework [10] where the shaded box highlights the newly defined component for QoS-related concerns, whereas the boxes with the striped pattern highlight the components that have been modified to handle QoS aspects. In the following we describe the main components.

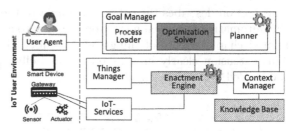

Fig. 1. Overview of our framework.

The *Goal Manager* is responsible for parsing the user goal and starting the EC formation process. It has three sub-components: (i) the Process Loader, responsible for specifying the user goal type and the spatial boundaries, and for loading the DO process corresponding to the specified goal type; (ii) the

Optimization Solver (that will be detailed in Sect. 3.1); (iii) the Planner responsible for the refinement of abstract activities in the loaded process. The *Things Manager* is responsible for managing available IoT things and DOs. It answers queries about available IoT things, their capabilities and locations; dynamically instantiates needed DOs, and handles co-relations among them. The *Enactment Engine* is mainly responsible for enacting the ECs. It (i) forms and enacts the ECs; (ii) sends instructions to IoT things (e.g., get sensor readings) through the Things Manager; (iii) handles the injection of the plans received by the Planner in place of the abstract activities and (iv) executes the final refined process that achieves the user goal. The *Context Manager* is responsible for maintaining the system knowledge. It retrieves data from the knowledge base (KB), parses received context from the Enactment Engine (e.g., new things states), and updates the KB. The *Knowledge Base* holds the internal system knowledge and includes repositories storing things operational states (e.g., if lights are turned on or off), the designed DOs, and the associations among things, DOs and corresponding capabilities. The *IoT Services* component enables the management and interaction with things, and it relies on the Amazon AWS-IoT cloud platform[1].

To make IoT things and services available in IoT-FED, a developer needs to do two main operations: (i) *register things in the AWS-IoT platform;* (ii) *model things, services and applications as DOs.* The REST endpoints generated by the platform are invoked in the DOs processes activities.

3   QoS-Based Approach

Our approach provides mechanisms for determining the near-optimal IoT-EAs that jointly satisfy functional and extra-functional requirements. In this section we use the SL scenario described in Sect. 2.1, where things cooperate for reaching the goal to set a predefined light level in a lecture room.

3.1   Overview of the Approach

This section describes the extensions made to the IoT-FED approach to enable the automatic QoS-based formation of EAs. To allow developers to specify QoS-related characteristics of things, we extended the Domain Objects formalism. This extension clearly impacts on the modelling phase of domain objects (see the shaded box in Fig. 2).

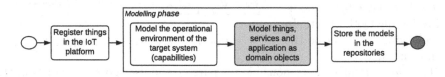

Fig. 2. IoT-FED extended guideline.

---

[1] https://aws.amazon.com/it/iot.

The specification of QoS-related characteristics, indeed, is performed at the level of DOs. In particular, each thing is associated to an arbitrary number of metrics inherited from its producer. Thus, we enhanced the specification of DOs (e.g., those representing real world things in the environment, value-added services or user applications) by adding QoS-related attributes.

Figure 3 reports an example of a domain-specific sensor (i.e., the Sensmitter[2]) expressed as a .xml file representing the corresponding light sensor's DO. In particular, it shows that the DO's state also contains QoS-related attributes (see lines **16–24** of Fig. 3), besides state variables. Specifically, regarding the SL scenario with the three categories of used devices, the specification of light sensors is augmented with three metrics: (i) power consumption (see lines **16–18** of Fig. 3), i.e., the energy consumed by sensors to provide measurements on the light level; (ii) sensing accuracy (see lines **19–21** of Fig. 3), i.e., the precision provided by sensors about their estimations; (iii) battery level (see lines **22–24** of Fig. 3), i.e., the state of the device's battery that can be dynamically updated. Lamps and curtains also include the power consumption in their specification, but differently from sensors, lamps show a lighting level that expresses their intensities, and curtains show a timing for opening/closing that denotes the efficiency of such devices. Note that metrics can be expressed in different units for sensors and actuators of different brands, however such units can be converted to a common reference unit in the DO model, thus to avoid misleading comparison.

```
1<?xml version="1.0" encoding="UTF-8"?>
2<tns:domainObject name="SensmitterLightSensor" xmlns:tns="http://.../">
3
4    <tns:domainKnowledge>
5        <tns:internalDomainProperty name="domainProperties/LightSensing">
6    </tns:internalDomainProperty>
7    </tns:domainKnowledge>
8    <!-- List of state variables -->
9    <tns:state>
10        <tns:stateVariable name="DeviceID" type="string">
11            <tns2:content type="anyType">Sensmitter_435</tns2:content>
12        </tns:stateVariable>
13        <!-- Other state variables here -->
14
15        <!-- QoS-related attributes -->
16        <tns:QoSAttribute name="PowerConsumption" type="integer">
17            <tns2:content type="anyType">2.5</tns2:content>
18        </tns:QoSAttribute>
19        <tns:QoSAttribute name="SensingAccuracy" type="integer">
20            <tns2:content type="anyType">8</tns2:content>
21        </tns:QoSAttribute>
22        <tns:QoSAttribute name="BatteryLevel" type="integer">
23            <tns2:content type="anyType">100</tns2:content>
24        </tns:QoSAttribute>
25    </tns:state>
26
27    <tns:process name="processes/PROC_SensmitterLightSensor"/>
28    <tns:fragment name="fragments/LS_senseLight"></tns:fragment>
29
30</tns:domainObject>
```

Fig. 3. Domain object model for the Sensmitter light sensor.

---

[2] https://www.senssolutions.se/.

The default setting of extra-functional requirements (i.e., min, max, threshold value) is enabled by the developers in the setting of the SL application. However, end-users may have different preferences while using the available things, hence they can modify such requirements. This is later translated into the QoS-based optimisation problem that guides the formation of the most suitable EAs.

The aim of our approach is to verify if an EA can be formed to achieve the given (functional and extra-functional) goal in the specified spatial boundaries. In particular, this is strictly related to the refinement of abstract activities. We recall that the refinement process consists of the automated resolution of a fragments composition problem. It is transformed into a planning problem, and AI planning-based techniques are used to solve it.

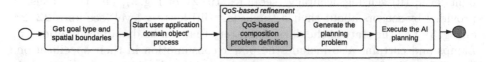

Fig. 4. IoT-FED extended process.

In particular, we enhanced the fragments composition problem in such a way that it also considers the QoS-related characteristics of devices. In Fig. 4 we provide an abstraction of the IoT-FED extended process (see the shaded box in Fig. 4). This way, the generated planning problem considers both extra-functional requirements and QoS-based characteristics expressed by DOs. Indeed, the specification of QoS-related characteristics in the DOs, together with the setting of extra-functional requirements (i.e., min, max, threshold value), leads to multiple architectural alternatives and trade-off analyses for the selection of near-optimal EAs. The mentioned QoS-based optimization problem is defined and solved by the **Optimization Solver** component (Fig. 1).

Figure 5 depicts a simplified example of the SL application execution. The Smart Light Process denotes the specification of the user application, and it represents the *User Application* DO. The QoS-based requirements guide the refinement of the encountered abstract activities (i.e., *Detect Light Level, Set Light Level*). For instance, the refinement of the *Set Light Level* abstract activity (i.e., goal G2 in Fig. 5) includes the fragment *Handle Devices* that is provided by the *Device Manager* DO (see Step 1 of Fig. 5). If the selected DO is not instantiated, then such operation is performed by the Things Manager component. The execution of this fragment implies the co-relation between the two instantiated DOs (i.e., *User Application* and *Device Manager*). The settled extra-functional requirements are passed to the Device Manager, see the QoS input data in the *Receive Device Request* activity. Subsequently, it will be considered for the refinement of the *Light Actuating* (i.e., goal G4 in Fig. 5) abstract activity. Eventually, the fragments composition (returned for this last refinement) is made by two fragments provided by those actuators in the room whose QoS-related characteristics are compliant with the QoS-based optimisation problem (see Step 2

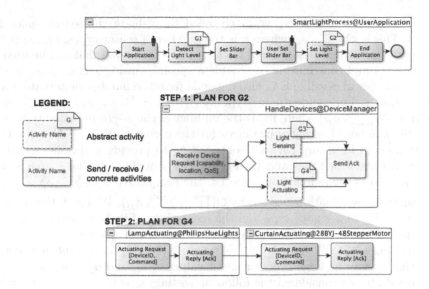

Fig. 5. Smart Light execution example.

of Fig. 5). Specifically, the fragments *Lamp* and *Curtain Actuating*, respectively provided by the *Philips Hue Lights*[3] and the *Stepper Motor*[4] DOs are selected, composed and injected in place of the abstract activity they refine.

3.2 Deriving QoS-Based Optimal IoT-EAs

The QoS-based search for alternative EAs initially deals with the issue of finding a set of devices (D) that implement the functionalities required by the application, but also fulfilling the stated requirements. Note that considering the requirements leads to trade-off analysis that takes into account the dependencies among the QoS-based properties, thus reducing the solution space. Then, given this reduced solution space (i.e., a set of devices), it is the planner to look for the optimal EAs. More formally, the problem can be expressed as follows: *Look for an EA_{opt} derived by an optimal selection of devices D_{opt}.*

To this extent, we defined an optimisation problem. It may also be modified by adding some constraints, such as costs and further domain-specific characteristics, e.g., the charging level of available devices. In the constrained case, we assume that there is a cost/restriction associated with each EA for providing a certain QoS level. In our case study, for example, we can introduce a constraint regulating the charging level of devices before being selected, e.g., activate lamps or curtains showing an initial battery level larger than 80%.

The number of different EAs (generated from the D_{opt}) is conditioned to the number of sensors and actuators, plus their instances. Since sensors are selected

---

[3] https://www2.meethue.com/en-us.
[4] https://bit.ly/2VmRegr.

before looking for actuators, we firstly need to evaluate the search space for sensors. This is $\mathcal{O}(\sum_{i=1}^{n} s_i)$ where n is the number of sensor types, and s_i is the number of sensor instances (related to the $i-th$ sensor type) that can be used to form any EA and contributing to provide a specific sensing service (e.g., light).

The number of possible EAs also depends from the number of actuators and their instances. For each actuator type a_j (with $j = \{1, \ldots, k\}$) we get a complexity of $\mathcal{O}(\sum_{i=1}^{m_j} a_{ji})$ where m_j is the number of the $j-th$ actuator type, and a_{ji} is the number of actuator instances for the corresponding $j-th$ type, that can be used to form any EA and contributing to provide a specific actuating service. All actuator types and their instances contribute to the search space. When actuators are individually selected, the complexity is $\mathcal{O}(\sum_{j=1}^{k} \sum_{i=1}^{m_j} a_{ji})$, whereas their combination is given by $\mathcal{O}(\prod_{j=1}^{k} \sum_{i=1}^{m_j} a_{ji})$. We recall that a_j represents the $j-th$ actuator type and the complexity of its instances is inherited from the definition above. Thus, the size of the solution space for the optimisation problem is $\mathcal{O}(\sum_{i=1}^{n} s_i \times \sum_{j=1}^{k} \sum_{i=1}^{m_j} a_{ji} \times \prod_{j=1}^{k} \sum_{i=1}^{m_j} a_{ji})$, and it becomes clear that it may be huge even for small values of s_i, and a_j. For example, in our case study, we considered the following setting: $s_i = 5$, $n_1 = \ldots = n_5 = 20$, $a_j = 2$, $m_1 = 3$, $m_2 = 2$, and the size of the solution space is $100 * 5 * 6 \simeq 3k$ options which makes an exhaustive search computationally expensive.

To address this challenge, we describe a near optimal solution technique that takes as input the specification of all the available devices, in the user spatial boundaries, whose fragments (exposed by the corresponding DOs) are suitable for the resolution of the planning problem. Such devices are analysed and discarded from the optimal set whenever their QoS-related characteristics do not fulfil the stated requirements. This set of devices, namely D_{opt}, is provided as output, and it contributes to the domain for the planning.

An optimal selection of devices is performed taking into account the application's settings (also editable by the users). If minimisation or maximisation is required, then an exhaustive search is necessary. On the contrary, if threshold values are set, then it is needed to look for the subset of sensors that fulfil such requirements. This way, the overall set of selected devices for both sensors and actuators is guaranteed to fulfil the stated extra-functional requirements.

4   Experimentation

This section reports our experimental results for the SL case study. We are interested to evaluate the QoS-based characteristics while selecting things (i.e., sensors and actuators). The scalability of the approach is also investigated.

4.1   Experimental Setup and Results

Table 1 reports the QoS-related characteristics of different brands of light sensors, lamp and curtain actuators, respectively. Our case study includes five brands of light sensors showing a power consumption (pc) varying from 1 to $5 \, \mathrm{W}$[5], and

---

[5] See, e.g., https://bit.ly/2IC6jtd.

a sensing accuracy (sa) is spanning from 2 to 10 and denoting an increasing precision. These two QoS-related characteristics are complementary, in fact a higher accuracy is given by a larger power consumption. Lamp actuators are of three different brands where power consumption varies between 10 to 20 W[6], whereas their light level (ll) is spanning from 4 to 8 and it indicates an increasing brightness. As another example, curtains are of two brands with an associated power consumption of 7 and 9 W[7], and a discrete timing for opening/closing (toc) equal to 8 and 12 s, respectively. All these numbers represent an estimation of QoS-related characteristics for arbitrary things, however their actual setting is part of the modelling step, and further numerical values can be considered when more accurate specification of things is available.

Table 1. QoS-related characteristics.

	Light sensors					Lamps			Curtains	
	LS_1	LS_2	LS_3	LS_4	LS_5	LA_1	LA_2	LA_3	CA_1	CA_2
pc	1	1.8	0.5	5	2.5	10	20	15	7	9
sa	4	7	2	10	8	-	-	-	-	-
ll	-	-	-	-	-	4	8	6	-	-
toc	-	-	-	-	-	-	-	-	12	8

All experimental results are obtained by using a laptop equipped with a dual-core CPU running at 2.7 GHz, and 8 Gb memory. In the following we discuss three main experiments that have been performed to evaluate different aspects of the SL case study. For all experiments we report the average values calculated over one hundred runs of the SL application. Besides, the execution time of the overall process is showed to demonstrate that its latency is affordable. In fact, we anticipate that all execution times, measured from when the user starts the SL application to the enactment of the QoS-based formed EA, vary up to 2.14 s, even when handling up to one hundred devices.

Exp_1: evaluation of QoS-related characteristics for sensors only. This experiment is aimed to understand the savings when adding extra-functional requirements for a specific device type. In our case study, we evaluated what happens when incrementally adding requirements (expressed with threshold values) to the power consumption and sensing accuracy of sensors. Obviously, we achieve a consistent power consumption saving (up to 50%) when considering constraints on it; however, when also including sensing accuracy, we still get 35% of savings that is a remarkable improvement. In this last case, the sensing accuracy increases, as expected, and this is due to the trade-off analysis among these two metrics. More in general, the requirements can be separately considered and lead to optimisation problems that provide different solutions.

Table 2. QoS-based optimisation for sensors.

	noQoS	QoS(pc)	QoS(pc, sa)
Power consumption	233.1	117.7	140.8
Sensing accuracy	6.41	4.63	5.53
Execution time	1.96	1.97	2.14

Table 2 reports the values of Exp_1, and it is structured as follows. Rows include the metrics we are considering to quantify the QoS-based savings, specifically: (i) the power consumption

---

[6] See, e.g., https://bit.ly/2TibLWj.

[7] See, e.g., https://bit.ly/2NYwPKF.

of the sensors used in the EAs; (ii) the sensing accuracy of adopted sensors; (iii) the execution time (expressed in seconds) for forming and enacting EAs. On the columns we distinguish three cases: the first one is without setting any constraint on QoS-related characteristics (i.e., *noQoS* in Table 2), the second is when setting the power consumption of sensors being less than 2 W (i.e., *QoS(pc)* in Table 2), and the third case is when also establishing that the sensing accuracy has to be larger than 3 (i.e., *QoS(pc, sa)* in Table 2). We can notice that QoS-based savings are relevant for our case study, in fact power consumption goes from 233 to 118. This implies a modification in the sensing accuracy that instead decreases (from 6.41 to 4.63), due to the selection of light sensors that consume less. However, the value for the sensing accuracy slightly improves to 5.53 when setting the threshold to that metric. Execution times also slightly increase across experiments when adding QoS-related constraints, but the largest gap is equal to $2.14 - 1.96 = 0.18$ s.

Exp$_2$: evaluation of QoS-based characteristics for all devices. This experiment investigates the savings when adding extra-functional requirements for both sensors and actuators. In our case study, we evaluated QoS-based savings when adding threshold values to the power consumption of all devices and progressively considering further aspects for light sensors, curtains, and lamps.

Table 3. QoS-based optimisation for sensors and actuators.

	noQoS	QoS_1	QoS_2	QoS_3
Power consumption	1946.5	1792.4	1588	1828
Sensing accuracy	6.37	4.35	4.29	4.45
Execution time	1.92	1.91	1.88	1.91
Lighting level	6.12	6	4.86	6
Time opening/closing	9.85	9.91	8	8

Table 3 reports the values of *Exp$_2$*, and it is structured as follows. Similarly to Table 2, the first three rows report power consumption (that is measured taking into account all devices), sensing accuracy, and execution time. Last two rows extend the evaluation to the following metrics: (i) the lighting level of lamp actuators used in the EAs; (ii) the time for opening/closing curtain actuators involved in the EAs. On the columns we present four different cases. The first one is without QoS-related constraints, i.e., *noQoS* in Table 3. The second (denoted by QoS_1 in Table 3) is a combination of: (1) power consumption of sensors (required to be less than 2 W), lamp actuators (required to be less than 18 W), curtain actuators (required to be less than 10 W); (2) lighting level of lamp actuators (required to be larger than 5). The third case (i.e., QoS_2 in Table 3) keeps the same threshold values for the power consumption, but it requires a minimisation of time for opening/closing curtains. Finally, the forth case (denoted by QoS_3 in Table 3) is a combination of the previous two cases where thresholds for power consumption, lighting level and time for closing/opening are jointly considered.

Obviously, we can notice that in all QoS-based optimisation procedures power consumption shows an improvement with respect to *noQoS*, in fact it goes from 1946.5 up to 1588 in the best case. As drawback, the sensing accuracy decreases and goes from 6.4 to values around an average of 4.3 (that is larger than the stated threshold). Execution times are very similar in all cases, and this supports the efficiency of QoS-based computation. Lighting level varies across cases and achieves its worst value (i.e., 4.86, see Table 3) when not constrained by any threshold. Finally, the time for opening/closing is also subject to some variations that steer it down in cases where such metric is explicitly optimised, i.e., in the last two columns of Table 3 where it shows a value of 8 vs the initial 9.85 (i.e., when measured with no QoS-based constraints). Figure 6 depicts the number of alternative EAs. We can notice that in case of not considering QoS-based requirements there are almost 50 different EAs that are enacted.

As expected, the handling of QoS-related requirements implies a reduction in the number of valid EAs of roughly 60%, in fact the average value of EAs in QoS scenarios is around 12. Obviously, QoS_3 is the one showing the lowest value, since it represents a combination of requirements set for QoS_1 and QoS_2. Power consumption (see Table 3) is reported on top of bars in Fig. 6 to remark the variations in QoS-based savings.

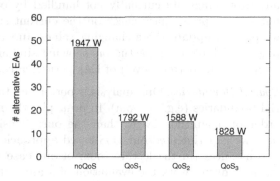

Fig. 6. Variations in the selection of EAs.

Exp_3: scalability of the approach. We added ten and twenty light sensors instances for each of the considered sensor brand, thus to evaluate the scalability of the approach when considering up to 50 and 100 light sensors, respectively.

Table 4. Scalability of the approach.

	noQoS	QoS(pc)	QoS(pc, sa)
#sensors = 5	1.96	1.97	2.14
#sensors = 50	2.01	1.98	1.99
#sensors = 100	2.10	2.05	2.07

Table 4 shows the execution times (expressed in seconds) when varying the number of sensors on the rows, and the cases of Exp_1 in the columns. We found that in all cases the execution time values vary within a narrow interval, i.e., from 1.96 to 2.14 s. This supports the scalability of our approach since the QoS-based computation does not largely affect the process of forming and enacting EAs. The number of devices does not affect the scalability of the approach, since the planner component of our platform (see Fig. 1) only considers the device brands and it is not checking their instances when computing plans (i.e., fragments compositions).

Summarising, these three experiments provide a quantitative evaluation of our approach and point out two main findings: (i) the effectiveness, since both Exp_1 and Exp_2 clearly show QoS-based savings; (ii) the scalability, in fact Exp_3 indicates that in the worst case the application of the approach takes 2.14 s, and this can be considered affordable for those classes of IoT systems that do not expose safety or hard real time constraints.

4.2 Discussion

Our approach includes a set of limitations that we discuss in the following.

Runtime Monitoring. There are some QoS-related characteristics associated to things that may change over time, e.g., the battery level of devices decreases when they are in use or increases after charging. These aspects of runtime evolution of things are currently not handled by our approach that instead computes some preliminary check on the current status of devices only. However, we plan to update these changing values and trigger a QoS-based adaptation (e.g., switching among actuators showing similar QoS-based characteristics but with different battery level) of EAs periodically.

Spatial Boundaries. Our analysis is performed taking into account the user spatial boundaries (e.g., a room). In principle, the number of things can scale with order of magnitude larger than the ones considered in this paper. However, here we experimented our QoS-based approach by varying the number of sensor instances (in the lecture room of our case study) up to one hundred. We leave as future work the evaluation of scaling the number of actuators, but we expect that this does not affect too much our computation due to the intrinsic nature of the planner component that reasons on device types (brands) instead of instances.

Requirements Specification. It may happen that the QoS-based optimisation problem is not able to provide a solution due to invalid requirements. However, there might be some options that do not deviate largely from users' expectations, and we plan to provide these alternatives as feedback to users that may decide to change their initial settings. Moreover, we plan to introduce weights associated to users' preferences on the type of available things. For example, in the SL application it may happen that users get disturbed by the curtains opening and closing, hence the activation of lamps is preferred.

Further Architectural Layers. Our approach currently allows the specification of QoS-related characteristics for the sensors and actuators only, because they are the main components for building the EAs. However, between these two layers there are further architectural layers, such as different middleware, operating systems, and communication protocols that contribute to the QoS of the IoT system. As future work we plan to extend our approach to embed these layers in the specification of QoS-related characteristics. An option can be to integrate benchmarks modelling the delay of these layers in our optimisation problem.

Threats to Validity. Our experimentation may be internally biased from the settings of input parameters, QoS requirements, and executions of the SL application. Both input parameters and QoS requirements lead to specify different QoS optimisation problems, but the overall procedure is not affected. As opposite, we found relevant to execute multiple runs of the SL application and we experienced no variations between 50 and 100 runs, hence this latest number has been considered to smooth biases in the output results. As external threats to validity, we are aware that the application of the approach to other case studies has not been performed, but we leave this point as part of our future work.

5   Related Work

The work presented in this paper is related to two main streams of research that we discuss hereafter, specifically the modelling of IoT architectures and their QoS-based analysis.

In [5] a reference architecture to plug and produce industrial IoT systems (whose architectural decisions are tackled in [15]) is presented, and it has the goal to reduce industrial device commissioning times across vendor products. Differently from our approach, the evaluation of IoT architectures in [5,15] builds upon some industrial (communication protocol and controller description) standards. On the contrary, our formalism (based on DOs) is aimed to specify any QoS-related characteristic, by setting QoS-based criteria, such as minimisation, maximisation, or a specific threshold value.

In [16] a framework for self-architecting service-oriented systems is proposed, and QoS-based analysis is performed by quantifying the execution time and availability of the service providers. In [17] QoS-based optimisation of service-based systems is performed through modelling the application with a Discrete Time Markov Chain (DTMC) and using a probabilistic model checker to rank the configurations based on the required extra-functional requirements. In [18] an approach for QoS-based feedback on service compositions is presented, and it makes use of design-time and runtime knowledge to manage QoS data over time [19], thus to support software architects while devising a service composition that best fits extra-functional requirements. Our approach mainly differs from these works [16–19] in considering the issues of the IoT domain where services may show QoS-based characteristics that are not platform-independent and time-varying. This heterogeneity makes more complex the QoS-based optimisation problem. In [20] models at runtime and statistical techniques are combined to realise adaptation of IoT systems, specifically quality models provides a probabilistic estimate of different adaptation options. Our approach differs in the specification of QoS-related characteristics that are explicitly modelled at the architectural level and contribute to the selection of devices fulfilling functional and extra-functional requirements.

In recent years, research has been done on the usage of business process-based technologies in the IoT context. Indeed, Business Process Management Systems (BPMS) approaches have become an efficient solution for the coordinated management of devices, as reported in [21]. At the same time, interesting research challenges arise from this novel research field [22]. From the one side, workflow management systems (WfMS) for industrial IoT have been realized to execute and monitor IoT-based processes [23]. From another side, standard workflow languages (e.g., BPMN 2.0) have been extended to support sensors/actuators specific activities and IoT communication paradigms [24]. In our approach, the use of the APFL and the abstract activities refinement mechanism enables the dynamic execution of IoT applications. Moreover, APFL has been extended to support the specification of QoS-related characteristics of things, inherited from their producers and enabling QoS-based formation of software architectures. To the contrary, APFL extensions to support things activities and IoT communication paradigms were not necessary. This is due to the use of the DOs formalism that allows developers to work at an abstract level without dealing with the heterogeneity of things and their communication protocols.

Summarising, we can conclude that, to the best of our knowledge, there is no work that incorporates QoS-related characteristics in the modelling of IoT software architectures and exploits this specification to jointly optimise functional and extra-functional requirements.

6 Conclusion

In this paper we presented an approach to consider QoS-related concerns as first class citizens in the process of forming software architectures in the Internet of Things. We extended a modelling language for enabling the specification of QoS-related characteristics of things (tags, sensors, actuators, objects, and devices). This information is exploited in the automatic formation of EAs since a QoS-based optimisation problem is adopted, and devices are selected taking into account extra-functional requirements. The approach is applied to a case study and the conducted experimentation provides three main lessons learned: (i) when introducing extra-functional requirements, the savings may be relevant; (ii) when considering multiple QoS-related characteristics, trade-off analysis is suitable to balance among contradicting QoS-based goals; (iii) the scalability of the approach is preserved when considering a realistic number of devices. As future work, besides addressing the limitations that have been discussed in the experimentation, we also plan to further investigate the effectiveness of our approach when involving real-world things and industrial case studies.

Acknowledgments. This work has been partially supported by the MIUR PRIN project titled "Designing Spatially Distributed Cyber-Physical Systems under Uncertainty (SEDUCE)".

References

1. Atzori, L., Iera, A., Morabito, G.: The internet of things: a survey. Comput. Netw. **54**(15), 2787–2805 (2010)
2. Gubbi, J., Buyya, R., Marusic, S., Palaniswami, M.: Internet of Things (IoT): a vision, architectural elements, and future directions. Future Gener. Comput. Syst. **29**(7), 1645–1660 (2013)
3. Lee, I., Lee, K.: The Internet of Things (IoT): applications, investments, and challenges for enterprises. Bus. Horiz. **58**(4), 431–440 (2015)

4. Khan, R., Khan, S.U., Zaheer, R., Khan, S.: Future internet: the internet of things architecture, possible applications and key challenges. In: International Conference on Frontiers of Information Technology (FIT), pp. 257–260 (2012)
5. Koziolek, H., Burger, A., Doppelhamer, J.: Self-commissioning industrial IoT-systems in process automation: a reference architecture. In: International Conference on Software Architecture (ICSA), pp. 196–205 (2018)
6. MacGillivray, C., Turner, V., Shirer, M.: Explosive Internet of Things Spending to Reach $1.7 Trillion in 2020. IDC Corporate USA (2015)
7. White, G., Nallur, V., Clarke, S.: Quality of service approaches in IoT: a systematic mapping. J. Syst. Softw. **13**, 186–203 (2017)
8. Alkhabbas, F., Spalazzese, R., Davidsson, P.: Architecting emergent configurations in the Internet of Things. In: IEEE International Conference on Software Architecture (ICSA), pp. 221–224 (2017)
9. Ciccozzi, F., Spalazzese, R.: MDE4IoT: supporting the internet of things with model-driven engineering. Intelligent Distributed Computing X. SCI, vol. 678, pp. 67–76. Springer, Cham (2017). https://doi.org/10.1007/978-3-319-48829-5_7
10. Alkhabbas, F., De Sanctis, M., Spalazzese, R., Bucchiarone, A., Davidsson, P., Marconi, A.: Enacting emergent configurations in the IoT through domain objects. In: Pahl, C., Vukovic, M., Yin, J., Yu, Q. (eds.) ICSOC 2018. LNCS, vol. 11236, pp. 279–294. Springer, Cham (2018). https://doi.org/10.1007/978-3-030-03596-9_19
11. Bucchiarone, A., De Sanctis, M., Marconi, A., Pistore, M., Traverso, P.: Design for adaptation of distributed service-based systems. In: Barros, A., Grigori, D., Narendra, N.C., Dam, H.K. (eds.) ICSOC 2015. LNCS, vol. 9435, pp. 383–393. Springer, Heidelberg (2015). https://doi.org/10.1007/978-3-662-48616-0_27
12. Bucchiarone, A., De Sanctis, M., Marconi, A., Pistore, M., Traverso, P.: Incremental composition for adaptive by-design service based systems. In: International Conference on Web Services (ICWS), pp. 236–243 (2016)
13. Bertoli, P., Pistore, M., Traverso, P.: Automated composition of web services via planning in asynchronous domains. Artif. Intell. **174**, 316–361 (2010)
14. Bucchiarone, A., De Sanctis, M., Marconi, A.: ATLAS: a world-wide travel assistant exploiting service-based adaptive technologies. In: Maximilien, M., Vallecillo, A., Wang, J., Oriol, M. (eds.) ICSOC 2017. LNCS, vol. 10601, pp. 561–570. Springer, Cham (2017). https://doi.org/10.1007/978-3-319-69035-3_41
15. Malakuti, S., Goldschmidt, T., Koziolek, H.: A catalogue of architectural decisions for designing IIoT systems. In: Cuesta, C.E., Garlan, D., Pérez, J. (eds.) ECSA 2018. LNCS, vol. 11048, pp. 103–111. Springer, Cham (2018). https://doi.org/10.1007/978-3-030-00761-4_7
16. Menasce, D., Gomaa, H., Sousa, J., et al.: SASSY: a framework for self-architecting service-oriented systems. IEEE Softw. **28**(6), 78–85 (2011)
17. Calinescu, R., Grunske, L., Kwiatkowska, M., Mirandola, R., Tamburrelli, G.: Dynamic QoS management and optimization in service-based systems. IEEE Trans. Softw. Eng. **37**(3), 387–409 (2011)
18. Caporuscio, M., Mirandola, R., Trubiani, C.: QoS-based feedback for service compositions. In: International Conference on Quality of Software Architectures (QoSA), pp. 37–42 (2015)
19. Mirandola, R., Trubiani, C.: A deep investigation for QoS-based feedback at design time and runtime. In: International Conference on Engineering of Complex Computer Systems (ICECCS), pp. 147–156 (2012)
20. Weyns, D., Iftikhar, M.U., Hughes, D., Matthys, N.: Applying architecture-based adaptation to automate the management of internet-of-things. In: Cuesta, C.E.,

Garlan, D., Pérez, J. (eds.) ECSA 2018. LNCS, vol. 11048, pp. 49–67. Springer, Cham (2018). https://doi.org/10.1007/978-3-030-00761-4_4

21. Chang, C., Srirama, S.N., Buyya, R.: Mobile cloud business process management system for the internet of things: a survey. ACM Comput. Surv. **49**(4), 70:1–70:42 (2017)

22. Janiesch, C., et al.: The internet-of-things meets business process management: mutual benefits and challenges. CoRR, vol. arXiv:1709.03628 (2017)

23. Seiger, R., Huber, S., Schlegel, T.: Toward an execution system for self-healing workflows in cyber-physical systems. Softw. Syst. Model. **17**(2), 551–572 (2018)

24. Domingos, D., Martins, F., Cândido, C., Martinho, R.: Internet of things aware WS-BPEL business processes context variables and expected exceptions. J. UCS **20**(8), 1109–1129 (2014)

A Survey on Big Data Analytics Solutions Deployment

Camilo Castellanos[1](✉), Boris Pérez[1,2], Carlos A. Varela[3],
María del Pilar Villamil[1], and Dario Correal[1]

[1] Systems Engineering and Computing Department,
Universidad de los Andes, Bogotá, Colombia
{cc.castellanos87,br.perez41,mavillam,dcorreal}@uniandes.edu.co
[2] Systems Engineering and Computing Department,
Universidad Francisco de Paula Santander, Cúcuta, Colombia
borisperezg@ufps.edu.co
[3] Computer Science Department,
Rensselaer Polytechnic Institute, Troy, NY, USA
cvarela@cs.rpi.edu

Abstract. There are widespread and increasing interest in big data analytics (BDA) solutions to enable data collection, transformation, and predictive analyses. The development and operation of BDA application involve business innovation, advanced analytics and cutting-edge technologies which add new complexities to the traditional software development. Although there is a growing interest in BDA adoption, successful deployments are still scarce (a.k.a., the "Deployment Gap" phenomenon). This paper reports an empirical study on BDA deployment practices, techniques and tools in the industry from both the software architecture and data science perspectives to understand research challenges that emerge in this context. Our results suggest new research directions to be tackled by the software architecture community. In particular, competing architectural drivers, interoperability, and deployment procedures in the BDA field are still immature or have not been adopted in practice.

1 Introduction

With recent big data proliferation, enterprises can use analytics to extract valuable insights from large-scale data sources, something not possible a few years ago. Traditional big data analytics (BDA) methodologies [1,2] involve three knowledge domains: business, analytics, and technology. In the business domain, business users have to define the business goals to drive the analytics project. In the analytics domain, these business goals are translated by data scientists into specific analytics tasks such as data cleaning, model building, and evaluation. This model development is performed within the data lab. Finally, in the technology domain, the IT (Information Technology) team take the analytics model

© Springer Nature Switzerland AG 2019
T. Bures et al. (Eds.): ECSA 2019, LNCS 11681, pp. 195–210, 2019.
https://doi.org/10.1007/978-3-030-29983-5_13

as an input for software implementation and deployment in the production environment respecting Quality Attributes (QA). This migration of the analytics model from data lab to production environment is called a *BDA deployment*.

Despite the growing interest of companies in BDA adoption, actual deployments are still scarce. Chen et al. in [3] coined this phenomenon as the "Deployment Gap". Later, Chen et al. in [4] summarized a set of technical, organizational, and technology challenges that must be handled when developing BDA projects. Previous works have tackled BDA adoption and challenges in analytics practices, and they will be reviewed in Sect. 2, but little research has been carried out to identify practices, behavior, and procedures from the perspective of software engineering and architecture.

The aforementioned aspects motivate the development of a survey whose objective is to identify the practices, techniques, and tools used in the design, development, and deployment of BDA projects from a software architecture perspective. We conducted a survey among practitioners following a methodology proposed by Kitchenham et al. in [5] defining objectives, designing, developing, and evaluating the survey, then obtaining data, and finally, analyzing the results. We collected answers from 76 practitioners engaged with cross-industry BDA projects in Colombia. The objectives of this survey are framed in the BDA development and deployment context, and they are stated as follows: (i) To determine used practices and methods. (ii) To determine used techniques and tools. (iii) To identify perceived challenges. (iv) To identify considered quality attributes.

The remainder of this paper is structured as follows: Sect. 2 reviews related work. Section 3 describes our research methodology. Section 4 presents the survey results. Section 5 discusses the findings. Section 6 presents the threats to validity. Finally, Sect. 7 draws conclusions and describes future work.

2   Related Work

Chen et al. [3] identified 11 factors which affect BDA adoption, and these factors include organizational, innovation, and technology. They presented the status and strategies to deploy BDA solutions based on 25 European enterprise case studies, but specific behaviors, practices, and tools used in the current deployment of such solutions were not reviewed.

Previous industry surveys (e.g. [6,7]) have focused on understanding analytics practices using questionnaires directed to a wide number of data scientists. They reported trends about algorithms, tools, data scientist roles, and analytics deployments. These works confirmed low rates (half of the respondents) of analytics projects being deployed, and delayed time of deployment—25% of deployments take months or even years. On the other hand, the survey results presented in [8] were focused specifically on the deployment of BDA solutions. That survey inquired about procedures for packaging, retraining and monitoring BDA solutions, finding that 50% of their respondents stated the level of difficulty of analytics model deployment was more than six (from 1 to 10). Real-time scoring showed a higher level of difficulty, and projects with issues on data quality and pipeline development presented also delayed deployment. Those surveys offer important statistics about deployment and operation of analytics solutions, but they are not framed in the BDA life cycle, and they do not consider either software engineering or architecture, highly implicated in those processes.

LaValle et al. presented in [9] challenges and opportunities in business analytics, and highlight the need for analytics capabilities to achieve competitive advantages and make informed decisions. In addition, they compared analytics adoption level, practices, and challenges to organization performance to offer some recommendations to improve analytics adoption across the organization. Although their research analyses general organizational and technology facets, detailed practices and techniques related to deployment, software engineering and architecture are not considered.

3 Methodology

According to Easterbrook et al. [10], the research method depends on the research questions. Based on the above, we decided to use a survey research method to identify the practices in industry and academy about how they develop and deploy BDA solutions. This survey follows the methodology proposed by Kitchenham and Pfleeger [5] for survey designing in empirical software engineering.

3.1 Research Questions

We formulate the research questions (RQs) of this survey based on the objectives presented in Sect. 1.

RQ1: *What are the practices, methods, techniques, and tools used in BDA development and deployment?* By answering this question, we intend to characterize practices, techniques and tools used in BDA design, development, deployment, and operation.

RQ2: *What are the main challenges faced in BDA development and deployment?* By answering this question, we aim at identifying the challenges practitioners have to face in this context.

RQ3: *What are the main quality attributes considered in BDA modeling, evaluation, and deployment stages?* By answering this question, we aim at characterizing QAs which drive BDA's software architecture.

3.2 Sample and Population

In our survey, the target population entails practitioners who have participated in BDA projects, playing a range of roles such as project manager, business expert, requirements engineer, data scientist/analyst, data engineer software designer/developer, software/IT/solution architect and IT administrator. We employed *Convenience sampling* (a non-probabilistic sampling method [5]) for selecting the population because of our access to participants involved in BDA projects. Participants were available through the master programs in Information Engineering and IT Architecture offered by Universidad de Los Andes, and the Colombian Center of Excellence and Appropriation in Big Data Analytics (CAOBA). These participants were involved in industry BDA projects and they were available to collaborate in this research. The master students were signed up for IT Architecture and Data Science Applied courses.

Inclusion and exclusion criteria enable us to choose valid answers regarding experience in BDA practice and consistency. This survey considered the following Inclusion criteria: (i) The respondent has industry experience in BDA projects, and (ii) The respondent has academic experience in BDA projects. The exclusion criteria were (i) There are inconsistent (i.e. contradictory) answers and, (ii) respondents that answered less than 50% of the questions.

3.3   Survey Design

This survey can be classified as descriptive research because: (1) This survey was preplanned and structured, and (2) the information collected can be statistically inferred over a population. This type of research uses closed-ended questions allowing us to get a better understanding of opinion or attitude by a group of people on a specific topic.

This survey is a self-administered questionnaire, where a research participant is given a set of questions to answer via paper-based questionnaire. Our survey includes an opening paragraph to introduces the purpose, concepts, and considerations needed to answer the instrument. The questionnaire was reviewed externally by two other researchers and they checked the content, meaning, and understandability. Additionally, 9 practitioners on BDA projects answered a pilot to refine the instrument and estimate the time needed to complete the survey.

Our questionnaire consisted of 5 parts and 24 questions as presented in Fig. 1 written in Spanish, the participant's native language. Eighteen questions corresponded to closed-ended questions with single choice, and seven questions included multiple-choice grids to specify the respondent's level of agreement or disagreement on a Likert scale. All questions were mandatory. The 5 parts of the survey were: (a) demographic questions, (b) questions about practices, behavior and challenges in BDA context, (c) questions about techniques and tools used in BDA projects, (d) questions about BDA deployment, and (e) questions about how practitioners dealt with quality attributes. Figure 1 also details how each questionnaire's part is related to the Research Questions (RQ).

Demographic questions asked for job, role, level of education and experience of the subjects. These questions also asked for company information like industry sector, size, experience, and maturity. This first section helped us to understand the participants' background. Remaining parts were used to collect data about the general perception of deployment of BDA projects.

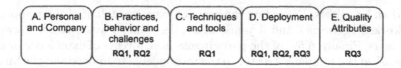

Fig. 1. Questionnaire sections and Research Questions

Data analysis were done through the following steps: (i) collection of responses into a single spreadsheet, (ii) analysis of the spreadsheet using descriptive statistics for quantitative answers for each given response, and (iii) identification of key findings from results of the statistical analyses. In order to enable the fully replication of this research, a package with the questionnaire and raw answers is publicly available[1].

4 Survey Results

This Section reports the survey results based on collected data, and the following four subsections address the questionnaire's sections detailed in Fig. 1.

In total, 115 answers were collected of which 39 (33.9%) were excluded by criteria detailed in Sect. 3.2. The remaining 76 (66.1%) valid answers were further analyzed. Hereinafter the 76 subjects who respond valid answers are denominated "respondents".

4.1 Personal and Company Data

This subsection describes the background information of the respondents. This background can influence the perspective and perception of BDA development and deployment process. This information includes respondent's profession, the role played in BDA projects, educational background and specific experience in this kind of projects.

Regarding respondent's profession, the vast majority of them (84.2%) are IT professionals, followed them by mathematicians/statistics (5.2%), engineers Non-IT and business administrators (3.9%).

The respondent's role played in BDA allows us to know how is represented the stakeholders introduced in Sect. 1, IT managers corresponds to 26.3%, software architects: 19.7%, developers: 15.7%, data scientists: 14.4%, and IT operators: 6.5%.

We also asked respondents the level of education. Most of them (40.7%) hold an M.Sc degree, 35.5% have a B.Sc. degree, 22.3% a specialization degree and one respondent holds a Ph.D. degree.

The question related to work experience in BDA projects shows that most of the respondents are in junior level hence 67.1% have got involved between 1 and 2 projects, 22.3% have participated between 3 and 5 projects, and 10.5% in

---

[1] https://storage.cloud.google.com/ccastellanos/BDA-Survey-package.zip.

more than 5 projects. Regarding the years of experience, half of the respondents have worked between 1 and 3 years, 32.8% less than 1 year, 10.5% between 3 and 6 years. Finally, 6.5% of the participants have 6 years of experience or more.

We asked the company's sector to the respondents to understand the business environment in which BDA projects are developed, and education (23.6%) is the most common sector, technology is the second-most popular sector with 22.3%. Both Financial and Government sectors are in the third place with 13.1% of participation, while Communication (9.2%) and Transport (5.2%) sectors complete the list of the top six.

Questions 8 and 9 inquire about the company size and experience by measuring the number of employees and projects undertaken within the company. Most respondents (63.1%) work in large companies (more than 250 employees), 18.4 in small (between 11 and 50), 13.1% in medium (between 51 and 250 employees) and only the 5.2% in micro-enterprises (less than 11 employees). With regard to the number of BDA projects, 47.3% of all participants work in companies with 1 to 3 projects, 15.7% in companies with more than 9 projects, and 14.4% in companies between 4 and 6 projects. Finally, 4 respondents answer that their companies have not developed such projects (5.2%), and 2.6% (2 out of 76) between 7 and 9 projects.

To know the appropriation level of BDA in the Companies, we asked the current status of BDA projects. As a result, pilot projects were reported in progress by 32.8% of respondents, 23.6% have at least an active program in production, 17.1% in exploration, 9.2% have no a plan and 5.2% have a defined plan to be implemented.

4.2   Practices, Behavior, and Challenges

Figure 2 depicts the perception of collaboration and teamwork among the stakeholders involved in the BDA environment. This perception is measured ranging from 1 to 5 (1-Difficult and disjointed and 5-Very fluid and articulated). Analytics and IT collaboration and teamwork have the best scoring with a rank greater than 3 for 56.5% of the respondents. Business/IT, and Business/Analytics interactions report the worst rating with only 26.3% and 22.3% of positive evaluations (i.e. greater than 3) respectively.

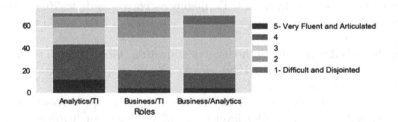

Fig. 2. Collaboration and teamwork.

We also inquired about the difficulty to carry out each BDA phase to identify the most challenging activities in the BDA life cycle regarding traditional methodologies [1,2]. This difficulty score ranges from 1 to 10, and the results are presented in Fig. 3 as boxplot graphs, including mean ($\bar{x}$) and standard deviation (σ). Six out nine activities observe the highest medians (8 points of difficulty): *(1) Define project's business goals, (3) Align analytics tasks to business goals, (4) Collect data, (5) Prepare data, (8) Deploy BDA solution* and *(9) Operation*. Among these six activities, those that present the highest means are: *(1) Define project's business goals* ($\bar{x} = 7.7, \sigma = 2.1$), *(3) Align analytics tasks to business goals* ($\bar{x} = 7.2, \sigma = 2.4$), and *(8) Deploy BDA solution* ($\bar{x} = 7.6, \sigma = 1.9$). The boxplots of these three challenging activities show that *(8) Deploy BDA solution* activity has the smallest Interquartile Range (between 7 and 9) while the other two activities exhibit more dispersed values. It implies that deployment activity presents jointly the highest mean and the least disperse difficulty score.

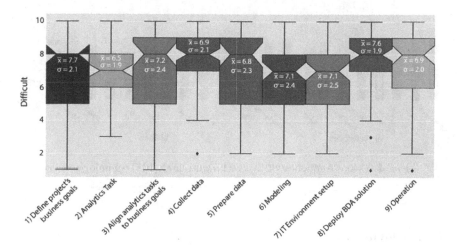

Fig. 3. Level of difficulty to perform BDA activities

4.3   Techniques and Tools

We asked respondents to categorize the usage of an arrangement of techniques to know how data scientists deal with and work with a myriad of options. Figure 4b describes the frequency of use of analytics techniques/algorithms to build analytics models in a scale from 1 (rarely used) to 5 (frequently used). The five most popular techniques are, in descending order: aggregations (sum, count, means, etc.), regression, clustering, anomalies (detection) and Principal Component Analysis (PCA). Aggregations are not actually ML algorithms, but they are the most used when data analysis is required. The most novelty techniques such as Deep Learning and Support Vector Machines (SVM) present a low level of usage in the respondents' context.

In addition to the techniques, we also asked about technology tools usage in BDA development through the same scale from 1 to 5 and Fig. 4b summarizes the results obtained. It is worth noting that this question comprised from spreadsheets to distributed processing engines including self-service Business Intelligence (BI) tools. This can be explained by the data scientist's need to explore, model, visualize and process data. Excel and Standard Query Language (SQL) to access relational databases predominate in the respondent's toolbox with 78.9% of high use frequency. The following eight-most used technologies are in descending order: Tableau, R, Power BI, Click view, Spark, SAS, IBM SPSS and Oracle Data mining. Except in the case of R, big data and ML open source frameworks such as Apache Spark, Scikit Learn, and Mahout are not widely utilized. And some IT big players such as Microsoft (Power BI), SAS, IBM (SPSS) and Oracle rank in the top ten of the technology preferences.

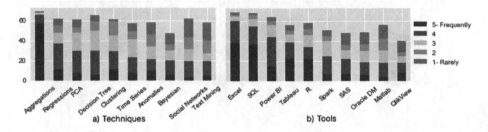

Fig. 4. Usage frequency of (a) Techniques and (b) Technology tools

4.4   Deployment

In Fig. 5a the frequency of BDA deployments on a production environment is shown. As can be noted, few times a year (34.2%), several times a year (18.4%) and "None yet" (18.4%) are the predominant answers, thus confirming the low frequency in our study's context.

During maintenance and operation stages is necessary to retrain/adjust models and software to have up-to-date services. Figure 5b depicts the procedures used to do such retraining. 22.3% of respondents retrain the model in data lab environments and they upgrade the production model using a manual procedure. Other respondents group reports that they do not retrain models, but they have to rewrite the code (18.4%), 14.4% retrain the model and export the new parameters to production, and only the 6.5% use a DevOps approach.

The respondents were consulted about the procedure or methodology to package/migrate the analytics models and data transformations from the data lab to production and Fig. 6a shows these results. Noteworthy, 31.5% of the respondents did not know or answer which deployment procedure is used. The 28.9%

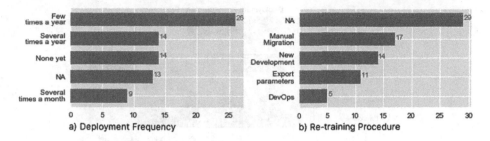

Fig. 5. Frequency of (a) BDA deployment in productive environment and (b) Re-training procedure.

of respondents reported they do not have a procedure because they have a single environment of BDA, use an ad-hoc procedure (25%), or have to rewrite whole source code (9.2%). Only 1 respondent (1.3%) reported the use of interoperable models such as PMML or PFA.

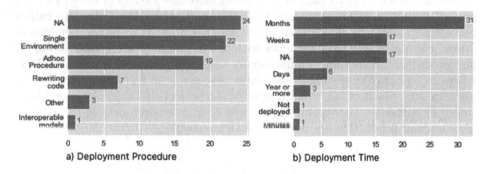

Fig. 6. Frequency of (a) Deployment procedure and (b) Deployment time.

To gain first-hand knowledge about the lag time in the deployment of BDA solutions, we also asked the time elapsed between model development and its deployment in production. Figure 6b details the time scales invested in this deployment. The most common time scale is *months* (40.7%), followed by *weeks* (22.3%), and in a lower proportion, *days* (7.8%).

To understand the relationship between deployment procedure and frequency, we compare such questions results in Fig. 7. Ad hoc procedure is the most common both in monthly (44.4%, 4 out of 9) and yearly deployments (42.3%, 11 out of 26). Although maintaining a single environment is highly used (35.7%, 5 out of 14) in projects with several deployments a year, also it is the most common procedure (50%, 7 out of 14) among projects which have no deployments yet. Specifications for sharing and interoperating predictive models are not used or scarcely used, displaying a lack of knowledge about these de facto standards.

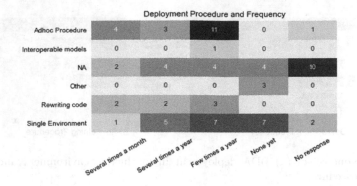

Fig. 7. Deployment procedure/methodology and frequency.

Figures 8 and 9 compare the appropriation level of the company with the deployment time and deployment procedure. Companies with active BDA programs take weeks 46.6% (7 out of 15) and months 24.6% (4 out of 11). While organizations with a BDA plan to be implemented take months (4 out of 4), pilot project exhibits monthly deployment (53.8%), and companies in the exploration phase take months to deploy their applications. Considering deployment procedures, it is noticeable that companies with active programs use mainly (50%) ad hoc procedures. Something similar occurs with companies with project pilots, where 28% (7 of 25) use ad hoc procedures, no-answer 28% (7 of 25), and rewriting code 20% (5 out of 25). Finally, most of the projects in the exploration phase (53%) or without a BDA plan (71.4%) use a single environment approach (i.e. data lab and production are the same environment).

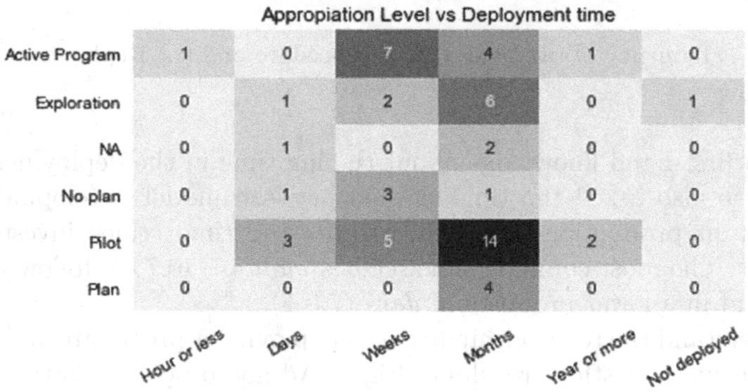

Fig. 8. Appropriation level and deployment time.

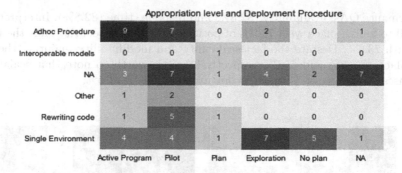

Appropriation level and Deployment Procedure					
Adhoc Procedure 9	7	0	2	0	1
Interoperable models 0	0	1	0	0	0
NA 3	7	1	4	2	7
Other 1	2	0	0	0	0
Rewriting code 1	5	1	0	0	0
Single Environment 4	4	1	7	5	1
Active Program	Pilot	Plan	Exploration	No plan	NA

Fig. 9. Appropriation level and deployment procedure.

4.5   Quality Attributes

The quality attributes drive the architecture of software solutions. In BDA context, it is also true. Hence it is valuable in this research to know how stakeholders deal with the trade-offs among quality attributes. For this reason, we formulated a set of questions oriented to answer RQ1.

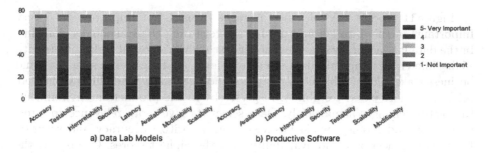

a) Data Lab Models	b) Productive Software

Legend: 5- Very Important; 4; 3; 2; 1- Not Important

Fig. 10. Quality attributes relevance in the (a) Data lab and (b) Productive software solution.

Figure 10a details the weights of relevance (from 1 to 5) for each QA when analytics techniques and models are selected, built and evaluated in the data lab environment. The most weighted QA is accuracy with 84.2% of positive ratings (i.e. greater than 3), followed by testability (77.6%), interpretability (73.6%), and, security (69.7%) and response time (65.7%) complete the top 5. Availability and scalability observe the lower ratings (63.1%, 60.5%, and 57.8% respectively) of relevance inside the data lab.

On the other hand, the same question about QA's relevance was made, but in the production environment to compare the quality's priorities. Figure 10b shows that accuracy continues in the first place with 88.1% of respondent's positive ratings (i.e. greater than 3). The second and third places are occupied by performance QAs: availability (82.8%) and response time (82.8%). Interpretability fall to fourth place with 78.9% of positive ratings and security ends the top 5 list with 73.6%. Despite the fact scalability and modifiability maintain the last two places (65.7% and 55.2% respectively), it is worth to note that scalability increases the rating of *Very important* from 17.1% to 31.5%.

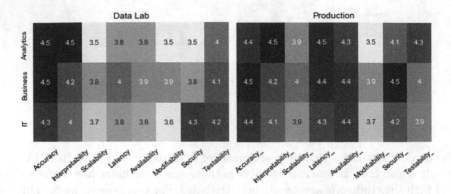

Fig. 11. Quality attributes relevance regarding stakeholder domains.

Figure 11 reports QA relevance averages (from 1-Not Important to 5-Very Important) in the data lab and production regarding the stakeholder domains. In the data lab, accuracy observes the highest relevance for all stakeholders with slight differences in magnitude. On a second level, analytics (data scientists) and business stakeholders rank interpretability and testability, while IT stakeholders prioritize security and testability, respectively. In the production environment, the picture changes significantly. Data scientists give more relevance to interpretability and latency, while business users prioritize accuracy and security. IT users rate accuracy and availability with the highest scores. Comparing the relevance scores between data lab and production, the differences in latency, availability, scalability, and security for all stakeholders are remarkable, evidencing a clear change of QA consideration between environments.

Fig. 12. Scaling approaches.

Finally, we included a question to know how is the scalability capacity to support the BDA context and Fig. 12 summarizes the respondent's answers.

The most noticeable result is that most of the respondents do not know/do not respond (32.8%, 25 out of 76), which could reflect the lack of knowledge or interest about the technical capabilities to support big data processing. Vertical scaling based on robust appliances is the most used approach with 22.3%. Distributed batch processing using big data frameworks such as Hadoop or Spark is used by 21.1% of respondents, 14.4% declared do not have scaling capabilities because they only work with small data. Distributed streaming processing is only required by 9.2% of the respondents.

5 Discussion

The BDA adoption and appropriation among companies is incipient as shown by results in which 47% have only developed between 1 and 3 projects, and only 23.6% have an active BDA program. This situation is slightly better compared to a report presented by the Colombian IT Ministry [11] that calculates the adoption of big data technologies of 16.8% in big enterprises. Compared to a previous worldwide report in 2016 [7], our survey reports better levels of appropriation in terms of the proportion of active programs in organizations (23.6% versus 17%), pilot programs (32.8% versus 17%) and "no–BDA plans" (9.2% versus 23%). In contrast, we find lower indicators regarding organizations in phases of exploration (17.1% versus 32%) and plans to be implemented (5.2% versus 11%). These results could suggest a growing interest in companies for BDA adoption and their respective progress over time.

This survey found that classic analytics techniques such as aggregations, regression, and clustering are the most used by companies. These results are similar to previous studies [6,7], the only exception is that in our survey, the decision tree is not ranked in the top three of the most used algorithms. The most basic tools like Excel and SQL scripts are in the first places, followed by Tableau and R. These preferences are different from specific data science studies where R, SPSS, SAS, and Tableau occupied the top positions. This can suggest unfamiliarity or lack of skills in data science-oriented tools in the Colombian context. This survey also reports a lack of standard procedures to deploy and operate BDA solutions which frequently implies manual code rewriting and configuration, confirming findings presented previously in [8]. It is noticeable the lack of knowledge and use of de-facto standards (1.3%) for sharing analytics models across technologies (such as PMML or PFA) compared to previous studies (19%) such as [8], what can promote the cumbersome and delayed process of putting analytics services in operation. These findings allow us to argue that DevOps practices in these specific domains are still unknown, immature, or under-used, and some recent works such as [12,13] have addressed this concern.

Activities involved in BDA development, such as business objectives and analytics goals definition, data collection, and deployment, are considered "hard" on average. Specifically, deployment seems to be a challenging stage, probably due to different factors such as software development driven by competing QAs in different environments, tools heterogeneity, and the lack of mature deployment procedures, even in organizations with active BDA programs. These factors have also been identified in previous works [7,8]. Teamwork and collaboration between data scientists and IT stakeholders are better ranked compared to business/IT and business/data scientist interaction.

In terms of deployment challenges, our results confirm issues in different facets: scarcity of deployments into production leading to low operationalization of BDA solutions and long delays for deployment which range from weeks to months (63%). This scenario can be caused partly by technical reasons such as inadequate tools, and inadequate procedures to deploy and retrain BDA solutions in production environments. These findings coincide with conclusions reported in [7] and [8] where they reported low rates of deployment, lack of procedures to deploy BDA solutions, and long deployment times. Even companies in a more mature BDA stages (i.e. with active programs) reported deployment times from weeks to months.

Relevant QAs during the data analytics modeling are not the same as those during the software development phase. The reason for this is that both artifacts (models and software) pursue different objectives, while the analytics model's quality is measured by the accuracy, interpretability, and testability, BDA software must achieve expected performance metrics such as availability, response time, and scalability. This can lead to competing drivers when the software architect makes decisions (i.e. patterns, tactics, technologies) which may differ for the same analytics solution in different environments. This situation could also lead to heterogeneity of technology tools reported along the BDA life cycle.

6   Threats to Validity

In our study, the research methodology was validated to avoid biases as much as possible. In the following, construct validity, internal validity, external validity and reliability are presented together with their mitigation strategies as reported by Runeson and Martin schema [14].

Construct Validity. It reflects the relation between operational measures studied and researcher's main idea, according to the research questions [14]. The phrasing used in sentences for closed-ended questions could be the most recurrent threat in questionnaire-based surveys. In order to mitigate this thread, we first piloted the survey internally several times and then piloted the survey externally with practitioners involved in BDA projects through an online survey what allow as to refine the used language.

Another risk is related to participants did not finding any suitable response in the set of available ones. For this, our strategy was included an "Other" answer for each question. In our results, we had a relatively low number of respondents using this alternative answer.

Internal Validity. It reflects the presence of causal relations affecting the investigated factor [14]. For this, we performed analysis of the data using basic descriptive statistics and performed cross-analysis of the responses of each participant.

We also provided definitions that are used consistently in the survey allowing the respondents to fully understand the questions asked.

External Validity. It reflects the possibility of generalize the findings, and to discover if the findings are of interest to other people outside the investigated case [14]. For our study, a potential threat refers to the demographic distribution of response samples. We applied Convenience sampling to helped us in selecting study participants. However, we are aware that this sampling technique could have had a negative impact on the size of the set of respondents. To mitigate this potential threat, we ensure that the set of respondents were an heterogenous sample in terms of demographic information, such as professional experience, educational background, number of projects, etc. (Sect. 4.1).

Reliability. It reflects the independence between the extracted data and the obtained results [14]. To mitigate this threat, we employed observer triangulation, having all authors participating in the data extraction and analysis processes. Due to the non-statistical nature of convenience sampling used in this study, we cannot give strong inferences, and we also avoid performing any statistical correlation analysis because we are aware our sample size is small and too centered in practitioners who have participated in BDA projects. Despite of this fact, our results can open new discussions and research lines.

7 Conclusions

We have presented an empirical study of how practitioners deal with the development and deployment of BDA solutions. We first developed and evaluated a pilot to design a paper-based survey. The data extracted from the questionnaires' answers provide clues for understanding activities, behavior, practices, and challenges faced by practitioners.

Our results open new research directions within the software architecture and software engineering community related to BDA procedures, methodologies, and design. The definition of the project's business goals, alignment between business goals and analytics task, and solution deployment were reported as the most challenging activities in BDA life cycle. We found communication and interoperability concerns across knowledge domains within BDA life cycle. Our results also found competing QAs (e.g. testability and interpretability vs performance) when developing analytics models compared to BDA software. Heterogeneity of technology tools and immature or little-known deployment procedures could lead to delayed and sporadic deployments which hinder BDA appropriation.

Regarding the practice of software architecture, our results offer insights about how to plan and design BDA solutions regarding the related challenges and procedures, and the deployment barriers to be tackled in advance. In addition, the most common methodologies, techniques, and tools in the industry could be a starting point to define a BDA adoption road map.

As future work, we can extend this survey by applying it on a wider and varied population in a regional or worldwide scale. We are researching on methodologies and frameworks in the BDA context which consider separation of concerns among the knowledge domains to reduce the deployment gap by integrating and interoperating business, analytics, software, and IT specifications.

Acknowledgment. This research is supported by Fulbright Colombia and the Center of Excellence and Appropriation in Big Data and Data Analytics (CAOBA), supported by the Ministry of Information Technologies and Telecommunications of the Republic of Colombia (MinTIC) through the Colombian Administrative Department of Science, Technology, and Innovation (COLCIENCIAS) within contract No. FP44842-anexo46-2015.

References

1. Chapman, P., et al.: CRISP-DM 1.0 step-by-step data mining guide. Technical report, The CRISP-DM consortium, August 2000
2. IBM: Foundational methodology for data science (2015). http://www-01.ibm.com/common/ssi/cgi-bin/ssialias?htmlfid=IMW14824USEN. Accessed 11 July 2017
3. Chen, H.M., Kazman, R., Matthes, F.: Demystifying big data adoption: beyond IT fashion and relative advantage. In: Twentieth DIGIT Workshop, Texas, US, pp. 1–14 (2015)
4. Chen, H.M., Schütz, R., Kazman, R., Matthes, F.: How Lufthansa capitalized on big data for business model renovation. MIS Q. Exec. **1615**(14), 299–320 (2017)
5. Kitchenham, B.A., Pfleeger, S.L.: Personal opinion surveys. In: Shull, F., Singer, J., Sjøberg, D.I.K. (eds.) Guide to Advanced Empirical Software Engineering, pp. 63–92. Springer, London (2008). https://doi.org/10.1007/978-1-84800-044-5_3
6. Rexer, K.: 2013 data miner survey. Technical report, Rexer Analytics (2013)
7. Rexer, K., Gearan, P., Allen, H.: 2015 data science survey. Technical report, Rexer Analytics (2016)
8. Dataiku: building production-ready predictive analytics (2017). http://asiandatascience.com/wp-content/uploads/2017/12/Production-Survey-Report.pdf. Accessed 11 July 2017
9. LaValle, S., Lesser, E., Shockley, R., Hopkins, M.S., Kruschwitz, N.: Big bata, analytics and the path from insights to value. MIT Sloan Manag. Rev. **52**(2), 21 (2011)
10. Easterbrook, S., Singer, J., Storey, M.A., Damian, D.: Selecting empirical methods for software engineering research. In: Shull, F., Singer, J., Sjøberg, D.I.K. (eds.) Guide to Advanced Empirical Software Engineering, pp. 285–311. Springer, London (2008). https://doi.org/10.1007/978-1-84800-044-5_11
11. Katz, R.L.: El Observatorio de la Economía Digital de Colombia. Technical report, Ministerio de Tecnologías de la Información y las Comunicaciones (2017)
12. Castellanos, C., Correal, D., Rodriguez, J.-D.: Executing architectural models for big data analytics. In: Cuesta, C.E., Garlan, D., Pérez, J. (eds.) ECSA 2018. LNCS, vol. 11048, pp. 364–371. Springer, Cham (2018). https://doi.org/10.1007/978-3-030-00761-4_24
13. Lechevalier, D., Ak, R., Lee, Y.T., Hudak, S., Foufou, S.: A neural network meta-model and its application for manufacturing. In: 2015 IEEE International Conference on Big Data (2015)
14. Runeson, P., Höst, M.: Guidelines for conducting and reporting case study research in software engineering. Empir. Softw. Eng. **14**(2), 131 (2008)

Assessing the Quality Impact of Features in Component-Based Software Architectures

Axel Busch[1]([✉]), Dominik Fuchß[1], Maximilian Eckert[2], and Anne Koziolek[1]([✉])

[1] Karlsruhe Institute of Technology, Karlsruhe, Germany
{busch,koziolek}@kit.edu, dominik.fuchss@student.kit.edu
[2] SAP Customer Experience, Munich, Germany
maximilian.eckert@sap.com

Abstract. In modern software development processes, existing software components are increasingly used to implement functionality instead of developing it from scratch. Reuse of individual components or even more complex subsystems leads to more cost-efficient development and higher quality of software. Subsystems often offer a variety of features whose use is associated with unclear effects on the quality attributes of the software architecture, such as performance. It is unclear, whether the quality requirements for the system can be met by using a certain feature of a particular subsystem. After initial selection, features must be incorporated in the target architecture. Due to a multitude of possibilities of placing the subsystem in the target system to be used, many architectural candidates may result which have to be evaluated in existing decision support solutions. The approach presented here enables software architects to automatically evaluate with the help of software architecture models the effects on quality of using individual features in an existing software architecture. The result helps to automatically evaluate design decisions regarding features and to decide whether their use is compatible with the quality requirements. We show the benefits of our approach using different decision scenarios driven by features and their placement alternatives. All scenarios are automatically evaluated, demonstrating how decisions can be made to best meet the requirements.

Keywords: Automated design decision optimization ·
Quality impact of features · CBSE

1 Introduction

Modern software systems support an increasing number of functionalities. The influence of the software architecture on the subsequently attainable software quality has been shown to be one of the critical factors. Therefore, it is important to consider quality attributes at design time. A subsequent change of the software architecture to implement certain functionalities without considering

T. Bures et al. (Eds.): ECSA 2019, LNCS 11681, pp. 211–219, 2019.
https://doi.org/10.1007/978-3-030-29983-5_14

the quality properties in advance can easily lead to high refactoring costs. For this reason, software architects want to evaluate their design decisions regarding the software architecture at an early stage. In particular, use of the paradigm of component-based software design has shown that there already are approaches that produce very promising results in predicting quality properties during the design phase, an example being the Palladio approach [12]. Such approaches benefit from modern software development, in which most of the functionalities are not longer developed from scratch, but are often reused in the form of libraries or subsystems. Such libraries often provide many features, i.e. function compositions that fulfill concerns. By reusing libraries or subsystems, not only the pure functionalities or the features are reused, but also their quality. Using such software artifacts reduces development time and the risk of recurring, already solved errors in a new development. Nevertheless, prediction of quality attributes at design time for reusing different systems is not trivial, especially when software developers have to decide among several similar systems or solutions. In addition to the supported features, the systems also differ in their quality attributes. When making decisions, the software architect is therefore facing the task of designing the right system to meet both the functional and quality requirements. Existing approaches for supporting design decisions with the quality attributes of software architectures, such as ArcheOpteryx [1], ArcheE [4], and PerOpteryx [11], already allow for an automatic exploration of architecture candidates with regard to different degrees of freedom. However, none of the approaches mentioned above provides decision support for evaluating the impact of using particular features on the quality attributes of the overall system. Nor do the approaches mentioned entail any recommendations which subsystem might be the best solution in order to maintain the defined quality properties.

We base on PerOpteryx and extend the approach for optimizing software architectures in the design phase or in evolution scenarios by regarding the features and the quality of solutions of the same type. This automatically supports the decision-making process of the software architect when features should be evaluated in terms of quality attributes regarding different implementations of functionally similar solutions. These extensions enable software architects to automatically analyse and optimize the effects of the implementation of functional requirements on quality attributes of the software system, such as performance, reliability, and monetary costs in the design phase. Furthermore, we can analyze whether the configuration of placement and assembly of the new features affect the quality attributes. The result of the automatic analysis and optimization helps software architects to choose the optimal solution among different functionally similar systems. This increases the efficiency of software development by reducing early wrong decisions, improves the quality of the resulting system, and reduces the risk of project delays or the failure of software projects.

2   Background

2.1   Design Space Exploration: PerOpteryx

We apply our methodology based on PerOpteryx [11], but the concepts are not limited to this approach. The PerOpteryx approach explores the huge set of software architecture configurations, in which each configuration is a specific combination of all possible design decisions. Thus, PerOpteryx supports making well-informed trade-off decisions for performance, reliability, and costs. For the design space exploration, PerOpteryx makes use of so-called *degrees of freedom* of the software architecture that can either be predefined and derived automatically from the architecture model or be modelled manually by the architect. As an example of a manually modelled degree of freedom, let us consider that some of the architecture's components offer standard functionality, for which other implementations (i.e. other components) are available. In this example, let us assume there is a available component `QuickDatabase` that can replace a `Database`. Assuming that `QuickDatabase` demands less resources but is more expensive than `Database`, the resulting architecture model has better response times but higher costs. The degrees of freedom span a design space and can be explored automatically. Together, they define a set of possible architecture models. Each of these possible architecture models is defined by choosing one design option for each degree of freedom instance (DoFI). We call such a possible architecture model a *candidate model*. The set of all possible candidate models corresponds to the set of all possible combinations of design options. We call this set of possible architecture models the *design space*.

Using the quantitative quality evaluation provided by the PCM analysis tools, PerOpteryx can determine performance, reliability, and cost metrics for each candidate model. The quality evaluation for a quality attribute can be expressed as a *quality evaluation function* from the set of valid PCM instances to the set of possible values of the quality metric. In addition to the evaluation functions, PerOpteryx requires a specification of whether a quality is to be maximized or minimized. Based on the DoFIs (as optimization variables) and the quality evaluation functions (as optimization objectives), PerOpteryx uses genetic algorithms and problem-specific heuristics to approximate the Pareto front of optimal candidates. Details on the optimization are not required for the discussion in this paper, but can be found in [9,10].

In its previous version described in this section, PerOpteryx does not support the analysis of the effect of reusing particular features of subsystems that require more complex modifications on the architecture model. The effects of using a single feature or a combination of features across the boundaries of multiple solutions cannot be studied meaningful by the previous PerOpteryx.

2.2   Feature Completion Meta Model

For the automatic evaluation of the effect of individual features when reusing components on the quality attributes of the overall system, we use the meta model from [7]. The meta model offers entities for structuring similar systems with the same underlying features. It consists of three parts, the feature completion definition, solution definition, and transformation description. The feature completion definition part consists of a `FeatureCompletionRepository` that stores all predefined `FeatureCompletions`. Such a feature completion is an abstract entity that can be decomposed into its basic elements, namely the *Feature Completion Components* (FCC). These basic elements define the abstract architecture of a feature completion (FC) that any realizing feature completion solution such as a MySQL DB for the DBMS FC must apply. Abstraction allows the automatic integration of inhomogeneous architectures of similar solutions into a target architecture. Similar to the more concrete software components, abstract FCCs can require each other's services or offer services themselves. Additionally, we define a model for `FeatureObjectives`. This model combines features in groups. The task of these groups is to represent interchangeable or mutually exclusive features. Let us consider a DBMS example. The FC DBMS could consist of two FCCs (simplified) - the unit for reading and retrieving structured data (i.e., `StructuringDataUnit`) and the unit for actually storing these data (i.e., `DataStorageUnit`). Correspondingly, `StructuringDataUnit` would offer services that require and provide unstructured data, while `DataStorageUnit` would require and provide the unstructured data for storage purposes. All the systems of the class of DBMS on the market would then be applied to this architecture (solution definition). For this, we use annotations that identify the integration points of the completion solutions in the target software architecture. Using an inclusion mechanism, which is also provided in the meta model (transformation description), the different solutions of the same feature completion can then be automatically included into the target architecture. Given the annotated components and transformation descriptions, the integration engine determines how a feature completion solution has to be integrated into the target software architecture.

2.3 Feature Completion Integration Mechanism

We can use two different types of integration mechanisms to incorporate the appropriate features in the target system. The first one is the `Adapter-InclusionMechanism`. Whenever a connection is to be established between a component in the target system and in the solution system, a new adapter component is (automatically) generated. This adapter component requires the interface of the solution component. Furthermore, it requires and provides the interface of the target component. The provided interface of the target component is connected to the corresponding required interface of the adapter. The adapter is then connected to the solution component using the corresponding interface. For each call to the provided interface, the adapter delegates the call to the target component and an external call to the subsystem component. Afterwards, the calls to the target component and its assembly contexts, respectively, are redirected to that of the adapter. As a result, the feature is incorporated in the system and can be used. In addition, the architect can also define the interfaces and signatures for which this mechanism should be performed. The second integration mechanism is the BehaviorInclusionMechanism. This mechanism allows a more fine-grained definition of how a feature should be built into the software architecture. Thus, it is possible to define that a call to the solution is to be executed in specific control structures of an RDSEFF. It is also possible to describe that at the beginning or at the end of a method call, this call is executed in the solution system.

3   Approach

Our approach consists of two parts: First, we demonstrate modelling of the features supported by the subsystem and the alignment of the features with its executing components. Second, candidates are created, evaluated, and optimized together with the target system architecture using degrees of freedom, which are spanned using the possible features and their configuration.

A subsystem provides services that can be reused in the target system. Only services that are provided by the subsystem via system external interfaces can be reused by the target system. Features will either be realized by FCCs as a whole (i.e. all provided interfaces of an FCC) or by a subset of these interfaces. In addition to system external interfaces, internal interfaces of the subsystem can also implement features. These features may be required by other features in order to implement their actual functionality. From this set of candidates, the software architect can then select the best candidate according to the project requirements.

Using the subsystem features and its associated architecture, the optimizer first generates the degree of freedom instances. If a particular solution supports a feature, it can be used and vice versa. The selection of a feature opens up further degrees of freedom, such as the position in the target system or the allocation of the solution itself. In addition, the three degrees of freedom, namely components exchange, component allocation, and development of hardware resources are included in the DoFI. In the next step, the software architecture candidate is created and integrated according to the previously generated DoFI. The evaluation required for the optimization is then performed according to the quality attributes (e.g., performance, reliability, cost) defined before. In the end, the software architect selects the best candidate from the resulting set of Pareto-optimal architecture candidates.

In order to extend the approach to decision support in software architecture design PerOpteryx by the approach described, we have adapted three parts: First, the meta model for the definition of reusable subsystems must be extended by the possibility of modelling supported features by a particular class of subsystems. Secondly, the degree of freedom model must be extended to include the existence or non-existence of features when creating architecture candidates. Depending on the solution and the features supported by this solution, the architecture candidates must be created. In addition, we need a degree of freedom modelling of placement configurations of the feature in the target architecture. Finally, the model weaving mechanism must be extended so that the corresponding model (with the selected set of features and the associated solution) is created according to the architecture candidate created previously.

4   Evaluation

This evaluation is to demonstrate the applicability and benefits for several scenarios of (real-world) application environments. With our automated approach, we show how trade-off decisions to select features can be supported automatically with regard to the expected software quality and what effects these decisions may have on the software architecture. For our scenarios, we consider the purpose of *logging*, which is often implemented in practice using the log4j framework. We first model the feature completion corresponding to logging frameworks, including different features and apply the defined structure to two real-world logging solutions, log4j version 1 and log4j version 2. The presented scenarios cover several facets of the design questions that arise from the use of a specific feature in the target architecture such as feature selection, solution selection, feature placement.

4.1   Target System

To demonstrate our approach, we use the model of a community case study, namely the Modular Rice University Bidding System (mRUBiS) [13]. mRUBiS implements a trading and auction platform modelled on the real auction platform ebay.com. mRUBiS has a component-based software architecture and is fully implemented in Enterprise Java Beans 3 (EJB3). The domain model is modelled in the Eclipse Modeling Framework (EMF). As execution engine, mRUBiS uses a GlassFish application server. mRUBiS supports several shops in which goods can be offered for sale. Sellers can offer new items for sale within their shops and check the current inventory. Buyers can register on the platform, log in, search for items using different categories, bid on items, and submit reviews. The mRUBiS model internally consists of nine software components that provide the services. Using `ItemService`, buyers can search for items and place bids. To do this, buyers must first register using the `Authentication` component. The request is then processed using the `Query` component and the `Database` component. Submitted bids are stored in the database using `Persistence`. `UserInfo` lets buyers edit information about their user profile. Sellers use the `Inventory` component to add new items to their shop. This request is forwarded to the database and processed using the query component. `ManageItems` checks the inventory and is then forwarded to the database via `BasicQuery`. The architecture model of mRUBiS has annotations to simulate performance analysis (using (RD)SEFFs) and cost estimation.

4.2   Logger Solutions

A logger collects and records system events, activities, and (inter-)actions over a period and enables tracking and monitoring, statistical analysis or debugging and error recovery. Three feature completion components (FCCs) model the abstract structure of loggers, the `Collector`, `Appender`, and `Formatter`. These components abstract the functionalities and dependencies of the subsystem's software components. In the case of a logger completion, the `Collector` represents the entry point of the logger and receives the log messages. The data are forwarded to the FCC `Appender`, which uses the FCC `Formatter` to convert the logs into a suitable format (e.g. XML) and stores them on a specified write target (e.g. hard disk). Each of the FCCs can have a set of provided and required perimeter interfaces. In the case of the logger completion, the FCC `Collector` comes with several provided perimeter interfaces, while the FCC `Appender` consists of one required perimeter interface. The required perimeter interface of the FCC `Appender` requires an interface to a database if the feature *database logging* is a desired feature. For the evaluation, we model two solutions, namely *log4jv1* and *log4jv2*, and annotate them to the logger completion [8]. These solutions represent variants of the same completion, since they build on each other, but differ in their quality attributes as well as in their realized set of features. *log4jv2* supports a broader range of features and, thus, both versions can be regarded as two different solutions for the logger completion[1]. The two solutions offer both core features, which makes them logging systems. This includes features, such as *FileLogging* and *SQLDatabaseLogging*. However, *log4jv2* offers additional features that we consider as optional. One of these is *AsyncLogging*. For this paper we have concentrated on a subset of all provided features

4.3   Scenario-Based Evaluation

We studied several scenario-based examples to demonstrate the applicability and benefits of the proposed approach. The scenario covers different design issues in terms of feature alternatives, solution selection, and placement choice. The simulation series considers more than 1000 architecture candidates and evaluates performance and cost of each candidate to find the Pareto-optimal solutions. Here, we evaluate a set of feature alternatives an architect has to consider. The scenario is relevant, but not limited to the requirements engineering phase. Different functional and quality requirements of features must be balanced against each other. Early evaluation of the quality effects of feature alternatives that implement the requirements helps to discuss their

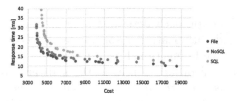

Fig. 1. Comparison of feature alternatives

---

[1] Please note that the approach is not limited to systems that build on each other and are related in their architecture.

prioritization with stakeholders on a sound data basis. In particular, we compare the features *FileLogging*, *SQLDatabaseLogging*, and *NoSQLDatabaseLogging*. As SQL database, we use MySQL v. 5.7.20 and as NoSQL database, we use MongoDB v. 3.4.10. Both DBMS are configured in the standard configuration. To analyze the scenario, we annotate the components `ItemService`, `Query`, and `BasicQuery` of the *mRUBiS* system with logging. Figure 1 shows the result of the evaluation. The diagram depicts the Pareto-optimal candidates for each feature alternative found by the design space exploration. The candidates with *File* logging show the best quality in terms of response time. The *NoSQL* alternative reaches 7.8% (average) higher response times. The *SQL* alternative is outperformed by the others, namely by 28.4% (average) through NoSQL and by 38.46% through File logging. It should be noted that *NoSQL* and *SQL* logging alternatives also result in slightly increased costs, which is due to the additional database component required by both alternatives. With the results, an architect can decide, which write target of the logger meets the requirements best.

5   Related Work

There are numerous papers that present variability models to define a common architecture for similar solutions. In [3] Atkinson et al. propose their KobrA approach that focuses on component-based product line development. The main component of the KobrA method is a framework that encapsulates a generic description of a family of applications. Here, not only the common parts of an architecture are relevant, but also all differences. They are considered by including all possible characteristics in decision models. These describe options that distinguish between the individual characteristics. If a concrete application is to be developed, the generic framework is instantiated and all decision models are solved. This results in a concrete instance, but does not influence the level of abstraction. There are similar approaches to modeling variability in software (architectures), such as Product Line Software Engineering (PuLSE) [5], the product line design process [6] by Bosch, the FAST [14] approach, or the algebraic language SPLA [2].

6   Conclusion

The approach described here presents a solution for the automatic evaluation and optimization of software architectures in the decision-making process about reusable functionalities. It supports decisions for the selection of features, configuration of features in the software architecture, and different solutions and effects on the quality attributes of the software architecture. The approach is aimed at supporting the software architect in evaluating the effects of features on the quality attributes at development time, even before the actual implementation has been carried out. Through early evaluation, suboptimal decisions can be discarded before implementation, thus supporting more cost-efficient software development. We demonstrated the advantages of this approach using a scenario from real-world systems. We modeled, analyzed, and optimized different design decisions based on scenarios. The results shown can be used in the next step to implement the software architecture.

References

1. Aleti, A., Bjornander, S., Grunske, L., Meedeniya, I.: ArcheOpterix: an extendable tool for architecture optimization of AADL models. In: MOMPES 2009 (2009)
2. Andres, C., Camacho, C., Llana, L.: A formal framework for software product lines. Inf. Softw. Technol. **55**, 1925–1947 (2013)
3. Atkinson, C., et al.: Component-Based Product Line Engineering with UML. Addison-Wesley Longman Publishing Co., Inc., Boston (2002)
4. Bachmann, F., Bass, L., Klein, M., Shelton, C.: Designing software architectures to achieve quality attribute requirements. In: SW Proceedings (2005)
5. Bayer, J., et al.: PuLSE: a methodology to develop software product lines. In: SSR 1999, ACM (1999)
6. Bosch, J.: Design and Use of Software Architectures: Adopting and Evolving a Product-line Approach. ACM Press/Addison-Wesley Publishing Co., Boston (2000)
7. Busch, A., Schneider, Y., Koziolek, A., et al.: Modelling the structure of reusable solutions for architecture-based quality evaluation. In: CloudSPD 2016. IEEE (2016)
8. Eckert, M.: Konditionale Platzierung von Architekturelementen zur Optimierung von Software-Architekt. Master's thesis, Karlsruhe Institute of Technology (2018)
9. Koziolek, A.: Automated Improvement of Software Architecture Models for Performance and Other Quality Attributes. KIT, Karlsruhe (2013)
10. Koziolek, A., Koziolek, H., et al.: PerOpteryx: automated application of tactics in multi-objective software architecture optimization. In: QoSA-ISARCS 2011 (2011)
11. Martens, A., Koziolek, H., et al.: Automatically improve software models for performance, reliability and cost using genetic algorithms. In: WOSP/SIPEW ICPE 2010 (2010)
12. Reussner, R.H., Becker, S.: Modeling and Simulating Software Architectures: The Palladio Approach. The MIT Press, Cambridge (2016)
13. Vogel, T.: mRUBiS: an exemplar for model-based architectural self-healing and self-optimization. In: SEAMS 2018. ACM (2018)
14. Weiss, D.M., Lai, C.T.R.: Software Product-line Engineering: A Family-Based Software Development Process. Addison-Wesley, Boston (1999)

Components and Design Alternatives in E-Assessment Systems

Michael Striewe[✉]

paluno - The Ruhr Institute for Software Technology,
University of Duisburg-Essen, Essen, Germany
michael.striewe@paluno.uni-due.de

Abstract. In the domain of e-learning and e-assessment, many different components are used to realise particular system features. Even for similar features using similar components there are different ways of realisation in terms of connection and integration. This paper presents results from literature review and design-space explorations that result in a catalogue of components and an overview on design alternatives.

1   Introduction

Following a general trend in recent decades, educational systems transformed in three generations from monolithic blocks via modular systems to service oriented frameworks [1]. Recent movements towards cloud based solutions are considered a fourth generation by some authors [2]. While these developments concern the general structure of systems, one can also analyse more closely the details of system design: There are different ways on how to connect components and the design of a given system may pose constraints on how to integrate additional e-assessment features. This paper makes two contributions: It provides a catalogue of system components commonly found in e-assessment systems and an overview on design alternatives in the context of component integration. Similar ideas have been explored for different aspects of system integration in the domain of e-learning [3,4] and intelligent tutoring systems (ITS) [5] in a less general way.

2   Component Catalogue

The component catalogue reports on different kinds of components found in the literature, that typically appear in the context of educational systems and that may be integrated with other components in a system offering e-assessment features. The overview serves as a baseline for subsequent considerations on design alternatives. The literature study particularly included (amongst other sources) a systematic review of papers from the *Int. Conf. on Technology Enhanced Assessment* (formerly known as *Int. Conf. on Computer Assisted Assessment*), the *IEEE Global Engineering Education Conf.*, the *Int. Conf. on Intelligent Tutoring Systems*, the *IEEE Trans. on Learning Technology* and the *Special Issue on*

© Springer Nature Switzerland AG 2019
T. Bures et al. (Eds.): ECSA 2019, LNCS 11681, pp. 220–228, 2019.
https://doi.org/10.1007/978-3-030-29983-5_15

eLearning Software Architectures issued by *Science of Computer Programming*. In the review, 36 publications have been identified as relevant, as they provide enough information about architecture and component design. 13 components have been extracted and grouped in four categories (see Table 1).

2.1 Frontend Components

Since e-assessment systems receive input, frontends of various kinds naturally form a category that also was identified earlier by other authors (e.g. [24]). A *student frontend* displays assessments to students and retrieves their answers. Systems often provide one single student frontend component that is extensible by plug-ins. However, there may also be cases in which a system offers e.g. one browser-based frontend for general purpose and one app-based frontend specifically designed for mobile devices. A *teacher frontend* aggregates features related to the organizational aspects of assessments (e.g. administration, authentication, and assessment scheduling). An *authoring tool* allows to create assessment items, item pools, and grading schemas. Notably, the naming difference between the teacher *frontend* and the authoring *tool* is intended. While the former is often designed as a closely coupled system component, the latter is often designed and perceived as a standalone tool.

2.2 Educational Components

The core of e-assessment systems are their features for generating contents, providing advice, and evaluating answers. An *assessment generator* prepares an assessment for delivery to the student. This often includes selecting appropriate items from an item pool in case of adaptive system behaviour, but can also appear in non-adaptive context in which nevertheless a particular exam must be delivered to a student. An *item generator* fills item templates with actual content. Consequently, it is not used in contexts using fixed items and in which any adaptations are performed by the assessment generator mentioned above. A *pedagogical module* provides advice as a human teacher would do. A typical action is to provide hints to students while they work on an assessment item. Consequently, these components primarily occur in systems that focus on learning or tutoring instead of formal evaluation of student performance. An *evaluator component* analyzes submissions, identifies mistakes and generates feedback. It is hence somewhat similar to the pedagogical module (and may be used by these modules), but it may be much simpler in that it just applies a grading schema to a solution without being able to provide any hint on how to improve a wrong solution. A *domain-specific expert system* is a component that is not specific for the purpose of e-assessment, but is able to solve general problems in a particular domain. It may be connected to evaluator components to enable complex analyses or to item generators to allow for sophisticated generation mechanisms.

Table 1. Overview on the component catalogue.

Component name and synonyms	Features/functionality/ contents/structure	References in literature
Frontend components (see Sect. 2.1)		
Student frontend (also: student LMS, student VLE, student CMS, student agent, or learning interface)	Get and display assessments, retrieve and store answers	[2, 6–22]
Teacher frontend (also: teacher LMS, teacher VLE, teacher CMS, or admin agent)	Administration, authentication, assessment scheduling	[2, 6]
Authoring tool (also: itembank user interface)	Create contents	[10, 17–19, 21, 23]
Educational components (see Sect. 2.2)		
Assessment generator (also: instructional manager, curriculum agent, task selector, tutoring component, or steering component)	Create assessments from item pool, individualize training	[2, 7, 9, 11–14, 16, 20, 22, 24–27]
Item generator (also: problem generator, item constructor, exercise generator)	Generate items/problems	[7, 8, 12, 17, 20, 27]
Pedagogical module (also: hint generator, tutoring engine)	Provides advice like teachers or hints	[5, 11–14, 16–18, 20, 22, 24]
Evaluator component (also: backend, checker, diagnose module, assessor, grader, marks calculator)	Analyse submissions and mistakes, create feedback	[6–10, 12–22, 25, 27, 28]
Domain-specific expert system (also: problem solver, domain component, knowledge agent)	Perform domain-specific operations or analyses	[8, 10, 12, 24]
Knowledge representation and storing components (see Sect. 2.3)		
Item bank (also: question bank, repository of questions, exercise database)	Assessment items including rules on how to grade responses and generate feedback or hints	[13–15, 20, 22, 23, 25]
Domain knowledge model (also: knowledge base)	Information on the assessment's domain (e.g. facts, concepts), organized by relations or rules	[5, 10–12, 16, 18, 20, 24]
Student model (also: learner model)	Information on a particular student (e.g. competency levels, overall scores), organized as records referring to an underlying competency structure	[5, 9–12, 14–16, 18, 20, 22, 24–26]
Connector components (see Sect. 2.4)		
Queue (also: spooler, middleware, service broker)	Connects frontend components and evaluator components for continuous data transfer	[6, 19, 28]
Data transfer component (also: notify and announce, reporting agent, assessment commit agent)	Bulk transfer of data, such as publishing results or archiving assessments	[2, 7]

2.3   Knowledge Representation and Storing Components

Almost every e-assessment system contains data storage for users, courses, or solutions. These basic features are out of scope here, but there are also components for storing more specific data. An *item bank* stores assessment items including rules on how to grade responses and generate feedback or hints. Authoring tools are typically the only components that have write access to an item bank, while problem generators and assessment generators may have read access. A *domain knowledge model* stores general facts or competency networks relating to the domain of the assessment. It is used in conjunction with expert systems and pedagogical modules. A *student model* reflects actual competencies or alike that relate to student capabilities or performance. Student models are most often used in conjunction with adaptive system behaviour.

2.4   Connector Components

In addition to fulfilling core requirements of e-assessment systems, some components are introduced for the sake of better software architectures. A *queue* can occur in two directions: (1) It may forward data from some frontend or steering components to evaluator components that possibly run on separate systems. (2) It may forward data from evaluator components to frontends. While this component does not add any educational value to a system, it may be crucial for several design alternatives on how to connect components. Different to a queue, a *data transfer component* is not concerned with continuous forwarding of data, but performs bulk transfer of data between components.

3   Design Alternatives

For the purpose of this paper, behavioural design defines which components are callers and callees or which components are used to (re-)direct calls from one component to another. Some alternatives in that area are discussed in Sects. 3.1 and 3.2. Similarly, structural design defines possible connections between components or the number of occurrences of components of a particular type within an architecture. Some alternatives in that area are discussed in Sects. 3.3 and 3.4.

3.1   General Component Behaviour

As in many other systems, it is possible to design components as *passive services* or *active agents*. Passive services are found in many e-assessment systems as explicit design decisions [1,6,27], while active agents are particularly common in the domain of intelligent tutoring systems [10,26]. In that particular domain they overcome the problem that students may not know how or when to trigger a certain feature (e.g. a request for a hint) from a passive service.

3.2 Grading a Response

A response to an assessment item is entered via a frontend component and processed by an evaluator component. The connection between them can be realized in different ways. All alternatives discussed below are independent of the number of evaluator components involved. System designers will surely use at least one alternative, but may use more within one system.

The *synchronous push* design corresponds to a plain method call. User interaction directly triggers the grading process and the user has to wait until it finishes. Systems in which grading tasks are short running and in which the next step depends on the previous result can employ this design. Its main benefit is its simplicity, as it does not require parallelism for single users. However, it is not suited for complex grading tasks that may be long-running or consume many resources. In these cases, students may have to wait for a system response or may even overload the server with requests.

The *asynchronous push* design also triggers the grading process directly, but without blocking user interaction. An example can be found in [27]. Although users are not blocked, a risk of system overload still exists, as many students can trigger grading processes at the same time.

In the *asynchronous pull* design input is stored in a queue and pulled from there by the evaluator component. Examples of this design can be found in [6,19,29]. Similar to the previous design, response times are kept low. However, there is an additional benefit in that many responses at the same time are less likely to overload server resources as they will just fill the queue and increase wait times until they are processed.

3.3 System Extensions

In component-oriented systems, extensions (e.g. adding new types of assessment items and grading functions) are possible by extending existing components and by adding a new one and connecting it properly to the existing ones. Systems that do not allow for extensions will not use any of the alternatives discussed below. Otherwise, a system may use one or more of the following alternatives.

An *encapsulated plug-in* implements the full feature set of the new component. It is written in the same language as the existing system and uses its data storage and other components. Usually the existing system offers an appropriate API to be used by plug-ins. The benefit is that a well-written plug-in API can ease plug-in development and assure a close integration. The API may also limit the plug-ins in what they do, which can protect the system from malicious components. This may also be a downside if some sophisticated features cannot be implemented that way. In addition, a badly-written plug-in API may cause problems in system maintenance or performance.

An *unrestricted plug-in* only implements a subset of the desired features directly. Besides connecting to the plug-in API of the existing system, it also connects to an own backend component that implements the missing part of the feature set. This design can be found in LMS as with the MOODLE External API

[30]. It overcomes the drawbacks mentioned above, as the backend component can implement arbitrarily complexe features. A drawback is that potentially critical data may leave the system. There is also a risk that the backend component may become a bottleneck with respect to system performance.

In the *external tool* design, the existing system redirects the user to an external tool via some standard API and receives a callback when the user has finished their duties there. This mechanism can be realized in learning management systems via the IMS-LTI standard [31]. This design actually avoids extending an existing system, but adds functionality by coupling it with another system. The design enforces a quite strict separation of data that can be a benefit and drawback at the same time: It improves privacy and simplifies data management but it also requires to establish a trusted connection between the tools.

In *API-based integrations*, there is an even more loose coupling. A system may use the *asynchronous pull* design and require all evaluator components reading from the queue to be *active agents*. An additional agent can then simply be added without the need for any kind of dedicated plug-in API. Instead, having a queue from which other components can read forms an implicit plug-in API.

3.4   Evaluator Granularity

Section 3.2 already discussed ways to invoke evaluator components. This section deals with design alternatives for structuring them internally. Each evaluator component will use one of the designs, but if there are many evaluator components, each of them may use a different one.

A *monolithic evaluator* is designed as a single block that receives a submission as input and returns grades and feedback as output. This is typically sufficient for short running synchronous grading tasks (e.g. [9,13]). The complete behaviour of the component can be modelled as a single process in this case. If entirely different grading procedures are necessary, two or more completely independent evaluator components can be employed following this pattern, as it is for example sometimes used for grading solutions in different programming languages [6,32].

If different grading procedures share some common elements, an *evaluator with sub-components* can be used. An example for this design can be found in [33], where the assignment database contains the sequence of modules to be applied to the submission. While some of the components may be relevant just for one type of assignments, others may be used for several assignment types. Similarly, the order of invoking these components may differ between assignment types. As an additional design choice, this pattern allows to use single-threaded processing within the evaluator or to call different sub-components in parallel threads. The main benefit of parallel processing is to speed up the grading process for a single solution and thus lowering the wait time for the student. On the downside, not all grading mechanism may be suitable for being split up into parallel tasks, as one grading step may require results from another grading step. Using several (single-threaded) evaluator instances in parallel may be an alternative, as it at least reduces the overall processing time in bulk processing.

4   Conclusions

The paper discussed a catalogue of components in e-assessment systems and design alternatives for four different aspects. Both catalogues are intended to serve developers of educational systems to make systematic design decisions and to serve software architecture researchers who are interested in domain specific architectural knowledge. All results can be used in a descriptive manner as a starting point for more detailed description and comparisons of systems in literature reviews or comparative studies. Moreover, the alternatives can be used in empirical analyses that elicit criteria for evaluating software architectures of e-assessment systems based on the design decisions they make.

References

1. Dagger, D., O'Connor, A., Lawless, S., Walsh, E., Wade, V.P.: Service-oriented e-learning platforms: from monolithic systems to flexible services. IEEE Internet Comput. 11(3), 28–35 (2007)
2. Gusev, M., Ristov, S., Armenski, G., Velkoski, G., Bozinoski, K.: E-assessment cloud solution: architecture, organization and cost model. iJET 8(Special Issue 2), 55–64 (2013)
3. Harrer, A., Pinkwart, N., McLaren, B.M., Scheuer, O.: The scalable adapter design pattern: enabling interoperability between educational software tools. TLT 1(2), 131–143 (2008)
4. García-Holgado, A., García-Peñalvo, F.J.: Architectural pattern to improve the definition and implementation of elearning ecosystems. Sci. Comput. Program. 129, 20–34 (2016)
5. Devedzic, V., Harrer, A.: Architectural patterns in pedagogical agents. In: Cerri, S.A., Gouardères, G., Paraguaçu, F. (eds.) ITS 2002. LNCS, vol. 2363, pp. 81–90. Springer, Heidelberg (2002). https://doi.org/10.1007/3-540-47987-2_13
6. Amelung, M., Krieger, K., Rösner, D.: E-assessment as a service. IEEE Trans. Learn. Technol. 4, 162–174 (2011)
7. Armenski, G., Gusev, M.: E-testing based on service oriented architecture. In: Proceedings of the 10th CAA Conference (2006)
8. Bridgeman, S., Goodrich, M.T., Kobourov, S.G., Tamassia, R.: PILOT: an interactive tool for learning and grading. In: Proceedings of the 31st SIGCSE Technical Symposium on Computer Science Education, pp. 139–143 (2000)
9. Cheniti-Belcadhi, L., Henze, N., Braham, R.: Implementation of a personalized assessment web service. In: Sixth International Conference on Advanced Learning Technologies (ICALT), pp. 586–590 (2006)
10. Costa, E., Silva, P., Silva, M., Silva, E., Santos, A.: A multiagent-based ITS using multiple viewpoints for propositional logic. In: Cerri, S.A., Clancey, W.J., Papadourakis, G., Panourgia, K. (eds.) ITS 2012. LNCS, vol. 7315, pp. 640–641. Springer, Heidelberg (2012). https://doi.org/10.1007/978-3-642-30950-2_100
11. El-Sheikh, E., Sticklen, J.: Generating intelligent tutoring systems from reusable components and knowledge-based systems. In: Cerri, S.A., Gouardères, G., Paraguaçu, F. (eds.) ITS 2002. LNCS, vol. 2363, pp. 199–207. Springer, Heidelberg (2002). https://doi.org/10.1007/3-540-47987-2_24
12. Goguadze, G., Melis, E.: Combining evaluative and generative diagnosis in ACTIVEMATH. In: AIED, pp. 668–670 (2009)

13. Gonzalez-Sanchez, J., et al.: A system architecture for affective meta intelligent tutoring systems. In: Trausan-Matu, S., Boyer, K.E., Crosby, M., Panourgia, K. (eds.) ITS 2014. LNCS, vol. 8474, pp. 529–534. Springer, Cham (2014). https://doi.org/10.1007/978-3-319-07221-0_67
14. Hatzilygeroudis, I., Koutsojannis, C., Papavlasopoulos, C., Prentzas, J.: Knowledge-based adaptive assessment in a web-based intelligent educational system. In: Sixth International Conference on Advanced Learning Technologies (ICALT), pp. 651–655 (2006)
15. Kenfack, C., Nkambou, R., Robert, S., Tato, A.A.N., Brisson, J., Kissok, P.: A brief overview of logic-muse, an intelligent tutoring system for logical reasoning skills. In: Micarelli, A., et al. (eds.) Intelligent Tutoring Systems, ITS 2016, LNCS, vol. 9684, pp. 511–513 (2016). https://doi.org/10.1007/978-3-319-39583-8
16. Martens, A.: Time in the adaptive tutoring process model. In: Ikeda, M., Ashley, K.D., Chan, T.-W. (eds.) ITS 2006. LNCS, vol. 4053, pp. 134–143. Springer, Heidelberg (2006). https://doi.org/10.1007/11774303_14
17. Martin, B.: Authoring educational games with greenmind. In: Woolf, B.P., Aïmeur, E., Nkambou, R., Lajoie, S. (eds.) ITS 2008. LNCS, vol. 5091, pp. 684–686. Springer, Heidelberg (2008). https://doi.org/10.1007/978-3-540-69132-7_77
18. Murray, T.: Having it all, maybe: design tradeoffs in ITS authoring tools. In: Frasson, C., Gauthier, G., Lesgold, A. (eds.) ITS 1996. LNCS, vol. 1086, pp. 93–101. Springer, Heidelberg (1996). https://doi.org/10.1007/3-540-61327-7_105
19. Richter, T., Boehringer, D.: Towards electronic exams in undergraduate engineering. In: IEEE Global Engineering Education Conference (EDUCON), pp. 196–201 (2014)
20. Rickel, J.W.: Intelligent computer-aided instruction: a survey organized around system components. IEEE Trans. Syst. Man Cybern. **19**(1), 40–57 (1989)
21. Siddiqi, R., Harrison, C.J., Siddiqi, R.: Improving teaching and learning through automated short-answer marking. TLT **3**(3), 237–249 (2010)
22. Weng, M.M., Fakinlede, I., Lin, F., Shih, T.K., Chang, M.: A conceptual design of multi-agent based personalized quiz game. In: 11th IEEE International Conference on Advanced Learning Technologies (ICALT), pp. 19–21 (2011)
23. Davies, W.M., Howard, Y., Davis, H.C., Millard, D.E., Sclater, N.: Aggregating assessment tools in a service oriented architecture. In: 9th International CAA Conference (2005)
24. Devedzic, V., Radovic, D., Jerinic, L.: On the notion of components for intelligent tutoring systems. In: Goettl, B.P., Halff, H.M., Redfield, C.L., Shute, V.J. (eds.) ITS 1998. LNCS, vol. 1452, pp. 504–513. Springer, Heidelberg (1998). https://doi.org/10.1007/3-540-68716-5_56
25. Kurup, M., Greer, J.E., McCalla, G.I.: The Fawlty article tutor. In: Frasson, C., Gauthier, G., McCalla, G.I. (eds.) ITS 1992. LNCS, vol. 608, pp. 84–91. Springer, Heidelberg (1992). https://doi.org/10.1007/3-540-55606-0_12
26. Neji, M., Ben Ammar, M.: Agent-based collaborative affective e-learning framework. Electron. J. e-Learn. **5**(2), 123–134 (2007)
27. Zschaler, S., White, S., Hodgetts, K., Chapman, M.: Modularity for automated assessment: a design-space exploration. In: Combined Proceedings of the Workshops of the German Software Engineering Conference (SE) (2018)
28. Iffländer, L., Dallmann, A., Daniel-Beck, P., Ifland, M.: PABS - a programming assignment feedback system. In: Proceedings of the Second Workshop "Automatische Bewertung von Programmieraufgaben" (2015)
29. Striewe, M.: An architecture for modular grading and feedback generation for complex exercises. Sci. Comput. Program. **129**, 35–47 (2016)

30. Casany, M.J., et al.: Moodbile: a framework to integrate m-learning applications with the LMS. J. Res. Pract. Inf. Technol. **44**(2), 129–149 (2012)
31. IMS learning tools integration specification. IMS Global Learning Consortium Std., Rev. 1.1.1 (2012)
32. Núñez, A., Fernández, J., Garcia, J.D., Prada, L., Carretero, J.: M-PLAT: multi-programming language adaptive tutor. In: Eighth IEEE International Conference on Advanced Learning Technologies (ICALT), pp. 649–651 (2008)
33. Pardo, A.: A multi-agent platform for automatic assignment management. In: Proceedings of the 7th Annual Conference on Innovation and Technology in Computer Science Education (ITiCSE), pp. 60–64 (2002)

Industry Track

A Four-Layer Architecture Pattern for Constructing and Managing Digital Twins

Somayeh Malakuti(✉), Johannes Schmitt, Marie Platenius-Mohr, Sten Grüner,
Ralf Gitzel, and Prerna Bihani

ABB Corporate Research Center, Ladenburg, Germany
{somayeh.malakuti,johannes.o.schmitt,marie.platenius-mohr,
sten.gruener,ralf.gitzel,prerna.bihani}@de.abb.com

Abstract. The promise of a digital twin is to make asset lifecycle information accessible by providing a single access point to the information. Thereby, it reduces the required time and effort and enables new data-intensive use cases. This paper provides an abstract four-layer architecture pattern to construct digital twins and to incorporate information from various kinds of sources. The pattern is designed to be flexibly extensible with new information sources and can flexibly support new kinds of proprietary or standard information. We discuss various alternatives to implement the pattern and provide an example realization based on microservices and OPC UA.

Keywords: Digital twin · Microservice · OPC UA · Information model

1 Introduction

A major problem of industrial systems are *information silos*. The information related to different lifecycle phases of an asset (e.g, a device, a production cell) is scattered across multiple information sources. These information sources are often maintained by different internal and external organizations and are interfaced by various applications. This leads to a broken information flow across the lifecycle of the assets because these information sources do not properly exchange information; some information may be duplicated or inconsistent while some others may be missing. As a result, significant amounts of time are usually required to find the relevant information, to convert the information to a suitable format, to pass the information to different tools, etc.

Digital twins can be seen as a promising solution for providing access to the lifecycle information of their assets. The underlying definition of the trend has evolved over time. Initially, a digital twin was considered to be a high fidelity mathematical model of a physical device that could simulate the device as closely as possible. This definition has been enriched over the time to be an evolving

The authors were partially supported by German Federal Ministry of Education and Research in the scope of the BaSys 4.0 project (01IS16022).

T. Bures et al. (Eds.): ECSA 2019, LNCS 11681, pp. 231–246, 2019.
https://doi.org/10.1007/978-3-030-29983-5_16

digital profile of the historical and current behavior of an asset together with all of its properties, where an asset is anything of value for an organization such as a physical device, a subsystem, a plant, or a software entity[1]. The information fragments contained in a digital twin are use case specific and often originate from different lifecycle phases. Typically, it encompasses elements such as ordering details, engineering parameters, operational information, and maintenance information.

Depending on the use case, differences arise in what kind of information must be collected, where it is found, and what it is used for. To have a unified solution, this paper proposes a four-layer architecture pattern to collect information about an asset from various information sources, to construct the digital twin of the asset and to aggregate the information in it. The pattern is designed to be flexibly extensible with new information sources and can support new kinds of proprietary or standardized information. We outline various alternatives to realize this pattern and sketch an example implementation, which is validated using our industrial use case, based on microservices and OPC UA [1] technologies.

In the next section, we describe an industrial use case for digital twins from ABB. Section 3 lists requirements for a solution to create and manage digital twins. Section 4 introduces our four-layer architecture pattern for such a solution, while Sect. 5 discusses a concrete realization of this architecture. Section 6 outlines the related work, and Sect. 7 concludes the paper with a discussion about the future directions of our research.

2   An Industrial Use Case in the ABB Company

Variable speed drives are a common asset in industrial plants to control the speed of motors. In our real-world example, we show digital twins for both the drive instance and its type. The latter contains type-design information such as CAD drawings, simulation models, and documentation. The former is the actual device used by a specific customer. While all of this information could be stored in a single digital twin, this would result in a massive amount of information replication as the type information is the same for all instances. Therefore, we envision two digital twins – one for the instance and one for the type. Since they are related to each other, this relation is also established among their digital twins.

The bottom part of Fig. 1 shows the case where the information related to different lifecycle phases of the drive and its type is scattered across multiple information sources. Here, the information about drive types is maintained in the so-called *Product Type Database*. Various proprietary applications are used, for instance the *Device Selection Tool* is used to select a specific drive type based on desired settings of customers. Information about the installations such as associated customers, plants, purchased devices and warranty information is maintained in a so-called *Installed-base Database*. The operational parameter

---

[1] https://www2.deloitte.com/insights/us/en/focus/industry-4-0/digital-twin-technology-smart-factory.html.

information of each drive is maintained within the drive firmware itself and served via an OPC UA (IEC 62541 [1]) server; hence, the drive is labeled as an *OPC UA-Enabled Drive*. Further information may be provided by *External Platforms*, e.g. production information for drive components manufactured by external suppliers.

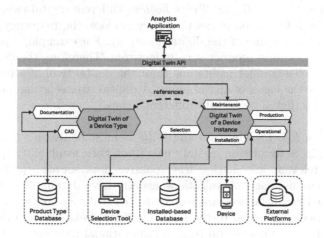

Fig. 1. A digital twin example

As depicted in Fig. 1, the digital twin is considered a means to provide a single entry point to the information of a drive and its type. Each digital twin contains information about the relevant asset. Having a digital twin in place helps to not only easily access the information but can even add further intelligence to the system. For example, there may be an analytics application which receives inputs about a drive's type, initial drive selection parameters, and operational values from the drive's digital twin to calculate its current health status.

3   Requirements

Based on our interviews with internal domain experts and evaluation of existing proposals for digital twins, we identified the following requirements to be fulfilled by a digital twin solution.

R1, Supporting Multiple Information Sources: To make a digital twin solution usable in practice, it must be possible to collect information from diverse sources and feed them to the relevant digital twins. Since the information sources are already operating for many years, only seamless extensions are allowed for enabling them to exchange information with digital twins.

R2, Supporting Modular Extension of Digital Twins: Information pieces are developed and delivered separately during the lifecycle of an asset. For example, when a new drive is installed in a plant, service information is only added once maintenance services take place. Therefore, it must be possible to incrementally extend the relevant digital twin content upon the availability of new information.

R3, Supporting Various Digital Twins Logics: Different digital twins may differ in terms of the information pieces that they enclose, the frequency of information updates, the lifetime of the digital twin, etc. For example, a product type exists before a concrete product is manufactured. Therefore, the digital twin of a product type has a different lifetime than the digital twin of a product itself. We name these the logics of digital twins. A digital twin solution must facilitate defining various digital twins with different logics.

R4, Supporting Information Push and Pull: It must be feasible to actively add information pieces to relevant digital twins upon their availability (push-based), or to query relevant information from passive data sources (pull-based). For example, in our use case, organizations usually have databases in which information related to all devices are stored; for each device, relevant information must be queried and added to the relevant digital twin. Each device may also actively bring more information (e.g., its operational parameters) to its digital twin.

R5, Syncing Information Between Digital Twins and Information Sources: The information enclosed by digital twins may be modified over time. To maintain information consistency, it must be possible to sync information between digital twins and the information sources. A special case is syncing information between a digital twin and the corresponding asset so that the information of the digital twins can be updated based on the actual information of the assets.

R6, Supporting Various Information Formats: Information pieces might be expressed in proprietary formats or based on different standards to facilitate interoperability across organizations. It must be feasible to collect and convert the information pieces and/or an entire digital twin to the desired format in a permanent way or on the fly when needed. The knowledge about which information formats are supported and processable by a certain component needs to be retrievable by the digital twin solution.

R7, Offering Dedicated Interaction Mechanisms for Each Information Piece: Each proprietary or standardized information piece requires a suitable user interface to display information and allow user-interaction.

R8, Identifying Digital Twins and Their Corresponding Asset: Since industrial systems may consist of thousands of assets (e.g. installed devices), it is necessary to provide a means to uniquely identify the assets and their corresponding digital twins on the network. Usually multiple identification schemes are in place within one organization, meaning that the information pieces collected from various sources might have different identification schemes. Therefore, means are needed to map these identifiers to each other in order to identify the multiple information pieces that are relevant to a given asset.

R9, Offering Digital Twin APIs: Suitable APIs must be offered to applications to access and manipulate information stored within digital twins.

The above-listed requirements mainly cover functional aspects of a digital twin solution. Several non-functional requirements such as security and distribution are also relevant, but out of the scope of this paper.

4 The Architecture Pattern for Digital Twins

Since collecting lifecycle information from various sources and making it accessible via digital twins is a recurring problem in companies, we propose an architecture pattern for managing digital twins and their information sources. This helps various business units or companies to adopt a unified solution for implementing their digital twins.

Figure 2 shows our four-layer architecture pattern for a digital twin solution. The bottom level is the *Information Providers* layer, which consists of various information sources (satisfies *R1*). The *Model Providers* layer is responsible for gathering and processing information pieces from the *Information Providers* layer, and feeding it to the *Digital Twin Providers*. In our pattern, we refer to information pieces as models, since they can be expressed in various proprietary or standard formats. The *Digital Twin Providers* layer creates and manages digital twins. Various applications, e.g. viewing and analytics applications, can be located at the *Applications* layer, which can access and manipulate digital twins.

This pattern does not make any assumption on the cardinality and distribution of the depicted components. We leave these decisions to the implementations of this pattern based on the quality attributes of the specific use cases. In Sect. 5, we list a set of design alternatives for our use case.

4.1 The Information Providers Layer

We distinguish among the following kinds of information sources.

Applications/Tools: Digital twins must include the output of various tools that exist in organizations. For example, in ABB, dedicated tools exist to select drives suitable for a specific application along with their connected motors, and to parameterize them. The output of these tools is usually stored as files in a specific format, and/or in some kind of databases.
Devices: The operational parameters of devices (e.g., temperature or speed), which are defined within the firmware software of the devices, are another source of information. It is becoming commonly accepted that future Industrial Internet of Things (IIoT) devices will be delivered with an embedded

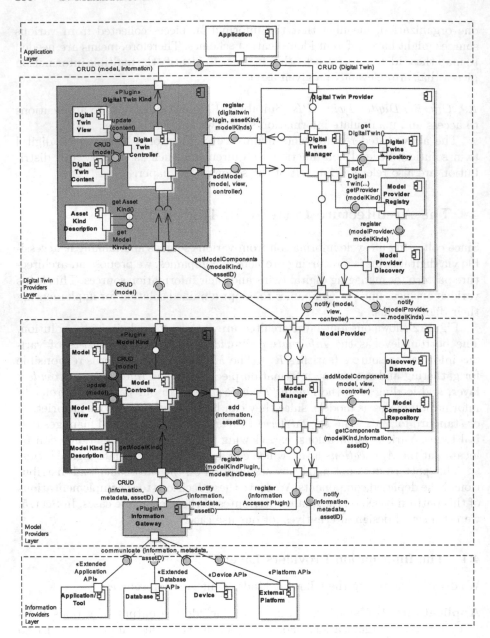

Fig. 2. The architecture pattern

information model in the OPC UA [1] format for defining at least the operational parameters and methods of the devices. Such devices already implement the functionality to sync this information with the relevant information within their firmware. The operational parameters of the devices can be discovered and added as part of the devices' digital twin.

Databases: There are different databases such as *Product Type Database* and an *Installed-base Database*, which contain various information about device types and their installations. These databases usually offer APIs, which can be used in a seamless manner to exchange information with digital twins.

External platforms: The information about a device and its type may be scattered in multiple IoT platforms, possibly owned by different companies. Such platforms are also sources of information that is described in a standard/agreed format or in the proprietary format of the source platform.

In addition to these, we have two special kinds of information providers:

Digital twin applications: The applications using information about digital twins (the top layer of Fig. 2) may also modify the content of digital twins. For example, an application may suggest new maintenance services to be performed on a device and this information can be included in the digital twin of the device. These modifications take place using the digital twin APIs and, if needed, are communicated to the relevant information providers.

Digital twins: Other digital twins provided by the same or different IoT platforms may also be a source of information. For digital twins within one platform, we assume that the information exchange among them takes place within the context of specific applications located at the *Applications* layer. These applications make use of the APIs offered at the *Digital Twin Provider* layer to access digital twins and establish information links among them.

4.2   The Model Providers Layer

We adopt a plugin-based architecture to make the *Model Providers* layer extensible with new kinds of information sources and new kinds of models at runtime (satisfies *R2*). The *Information Gateway* plugin at the bottom part of this layer interacts with information sources to retrieve and/or update information. Dedicated plugins can be defined for each kind of information source.

The *Model Kind* plugin defines necessary components to provide and manage different kinds of models (satisfies *R6*). There is the so-called *Model Kind Description*, describing which kind of model is supported by particular plugins; example model kinds are documentation, CAD drawing, operational parameters, and maintenance. Dedicated plugins may be provided for each model kind. The model descriptions will later on be used at the *Digital Twin Provider* layer to match the models to the relevant digital twin.

Within the *Model Kind* plugin, we adopt the Model View Controller (MVC) pattern [2] to manage each model that is to be included in a digital twin. The information content corresponds to the *Model* component of this pattern. Since each model is defined based on a specific standard or in a proprietary format, there is a dedicated *View* associated to each model to visualize its content in a suitable format. Each model is also associated with a *Controller*, which communicates with the respective view and also populates the model by interacting with *Information Gateway* (view and controller satisfy *R7*). The interactions with *Information Gateway* may be for creating, reading, updating or deleting (CRUD) information, as well as receiving notifications about the changes in the source information.

The *Model Provider* component is the core component, in which other components are plugged in. Here, *Model Manager* instantiates the MVC components when needed, and keeps a reference to them in *Model Components Repository*. *Model Manager* interacts with the *Digital Twin Provider* layer through its APIs; for example, it receives commands to construct a model, or to provide a model to *Digital Twin Manager*. The information exchange with the *Digital Twin Provider* layer can be push- or pull-based; i.e. the information is actively pushed to, or can be queried by the *Digital Twin Provider* layer, respectively (satisfies *R4*).

Once the models are constructed and added to the relevant digital twins, the associated *Controller* component may also be the recipient of the commands from the *Digital Twin Provider* layer; for example, to update the content of the model in a special frequency.

The availability and multiplicity of model providers may change during the lifetime of a digital twin. To be able to cope with such changes, our architecture opts for a mechanism to discover model providers. The necessary information to perform such a discovery is provided as *Discovery Daemon*, which notifies the *Model Provider Discovery* component in the upper layer.

4.3   The Digital Twin Providers Layer

The core part of this layer is the *Digital Twin Manager*, which is responsible for managing the lifecycle of digital twins, i.e. construction and destruction. It discovers model providers and their supported model kinds via the *Model Provider Discovery* component, which registers the providers at the *Model Provider Registry*. This registry allows *Digital Twin Manager* to retrieve the matching model provider for a given model kind.

There can be different kinds of digital twins within one system. For example, in our use case, we distinguish between the digital twin of a drive type and that of a drive instance. Each contains different kinds of models collected from different information sources. We adopt a plugin-based architecture to make the *Digital Twin Providers* layer extensible with new kinds of digital twins (satisfies *R3*). Here, *Asset Kind Description* specifies desired model kinds for each kind of digital twin. For example, for the digital twin of a drive type, documentation models and CAD drawings are model kinds of interest.

Similarly to each individual model, we also adopt the MVC pattern to manage each kind of digital twins. Here, the actual *Digital Twin Content* forms the model component of the pattern. The content of a digital twin is the aggregation of the models collected from the *Model Providers* layer, as well as an identification mechanism to bind these models together (satisfies *R8*, see Sect. 5 for details). A *Digital Twin Controller* component associated with each digital twin instance updates the model and interacts with the *Digital Twin View* component.

The point of time at which a digital twin must be constructed is use case specific. For example, users may explicitly construct a digital twin via a dedicated *Application* and start collecting information from model providers; another way is to automatically construct a digital twin upon the presence of its first constituent model. Either way, the *Digital Twin Manager* instantiates a *Digital Twin Controller* and passes the control to it to proceed with content acquisition from model providers.

The information about digital twins and their MVC components are maintained in the *Digital Twin Repository*. Suitable APIs are offered to applications to access and manipulate digital twin information.

4.4   The Applications Layer

Various use case specific applications may be developed to work with digital twins. These applications may work at the level of digital twins to create, read, update, and delete (CRUD) digital twins; or, they may work with the information contained within digital twins. For the latter case, the applications may directly interact with the respective *Digital Twin Controller*, and for the former case with *Digital Twin Manager*, both of which provide appropriate APIs (satisfies *R9*).

5   A Concrete Architecture Example

This section discusses an example implementation of the architecture pattern for our use case in Sect. 2. We have implemented our example in OPC UA [1] technology. OPC UA is becoming the de facto machine-to-machine communication protocol for industrial automation systems, which also offers an object-oriented information modeling mechanism as well as a service-oriented architecture to access the information. One faces various alternatives in implementing our abstract architecture. Figure 3 summarizes some alternatives and our decisions for our use case. We will return to them after we explain the concrete architecture, as depicted in Fig. 4, in the following subsection.

5.1   The Model Providers Layer

Since various pieces of information are delivered by different organizations, we define a separate model provider for each information provider, so that we can flexibly extend our implementation with new information providers. One may consider different cardinalities in other use cases; for example, a use case may require that one model provider accesses many information providers, or vice versa.

In our use case, we have the following kinds of information providers: (a) Two existing databases, i.e., *Product Type Database* and *Installed-base Database*, (b) the *Device Selection Tool* that generates information about the initial parameterization of drives, (c) a drive with embedded OPC UA server, and (d) an external platform providing production information.

Category	Decision Point	Alternatives	Adoption in the Prototype
Information Provider Layer	Cardinality of Model Providers w.r.t Information Providers	1:1, 1:n, m:1, m:n	1:1, one model provider per information provider
	APIs to Information Providers	Standard vs. Proprietary	OPC UA standard API to access device, proprietary APIs to access other information providers
Model Provider Layer	Cardinality of Model Providers w.r.t Models	1:1, 1:n, m:1, m:n	1:1, one model provider provides one type of model, except for type-specific models, which is 1:n
	Model Content w.r.t Information Providers	Copy vs. Reference	Referencing the operational parameters of the drive, copying the rest
	Model Content Format	Proprietary vs. Standard	Proprietary models
	View Execution	Server-side vs Client-side	Client-side execution of HTML pages
	View Kind	Desktop-based vs. Web-based vs. Native Mobile-based	Web-based views
	Model Provider Distribution	Distributed vs. Centralized	Distributed microservices
Digital Twin Provider Layer	Distribution	Centralized vs. Distributed	One Digital Twin Manager centralized instance
	Cardinality of Model Providers w.r.t Digital Twin Providers	1:1, 1:n, m:1, m:n	m:1, multiple Model Provider microservices, one centralized Digital Twin provider
	Cardinality of Digital Twin w.r.t. Asset	1:1, 1:n, m:1, m:n	1:1, one digital twin for each device
	Communication Kind	Pull-based vs. Push-based	Pulling installation and type information, Pushing drive operational model and maintenance model
	Information Storage	Any storage such as OPC UA servers, MongoDB, etc.	OPC UA servers
	Digital Twin Content w.r.t Model Providers	Copy vs. Reference	Proxy objects in OPC UA server referencing original model objects; using REST URIs to access controllers
	Digital Twin Content Format	Proprietary vs. Standard	Proprietary by default with the possibility to be transformed to a standard format on demand
	Model Provider Discovery	Automatic vs. Manual	Automatic via mDNS discovery mechanism, manual by configuration files
	Distribution	Centralized vs. Distributed	One Digital Twin Manager centralized instance
	Deployment	Device vs. Edge vs. Cloud	On the edge
	Construction and Destruction	Manual vs. Automatic	Automatic upon the appearance of the device on the network, also manual on user requests
	APIs to Applications	Standard vs. Proprietary	Standard OPC UA APIs, REST API
Application Layer	Deployment	Device vs. Edge vs. Cloud	On-premise

Fig. 3. Example alternatives for implementing the pattern

For the sake of extensibility, we adopt microservices to implement each model provider. We use the web-based API of the existing databases to access their information. The model provider that accesses the *Product Type Database* has two plugins for the MVC components because it provides two kinds of models: documentation and CAD drawing. Other model providers offer one type of model; hence, they have one MVC plugin.

The model provider that accesses the *Device Selection Tool* must read the output files of this tool. To access the files on the file system, we define a so-called *Digital Twin Monitored Folder*, where the files must be stored. The existing tool is extended with an add-in to store their results in this folder.

Since we adopt OPC UA as the technology to implement digital twins, the OPC UA drive can be seen as a *native* model provider: An information provider

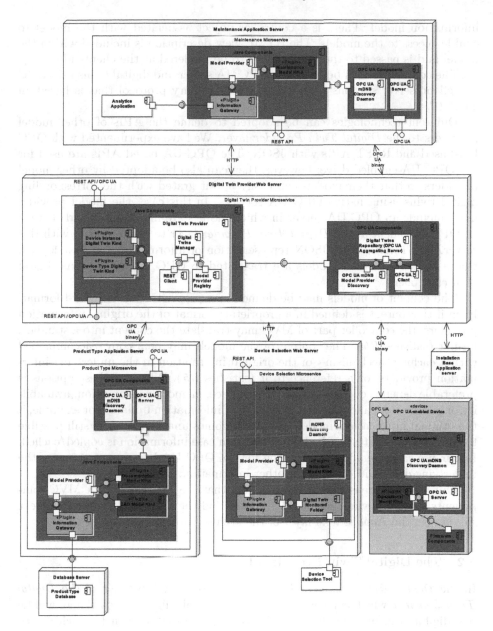

Fig. 4. An example concrete architecture

that provides the necessary MVC components, which can be directly integrated into a digital twin, is regarded in our architecture as a native model provider. In terms of the necessary MVC components, the embedded OPC UA server of the drive provides the operational parameters of the drive as an OPC UA information model. There is a controller object associated with the model to enable access to the models. The HTML view description is included within the model and is passed to the upper layers to be rendered at the client-side.

The communication between the OPC UA server and digital twins uses OPC UA client/server sessions using the OPC UA binary protocol that is based on TCP/IP.

Different technologies can be adopted to define the APIs of other model providers to the *Digital Twin Provider* layer. We have experimented with OPC UA-based and REST APIs with JSON. The OPC UA-based APIs are used for the OPC UA-enabled drive; however, they can also be adopted by other model providers so that their models can easily be integrated with the corresponding digital twins using native OPC UA services. In this case, the model provider must include an OPC UA server in which models are maintained, and there is an OPC UA client at the *Digital Twin Provider* layer to communicate with this server. REST APIs with JSON representation of information can be adopted, where the JSON-based models are translated to OPC UA objects via digital twin controllers.

The content of models may be defined in a proprietary or standard format. Even if the content is defined in a proprietary format of the original information providers, the controller part of MVC may translate the content into a standard format (satisfies *R6*). The content of the models may be a copy—accompanied with a caching mechanism—of the original information in the underlying information providers, or a reference to it (satisfies *R5*). Which of these options is preferable depends on the desired performance, memory consumption, availability of information, and required frequency of information update. For example, if the original information/model provider becomes unavailable, it is still possible to work with the latest cached information in case information is copied/cached. In our use case, we adopt referencing for the OPC UA-based parameters of the underlying drive and copying for other information.

Our architecture is web-based, meaning that the view part of the MVC components is defined via a set of HTML files, and they are rendered at the client side, i.e. in the *Applications* layer of the architecture.

5.2   The Digital Twin Providers Layer

In the *Digital Twin Providers Layer*, there is only one instance of the *Digital Twin Manager* which can centrally manage multiple digital twins. There will be one digital twin instance for each device and one digital twin for each device type. Hence, there are two *Digital Twin Kind* plugins in our realization.

The choice of technology for storing digital twins depends on the scale of the system and desired non-functional requirements such as performance. We make use of a so-called OPC UA aggregating server to store digital twins, and to aggregate underlying models in digital twins. An OPC UA aggregating server is a special OPC UA server, which concentrates the information of underlying servers and may add more logics on top, e.g. to compute historic information.

In our implementation of the aggregating server, only a reference to the actual information in the underlying model providers is maintained, and actual information is retrieved from the underlying model providers on demand.

Since the underlying model providers can communicate via OPC UA or REST APIs, there are dedicated clients in the *Digital Twin Provider* to facilitate the communications. We adopt the multicast DNS (mDNS) [3] discovery mechanism to automatically discover the appearance/disappearance of microservices. Each model provider microservice makes use of its *mDNS Discovery Daemon* to announce its presence as well as its list of supported models to the *Model Provider Discovery* component. The microservices keep announcing themselves on a regular basis while they are alive. The *Model Provider Discovery* component will update the *Model Provider Registry* as soon as new microservices announce themselves or previously present microservices disappear. In an OPC UA realization, the disappearance of a microservice will be noted by a closed client connection, which could also trigger an update of the registry.

The *Digital Twin Manager* can interact with multiple model providers. The interactions can be push-based or pull-based (satisfies *R4*). In the latter case, the *Digital Twin Manager* requests models from the available model providers; in the former case, model providers proactively push the models upon their availability.

Digital twins may be constructed either manually upon user requests in the *Application* layer or automatically upon the availability of a specific model. The latter is implemented in our use case when a drive is installed in the network, its presence is detected via mDNS, and its embedded OPC UA information model is considered as the first model to be included in the digital twin of the drive. Afterwards, the corresponding digital twin controller pulls other models from the available model providers and adds them to the corresponding digital twin.

5.3   The Applications Layer

There is one microservice in this layer, which contains an analytics application. There are Java components that interact with the *Digital Twin Provider* microservice via REST APIs to receive necessary information from within the digital twin of a device and its type. This information is provided to a Python application for further analysis, and the results of the analysis are stored back in the so-called maintenance model. This means that, in addition to consuming digital twin content, the application is also a model provider for the digital twin. To be able to easily aggregate the maintenance model into the digital twin of the corresponding device, we have an OPC UA server within the *Analytics* microservice, which stores the maintenance model.

5.4   A Common Identification Mechanism

It is usually the case that each information provider adopts its own specific scheme to uniquely identify information pieces. For example, in our use case, within the *Product Type Database* there is a unique alphanumeric ID to designate each type, but there are several aliases for one type ID; within the *Installed-base Database* there is a numeric identifier for each installation, all its contained devices, services performed on the devices, etc.; each manufactured device has a serial number and type information included, which follows a specific format. Since the information providers are usually developed and managed by separate organizations, it is not practical to enforce one unique way of identification on all of them. Instead, we need to define how the various identifiers can be mapped to each other.

Since in our use case we assume that there is one digital twin per device, we take the device serial number as the key identifier for the digital twin to which various identifiers must be mapped. Each information provider must be extended to provide a mapping between its internal identifier and the associated serial number, and this mapping must be communicated to the digital twin when a new model is provided to the *Digital Twin Providers* layer. This approach enables us to communicate with the underlying information provider using its own identifier and yet aggregate multiple models together within one digital twin.

Each model that should become a part of a digital twin must have dedicated fields defining its identifiers. Figure 5 shows the generic structure for defining identifiers in different models. Here, an abstract class *Model* contains identifiers that are manda-

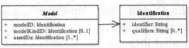

Fig. 5. Identifiers as part of any model

tory for every model, since all models inherit from this class. The property *modelID* is used to define the unique identifier of the model itself. The property *modelKindID* is used to keep the identifier of the model kind, if any. If there is, for example, any standardized model kind description, a reference to that description could be stored in this property. The key identifier (serial number in our use case) and further optional local asset identifiers within each information provider can be stored in *assetIDs* collection.

All these identifiers are defined in the class Identification, which has a property to keep the value of the identifier, accompanied with zero or more qualifiers in the qualifiers collection. The qualifiers provide additional information about the identifier, e.g., whether it is a serial number. This mechanism allows using different formats for various identifiers while preserving their semantics. The object-oriented definition of model identifiers presented in Fig. 5 allows a straightforward mapping to the selected implementation technology used by model providers, e.g., OPC UA or REST APIs with JSON.

6 Related Work

In [4] we discussed various architectural aspects of digital twins. The pattern proposed in this paper illustrates a concrete realization of these architectural aspects. Alam and Saddik describe C2PS [5], a "digital twin architecture reference model" for cloud-based cyber-physical systems. However, they focus on network communication aspects and controller design. They do not address how to create a digital twin from the information modeling perspective, nor do they consider various information sources. Gabor et al. [6] present the definition of an architectural framework for digital twins as well. In contrast to our approach, their digital twin is mainly about the simulation of real asset, and their framework is limited to it. Likewise, Delbrügger et al. [7] focus on a digital twin that simulates a factory and introduce a navigation framework that aims to improve movement paths.

In [8], a service oriented application for knowledge navigation is presented. The architecture of the application linking different data sources is outlined briefly without mentioning the approach of how to link those data source together. In [9], a twin platform based on a data-centric middleware is defined, whose architecture mostly focuses on communication and data transfer between the physical assets and simulation and not the general management of digital twins.

General cloud providers also started supporting digital twins and include them as a service into their IoT solutions. For example, Microsoft's Azure Digital Twins platform[2] enables creating digital twins and populating them with data. However, all information models to be included must follow a specific data format; they do not yet provide the flexibility to extend the system with new information sources and different kinds of information models. In general, Azure Digital Twins comes with one concrete solution and does not provide many degrees of freedom regarding different architectural alternatives. Asset Administration Shell (AAS) is the digital twin for Industrie 4.0 systems [10]. Our pattern can be adopted to implement AAS by flexibly collecting information and generating the so-called submodels for AAS.

7 Conclusions and Future Work

In this paper, we proposed an architecture pattern to construct the digital twin of an asset considering its various information sources. The pattern is designed for flexible extension with new information sources and supports new kinds of proprietary or standard information. We outlined the alternatives to realize this pattern and described a microservices- and OPC UA-based example implementation, which was validated based on an industrial use case from ABB.

In the future, digital twin solutions have to take into account composite structures, e.g., devices that consist of multiple other devices, each having its own digital twin, leading to composite digital twins. Our architecture pattern needs to be validated with respect to such scenarios.

---

[2] https://azure.microsoft.com/en-us/services/digital-twins/.

References

1. OPC Foundation: IEC 62541–1: OPC Unified Architecture - Part 1: Overview and concepts (2016). https://webstore.iec.ch/publication/25997
2. Buschmann, F., Meunier, R., Rohnert, H., Sommerlad, P.: Pattern-Oriented Software Architecture: A System of Patterns. Wiley, New York (1996)
3. Internet Engineering Task Force (IETF): Multicast DNS. http://www.ietf.org/rfc/rfc6762.txt
4. Malakuti, S., Grüner, S.: Architectural aspects of Digital Twins in IIoT systems. In: Proceedings of the 12th European Conference on Software Architecture (ECSA 2018): Companion Proceedings, p. 12. ACM (2018)
5. Alam, K.M., El Saddik, A.: C2PS: A digital twin architecture reference model for the cloud-based cyber-physical systems. IEEE Access 5, 2050–2062 (2017)
6. Gabor, T., Belzner, L., Kiermeier, M., Beck, M.T., Neitz, A.: A simulation-based architecture for smart cyber-physical systems. In: IEEE International Conference on Autonomic Computing (ICAC), pp. 374–379. IEEE (2016)
7. Delbrügger, T., Lenz, L.T., Losch, D., Roßmann, J.: A navigation framework for digital twins of factories based on building information modeling. In: 22nd IEEE International Conference on Emerging Technologies and Factory Automation (ETFA), pp. 1–4. IEEE (2017)
8. Padovano, A., Longo, F., Nicoletti, L., Mirabelli, G.: A digital twin based service oriented application for a 4.0 knowledge navigation in the smart factory. IFAC-PapersOnLine 51(11), 631–636 (2018)
9. Yun, S., Park, J., Kim, W.: Data-centric middleware based digital twin platform for dependable cyber-physical systems. In: 2017 Ninth International Conference on Ubiquitous and Future Networks (ICUFN), July, pp. 922–926 (2017)
10. Plattform Industrie 4.0: Details of the Asset Administration Shell – Part 1: The exchange of information between partners in the value chain of Industrie 4.0 (2018). https://www.plattform-i40.de/PI40/Redaktion/EN/Downloads/Publikation/2018-details-of-the-asset-administration-shell.html

Tool Support for the Migration to Microservice Architecture: An Industrial Case Study

Ilaria Pigazzini[1]([✉]) [iD], Francesca Arcelli Fontana[1] [iD], and Andrea Maggioni[2]

[1] Department of Informatics, Systems and Communication,
Università of Milano-Bicocca, Milan, Italy
i.pigazzini@campus.unimib.it, francesca.arcelli@unimib.it
[2] ALTEN Italia, Milan, Italy
andrea.maggioni@alten.it

Abstract. With the introduction of microservice architecture, many investigate how to migrate their legacy systems into this architectural paradigm. The migration process requires the recovery of the project architecture to be migrated together with the knowledge necessary to understand how to decompose the code and obtain new microservices. At the moment, this process is realized mostly manually. This paper introduces an approach to identify candidate microservices in monolithic Java projects, implemented in a tool named Arcan and the validation of the approach in an industrial setting. The approach involves static analysis of the system architecture, architectural smell detection and topic detection, a text mining method used here to model software domains starting from code analysis. We report the feedbacks we get from an experienced industrial developer who carried out the migration described in the case study. From this collaboration with industry we collected useful information to enhance the approach, improve the tool and replicate the study.

Keywords: Architectural smells · Architecture migration ·
Microservices · Topic detection · Architecture recovery

1 Introduction

In the past few years the microservices field has received large attention, both from industrial and academia world [11]. Microservice architecture is an architectural style that structures an application as a collection of small, loosely coupled and self-contained components, called services, which implement specific business capabilities [23]. These components communicate through lightweight protocols and are usually developed by dedicated teams which take care of their entire life cycle, enabling independent deployment. A single component (service) in this architecture is elastic, resilient, composable, minimal, and complete; moreover it is easy to replace it and focused on a single business capability. Services can be developed with different programming languages and by different teams

© Springer Nature Switzerland AG 2019
T. Bures et al. (Eds.): ECSA 2019, LNCS 11681, pp. 247–263, 2019.
https://doi.org/10.1007/978-3-030-29983-5_17

of developers, which makes them ideal in a business environment in continuous evolution. The characteristics of the services enable selective scaling, which means that the number of instances of each service can be chosen and tailored depending on the particular need; moreover they enable continuous and fast delivery. For these reasons, many legacy existing projects are moving from their original monolithic architecture to embrace this new paradigm.

The migration consists in various steps aimed at refactoring and decomposing the current codebase in independent domain components. At the moment, these tasks are usually carried out manually [17] with the partial support of software analysis tools to navigate the code under inspection. In addition to being time consuming, this process requires specialized personnel on software analysis with knowledge about the system to be refactored. Moreover, in large legacy software the documentation of the architecture and code design is often missing or does not reflect the actual implementation. In a survey conducted on 18 practitioners, Di Francesco et al. [10] collected feedbacks on migration to microservices experiences. The questions regarded the activities carried out during the migration: reverse engineering, architecture transformation and forward engineering. Concerning in particular the reverse engineering phase, the majority of the interviewed agreed that understanding the existing system, in particular by identifying its functionalities and subdomains, is very important to architect the new system. Moreover, the authors identified challenges regarding the high level of coupling of the existing system, the problems in identifying the candidate microservices and the system decomposition. They suggest that a tool able to support practitioners in these activities during migration could be particularly useful.

Hence, we started a collaboration between academy and a company (Alten, Italia) in order to experiment how a tool, developed at the ESSeRE Lab of the University of Milano Bicocca[1], could be useful in order to support the migration towards microservices of a project of the company. The tool called Arcan has been previously developed for architectural smell detection [4] and then extended to support the migration process. This extension of the tool will be introduced for the first time in this paper, together with the description of how the tool has been used in the industrial setting.

The outcome of this study can be useful both for the academia and the industries, since the feedbacks on the tool can be exploited in order to improve or extend the tool on behalf of the ESSeRE Lab and from the company to identify a useful support to be used during the migration process. Moreover, other companies could be interested to replicate this study and exploit the Arcan tool in the migration process of existing systems.

The new extension of Arcan is focused on the detection of features and domains from existing Java codebases in order to support the migration from monolithic to microservices architecture. The techniques applied to detect candidate microservices vary from graph algorithms to topic detection, where the latter has been previously used in the literature in different contexts such

---

[1] http://essere.disco.unimib.it/wiki/arcan.

for example to analyze code in the context of public projects/repositories labelling [18,24,27]. In particular the application of Latent Dirichlet Allocation [7] algorithm has been used in our approach to identify services depending on the application domain. The results consist in information on the Java classes and packages that should belong to the same candidate microservice due to their relationships in the monolithic application.

Hence, the main contributions of this work are:

- development of a new extension of a tool to support the migration from monolithic to microservice architecture through architectural smells detection, graph analysis and topic detection algorithms;
- discussion of an industrial case study, where the tool has been used and evaluated by an experienced practitioner.
- different lessons learned on the usefulness of the tool in real industrial setting, stimulating the university/industry collaboration in this context.

The paper is structured as follows: Sect. 2 presents related works on microservices migration, Sect. 3 explains the migration approaches implemented in the tool, Sect. 4 discusses the industrial case study and finally Sect. 5 presents conclusions and lessons learned.

2 Related Works

The discussion on how to migrate from monolithic architectures to microservices produced several practical guidelines to help developers in this process: they usually come from direct experiences in the industry [8], but also from research in academia. We describe below some of the most recent proposed approaches. Balalaie [5] present a catalog of migration patterns to support the migration from non cloud-native architectures to microservices architectures.

Mazlami [21] propose a formal approach to identify components of monolithic applications that can be turned into microservices. Their extraction model represents the system under analysis as a weighted graph on which they run graph clustering algorithms. They introduce three extraction methods which differ in how the edge weights of the graph are computed. Mishra [22] propose an approach to enable the migration from the monolith to microservices by exploiting *data flows analysis*. Their approach exploits the existing data schema joined with other information obtained by using profiling tools to understand the data flow and access patterns: this information is used to propose functional modules, that are candidate microservices. Furda [12] proposes a set of refactoring and architectural pattern-based migration techniques relevant to microservice architectures. Baresi [6] proposes a solution to find the adequate microservices granularity based on the semantic similarity of foreseen/available functionalities described through OpenAPI specifications.

The approaches introduced above do not provide tool support, while in this paper we introduce a tool to support the microservice migration process. On the other hand, Gysel [15] proposed *Service Cutter* which is a method and tool framework for service decomposition based on 16 coupling criteria distilled from the literature and industry experience. The tool is able to extract coupling information from engineering artifacts such as domain models and use cases, represented as an undirected, weighted graph to find and score densely connected clusters. The tool exploits graph clustering algorithms to suggest candidate service cuts which should reduce coupling between services and raise their cohesion. The tool that we introduce in this paper differs from Service Cutter since we collect information on candidate microservices with other techniques such as architectural smell detection and topic detection. Moreover our graph investigation is based on graph algorithms and exploits the information coming from the analysis of the Java bytecode of the project. For what concerns the detection of architectural smells during the migration process, Carrasco [9] introduced 9 common pitfalls that divides in 5 architectural and 4 migration bad smells. However, they do not offer a tool to automatically identify smells while we propose to exploit the Arcan tool in order to identify possible architectural smells before or during the migration process. Hence, with our work we provide a tool specifically for Java projects able to support the decomposition of the monolithic application allowing to identify the specific Java classes/packages to be considered during the migration process and we describe our experience in using it in an industrial case study. This work is different from the approaches previously described in this section which often are not implemented in a tool. Moreover, the experimentation in an industrial setting allows to get relevant feedbacks on the usefulness of the approach and the tool in order to improve it and replicate the study in other industrial projects.

3   Candidate Microservice Identification Through Arcan

In this section, we introduce the new extension of the Arcan tool in order to identify candidate microservices in Java projects. This extension has been exploited and evaluated in the industrial case study described in Sect. 4.

Arcan is a software analysis tool for architectural smell detection [13] in Java projects which relies on graph database technology: it bases all its computations on the *dependency graph* which is the representation of the project under analysis in form of a directed graph. The basic nodes represent the system entities, such as Java classes, packages and methods. Other nodes, that can be referred to as "supernodes", represent instances of architectural smells. When a particular structure is found in the graph, all the nodes involved are linked to a new supernode. Edges represent the relationships among the various entities. The tool allows to store the graph into a Neo4j[2] graph database, which also offers a browser to visualize and query the graph [3].

The new extension proposed in this work aims to offer a set of implemented functionalities to gather information on how to decompose the project starting from the code. We propose a migration approach through different steps:

---

[2] https://neo4j.com.

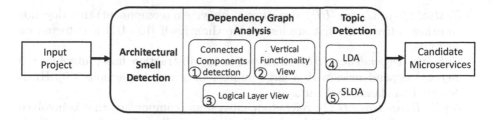

Fig. 1. Migration to microservices process

(1) architectural smell detection *(2)* dependency graph analysis *(3)* topic detection (see Fig. 1). All these steps produce information useful to identify candidate microservices. The three steps differentiate since the first offers hints on how to decompose the project under analysis taking in consideration the presence of architectural smells; the second aims to retrieve blocks of the project that are structurally independent and can be reused or transformed in microservices, while the third aims to identify the parts of the project which belong to the same "domain" in order to return a "semantic map" of the project. In this way a maintainer involved in the migration is able to collect hints and information of different kinds, and choose the decomposition solution which best fit the project under analysis. In particular, as shown in Fig. 1, the Dependency Graph Analysis step includes different methods to identify microservices, respectively: connected components detection of the dependency graph ① and generation of two views, Vertical Functionality ② and Logical Layer ③; while the Topic Detection step includes the analysis of the text coming from the code and execution of two *topic detection* algorithm to extract "hidden concerns", named Latent Dirichlet Allocation (LDA) ④ and Seeded Latent Dirichlet Allocation (SLDA) ⑤. At the end of the process, the available information regards the hidden modules in the monolithic architecture that can be exploited to forward engineer the future microservice architecture: the proposed solution aims to maximize the modules' cohesion to ease the activity of creating single-purpose services. In this paper, we do not address the problem of transforming the modular monolith into implemented microservices.

3.1   Architectural Smell Detection

The project architecture to be migrated could be eroded and hard to comprehend because of existing architectural smells/issues. For instance, a circular dependency among two architectural entities may make it harder to understand how they interact with each other and how to separate them to obtain single services. Hence it is useful to detect the presence of this kind of architectural smells which could hinder the identification of the services and should be removed before starting the migration process. In particular, we consider the identification of the following architectural smells (AS):

- *Unstable Dependency (UD)*: describes a subsystem (component) that depends on other subsystems that are less stable than itself [19]. UD is detected on packages.
- *Hub-Like Dependency (HL)*: arises when an abstraction has (outgoing and ingoing) dependencies with a large number of other abstractions [26]. HL is detected on classes and packages.
- *Cyclic Dependency (CD)*: refers to a subsystem (component) that is involved in a chain of relations that break the desirable acyclic nature of a subsystem's dependency structure. CD is detected on classes and packages. The cycles are detected according to their different shapes: tiny, circle, star, clique [1].

The details of the detection algorithms of these architectural smells can be found in [4]. A validation of Arcan results in terms of Precision, Recall and F-measure on two industrial projects is also available [4]. The detection results of Arcan were also inspected by practitioners on the analysis of four industrial projects [20]. Moreover, in this work we introduce the detection of a new smell through the Arcan tool named Feature Concentration.

- *Feature Concentration (FC)*: occurs when an architectural entity implements different functionalities in a single design construct [2]. FC is detected on packages.

The detection of Feature Concentration is crucial because, in addition to being a smell, FC is particularly indicated to support the identification of functionalities in the monolithic architecture. In particular it shows the functionalities of each package: each of them could be a candidate microservice.

3.2   Dependency Graph Analysis

The aim of this step is to obtain an indication on how the monolithic architecture should be decomposed by looking at the static structure of the project under analysis i.e. its dependency graph. This step consists of three methods, *Connected Components detection*, *Vertical Functionality View* and *Logical Layer View* (see Fig. 1). Both Views generation is based on an assumption: even if Java monolithic systems are considered a big mixture of lines of code, most of the times they are composed by well defined Java services such as REST services, JMS services, SOAP services, EJB services and Servlet/JSP services. The presence of these services is characterized by the use of dedicated Java libraries which enable their implementation. These can be detected by inspecting the dependency graph with graph queries and by executing graph algorithms. The following paragraphs go deeper in the description of the three methods.

Connected Components Detection. This functionality consists in applying the *Depth First Search (DFS)* algorithm [25] in order to find connected components (sets of Java classes or packages) in the graph by considering the undirected edges. The subgraph that can be generated has only nodes corresponding to the identified components. In Arcan, the algorithm is used to detect totally detached parts of code, which can be extracted independently from the project.

Vertical Functionality View. This view aims to isolate and show each functionality contained in the project under analysis in order to support the extraction of the interested parts of code as microservice candidates. This is obtained by running the *Depth First Paths (DFP)* algorithm [25]: by providing a specific set of source classes, the algorithm is able to compute for each source class the paths on the directed graph. The nodes of the paths represent the Java classes and the edges represent the dependencies among the classes. Then, every path is compared one to the other in order to find eventual "shared" classes i.e. classes that belong to more than one path. There are various ways to provide to Arcan the input source classes to be used as starting nodes for functionalities search.

(a) The simplest one, that can be used when the maintainer has zero knowledge about the project under analysis, is to choose the classes with no incoming dependencies. This means that such classes are never referred from other parts of code in the project, making them candidate entrypoints.

(b) The second way requires more information: it chooses classes with no incoming dependencies which refer to specific libraries. For instance if a class exploits the Java API for RESTful Web Services (JAX RS)[3], it may be a good candidate to find an hidden REST service inside the monolithic architecture. The tool already recognizes the libraries which implements the JEE Specification.

Logical Layer View. This view allows to divide the classes in groups depending on the layer they belong to. *Layers* refers to the ones of the three tier model, which organizes the code in presentation layer, application processing (business) layer, and data management (persistence) layer. The tool is able to separate and assign each class to its layer by looking at their external dependencies, in particular checking the Java implementation packages of the JEE specification. Unlike the vertical functionality view, the layered one offers a coarse grained representation of the project under analysis. In this way it is possible to understand the role of each class when the maintainer has no information about how the code is organized.

3.3   Topic Detection

Usually microservices are created depending on specific "domains" or "business concerns" of the project. When migrating from a monolithic architecture, it is not trivial to automatically extract such concerns from the code without human supervision. However, a possible solution to this problem could be reached through topic detection techniques, by considering code as text and by looking for *topics* that could correspond to services. In this work, the algorithms exploited to extract topics from code are **Latent Dirichlet Allocation (LDA)** [7] and **Seeded Latent Dirichlet Allocation (SLDA)**, a semi-supervised variant of the original LDA algorithm [16]. The latter algorithm allows the maintainer to provide some *seed* words so that the model is encouraged in finding evidence of some "expected" topics in the data. The idea behind the

---

[3] The Java API specification that supports the development of RESTful web service.

choice of the seeded algorithm is that developers may know some of the topics which could be hidden inside the monolithic system and enhance the results of the detection. The following paragraph describes the topic detection process.

(1) Document collection: a document is created by selecting comments and source code words from a single Java class, in particular the class name, its membership package name and the name of all its methods. Class attributes and variables are not included since often they do not distinguish a class from each other by belonging to a specific topic (e.g. "filename", "x", "a", "temp"). This step is implemented in Java language.

(2) Preprocessing: this step consists in manipulating the text contained in the documents to enhance the results of topic detection. In particular, the documents created starting from Java classes are *tokenized* i.e. their stream of characters is broken into words. After tokenization, *filtering* is applied. The resulting tokens are converted to lower cases and are analyzed in order to remove numbers, punctuation and stop words, which are the very common words in a language. This step is implemented in Python language.

(3) (Seeded) Latent Dirichlet Allocation: the last phase is the running of the topic detection algorithm. In order to run the LDA algorithms, the Python library *guidedLDA*[4] was used. This library was chosen because it lets the maintainer to define a set of *seed topics*. The output consists in the detected topics represented as word-topic distribution and the document-topic distribution, that is the proportion of words of each topic associated to a given document.

At the end of the process, the maintainer can collect hints about the semantics of the project to be migrated, in particular on which Java classes are associated to a specific domain.

4   Industrial Case Study

We now describe how the different functionalities/steps provided by Arcan to support the migration process have been exploited in an industrial project. The analysis was carried out by an experienced developer which executed Arcan on an industrial project and identified candidate microservices basing on the tool outcomes. Moreover, he provided several feedbacks on the migration techniques offered by Arcan and on the final candidate microservices solution that he was able to define thanks to the tool. The industrial project analyzed is a Java enterprise project developed to manage the collection of information for the initiation of legal proceedings. It is composed by 267 classes divided into 27 packages. The developer originally took part in the development of the analyzed project, in particular he managed the collection of requirements and the development process. Hence, he possessed remarkable knowledge on the design choices and business logic: we chose this particular case study because we were interested in valuable feedbacks on the quality of the solution proposed by Arcan.

---

[4] https://guidedlda.readthedocs.io/en/latest/.

Table 1. Detected architectural smells

# Unstable Dependency (UD)	# Hub-Like Dependency (HL)	# Cyclic Dependency (CD)		# Feature Concentration (FC)
10	1	Class 4	Package 2	22

Another validation of the Arcan tool on a simple case study named *Daytrader* is available[5]. Daytrader[6] is a project developed by IBM specifically to simulate the manual migration from a Java monolithic architecture to a microservice architecture. It was chosen to validate the Arcan algorithms since it offers the source files and some documentation on the pre and post migration architecture.

The following sections show the results obtained through the different migration steps implemented in Arcan. The developer followed the approach described in Sect. 3. The data generated by the tool are available[7].

4.1   Architectural Smells Detection

First, the developer executed Arcan to detect all the types of architectural smells described in Sect. 3.1. Table 1 shows the number of AS detected in the project under analysis. He could retrieve the most relevant information from the analysis of Cyclic Dependency and Feature Concentration smells, for the reasons described below.

Cyclic Dependency. The developer recognized four cycles as real issues for the monolithic application. However, he reported that *"Those cycles will not be a problem during the migration"* except for one cycle on classes. This particular smell involved 3 classes which are part of the central logic of the application, whose aim is to create entries on a calendar basing on a set of deadline rules. He foresaw that in the new architecture this logic will be completely redefined, in particular it will be divided into different services. He indicated the presence of the cycle as a possible obstacle to the decomposition of the application.

On the other hand, two of the four CD smells detected on classes resulted to be false positives. Both are cycles between an anonymous class and its corresponding container class and this Java feature always leads to the introduction of a tiny cycle.

Feature Concentration. The developer found the detection of this smell particularly useful. He was able to identify the main domain *entities* of the application, that represent the information managed by the application, since the smell

---

[5] https://drive.google.com/file/d/1YuIery5fzEykuqxufNNAub4xyPwZJhrS/view?usp=sharing.

[6] https://github.com/davemulley/daytrader-ee6.git.

[7] https://drive.google.com/drive/folders/1kLJXMPXhG2U8pIrqG_MWVU0STSCdIsMN?usp=sharing.

instances affected the packages containing business application classes. Table 2 shows the identified entities. The approach he followed to identify entities starting from FC smell consists in: *(1)* spotting the affected packages from Arcan results; *(2)* exploiting the Neo4J browser to navigate the disconnected subgraphs and *(3)* extracting the entities associated to the different subgraphs.

4.2 Dependency Graph Analysis

The following section shows the results of the service detection using the *Vertical Functionality* and the *Logical Layer* views. The results of Connected Components detection are not discussed since the developer did not use it to build the final microservices solution; the detected components did not gave him interesting hints on the business concerns/functionalities (see Sect. 4.4).

Vertical Functionality View Results. The developer chose to run the generation of the vertical view with the two possible kinds of input offered by Arcan: classes with no incoming dependencies and classes with no incoming dependencies depending from specific JEE libraries (see Sect. 3.2). The view generation with the first type of input returns a csv file containing all the directed paths starting from the classes without incoming relations. In this case study the total number of detected paths was 69: the developer found the use of this information expensive in terms of time, hence moved forward with the next analysis. The second type of input computes DFS paths from nodes which have been identified as *Web* and *Web Service* in JEE Specifications. The results of the second view generation returned a total of 3 paths. In this case, he reported that one of the paths was useful during the analysis; it helped in identifying the service regarding the components which manage the entity called *Attachments*, where *Attachments* represents the files uploaded on the application and saved on a Mongo Database.

Logical Layer View Results. Table 3 shows the results of the service detection process using the *Logical Layer View* functionality. The table shows the different layers and the number of classes assigned to each layer and the value of True Positives (TP) and False Positive (FP) class assignments, which the developer used to compute Precision. By analyzing the *false positive* results, the developer reported that Arcan can not assign the correct layer to the classes which use the Spring framework[8] classes, both for the Persistence layer and for the Web layer. The matching rules implemented in this first version of the *Logic Layer Detection* algorithm have been thought basing on *old* functionalities of the Java Enterprise Edition, which are used in many legacy projects. In more recent Java application Spring is a popular framework, hence the developer suggested us to introduce new rules taking in consideration the use of Spring to achieve higher *precision* value on the layer-class assignation.

---

[8] https://spring.io/.

Table 2. Main entities

Entity	
Event	User
DeadlineItem	Suspension
Attachment	Notification
Society	Proceedings
CronologyChange	

Table 3. Logical Layer Results

Layer	Number of classes	EVAL TP	FP
Persistence	1	0	1
Web	8	6	2
Core	267	207	60
Precision: 77,2%			

4.3 Topic Detection

This step consisted into two main parts. First the developer ran the *Document collection* generation of Arcan, which reads the Java source files and produces for each class a csv file which contains the meaningful words contained in the class. In total Arcan produced 267 files which contain 418 different words. Then the developer executed the two versions of the LDA algorithms.

From the first run of the classic LDA algorithm, he noticed the noise produced by some words belonging to technical aspects of the libraries used in the application e.g. the HTTP methods connected to the "Spring Controller" of Spring Framework. Hence, he excluded 119 words from the vocabulary and added them to the stopwords file (see Sect. 3.3). This because he was interested in retrieving information referring to the business logic contained in the project respect to the technical one. The excluded words can be consulted in the available folder (see footnote 7). Once the developer modified the stopwords file, he proceeded with the run of both LDA algorithms and compared their results. Both algorithms needed a parameter setting as input, in addition to the document collection. The choice of all the parameters except for the number of topics (which was chosen by the developer) was guided by the state of the art of the topic detection field [14]. The parameters are:

- ⋄ **number of topics:** 10
- ⋄ **alpha** - prior weight of each topic in a document: 0.01
- ⋄ **beta** - prior weight of each word in a topic: 0.1.

Latent Dirichlet Allocation Results: Table 4 contains the 10 topics retrieved by the classic LDA algorithm. The developer found the results interesting since the detected topics contain many words that recall the entities and functionalities of the application. For instance he found references to the functionality of the application which sends an alert when a *proceeding* is created by reading the words of topic 8: "creation", "proceedings", alert". Another example, words of topic 4 "user", "change", "roles" recall the application feature of changing the roles of a *user* inside the application.

Moreover, he was able to obtain the same information on the entities identified with the AS analysis (Table 2): he could label each topic (see column Entity

Table 4. Topic detection results

LDA			Seeded LDA	
Topic		Entity	Topic	
1	Proceedings deadline suspension attachment start state days management	Proceedings	1	Proceedings deadline date suspension reminder item payment days
2	User history username process provvedimento email finale change	User	2	Summary date proceedings comment voice data event description
3	Delibera subject collegio approvazione audizione provvedimenti area action	Key-Value	3	History event activity process analize society ragione date
4	User change roles summary cronology voice history date	User	4	State proceedings attachment society management document visible event
5	Access data impegni decisoria payment avvio procedimento turnover	Key-Value	5	Attachment cronology history object change interceptor resolver changed
6	Attachment proceedings reminder today date events notifications recipient	Notification	6	Subject impegni decisoria provvedimenti action istruttoria procedimento turnover
7	Proceedings deadline event summary date voice comment item	Suspension	7	User finale roles username email provvedimento data role
8	Event state proceedings history creation proceedings alert assigned	DeadlineItem	8	Delibera collegio access approvazione documents audizione data ammissibilita
9	Date documents response finale appeal atto determina document	Key-Value	9	Event deadline proceedings voice summary events simplified owner
10	Society data activity ammissibilita files status ragione sociale	Society	10	User date change today event audit state expire

in Table 4) and became aware of a new entity which, basing on his past knowledge, he called *Key-Value*.

Seeded Latent Dirichlet Allocation Results: In order to run the modified version of LDA, the developer defined 5 *Seed Topics*. He defined 4 of them on the basis of the entities collected through the AS detection step, while one (*Summary*) represented an entity expected by the developer:

1. proceedings, deadline, suspension, item (**Deadline**)
2. summary, voice, comment, attachment (**Summary**)
3. society, ragione, sociale, soggetto (**Societies**)
4. event, reminder, days (**Events**)
5. notification, recipient, sender, object (**Notification**).

Table 4 contains the results of the Seeded LDA analysis. The execution of SLDA was not considered useful by the developer because even if the algorithm retrieved quite the same information from the execution of classic LDA, he could not easily label each topic with a corresponding entity. Moreover, the *Summary* entity was not identified as expected by the developer (see Sect. 4.4).

After comparing the results coming from all the methods implemented in Arcan, the developer produced the final solution. Table 5 shows the candidates microservices, for each service there is a brief description of the functionality associated to it. As a results of the topic detection step, the developer chose to incorporate entity *Event, Deadline* and *Suspension* into a unique candidate microservice. Moreover, he introduced *Key-Value* and discarded *CronologyChange* on the base of his past knowledge on the project.

Table 5. Candidates microservices

Candidates microservices	
Proceedings	This service will manage the Proceedings, the main entity of the new system
Attachment	This service will manage the Attachment, an Attachment is a file associated to a Proceedings
Society	This service will manage the Societies which could be associated to a Proceedings
User	This service will manage the User authentication and the applications roles associated to a User
Notification	This service will manage a chat service
Deadline & Suspension	This service will manage the *Deadline & Suspension* logic
Key-Value	This service will manage a new type of entity called *Key-Value*; this entity will have only a few attributes (e.g. id, value, type). A *Key-Value* will be used by the Front-End part to display show some select tag at the final users

4.4   Discussion

We now discuss the results and feedbacks obtained from this case study on the microservice migration process through Arcan. The developer ran Arcan following the steps described in Sect. 3 in order to identify how many "business services" compose the industrial application under analysis. The AS detection was the preferred and most useful step for the developer in order to understand how the application was composed. He was able to identify the parts of code related to single *entities* which could become microservices (Table 2). Moreover the AS detection made him aware of a problem regarding a specific entity named *Deadline*: the creation of a *Deadline* requires the information present in *Suspension* and *Proceedings* and vice-versa, part of the problem was solved by incorporating entity *Deadline* with *Suspension*, while the Cyclic Dependency between *Deadline* and *Suspension* should be analyzed and possibly removed during the migration process in order to decouple the services. The Dependency Graph Analysis is the step which gave him less information, because the implemented methods are based on the idea that the application under analysis refers to a JavaEE standard architecture used in many legacy projects. The analyzed application is based on *SpringFramework* (see footnote 8), so Arcan could not assign the correct layer to the classes and put all of them in the *Core Layer*. Moreover he did not use the results coming from the Connected Component detection, because the microservices candidates proposed by the algorithm were not in accordance with his background knowledge. This tells us that in general we have to improve our current approach about graph analysis. Finally, the developer validated the topic detection step. He preferred the classic version of the LDA algorithm since in his opinion the resulting topics were more relevant respect to the seeded version. He supposed that the seeded LDA results are strictly connected to the chosen seed topics. The topic detection confirmed the results of the AS detection and provided additional information useful to establish the final solution (Table 5).

In conclusion, the developer stated that *"In general the migration process is not easy to carry out, since a deep knowledge of the project subjected to the migration is needed in order to have significant results. Arcan can be very useful: to retrieve knowledge about the project using the architectural smell detection and the vertical functionality view, and to extract more information about the services using the LDA algorithm."*

5   Conclusions and Lessons Learned

In this paper we showed how the application of different techniques such as architectural smells detection, dependency graph analysis and topic detection can help a maintainer to identify which parts of the code can be migrated to a microservice. In particular, in this work the Arcan tool has been exploited in an industrial case study in order to analyze Java projects and retrieve their dependency graph representing the internal architecture and identify candidate microservices through: *(1)* architectural smell detection, *(2)* dependency graph analysis and *(3)* Latent Dirichlet Allocation. An industrial case study has been discussed to manually validate the implemented techniques: an experienced developer successfully identified the candidate microservices through Arcan. The data provided by the tool are available (see footnote 7).

We collected important lessons learned from the collaboration with the industry. First of all, (1) we received positive feedbacks concerning the usefulness of the Arcan tool, which stimulate us to continue working in this direction and increase the collaboration with industry in this context; (2) we collected several feedbacks useful to the Arcan tool developers in order to enhance and extend the tool; (3) we understood that the analysis of some data are more time consuming than other, such as the information provided by the architectural smells detection and the dependency graph analysis with respect to topic detection. (4) We observed that AS detection and dependency graph analysis are suitable for a deep project comprehension, while topic detection could be exploited for the initial understanding of the project, when few knowledge is available to the practitioners. However, in the case study presented in this paper, topic detection results enhanced when the developer changed a setting (*stopwords* file) and executed the algorithm again: this suggests that the topic detection functionality works better when applied across multiple iterations. All these findings could lead the Arcan developers to the refinement of the current migration approach to fully exploit the potential of Arcan functionalities. Moreover, the current approach addresses only a step of the migration to microservices i.e. the information extraction from the current system. We aim to extend our work in order to support the concrete implementation of the services and provide a method to evaluate the quality of the migrated architecture, as studied by Carrasco [9]. Having a framework to evaluate the software quality before and after the migration could assist in making decisions during the migration phase. Starting from the obtained results, this work opens up to further extensions and studies. In fact our work presents some threats to validity, in particular the size of the case study, which is small in terms of number of classes/packages. Hence, as a first step we plan to extend the validation on more industrial projects of larger dimension, both in the same company or in other companies. For what concerns the possible enhancements of Arcan, it would be interesting to enrich the dependency graph of the tool with information from topic detection: in this way the graph would offer both knowledge on the structure and on the semantic of the system under analysis, through the overlapping of the two approaches which at the moment are considered separately. Regarding the Vertical Functionality View, a possible future development is the detection of common libraries and frameworks to implement Java services, such as Hibernate and Spring frameworks. This would extend the approach adopted until now, which only considers Java Enterprise API libraries.

References

1. Al-Mutawa, H.A., Dietrich, J., Marsland, S., McCartin, C.: On the shape of circular dependencies in Java programs. In: Proceedings of the 23rd Australian Software Engineering Conference (ASWEC 2014), pp. 48–57. IEEE, Sydney, April 2014
2. de Andrade, H.S., Almeida, E., Crnkovic, I.: Architectural bad smells in software product lines: an exploratory study. In: Proceedings of the WICSA 2014 Companion Volume, pp. 12:1–12:6. ACM, New York (2014)
3. Arcelli Fontana, F., Pigazzini, I., Roveda, R., Zanoni, M.: Automatic detection of instability architectural smells. In: Proceedings of the 32nd International Conference on Software Maintenance and Evolution (ICSME 2016). IEEE, Raleigh (2016)
4. Arcelli Fontana, F., Pigazzini, I., Roveda, R., Tamburri, D.A., Zanoni, M., Nitto, E.D.: Arcan: a tool for architectural smells detection. In: International Conference Software Architecture (ICSA) Workshops, Gothenburg, pp. 282–285, April 2017
5. Balalaie, A., Heydarnoori, A., Jamshidi, P., Tamburri, D.A., Lynn, T.: Microservices migration patterns. Softw. Pract. Exp. (2018)
6. Baresi, L., Garriga, M., De Renzis, A.: Microservices identification through interface analysis. In: De Paoli, F., Schulte, S., Broch Johnsen, E. (eds.) ESOCC 2017. LNCS, vol. 10465, pp. 19–33. Springer, Cham (2017). https://doi.org/10.1007/978-3-319-67262-5_2

7. Blei, D.M., Ng, A.Y., Jordan, M.I.: Latent Dirichlet allocation. J. Mach. Learn. Res. **3**, 993–1022 (2003)
8. Bucchiarone, A., Dragoni, N., Dustdar, S., Larsen, S.T., Mazzara, M.: From monolithic to microservices: an experience report from the banking domain. IEEE Softw. **35**(03), 50–55 (2018). https://doi.org/10.1109/MS.2018.2141026
9. Carrasco, A., van Bladel, B., Demeyer, S.: Migrating towards microservices: migration and architecture smells. In: Proceedings of the International workshop on Refactoring (IWoR), pp. 1–6. ACM (2018). https://doi.org/10.1145/3242163.3242164
10. Di Francesco, P., Lago, P., Malavolta, I.: Migrating towards microservice architectures: an industrial survey. In: IEEE International Conference on Software Architecture (ICSA 2018). IEEE, Seattle (2018)
11. Francesco, P.D., Malavolta, I., Lago, P.: Research on architecting microservices: trends, focus, and potential for industrial adoption. In: 2017 IEEE International Conference on Software Architecture (ICSA), pp. 21–30. IEEE, April 2017
12. Furda, A., Fidge, C., Zimmermann, O., Kelly, W., Barros, A.: Migrating enterprise legacy source code to microservices: on multitenancy, statefulness, and data consistency. IEEE Softw. **35**(3), 63–72 (2018)
13. Garcia, J., Popescu, D., Edwards, G., Medvidovic, N.: Identifying architectural bad smells. In: CSMR 2009, pp. 255–258. IEEE, Germany (2009)
14. Griffiths, T.L., Steyvers, M.: Finding scientific topics. Proc. Nat. Acad. Sci. **101**(Suppl. 1), 5228–5235 (2004)
15. Gysel, M., Kölbener, L., Giersche, W., Zimmermann, O.: Service cutter: a systematic approach to service decomposition. In: Aiello, M., Johnsen, E.B., Dustdar, S., Georgievski, I. (eds.) ESOCC 2016. LNCS, vol. 9846, pp. 185–200. Springer, Cham (2016). https://doi.org/10.1007/978-3-319-44482-6_12
16. Jagarlamudi, J., Daumé III., H., Udupa, R.: Incorporating lexical priors into topic models. In: Proceedings of the 13th Conference of the European Chapter of the Association for Computational Linguistics, EACL 2012, Stroudsburg, PA, USA, pp. 204–213 (2012). http://dl.acm.org/citation.cfm?id=2380816.2380844
17. Kecskemeti, G., Marosi, A.C., Kertesz, A.: The ENTICE approach to decompose monolithic services into microservices. In: 2016 International Conference on High Performance Computing Simulation (HPCS), pp. 591–596, July 2016
18. Linstead, E., Lopes, C., Baldi, P.: An application of latent Dirichlet allocation to analyzing software evolution. In: Seventh International Conference on Machine Learning and Applications, pp. 813–818. IEEE, December 2008
19. Martin, R.C.: Object oriented design quality metrics: an analysis of dependencies. ROAD **2**(3), 5–6 (1995)
20. Martini, A., Fontana, F.A., Biaggi, A., Roveda, R.: Identifying and prioritizing architectural debt through architectural smells: a case study in a large software company. In: Cuesta, C.E., Garlan, D., Pérez, J. (eds.) ECSA 2018. LNCS, vol. 11048, pp. 320–335. Springer, Cham (2018). https://doi.org/10.1007/978-3-030-00761-4_21
21. Mazlami, G., Cito, J., Leitner, P.: Extraction of microservices from monolithic software architectures. In: 2017 IEEE International Conference on Web Services, ICWS 2017, Honolulu, HI, USA, 25–30 June 2017 (2017)
22. Mishra, M., Kunde, S., Nambiar, M.: Cracking the monolith: Challenges in data transitioning to cloud native architectures. In: Proceedings of the 12th European Conference on Software Architecture: Companion Proceedings, ECSA 2018 (2018)
23. Newman, S.: Building Microservices, 1st edn. O'Reilly Media Inc., Sebastopol (2015)

24. Rama, G.M., Sarkar, S., Heafield, K.: Mining business topics in source code using latent Dirichlet allocation. In: Shroff, G., Jalote, P., Rajamani, S.K. (eds.) Proceeding of the 1st Annual India Software Engineering Conference, ISEC 2008, Hyderabad, India, 19–22 February 2008, pp. 113–120. ACM (2008)
25. Sedgewick, R., Wayne, K.: Algorithms, 4th edn. Addison-Wesley, Boston (2016)
26. Suryanarayana, G., Samarthyam, G., Sharma, T.: Refactoring for Software Design Smells, 1st edn. Morgan Kaufmann, Burlington (2015)
27. Wang, T., Yin, G., Li, X., Wang, H.: Labeled topic detection of open source software from mining mass textual project profiles. In: Proceedings of the First International Workshop on Software Mining, SoftwareMining 2012, pp. 17–24. ACM, New York (2012)

ACE: Easy Deployment of Field Optimization Experiments

David Issa Mattos[1]([envelope]) [iD], Jan Bosch[1] [iD],
and Helena Holmström Olsson[2] [iD]

[1] Department of Computer Science and Engineering,
Chalmers University of Technology,
Hörselgången 11, 412 96 Gothenburg, Sweden
{davidis,jan.bosch}@chalmers.se
[2] Department of Computer Science and Media Technology, Malmö University,
Nordenskiöldsgatan, 211 19 Malmö, Sweden
helena.holmstrom.olsson@mau.se

Abstract. Optimization of software parameters is a recurring activity in the life-cycle of many software products, from prototypes and simulations, test beds and hardware-in-the-loop scenarios, field calibrations to the evolution of continuous deployment cycles. To perform this activity, software companies require a combination of software developers and optimization experts with domain specific knowledge. Moreover, in each of life-cycle steps, companies utilize a plethora of different tools, tailored for specific domains or development stages. To most companies, this scenario leads to an excessive cost in the optimization of smaller features or in cases where it is not clear what the returned value will be.

In this work we present a new optimization system based on field experiments, that is aimed to facilitate the adoption of optimization in all stages of development. We provide two main contributions. First, we present the architecture of a new optimization system that allows existing software systems to perform optimization procedures in different domains and in different development stages. This optimization system utilizes domain-agnostic interfaces to allow existing systems to perform optimization procedures with minimal invasiveness and optimization expertise. Second, we provide an overview of the deployments, discuss the advantages and limitations and evaluate the optimization system in three empirical scenarios: (1) offline optimization with simulations; (2) optimization of a communication system in a test bed in collaboration with Ericsson; (3) live optimization of a mobile application in collaboration with Sony Mobile. We aim to provide practitioners with a single optimization tool that can leverage their optimization activities from offline to live systems, with minimal invasiveness and optimization expertise.

Keywords: Optimization · Black-box optimization · Field experiments · Software architecture

© Springer Nature Switzerland AG 2019
T. Bures et al. (Eds.): ECSA 2019, LNCS 11681, pp. 264–279, 2019.
https://doi.org/10.1007/978-3-030-29983-5_18

1 Introduction

Optimization is a recurring activity for many software products in a range of different domains. Companies continuously try to improve different aspects of their products in order to make them more desirable, maintain their products' competitive advantage or to overcome existing gaps with competitors. Some aspects that are often optimized are performance, accuracy, usage and user experience.

Traditionally, optimization techniques rely on mathematical or existing empirical models of the system. These optimization techniques are used in the early stages of the product/feature development. They require modeling or adapting an existing model to the desired scenario and the optimization is done within a simulation toolbox and with domain-specific optimization algorithms, such as the ones provided in Matlab[1]. These existing solutions are usually restricted to a particular programming or modeling language and each one has their own interface. However, if the simulation environment is customized and developed by the company themselves, it requires implementation and validation, or the acquisition of the optimization algorithms. In test beds and hardware- and software-in-the-loop laboratory scenarios, companies rely on a custom platform with optimization procedures that mix traditional optimization with statistical evaluation of observations [1, 2].

For field optimization, web-facing companies such as Microsoft, Google, Facebook, Amazon and LinkedIn, among others started running online experiments to optimize their systems [3–6]. In the website and mobile domain, companies such as VWO[2] and Optimizely[3] offer experimentation services for specific optimization situations such as A/B testing and multi-armed bandits. However, these companies do not offer solutions that can be adapted and used in different domains, such as in the embedded systems and communication domain. Moreover, the algorithms provided in the online domain only cover a subset of optimization experiments with a discrete and finite number of alternatives.

Embedded and cyber-physical systems are often deployed and used in uncontrolled conditions. Web and mobile systems users have uncertainties associated to user behavior. The results of all these deployment conditions, usage environments and user behaviors are complex interactions which are infeasible to model, replicate in a laboratory or optimize in pre-deployment activities. Ultimately this leads to a mismatch between pre-deployment optimal values and field observations. Additionally, in many real-world engineering problems, the evaluation of the system during the optimization procedure is limited by the costs or time required to compute an iteration, therefore restricting the choice of algorithms.

To avoid this complex optimization scenario, companies can choose to embed the algorithms in their applications. However, the introduction of optimization algorithms and heuristics inside an application is viewed with skepticism by many practitioners since they can create performance issues, are hard to validate without directly affecting

---

[1] http://mathworks.com.

[2] https://vwo.com/.

[3] https://optimizely.com.

the customer, introduce a significant amount of code that might not be justified by the gained benefits, require re-validation, re-testing and sometimes even re-certification of the software application, are difficult to update and replace, and require a knowledge that might not be available during product development [7, 8].

Optimization of systems throughout the entire lifecycle requires a range of different tools, techniques, algorithms and expertise that makes it impractical for large scale software development. These constraints require efficient optimization algorithms to be deployed in a different environment and communicate with the software application in consistent ways that can be utilized by software developers at different stages of product development.

To address these challenges, we present a new optimization system based on the optimization of expensive black-box systems, which is aimed to facilitate the adoption of optimization in all stages of development. We provide two main contributions. First, we present the architecture of a new optimization system called ACE (Automated Continuous Experiments), that allows existing software systems to perform optimization procedures in different domains and in different development stages. This optimization system utilizes domain-agnostic interfaces to allow existing systems to perform optimization procedures with minimal invasiveness and optimization expertise. Second, we provide an overview of the deployments, discuss the advantages and limitations and evaluate the optimization system in three empirical scenarios: (1) offline optimization with simulations; (2) optimization of a communication system in a test bed in collaboration with Ericsson; and (3) live optimization of a mobile application, in collaboration with Sony Mobile. We aim to provide practitioners with a single optimization tool capable of leveraging their optimization activities from offline to live systems, with minimal invasiveness and optimization expertise.

This work is part of a larger research project (as discussed in Sect. 3), with previously published results. The results of our industrial cases were previously published in [9] (in collaboration with Sony Mobile) and in [10] (in collaboration with Ericsson). The first publication focuses on the development and analysis of a field optimization algorithm with Sony Mobile. This algorithm, though with several modifications and extensions, was also used in the Ericsson case study. Since this approach is new in the mobile network optimization domain, the second publication consists of a problem framing and a description of the case study. This paper significantly differs from the previous publications in terms of its scope and presents novel content and results, focusing on the architecture of the experimentation system and discussing it in three deployment scenarios.

This paper is organized as follows. Section 2 presents background information regarding the optimization of expensive black-box systems. Section 3 discusses the research process and provides a brief description of the case studies discussed in the empirical cases. Section 4 discusses the architecture of the ACE optimization system. Section 5 presents the three empirical scenarios. Section 6 discusses related work. Lastly, Sect. 7 concludes the paper and discusses future research directions.

2   Background

Black-box software optimization refers to the problem where an algorithm needs to optimize software parameters based of an objective function in a system utilizing black-box interfaces. The algorithm can ask the system to evaluate a parameter set, but it only observes the system response, without any assumptions or a model of the system. The system's response can be stochastic or noiseless.

Online companies traditionally conduct experiments based on experiment design theory when optimizing their systems [3–6]. These experiments – usually sequential A/B testing or factorial experiments – are used to compare a finite and discrete number of alternatives [11]. For example, determining if a feature should be deployed to the whole user base, or selecting between multiple layout options. These techniques have the advantage of having comparable sample sizes (usually the number of active users or the number interactions with the system) for all variations in the statistical analysis at the expense of increase in the regret and the higher sample size for the optimization.

Multi-armed bandit algorithms provide a framework for black-box optimization with a finite and discrete number of alternatives. Multi-armed bandit algorithms dynamically change the sample size allocation to the best performing variation [12]. So at the expense of statistical power, this framework focuses on regret minimization and it enjoys wide use in the industry [13–15]. Multi-armed bandit algorithms are an active area of research and provide a number of algorithms for different optimization situations. Hierarchical methods are one of the extensions of the multi-armed bandit field for optimization in the continuous space [9, 16].

A prominent approach for the optimization of expensive functions is the Bayesian Optimization. This approach is a sequential approach which selects a parameter set, queries the black-box with this parameter set and then based on the response value it updates the statistical model for the next parameter set [17]. The two key components are the surrogate model of the objective function and the loss function used to describe the sequence of parameter sets to be tried.

Shang [18] presents an overview of black-box optimization methods. The report compares the Bayesian Optimization to the Gaussian Process with bandits hierarchical methods, such as the HOO [16]. It is concluded that even though Bayesian Optimization methods can provide better function approximations and faster convergence, they require the selection of better priors and hyper-parameters when compared to hierarchical methods, thus increasing the need for optimization expertise.

Finally, genetic algorithms have also been used in simulation and field experiments. Tamburrelli and Margara [19] proposed an infrastructure and a genetic algorithm to optimize HTML web pages in a large space. However, the proposed solution requires using non-validated assumptions of the hyper-parameters and of the mating strategies. Additionally, the solution requires a large space of unique users which restricts its application in real world scenarios to very large-scale software companies.

Although black-box optimization is an extensive research topic and multiple algorithms are available, few works have discussed architectures and deployment of such systems. We discuss and compare existing approaches to our work in Sect. 6.

3   Research Process

This research is part of a larger project where we aim to facilitate the adoption of continuous experimentation and leverage the development of optimization experiment solutions relevant to our industrial partners. We utilize a design science approach [20, 21], grounding our theory on developments from multiple domains, such as experiment design [11, 22], test bed and simulation experiments [1, 23, 24], black-box optimization systems [12, 15, 16] and optimization [15, 19, 25–28].

Our industrial collaboration occurs within the context of the Software Center[4]. Based on industrial cases, we iteratively developed artifacts such as an optimization system and algorithm, which we could refine and evaluate first using simulations and later using field studies. We built our case studies with companies sequentially and we have divided our research approach into three phases.

Phase One. The first phase consists of contextualizing, scoping, adapting and formalizing our existing research results to a specific company project. This initial step allows us to evaluate the feasibility of the project and the generality that this project would add to the research project. If our current solutions are able to address the problems, we implement them in the company and gather feedback at end of the data collection. In the case that our current methods are not able to handle the company project, we proceed to the next phase.

Phase Two. This phase consists of an iterative process where we develop, refine and deploy our solutions in the context of the company project. In this iterative process, we aim to identify company specific constraints while abstracting the solutions and research so that they may be used and applied in a wider range of applications and domains, including the ones we have previously worked on. This iterative process starts with simulations and integration activities while understanding the problem domain. Thereafter, we move towards a limited deployment of the solution to analyze the initial results and make necessary adjustments. Finally, we proceed to a full deployment where we collect empirical evidence and evaluate our approach with field data.

Phase Three. The last phase consists of gathering the qualitative and quantitative information obtained in the industrial case studies together with simulations and other empirical data, such as meeting notes, emails and comments. We try to abstract this information and formulate constructs and related them to existing research work. These constructs are reported in research publications and reviewed by our industrial collaborators. In this project we have an ongoing collaboration with two industrial partners, Sony Mobile and Ericsson, and the first company case started in September 2017. Sony Mobile is a subsidiary of the Sony Corporation and is a leading global innovator in information technology products for both consumer and professional markets. Ericsson is a Swedish multinational network and telecommunications company. The company provides services in software and infrastructure in information and communications technology, including mobile network infrastructure.

---

[4] https://www.software-center.se/.

4   The ACE System

This optimization system is capable of running traditional A/B experiments, multi-armed bandit experiments and optimization algorithms in a continuous space. It can run multiple simultaneous optimization jobs and has the ability to stop and resume an experiment at any time. The experimentation system, called ACE (Automated Continuous Experimentation), was inspired by the architectural framework and design decisions presented in [27, 28], however the proposed instantiation is not equivalent to previous works.

An overview of the experimentation system is shown in Fig. 1. The system is divided in three services that can be launched independently as Docker containers[5] and can be deployed locally or in as a cloud service. The main service consists of a Python backend application with five layers and it is responsible for the algorithms, variant assignment, data preparation and configuration of the experiment.

The first layer consists of an API layer. This layer utilizes the webserver NGINX[6] together with a Flask[7] API application. This layer is responsible for securing the connection and cross-checking authorization such as API keys and login information. The Flask API application is responsible for parsing the HTTP/HTTPS requests to the correct modules in the application layer.

The application layer consists of five modules. The configuration module is responsible for creating and updating the setting of an experiment, for example the number of variants, the number of dimensions, the precision and range of the search space, and algorithm parameters. The model update module is responsible for receiving new data points from the system under experiment (SuE) and updating the statistical model of the experiment. It receives the reward value and the corresponding arm value or variant that generated the particular reward. A reward can be a KPI metric, such as number of clicks to more complex ratios and performance estimations. However, reward metrics always have a positive direction (higher value is better). The arms request module is responsible for providing the SuE with a new arm value or variant to try. The new arm value can either be based on the statistical model or be a randomized assignment. The data presentation module receives requests to process and present the experiment data to the experiment owner. This module reads the experiment statistical model and processes visualization figures, provides an overview of the statistical model and identifies the best performing arms. The final module, the statistical comparison module, is independent of the algorithm and the statistical model of the experiment. This module reads the raw data directly in order to perform a statistical analysis of the experiment, after its conclusion. This module is based on current frequentist statistical methods and performs a parametric, non-parametric and factorial analysis for experiments in a discrete space.

---

[5] https://www.docker.com.

[6] https://www.nginx.com/.

[7] http://flask.pocoo.org/.

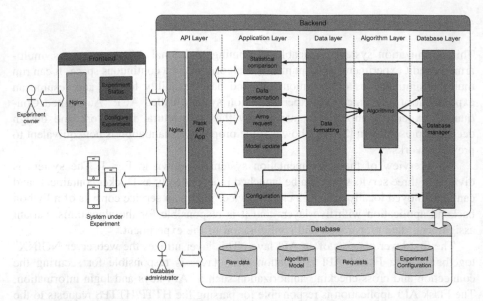

Fig. 1. Overview of the experimentation system. The services are represented in different colors, in blue the frontend, in green the backend and in orange the database service. The arrows indicate the flow of data in the software, from computed statistics of the algorithms statistical models to raw and processed data collected from the users and systems under experiment. (Color figure online)

The algorithm layer implements the experimental design algorithms, such as A/B tests, factorial experiments, discrete multi-armed bandits and continuous-armed bandits. The case studies presented in Sect. 5 utilize the algorithm LG-HOO described in [9].

The data layer is responsible for formatting and preparing the data according to the algorithm specification as defined through the configuration module. This step consists of removing duplicated data, pre-processing metrics, aggregating the raw data for the statistical analysis, and preparing the input and output of the statistical model to the application layer.

The database layer is responsible for securing a connection and interfacing the backend with the local or remote database. All connections from the backend to the database are processed in this module.

The second service consists of a group of MongoDB NoSQL databases, which store all experiment data, current status, variant requests and their replies, and the current statistical model of the experiment. This service is to kept separate from the backend service so that it can be deployed locally and store the data according to regional data legislation, such as the GDPR[8].

---

[8] https://ec.europa.eu/commission/priorities/justice-and-fundamental-rights/data-protection/2018-reform-eu-data-protection-rules_en.

The third service consists of an optional frontend service to configure a new experiment and to display information regarding the status of an experiment to the experiment owner. This service does not add functionality to the experiment execution but facilitates the usage of the interfaces to configure and launch an experiment and facilitates the visualization of the experiment data.

4.1 Experiment Configuration and Interfaces

The ACE system was developed with the following in mind: to minimize dependencies on the SuE, to keep the integration efforts to a minimum and to allow the ACE system to be integrated with applications from different domains. These constraints motivated the usage of HTTP/HTTPS POST requests for communication between the SuE and the backend service. The SuE can launch independently of ACE and run even in the case of a failure in ACE. In such situations, the default values and variants are used, instead of the suggested values given by ACE.

The configuration of the optimization experiment is done independently of the SuE and it can be updated without modifications in the SuE code. The configuration is done utilizing POST requests with the configuration in a JSON format. This configuration is then parsed in the backend and an initial statistical model for the experiment is created. These configuration requests can be made utilizing the frontend or accessing the interfaces directly with a tool such as curl or Postman. The configuration of an experiment requires specifying what data is going to be logged in the signals field, which of these values will be used as the objective or reward metric for the statistical model, the algorithm specification and its parameters, and the dimensions specifications.

Requesting and logging information in the ACE system follows a similar pattern. Note that requesting a new trial or variation and logging metrics are independent of the statistical model used by the algorithm. Therefore, the configuration and the statistical model can be updated to a new version without comprising the integration code in the SuE. This facilitates the update of an algorithm and its hyperparameters to fine-tune it to a particular case without the need for a re-deployment. Additionally, this scheme enables the developers to expose interfaces for metrics and parameters that might be of interest for future observation.

We divide an experiment iteration in four steps, as shown in Fig. 2. First, the developers implement the interfaces to ACE. Second, the experiment/optimization owner configures the experiment, specifying the algorithm details, search space, metrics to be used, etc. Third, the SuE requests trials from ACE. Finally, after the SuE runs the request trial it updates the statistical model in ACE. Steps three and four are repeated until the optimization experiment finalizes.

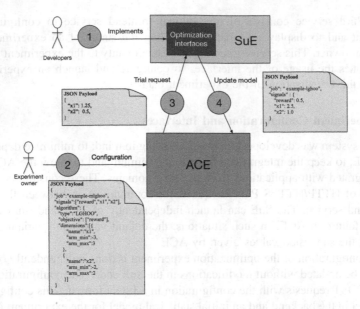

Fig. 2. Overview of the four steps to run an experiment.

5 Empirical Cases

Optimization of the Parameters of a PID Controller

This scenario shows how to optimize the parameters of a PID (proportional-integral-derivative) controller utilizing the ACE system in a simulation scenario. While simulation packages often provide optimization algorithms, and efficient algorithms for tuning control systems do exist, we provide an example where little domain knowledge and implementation effort is needed to optimize a PID system. Additionally, the use of the ACE system in simulation is the same as the use of the ACE system in testing scenarios and live systems, as discussed later.

The deployment of ACE in a simulation scenario consists of requesting a new trial at the beginning of every simulation iteration and updating the statistical model at the end of the iteration, similar to what is done with other simulation optimization scenarios. However, unlike most simulation package, the ACE system does not perform minimization procedures directly. We follow the recommendations and discussion provided in [29], where the authors recommend that all experiment and optimization designs utilize maximization objectives. Figure 3 shows how the ACE system can be integrated into a simulation environment. The results shown in Fig. 4 compares the results of this optimization procedure with an existing domain specific algorithm. In this case, we optimize three variables of the PID controller within 3000 simulation iterations. Note that in this case we utilize the same algorithm as that used in the Ericsson and Sony Mobile optimization experiments.

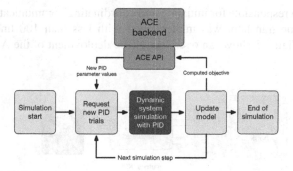

Fig. 3. Overview of the deployment of the ACE system in the PID controller simulation example

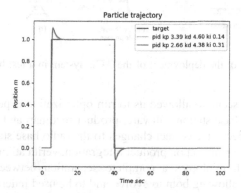

Fig. 4. Optimization experiment of a PID controller using the ACE system (in green) and using the domain specific heuristic twiddle (in orange). The ACE system is capable of learning the PID parameters comparable to a domain specific solution. The system dynamics is based on the project https://github.com/cheind/py-control (Color figure online)

Optimization of Radio Base Station Parameters in a Test Bed with Ericsson

One challenge faced by many mobile network operators is the optimization of the software parameters in a deployed radio base station [10]. The goal with this optimization procedure is to provide quality of experience (QoE) for a range of different applications, such as voice over LTE, uplink signal, video traffic, web browsing and online gaming. We deployed ACE in a test bed environment. The radio base station hardware is connected to a number of real user equipment that generates the profile traffic used in system testing and verification purposes. A full description of the domain, the optimization objective, the optimization variables and the different optimization experiments can be found in [10]. In order to modify software parameters and collect metrics from the radio base station, we utilized an existing command line interface program which mobile operators can use to configure and monitor their own mobile networks. We developed an intermediate translator that bridges the communication between the ACE system and a command line interface (CLI) program. The translator is also responsible for initiating and coordinating communication between the two systems. The translator was implemented with less than 100 lines of code in a Python script. Figure 5 shows an overview of the deployment of the ACE system with Ericsson.

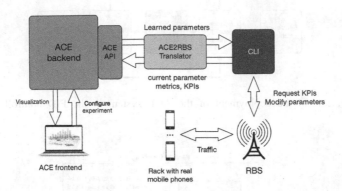

Fig. 5. Overview of the deployment of the ACE system in a test bed with Ericsson.

This deployment scenario allowed us to run optimization experiments without any changes to the radio base station software, product roadmap and to the test bed. This was an important aspect, since direct changes to the radio base station software and to the test bed will have an impact on product integration, verification and validation. This deployment approach reinforces a complete separation between the SuE and the optimization system, allowing both to evolve and to be used independently. One of the experiments that we ran shows an increase of 46.1% in the objective metric by changing two simultaneous optimization variables in 200 iterations.

Optimization Based on User Behavior with Sony Mobile
One of Sony Mobile's products is transitioning to data-driven development and aims to run experiments continuously throughout its development process. The product is a business to business solution, where the users of the software consists of employees of the company that requested the solution. The software development of this product spans development for web, mobile, backend systems and distributed embedded hardware. During the development of the product several assumptions were made, such as numerical, textual, and GUI constants that have a direct impact on the how the users interact with the system. The development team of this product wants to optimize these constants and to verify that these assumptions are based on actual user behavior metrics.

The ACE system was integrated with the SuE utilizing a proxy to route requests, since the ACE utilizes a different backend solution from the SuE. Figure 6 shows how the ACE system connects to the Sony Mobile product. This integration allows the product development team to control the connection and information exchange between users and the ACE system, adding an internal security layer and the ability to isolate the SuE from the ACE system when necessary. The integration between the mobile application and the ACE system was done utilizing existing HTTP libraries to perform the requests. This integration required a low effort from the development team, since endpoints to collect the required metrics and to modify the necessary parameters were already available in the system. The team estimates an integration effort with less than 10 line of code given the existing infrastructure.

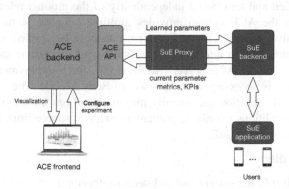

Fig. 6. Overview of the deployment of the ACE system in a live system with Sony Mobile.

With this deployment setup, we ran two optimization experiments. The first was the optimization of a text message shown in the application. This optimization experiment was conducted with a traditional A/B experiment method with user consistency. The goal was to identify which text message led more users to perform a particular task. The best performing variation increased the expected user action by almost 30%. The second experiment consisted of optimizing a parameter of one algorithm internal to the application. It was expected that this parameter would impact a particular user behavior. The experiment result showed that this parameter in the search space had little impact on the expected behavior. The estimation of the behavior with the algorithm parameter however led the development team to make informed decisions regarding the feature roadmap. Additional details of this second experiment and the algorithm used can be found in [9].

Discussion

The ACE system provides a unique way to optimize software parameters in deployed systems utilizing field data. The single interface and communication allow developers to easily expose variables and metrics to the experimentation system during development and launch an experiment at a later time after the system is deployed.

In the simulation case, we show how to integrate ACE with existing simulation models. This allows a company to use the same optimization system in different stages of the product development. In the case study with Sony, since the mobile applications access the ACE APIs directly, some code was necessary to connect the mobile application and the ACE system, however the communication overhead is considered minimal since as it happens only once a day. However, for the Ericsson case, the instrumentation and parametrization of the system was already in place. A CLI application can access the different metrics and counters and modify the existing parameters in the system. This allowed the connection of the ACE system without any modification in the existing code of the SuE, therefore it does not require to re-test and re-evaluate the deployment due to ACE. This shows the potential for optimizing systems without adding complexity to the product and making changes to the product roadmap. The optimization procedure occurs within defined boundaries and can be activated, modified and terminated independently of the product release cycle.

Even though the ACE system provides multiple benefits, some restrictions and downsides are also present. The ACE system can only be applied where instrumentation and parameterization interfaces are possible, and the system can have constant communication with the ACE server. Additionally, for a deployment in production additional security is necessary, as in the case of Sony Mobile. The ACE system only provides basic authentication and security measures and has not been evaluated under different attack conditions in order to prevent an external source from gaining access to the open interfaces in the SuE.

Threats to Validity

External Validity: In the system and architecture development, we aimed to minimize company specific cases as discussed in the research process. Company specific restrictions where implemented as separated systems, as discussed in the different deployment situations. Although we have shown empirical evaluations of the ACE system in the three distinct optimization problems in different domains, these domains are not exhaustive. Additional modifications to the architecture design might be necessary to allow the ACE system to be used in a broader optimization context.

Internal Validity: In terms of the architecture, its design and interface were iteratively discussed with the industrial collaborators to achieve a trade-off between generality of the proposed solution and problem specific needs. The researchers involved discussed the trade-offs to minimize confounding variables, specific to a company context, in the proposed solution while still preserving the generality of the solution. However, other alternative architecture and implementation solutions for the same optimization problem are possible. In terms of experimental design, the results and conclusion from the optimization are further subjected to other validity considerations.

6   Related Work

Google's Vizier [15] is a tool for black-box optimization that takes advantage of multi-armed bandit algorithms and of Bayesian Optimization. Google's work provides a high overview of the system and basic user workflow. The Vizier architecture is modular and has five main components: the database for persistence; the suggestion service to create new trials; an early stop service; an API for communication; and the evaluation workers that correspond to the SuE. While the ACE system shares several similarities with Google's Vizier in terms of its main processes, Vizier is described as an internal application at Google that is used to perform hyperparameter tuning of machine learning models and A/B testing case scenarios. Google's paper does not describe the different deployment scenarios and how it integrates with their existing products and workflows.

Tamburrelli and Margara [19] propose an infrastructure and a genetic algorithm to optimize HTML web pages in a large space. The work discusses a run-time framework that generates and selects population variants with its genetic algorithm. The run-time system is integrated with the existing website application in terms of primitive constructs. Although this strategy might have performance gains, compared to our proposed approach it is challenging to reuse in different contexts since it has a tight integration between the application and the run-time system.

In our previous work, we [27, 28] we present an architecture framework and architecture decisions to run optimization experiments in the context of a cyber-physical system. This architecture framework served as the basis for the initial steps and was iteratively modified as described in the research process in Sect. 3. The architecture is intended to be external to the application domain, and only connected to the monitor and effector interfaces. Those interfaces are equivalent to the request trial and updated model interfaces discussed in Sect. 4. The system provides basic metric analysis components, which enable the verification of global restrictions. An experiment coordinator handles the active experiment. Algorithms can be implemented in the version generator component that communicates with the effector interface. The cyber-physical system application example utilizes a domain specific heuristic for the multi-armed bandit problem to perform the optimization procedure.

Gerostathopoulos et al. [25, 26] discuss a tool for end-to-end optimization for black-box systems. The tool utilizes three sequential steps in the optimization. First it runs a factorial experiment, analyzed with an analysis of variance Second, it inputs the output of the first step into a Bayesian Optimization. And third, it compares the output of the Bayesian Optimization with the default values utilizing a t-test. Their system follows a similar pattern as ACE and Google's Vizier. It implements a webserver to control the workflow and interface with the database, the frontend client and middleware that interfaces with the system under experiment. However, the system is evaluated only in simulated scenarios, such as a traffic routing system and in just-in-time compilers in the Java Virtual Machine, and the paper does not describe the deployment strategy changes when integrating it with new existing systems.

7 Conclusion

Companies often seek to improve their products by optimizing their software in different stages of development. This work proposes a new black-box optimization system called ACE (Automated Continuous Experimentation), that can be used to run optimization field experiments in a range of different domains and stages of development, such as simulations, test beds and in deployed systems in addition to different domains. We present an overview of the ACE system architecture and we discuss different integration and deployment scenarios where the ACE system was integrated in one simulation project and two existing industrial products, in collaboration with Ericsson in a test bed scenario and Sony Mobile in a live system. In this context, we aim to provide practitioners with a single optimization tool that can leverage their optimization activities from offline to live systems and do so with minimal invasiveness and optimization expertise.

In future work, we plan to expand this architecture to different domains in order to increase the generality of the solution and add new components that facilitate its adoption and minimizes the need of additional code to connect the optimization system to the system under experiment. Towards the end of this larger research project, we plan to make all project artifacts, such as the algorithms and the ACE experimentation system available open-source in the repository https://github.com/davidissamattos/ACE.

Acknowledgments. This work was partially supported by the Wallenberg Artificial Intelligence, Autonomous Systems and Software Program (WASP) funded by the Knut and Alice Wallenberg Foundation and by the Software Center. The authors would also like to express their gratitude for all the support provided by Ericsson and Sony Mobile. We also would like to thank to the support and help from Anas Dakkak, Krister Bergh and Erling Mårtensson.

References

1. Piyaratna, S., et al.: Digital RF processing system for Hardware-in-the-loop simulation. In: 2013 International Conference on Radar, pp. 554–559 (2013)
2. Scholz, D., von Stryk, O.: Efficient design parameter optimization for musculoskeletal bipedal robots combining simulated and hardware-in-the-loop experiments. In: 2015 IEEE-RAS 15th International Conference on Humanoid Robots (Humanoids), pp. 512–518, December 2015
3. Tang, D., Agarwal, A., O'Brien, D., Meyer, M.: Overlapping experiment infrastructure. In: Proceedings of the 16th ACM SIGKDD International Conference on Knowledge Discovery and Data Mining - KDD 2010, p. 17 (2010)
4. Bakshy, E., Park, M., Eckles, D., Park, M., Bernstein, M.S.: Designing and deploying online field experiments. In: Proceedings of 23rd International Conference of World Wide Web - WWW 2014, pp. 283–292, September 2014
5. Kohavi, R., Deng, A., Longbotham, R., Xu, Y.: Seven rules of thumb for web site experimenters. In: Proceedings of the 20th ACM SIGKDD International Conference on Knowledge Discovery and Data Mining - KDD 2014, pp. 1857–1866 (2014)
6. Xu, Y., Duan, W., Huang, S.: SQR : balancing speed, quality and risk in online experiments. In: Proceedings of the 24th ACM SIGKDD International Conference on Knowledge Discovery & Data Mining - KDD 2018, vol. 1, pp. 895–904 (2018)
7. Sculley, D., et al.: Hidden technical debt in machine learning systems. In: Advances in Neural Information Processing Systems, pp. 2503–2511 (2015)
8. Issa Mattos, D., Bosch, J., Olsson, H.H.: Multi-armed bandits in the wild: pitfalls and strategies in online experiments. Inf. Softw. Technol. 113, 68–81 (2019)
9. Mattos, D.I., Mårtensson, E., Bosch, J., Olsson, H.H.: Optimization experiments in the continuous space. In: Colanzi, T.E., McMinn, P. (eds.) SSBSE 2018. LNCS, vol. 11036, pp. 293–308. Springer, Cham (2018). https://doi.org/10.1007/978-3-319-99241-9_16
10. Mattos, D.I., Bosch, J., Olsson, H.H., Dakkak, A., Bergh, K.: Automated optimization of software parameters in a long term evolution radio base station. In: IEEE 13th Annual International Systems Conference, pp. 1–8 (2019)

11. Kohavi, R., Longbotham, R., Sommerfield, D., Henne, R.M.: Controlled experiments on the web: survey and practical guide. Data Min. Knowl. Disc. **18**(1), 140–181 (2009). https://doi.org/10.1007/s10618-008-0114-1
12. Burtini, G., Loeppky, J., Lawrence, R.: A survey of online experiment design with the stochastic multi-armed bandit. pp. 1–49 (2015) arXiv:1510.00757
13. Urban, G.L., et al.: Morphing banner advertising. Mark. Sci. **33**(1), 27–46 (2014)
14. Li, L., Chu, W., Langford, J., Schapire, R.E.: A contextual-bandit approach to personalized news article recommendation. In: Proceedings of the 19th International Conference on World wide web - WWW 2010, p. 661 (2010)
15. Golovin, D., Solnik, B., Moitra, S., Kochanski, G., Karro, J., Sculley, D.: Google vizier. In: Proceedings of the 23rd ACM SIGKDD International Conference on Knowledge Discovery and Data Mining - KDD 2017, pp. 1487–1495 (2017)
16. Bubeck, S., Munos, R., Stoltz, G., Szepesvari, C.: X-armed bandits. Theor. Comput. Sci. **412** (19), 1832–1852 (2010)
17. Shahriari, B., Swersky, K., Wang, Z., Adams, R.P., de Freitas, N.: Taking the human out of the loop: a review of Bayesian optimization. Proc. IEEE **104**(1), 148–175 (2016)
18. Shang, X., Kaufmann, E., Valko, M.: Hierarchical bandits for "Black Box" optimization, Lille (2015)
19. Tamburrelli, G., Margara, A.: Towards automated A/B testing. In: Le Goues, C., Yoo, S. (eds.) SSBSE 2014. LNCS, vol. 8636, pp. 184–198. Springer, Cham (2014). https://doi.org/10.1007/978-3-319-09940-8_13
20. Hevner, A.R., March, S.T., Park, J., Ram, S.: Design science in information systems research. MIS Q. **28**(1), 75 (2004)
21. Gregor, S., Hevner, A.R.: Positioning and presenting design science research for maximum impact. MIS Q. **37**(2), 337–355 (2013)
22. Montgomery, D.C.: Design and Analysis of Experiments, 8th edn. Wiley, Hoboken (2012)
23. Krettek, J., Schauten, D., Hoffmann, F., Bertram, T.: Evolutionary hardware-in-the-loop optimization of a controller for cascaded hydraulic valves In: 2007 IEEE/ASME International Conference on Advanced Intelligent Mechatronics, pp. 1–6 (2007)
24. Zhao, Y., Dong, W., Zou, X., Tong, L., Zhu, G.: Analysis and design of power hardware-in-the-loop testing for 400-Hz inverters. In: Proceedings of 2017 12th IEEE Conference on Industrial Electronics and Applications. ICIEA 2017, pp. 1122–1126, February 2018
25. Gerostathopoulos, I., Uysal, A.N., Prehofer, C., Bures, T.: A tool for online experiment-driven adaptation. In: Proceedings - 2018 IEEE 3rd International Workshop on Foundations and Applications of Self Systems FAS*W 2018, pp. 100–105 (2019)
26. Gerostathopoulos, I., Prehofer, C., Bulej, L., Bures, T., Horky, V., Tuma, P.: Cost-aware stage-based experimentation : challenges and emerging results. In: 2018 IEEE International Conference on Software Architecture Companion, pp. 72–75 (2018)
27. Mattos, D.I., Bosch, J., Olsson, H. H.: Your system gets better every day you use it: towards automated continuous experimentation. In: 2017 43rd Euromicro Conference on Software Engineering and Advanced Applications (SEAA), no. Ml, pp. 256–265 (2017)
28. Mattos, I., Bosch, J., Olsson, H.H.: More for less: automated experimentation in software-intensive systems. In: Felderer, M., Méndez Fernández, D., Turhan, B., Kalinowski, M., Sarro, F., Winkler, D. (eds.) PROFES 2017. LNCS, vol. 10611, pp. 146–161. Springer, Cham (2017). https://doi.org/10.1007/978-3-319-69926-4_12
29. Deng, A., Shi, X.: Data-driven metric development for online controlled experiments. In: Proceedings of the 22nd ACM SIGKDD International Conference on Knowledge Discovery and Data Mining - KDD 2016, pp. 77–86 (2016)

Author Index

Printed in the United States
By Bookmasters